The Development of
the Communist Bloc

STUDIES IN HISTORY AND POLITICS

Under the editorial direction of Gerald E. Stearn

RUSSIA AND THE WEST FROM PETER TO KHRUSHCHEV

Edited by L. Jay Oliva, New York University

THE DEVELOPMENT OF THE COMMUNIST BLOC

Edited by Roger Pethybridge, University College, Swansea

CHURCH AND STATE IN AMERICAN HISTORY

Edited by John F. Wilson, Princeton University

Other volumes in preparation

STUDIES IN HISTORY AND POLITICS

The Development of the Communist Bloc

Edited with an introduction by

Roger Pethybridge

University College, Swansea

D. C. HEATH AND COMPANY: BOSTON

Englewood · Chicago · Dallas · San Francisco · Atlanta · London · Toronto

The aim of this book is to provide the college student and the general reader with an introduction to the affairs of the communist bloc. The period treated extends from the closing stages of the Second World War up to 1960, after which time the developing political outline becomes too indistinct for the contemporary observer to trace with any confidence.

Grateful acknowledgment is made to the authors, publishers and editors who have allowed me to reprint their materials. In particular I should like to thank the New American Library and George Allen & Unwin for their kind permission to use short extracts from my book, *A History of Postwar Russia.* Finally I wish to thank Mrs. E. Davies for her invaluable assistance in preparing this book for publication.

Roger Pethybridge

Library of Congress Catalog Card Number: 65-25436

Table of Contents

Introduction

The present account of the development of the Soviet bloc begins with the advance of the Red Army into Eastern Europe near the end of the Second World War. This is the conventional starting point, and the author does not wish to enter into a controversy regarding the date of the origin of the Soviet bloc. Nevertheless this introduction might serve as a useful setting for a brief survey of earlier Soviet efforts to communize areas of the world that did not form an integral part of Bolshevik Russia.

The formation of the Soviet bloc after 1944–1945 was not a unique phenomenon. It has in fact been preceded by several attempts, some of them successful, to sovietize other areas of the world. A short analysis of the ways in which Soviet Russia dealt with these areas of comparatively minor importance may help to shed some light on the major operation that was undertaken after the Second World War. We shall see that the Russians drew quite extensively on their experience from the years 1917–1944 when they came to deal with the situation in Eastern Europe in 1944.

From the Bolshevik Revolution of 1917 until the autumn of 1924 the prevailing Soviet policy with regard to the conversion of the rest of the world to socialism was based on Trotsky's theory of "permanent revolution," formulated in 1905. According to this theory, it was impossible for Russia to establish a stable socialist regime by her own efforts. Socialism had to be built on an international level through a chain of revolutions. Otherwise the Russian experiment, hampered internally by a backward economy and menaced externally by the superior might of capitalism, would soon turn out to be a failure. Prompted by this theory, the Bolsheviks welcomed any independent foreign uprisings that might bring them an ally who would eventually become a socialist brother in the supernational socialist world of the future. In 1919 they pinned their hopes in turn on the attempted uprisings in Berlin, Munich and Budapest. All three proved to be abortive. One of the reasons behind the success of the Bolshevik Revolution was the fact that Russia was isolated geographically from the victorious Allies by a wide belt of ex-enemy states. This was not the case in Germany. Unfortunately, Germany was not contiguous with Russia, which would have allowed the Red Army to lend direct support to the insurgents, as it was to do in Central Europe at the close of the Second World War. Finally, the established governments in Germany and Hungary had the advantage of knowing how their internal enemies would try to stage the revolt, closely following the lines laid down by the Soviet prototype.

In the years 1944–1948 East European statesmen were caught unawares by the revised form of communist revolution, directed almost completely from abroad, and carefully controlled, not spontaneous. How and why did the Russians change their theoretical views and their practical policies between 1919 and 1944 on the question of socialist revolutions abroad?

After the failure of all but the Russian communist revolution, the Russians began to revise their official line on the question of foreign uprisings. The infant Soviet Union was clearly too weak to impose Soviet republics on Western Europe from outside. Capitalism appeared to take on a new lease of life after the First World War. It was Stalin who took upon himself the task of replacing Trotsky's theory of "permanent revolution" by the new doctrine of "Socialism in One Country." Stalin maintained that in the light of her experience Russia should now concentrate primarily on building herself up as an industrial power so that she could become a strong bastion of socialism in a hostile world. Aid to foreign revolutions was relegated to second place. If Russia overextended herself, she would not only fail to instigate uprisings abroad; she would collapse internally as well. With this in mind, Stalin contended paradoxically: "An internationalist is he who unconditionally, openly and honestly . . . is ready to uphold and defend the U.S.S.R." (*Mastering Bolshevism*).

Such was the official Soviet line from 1924 until the Second World War. But although aid to foreign revolutions was relegated to second place, it was not excluded entirely. The vision of international communism was merely postponed, not abandoned. Postponed, that is, in Europe, but not in Central Asia between 1924 and the Second World War. Central Asia was geographically remote from the centers of capitalist power. China was the only country in this period which had a vital interest in preventing the Russians from taking over in areas like Outer Mongolia and Tannu Tuva, and she was too enfeebled to take any action.

It is not generally realized that the Soviet technique of controlled revolution from above (as opposed to spontaneous, independent uprisings of the sort envisaged by Trotsky) was applied in Central Asia long before it was used once again in Eastern Europe during and after the Second World War. Let us take one example among several. After the October Revolution in Petrograd the Khanates of Bokhara and Khorezm declared themselves independent from Russian rule, which had been imposed on them not very long before 1917. The Bolsheviks allied themselves with left-wing opinion in the Khanates, the reactionary rulers were forced out, and "People's Republics" were organized in 1919–1920. The title was significant. In conformity with the Marxist view of history, the feudal Khanates could not possibly become models of socialist society overnight. Somehow the bourgeois stage in history had to be inserted. Thus, from 1920 until 1924 artificially contrived "bourgeois" states were set up in the two areas, only to be knocked down again in the latter year, when the Khanates were admitted into the network of Soviet *Socialist* Republics. In seven years Bokhara and Khorezm had in Marxist theory, though not in practice, been transformed from backward feudal régimes into political entities of a kind that even Germany had not been ripe for in 1919! The political evolution of Eastern Europe from 1944 onwards, as it is described in the present book, went at a snail's pace in comparison, although to noncommunist observers it seemed to proceed at lightning speed.

The Russians were gradually widening their experience of communist take-overs. The period of considerable activity in Central Asia in the 1920s was followed by a lull in the 1930s until 1939, which witnessed the incorporation in the U.S.S.R. of the Baltic States and a large slice of eastern Poland. The Soviets did not merely occupy eastern Poland with their troops. A controlled political, social and economic revolution was carried out. Local city and rural committees were established, and elections to the new "People's Assemblies" held. There were no official communist candidates. Nominees of social organizations were put forward. But only four days after the elections the Assembly of Western Ukraine voted for the legal incorporation of eastern Poland into the Soviet Union, thus coating the bitter pill of Soviet military occupation. Just as in the rest of Eastern Europe a few years later, the local factory owners and landowners were expropriated.

Thus by the close of the Second World War Soviet politicians in general, and Stalin in particular, had acquired some measure of expertise with regard to controlled revolutions in areas adjacent to Soviet territory. Even before he established himself as sole ruler of the U.S.S.R., Stalin had played an important role in Central Asian affairs as Commissar of Nationalities. He naturally drew on his long experience when he came to deal with Eastern Europe after 1944. The story of his judicious management of successive controlled revolutions in this area is the subject of the present work.

The Soviet Union has often been accused of empire-building. Certainly no other country in the postwar world has increased in size and influence as fast as the U.S.S.R. In conclusion we may examine this accusation in very broad terms.

It is true that in the manner of nineteenth-century empire-builders the Soviet Russian nation had a keen interest in the economic benefits to be gained from territorial expansion and the acquisition of foreign protectorates. With this in mind the Bolsheviks considered it out of the question after 1917 to acquiesce in the separation of the national minorities, given the economic importance of Russia's borderlands. Similarly, Eastern Europe after 1945 was viewed at first as an economic mine from which riches could be extracted for the rehabilitation of warworn Russia. But economic motives were nearly always linked with others which did not loom so large in the considerations of nineteenth-century imperialists. The security of the Soviet fatherland was a major preoccupation, and small wonder. Capitalist intervention from all sides immediately after 1917 convinced the Russians of the need to retain the relatively new acquisitions of the Tsarist empire. Hitler's long thrust into Eastern Europe and Russia in the Second World War reminded them of the constant threat presented by the power vacuum between their own country and Western Europe. A third undeniable motive for expansion, although many noncommunist writers have ignored or refuted it, has been the Marxist vision of international socialism.

Soviet methods, too, have often been reminiscent of earlier techniques, but there have also been great differences. In earlier centuries empires were controlled by navies. The Russians have relied exclusively on land armies, and in the last resort still depend on their military might for their wide influence. Very few of the enormous territories now under Soviet influence have been won over to socialism without the initial presence of Russian troops. In another respect Soviet methods have differed greatly. In Eastern Europe the U.S.S.R. was dealing with highly developed peoples, all of them possessing their own national cultures. Nineteenth-century European powers concentrated on the undeveloped continents of the world. Neither the Turks nor the Austrians in their time, whose rule extended over far longer periods than Soviet influence, were able to replace virile nationalism in Eastern Europe with their own ways of life. History may well prove, and the last few years seem to indicate, that the Soviet Union may have no more success than they did. Communism now sways nearly forty percent of the world's population. The vital question for the future is—what sort of communism: Great Russian communism or truly international communism?

I.   *The Origins of Soviet Domination in Eastern Europe, 1944-1947*

SOVIET MILITARY EXPANSION IN EASTERN EUROPE

Postwar Soviet influence in Eastern Europe was initially established by the sheer force of military might, and in the last resort it is still based on military might today. In view of this fact it is important to note the way in which Soviet armies took over the power vacuum of Eastern Europe from the retreating Germans towards the close of the Second World War.

1944 marked the crossing of Russia's 1939 frontiers by the advancing Soviet armies. With many divisions held down in Western Europe by the Allied invasion, the German army in the East bore the brunt of Soviet assaults, which were no longer confined to a front of four hundred miles but now stretched over a distance of two thousand miles, from the Arctic Ocean to the Black Sea. In winter in the snows of Leningrad, in spring in the mud of the Ukraine, in summer on the plains of Belorussia and Rumania, in autumn in the Carpathian mountains and along the Hungarian plains, the Soviet troops proved their superiority. They had it within their power to capture almost any objective in Eastern Europe.

A main summer offensive was launched by the Russians just two and a half weeks after the Anglo-American invasion of Normandy. On June 23 they moved forward, not from the great wedge in southern Poland which had been opened up after the Ukrainian victories of 1943, but from the line farther east and to the north, in Belorussia. In less than a fortnight the Red Army pushed the Germans out of Belorussia. By the end of July the Vistula marked the no-man's land between the two armies. From August until the end of the year the main Russian front stood astride the center of Poland. Meanwhile in the south the Soviets struck out against Rumania, which then declared war on Nazi Germany.

Besides consolidating the fronts already held, Russian armies spread farther afield, moving through Hungary and Yugoslavia in the south and the Baltic states in the north. Thus practically the whole of Eastern Europe was systematically covered by Soviet troops, a factor which had great weight in the diplomatic talks between the Allies. After Roosevelt's insistence on a policy of unconditional surrender for Germany, there was no need for Stalin to rush his armies into Berlin. Vienna, not Berlin, was the strategic center of Eastern Europe, and by February 1945 Stalin had the Allies' word for it that Berlin would be within the Russian zone of occupation under any circumstances.

1

By the end of April Zhukov's armies had encircled Berlin, and Soviet patrols met up with the American First Army on the Elbe. Vienna had been taken by the Russians on April 13. Prague too was left to Stalin, because Eisenhower obligingly halted his troops on the Elbe and a few miles inside Czech territory. He believed, wrongly as it turned out, that the Nazis were building up a final defense in the Alps. Thus by the time war in Europe came to an end on May 7, 1945, Soviet armies had spread out over the whole of Eastern and most of Central Europe, thanks to their superior power and the adroit use of the political situation.

Having taken a brief look at Soviet military expansion, let us examine the problem it posed for Russia's allies, who had acted as bulwarks against the spread of Soviet communist influence since 1917.

Philip E. Mosely

AMERICAN POLICY TOWARD EAST CENTRAL EUROPE

The experience of World War II suggests that the only way in which the United States could have exercised a determining influence on the postwar status of East Central Europe was to appear there with large military forces.

In recent years it has often been argued that, if the American leadership had accepted the Churchill-sponsored project for an invasion of the Balkans in 1943, the later fate of East Central Europe might have been a very different one, for the need and opportunity for Soviet-style "liberation" would have been averted. The plans for a Balkan approach have remained obscure, as to forces proposed and limits of advance and schedule, but there has been no indication that they called for more than an advance northward to the Danube-Sava line. If carried out, this plan would presumably have brought Bulgaria within the British safety-zone for the Mediterranean, but it is probable that Yugoslavia would have remained under the control of Tito's forces. In any case, Poland and Czechoslovakia, Hungary and Rumania would have remained within the Soviet military theater, with all the consequences deriving therefrom. In addition, the SHAEF invasion of Western Europe could not have been carried out during 1944. It is possible that not only all of Germany, but also Denmark, the Netherlands, Belgium and perhaps France would have experienced Soviet-style "liberation."

There was much more to be said in favor of Churchill's proposals, in the summer of 1944, that the Anglo-American forces should advance through the Ljubljana Gap into Austria and perhaps into Western Hungary, but the American Joint Chiefs of Staff also overruled this proposal in favor of the invasion of southern France. By that time Hitler could no longer afford to withdraw forces from Western Europe to reinforce his hold on the Danube area, and So-

From "Hopes and Failure: American Policy Toward East Central Europe, 1941–47," *The Fate of East Central Europe,* ed. S. D. Kertesz, (Notre Dame, 1956) pp. 61–63. Reprinted by permission of University of Notre Dame Press.

viet forces were at the outskirts of Warsaw and on the eastern frontier of Hungary. An alternative campaign, discussed to some extent at the time, called for the use of Allied forces in Bulgaria and Albania, but this diversion of forces was also opposed by the American chiefs. It is easy, in retrospect, to say that the landing in southern France in August 1944 was unnecessary and that this force should have been directed against the Balkan or Danubian area. But who can blame a commander for making assurance doubly sure at a time when the decisive campaign in Normandy hung in the balance?

Churchill's persistent advocacy of a Balkan campaign had one unfortunate repercussion on American planning for the postwar status of East Central Europe. After the great debates of 1943 over strategy and the postponement of the Normandy invasion to May 1944 the American Joint Chiefs of Staff ruled, in the autumn of 1943, that the United States should take no responsibilities "in the area of the Balkans including Austria." It was many months before this veto against American participation in Austrian affairs was lifted. In May 1944 Ambassador John G. Winant, United States representative on the European Advisory Commission, took occasion to explain in person to President Roosevelt how serious it would be for the United States to refuse to participate in the reestablishment of an independent Austria. American abstention would leave Russia and Britain face-to-face as occupying or liberating powers and would result in the partitioning of Austria into two zones, thus nullifying the assurances which the three powers had given in their Declaration on Austria, of November 1, 1943. As a result,

the Joint Chiefs of Staff agreed in June 1944 that the United States could participate in the central control machinery for Austria, but maintained their refusal to consider accepting an American zone of occupation.

At the end of December 1944 as the time for negotiating concrete arrangements for Austria was drawing near, Winant reopened directly with Roosevelt the question of policy toward Austria. In a series of strong messages Winant explained that, if the United States was to have an effective voice in Austrian affairs, it must also have a zone to administer. At the end of December 1944, the Joint Chiefs of Staff reluctantly agreed that the United States would administer a zone in Austria; since the United States had agreed, in September 1944, to occupy the southern zone in Germany, bordering on its proposed zone in Austria, there was no longer any logistical reason for refusing to participate in the reestablishment of the Austrian state.

However, if Austria seemed to the military leadership to be a part of the "Balkans," and was thereby excluded for so long from political as well as military planning, how much prospect was there that any of the countries of East Central Europe would fall within the sphere of effective American action? Echoes of this persistent military position were heard at the crucial White House conference of April 23, 1945, called by President Truman to discuss the American attitude toward the flagrant Soviet violations of the Yalta agreements. At this conference Secretary Stimson argued that "the Balkans and their troubles were beyond the sphere of proper United States action"; he urged caution in opposing the Soviet flouting of the Yalta agreement on Poland and the Yugoslav seizure of Trieste.

3

EARLY SOVIET AIMS IN EASTERN EUROPE

Of all the problems discussed during the inter-allied talks at Teheran, Yalta, and Potsdam, the future of Eastern Europe was to have the most significance for postwar relations between the Soviet Union and her ex-allies. It is important at this point to make an assessment of Russian aims *as of 1944–1945* in this area, and to avoid assigning with the wisdom of hindsight any intentions that simply did not exist or else were only very dimly outlined at the time.

What were Stalin's thoughts on Eastern Europe at the end of the war? While it is impossible to pin them down with certainty, some interesting facts emerge. In the first place Stalin made it quite clear that the objectives of Soviet diplomacy were practically the same as they had been during the period of the Soviet-German Nonaggression Pact. During the whole course of the war Stalin affirmed that the territories Russia had annexed from Poland, Rumania, and Finland in 1939 and 1940 belonged to her on a permanent basis. At Teheran Stalin declared also that the Baltic States of Lithuania, Latvia, and Estonia, which had been annexed in 1940, had become member republics of the U.S.S.R. by virtue of the free vote of their peoples.

Far less explicit was the nature of Soviet plans for the territories through which the Red Army marched on its way to Berlin. It is very probable that Stalin had no long-term blueprint for Eastern Europe. We must try to put ourselves in his place and consider what this area of the world meant to him at this time. First and foremost, Eastern Europe had to be drawn into the Russian sphere of influence. For the second time in the twentieth century Germany had inflicted devastating losses on Russia, sweeping across the wide plains and defenseless territories of the small nations that separated her from the U.S.S.R. In 1944 Stalin was still thinking in terms of prenuclear strategy: even if Germany did not arise from the ashes and attempt to take her revenge, there was always the chance, to Soviet ways of thinking at least, that bourgeois governments would stage another intervention or else secure a ring of pro-capitalist states around Russian borders. Stalin's fear of Germany dominated his ideas on foreign policy at this time. We shall see this fear dominating his plans for Poland, the German gateway to Russia, and in his ideas on international co-operation in the postwar world.

Stalin was determined that the East European states would not fall under the control of domestic governments which might be hostile to the Soviet Union. This need was recognized by Russia's allies, and led to the Anglo-Soviet agreement on spheres of influence in the Balkans. It is doubtful whether Stalin in 1945 had any fixed intention of submitting the East European states to uncompromising communist rule. When the Soviet government stated on July 26, 1944, that it did not "pursue the aim of acquiring any part of Polish territory or of changing the social order in Poland," a claim that had previously been made with respect to Rumania, it was not necessarily indulging in double-talk.

In October of the same year Stalin expressed the opinion in a conversation with Mikolajczyk, the Polish premier, that communism did not fit the Poles as a nation. It seems that Stalin merely hoped that communist parties in Eastern Europe would wield sufficient influence to prevent the emergence of anti-Russian tendencies.

It would be rash to rely on Soviet statements alone as a guide to Soviet policy; but in this case practical Soviet moves lent credence to the opinion given above. These actions revealed a policy of great flexibility with regard to the future of the East European states, as illustrated by wartime relations between Moscow and the Yugoslav and Polish communists. In 1942 Tito was criticized for allowing his partisan movement to acquire "a communist character." In Poland a heated quarrel ensued between local communists who maintained a rigid, orthodox view of revolutionary tactics and their more flexible compatriots brought in from Moscow.

Stalin's geographical manipulations in Poland showed that at the beginning he had no precise plans for forcing a communist government on that country. He annoyed the Poles by refusing to make any concessions about their eastern frontier. Yet if Poland as well as Russia was to be communist, what need was there for Stalin to be so adamant? Soviet relations with communist parties in the Axis countries were also strained because of the crippling reparations which Stalin demanded from Hungary, Rumania, and Bulgaria amongst the East European states. There would have been little reason to ransack and antagonize Eastern Europe if Stalin had already envisaged the pattern of Soviet economic control that evolved in the area after the war. In the political sphere too, the Cominform appeared to be only a distant reality.

At the root of Stalin's behavior lay his aversion to spontaneous revolutions by any of the foreign communist parties. George Kennan thinks that the spirit of Trotsky, rather than that of Hitler or of any other capitalist demon, haunted Stalin the most. Having once ousted Trotsky and built up Socialism in One Country, a theory which in practice ensured his position as the head of the world communist movement, Stalin would have run counter to his whole previous way of thinking had he deliberately encouraged revolution in Eastern Europe. He had been against revolutions before 1939, when Russia's strength was growing rapidly. He was even more cautious in 1945, when his own country, the bastion of his personal power, lay in ruins.

The existence of a number of states outside Russia in which communist rule seemed a likelihood for the future created an entirely new set of problems for Stalin. At the end of the war he directed his attention chiefly to the rehabilitation of Russia, a problem with which he was perfectly familiar, while cautiously watching developments in Eastern Europe. It was only when his initial approach to Eastern Europe spelled danger that he extended Socialism in One Country to socialism in one zone, as Isaac Deutscher has called it. Stalin was to discover that the only way he could ensure undisputed Soviet influence in

Eastern Europe was to apply controlled revolution from above. In the long run totalitarian government is incompatible with flexibility, even when government is exercised indirectly over foreign states.

Leon Trotsky

PERMANENT REVOLUTION

The dictatorship of the proletariat which has risen to power as the leader of the democratic revolution is inevitably and very quickly placed before tasks that are bound up with deep inroads into the rights of bourgeois property. The democratic revolution grows over immediately into the socialist, and thereby, becomes a *permanent* revolution.

The conquest of power by the proletariat does not terminate the revolution, but only opens it. Socialist construction is conceivable only on the foundation of the class struggle, on a national and international scale. This struggle, under the conditions of an overwhelming predominance of capitalist relationships on the world arena, will inevitably lead to explosions, that is, internally to civil wars, and externally to revolutionary wars. Therein lies the permanent character of the socialist revolution as such, regardless of whether it is a backward country that is involved, which only yesterday accomplished its democratic revolution, or an old capitalist country, which already has behind it a long epoch of democracy and parliamentarism.

The completion of the socialist revolution within national limits in unthinkable. One of the basic reasons for the crisis in bourgeois society is the fact that the productive forces created by it conflict with the framework of the national state. From this follow,

on the one hand, imperialist wars, and on the other, the utopia of the bourgeois United States of Europe. The socialist revolution commences on the national arena, is developed further on the inter-state and finally on the world arena. Thus, the socialist revolution becomes a permanent revolution in a newer and broader sense of the word; it attains completion only in the final victory of the new society on our entire planet.

The above outlined schema of the development of the world revolution eliminates the question of the countries that are "mature" or "immature" for socialism in the spirit of that pedantic, lifeless classification given by the present program of the Comintern. In so far as capitalism has created the world market, the division of labour and productive forces throughout the world, it has also prepared world economy for socialist transformation.

The various countries will go through this process at different tempos. Backward countries, under certain conditions, can arrive at the dictatorship of the proletariat sooner than the advanced countries, but they come later than the latter to socialism.

A backward colonial or semi-colonial country, whose proletariat is insufficiently prepared to unite the peasantry and seize power, is thereby incapable of bringing the democratic revolution to its conclusion. On

---

Leon Trotsky, *On Revolution* (New York, 1931).

the contrary, in a country where the proletariat has power in its hands as the result of the democratic revolution, the subsequent fate of the dictatorship and socialism is not only and not so much dependent in the final analysis upon the national productive forces, as it is upon the development of the international socialist revolution.

The theory of socialism in one country which rose on the yeast of the reaction against October is the only theory that consistently, and to the very end, opposes the theory of the permanent revolution.

The attempt of the epigones, under the blows of our criticism, to confine the application of the theory of socialism in one country exclusively to Russia, because of its specific characteristics (its extensiveness and its natural resources) does not improve matters but only makes them worse. The break with the international position always leads to a national messianism, that is, to attribute special prerogatives and peculiarities to one's own country, which would permit it to play a rôle that other countries cannot attain.

The world division of labor, the dependence of Soviet industry upon foreign technique, the dependence of the productive forces of the advanced countries of Europe upon Asiatic raw materials, etc., etc., make the construction of a socialist society in any single country impossible.

The theory of Stalin-Bucharin not only contrasts the democratic revolution quite mechanically to the socialist revolution, but also tears the national revolution from the international path.

This theory sets the revolution in the backward countries the task of establishing an unrealizable régime to the dictatorship of the proletariat, thus introducing illusion and fiction into politics, paralyzing the struggle for power of the proletariat in the East, and hampering the victory of the colonial revolution.

The very seizure of power by the proletariat signifies, from the standpoint of the theory of the epigones, the completion of the revolution (to "nine-tenths," according to Stalin's formula) and the opening of the epoch of national reform. The theory of the *kulak* growing into socialism and the theory of the "neutralization" of the world bourgeoisie are consequently inseparable from the theory of socialism in one country. They stand and fall together.

By the theory of national socialism, the Communist International is degraded to a weapon useful only for the struggle against military intervention. The present policy of the Comintern, its régime, and the selection of its leading personnel, correspond entirely to the debasement of the Communist International to an auxiliary corps which is not destined to solve independent tasks.

The program of the Comintern created by Bucharin is thoroughly eclectic. It makes the hopeless attempt to reconcile the theory of socialism in one country with Marxian internationalism, which is, however, inseparable from the permanent character of the world revolution. The struggle of the Communist Left Opposition for a correct policy and a healthy régime in the Communist International is inseparably combined with a struggle for a Marxian program. The question of the program in turn is inseparable from the question of the two mutually exclusive theories: the theory of permanent revolution and the theory of socialism in one country. The problem of the permanent revolution has long ago outgrown the episodic differences of opinion between Lenin and Trotsky, which were completely exhausted by history. The struggle is between the basic ideas of Marx and Lenin on the one side and the eclectics of the Centrists on the other.

Philip E. Mosely

STALIN AT YALTA AND POTSDAM

Stalin's aims, heavily backed by unassailable military superiority in Eastern Europe, are reflected in the following account of the inter-allied diplomatic negotiations between 1943 and 1945.

The opposition of the military to the American acceptance of responsibilities in spheres lying outside their own theaters of command was reflected in political planning and action. Because of the reluctance of the President and the military to make political commitments regarding areas outside American direct control, the State Department was left adrift, to "make do" the best it could by means of notes and exhortations. One result was that, just as the Mediterranean was regarded as a wartime and postwar British sphere, East Central Europe, until Yalta and Potsdam, was also treated, between the British and Americans, as primarily a British concern. The location of the governments-in-exile in London, and their partial financial dependence on the British Government, made it plausible for many people in Washington to regard both the governments and their countries' problems as peculiarly a British concern. Suggestions that they would like to move to Washington were firmly rebuffed.

At both the Moscow and Teheran conferences, in late 1943, the American assumption was that the first and most important step was to secure Soviet support for certain basic policies, such as an agreed policy toward Germany and the establishment of the United Nations. Once the central problems of security were resolved to the mutual satisfaction of the "Big Three," "minor" problems, such as the future boundaries of Poland or the postwar regime of Yugoslavia, would, it was hoped, lose much of their urgency in Soviet eyes and could then be resolved in some way compatible with the internal independence of the East Central European nations.

At the Moscow conference of October 1943 the British raised the questions of restoring Soviet relations with the Polish government in London, of resolving the Tito-Mihailovich clash in Yugoslavia, and of promoting the creation of a Danubian confederation which might help the peoples of the area to defend themselves against a resurgent Germany. Molotov promptly accused Eden of wanting to rebuild a *cordon sanitaire* against Russia, and, after long discussion, the British agreed to drop this item from the agenda. Obviously, any idea of federation or confederation in East Central Europe was anathema to the Soviet leaders.

The more real issue of the Soviet-Czechoslovak twenty-year treaty of mutual defense, whose signature had been held up for many months by British objections, also caused sharp discussions at the Moscow Conference. After urging that this and similar postwar commitments should be deferred until the exile governments had returned to their homelands and had been confirmed as representing their people and until the question of the compatibility of separate alliances with the future United Nations could be studied, the British again gave in, and it was agreed that the Benes government would sign the Alliance, as it did in December 1943.

When the character of the postwar Polish

From "Hopes and Failures: American Policy Toward East Central Europe, 1941–47," *The Fate of East Central Europe*, ed. S. D. Kertesz, (Notre Dame, 1956), pp. 63–74. Reprinted by permission of University of Notre Dame Press.

and Yugoslav regimes came up for discussion, the British again bore the brunt of the argument. Mr. Hull, pressed for his opinion, said that he hoped his British and Soviet colleagues would talk it over and come to a meeting of minds. Molotov, quick as a rapier, then pressed to know if the United States would accept whatever the British and Soviet delegations agreed on. Hull, of course, evaded this invitation to "bow out" from the entire complex of East Central European problems, but he made it equally clear that the United States Government was not really concerned about this area of Europe, at least in comparison with the "big" issues. Certainly, this must have been the Soviet impression of the American position.

A similar tactic of playing down the American concern about the postwar prospects of East Central Europe was followed by President Roosevelt at the Teheran Conference, although he did not follow Churchill in endorsing the claim of the Soviet Government to recover the boundary of June 22, 1941. Again, he left it to the British representatives, despite their acceptance of the Curzon line as Poland's eastern boundary, to uphold the interest of the West in the postwar status of the peoples of East Central Europe.

If the most influential American leader was uncertain whether his country would be willing to guarantee any specific postwar settlements even in Western Europe, the pressure on Britain to accept Soviet-imposed decisions in the area of the Red Army's advance and thereby to gain some bargaining advantage for British interests elsewhere became almost irresistible. If no outside force could deter or dissuade the Soviet leaders from having their way in areas under their military control, then it was important for the British to accept the inevitable as early and as gracefully as possible and thereby to gain some counterpart, for example, through Soviet recognition of Britain's paramount interests in

the countries bordering on the Mediterranean. If the Soviet Government was determined on building its own sphere in East Central Europe, then London must secure in advance a Soviet promise to respect the British lifeline to the East.

This question became especially acute with the Soviet entry into Rumanian territory, in April 1944, and in May the British Government proposed, first to Moscow and then to Washington, that Russia have a controlling influence in Rumania and Britain in Greece. Shortly after, Churchill also proposed assigning Bulgaria to Russian control and Yugoslavia to British. Following strong protests by Secretary Hull, Roosevelt cabled Churchill that he preferred to see consultative machinery for the Balkans set up to resolve misunderstandings and to prevent the development of exclusive zones of influence. However, two days later Roosevelt yielded to Churchill's pressure and agreed that the proposed division of responsibility would receive a three-months' trial, after which it would be reviewed by the three governments.

Four months later, in October 1944, an even more elaborate Anglo-Soviet agreement was negotiated by Churchill and Eden at Moscow. According to one version, it assigned to Russia 75/25 or 80/20 preponderance in Bulgaria, Rumania and Hungary, while in Yugoslavia Russia was to share influence with Britain 50/50. When, at Yalta, American influence began to be exerted more positively in favor of the national independence of the peoples of East Central Europe, this shift occurred against a long record of general declarations seasoned with inaction and with a weather-eye cocked to detect Soviet reactions. The question always asked was whether it was worthwhile to risk a Soviet separate peace with Germany, later, a Soviet abstention from entering the war against Japan, in order to protest against Soviet actions which the United States was powerless to prevent. Perhaps the final outcome would have been the same, but those who were charged with negotiating were never given any valuable counters to use; they were left with the frustrating invitation to win over the Soviet Government to American views by means of words alone. When at Yalta the United States began shifting from passivity to active interest, its British partner was too far committed to a division-of-spheres policy to render strong support.

For East Central Europe the crucial year was 1944, which saw the conclusion of several armistices and the installation of massive Soviet power, backed by communist parties and the Soviet secret police, in most of the area. Unlike the Soviet role in determining surrender terms for Italy, the Western powers negotiated actively, if ineffectively, on the terms of the armistices. In the long negotiations on the Bulgarian armistice, for example, the author proposed that the Allied Control Commission operate under the "general direction" of the Soviet commander only during the period of hostilities against Germany. Several weeks of close negotiation in London, in the European Advisory Commission, ended when, during the Churchill-Eden visit in Moscow in October 1944, the British representatives agreed to abandon the provision for tripartite and equal control in the post-hostilities period. As a result, both the Bulgarian armistice of October 28, 1944, and, after it, the Hungarian armistice of January 20, 1945, provided that

During the period between the coming into force of the armistice and the conclusion of hostilities against Germany the Allied Control Commission will be under the general direction of the Allied (Soviet) High Command.

But they made no corresponding provision for the period between the surrender of Germany and the coming into force of the peace treaties. During the period between the armi-

stices of 1944 and the Yalta Conference of February 1945 it had become clear that the wartime policy of postponing to a peace conference the settlement of the specific issues of East Central Europe was no longer tenable. Reflecting both hope and alarm, the State Department staff, in preparation for Yalta, prepared detailed studies and recommendations in support of a positive United States policy designed to safeguard the internal independence of the one hundred million people of this area. In addition to specific recommendations for strengthening the American role in each of the countries, the State Department also prepared a draft Declaration on Liberated Europe and a detailed plan for creating a four-power Emergency High Commission for Liberated Europe, empowered to carry out the lofty intentions of the Declaration.

At Yalta Roosevelt put forward the draft Declaration, which, after a relatively brief discussion, was approved with minor changes. He decided not to present the proposal for establishing an Emergency High Commission. Why? On this the record is obscure. Perhaps he was fearful of jeopardizing Soviet participation in the war against Japan. Perhaps he disliked the inclusion of the French Provisional Government in the proposed four-power commission. In any event, the opportunity, perhaps the last during the war, to assure a more active and perhaps more effective participation by the United States in the wartime and postwar reshaping of East Central Europe was lost. The signing of the Declaration on Liberated Europe was, in itself, not enough to convince the Soviet leaders of the new and serious interest which the United States was now prepared to assert in the affairs of that region. Nor did the Yalta agreements on the affairs of Poland and Yugoslavia resolve the basic contradictions between the Soviet and American aims.

Between Yalta and Potsdam the cleavage between Soviet and Western aims in East

Central Europe grew ever wider. In violation of the Yalta agreement on Poland, in April the Soviet Government recognized unilaterally the unreconstructed Lublin regime. In violation of the Agreement on Zones of Occupation in Germany, in June it transferred a major part of the Soviet Zone to Polish possession. The United States withstood the Soviet pressure to admit the Lublin government to the San Francisco Conference, but by the June 1945 compromise, itself a compromise within the Yalta compromise, the Soviet leaders secured the substance of power within Poland for their puppet regime by giving only token representation to the parties and leaders which represented the great majority of the Polish people. Within Yugoslavia Soviet encouragement to the Tito regime blithely ignored both the substance of the Yalta agreement and the Anglo-Soviet agreement for a 50/50 sharing of influence, as the Yugoslav communists zealously consolidated their undivided control. At the end of February, in disregard of the Yalta Declaration and of strong American protests, Vyshinsky dismissed the Radescu government in Rumania and imposed the Communist-dominated Groza regime. Roosevelt's pleas and protests over Soviet actions in Poland and Rumania were dismissed abruptly by Stalin. By the time of Roosevelt's death the cleavage between Soviet actions and American hopes was complete.

Molotov's visit to Washington, on his way to the San Francisco Conference, gave occasion for the new President to review the Yalta agreements on East Central Europe and to consider what could be done to secure their fulfillment. At an important White House meeting on April 23, 1945, Truman received contradictory advice. Stettinius, Harriman, and Forrestal urged a strong stand, meeting the issue head-on. Leahy urged accommodation and Stimson argued that "the Balkans and their troubles were beyond the sphere of proper United States action," while Marshall warned that a break with Moscow might destroy the hope "for Soviet participation in the war against Japan at a time when it would be useful to us." President Truman felt that "our agreements with the Soviet Union so far had been a one-way street and that he could not continue." His firmer stand succeeded in some details but was to fail in its broader purpose. By June, through the Hopkins mission to Moscow the outward form of agreement on the new Polish Government was all that could be salvaged.

By the time of the Potsdam Conference the Truman administration was no longer shackled by the gnawing fear that through a "strong" policy on East Central Europe it might forfeit Soviet participation in the war against Japan, but the urgency of reaching agreement on post-hostilities policy toward Germany and a multitude of other pressing issues limited severely the pressure which could be exerted on behalf of the freedom and independence of the peoples of East Central Europe. Despite strong misgivings over placing so much German territory under Polish administration, the best that could be done was to leave open the final decision on the new western boundary. Even this agreement was promptly repudiated a few days later by the Soviet Government, which, in August 1945 guaranteed to Poland the annexation of the German territories which had been placed under its "provisional administration."

Despite State Department hopes that the Allied Control Commissions in Hungary, Rumania, and Bulgaria would henceforth be placed under three-power direction, the best that could be achieved was an agreement that directives would now be issued by the Soviet chairmen only after "coordination" with their British and American colleagues. Even this concession was promptly vitiated by Soviet action; sidestepping the Commissions, henceforth the Soviet commanders issued their orders, as military commanders, directly to the Communist members of the puppet regimes.

Stalin also agreed to freedom of movement and reporting for Western correspondents, but he firmly rejected plans for "internationalizing" the Danube and Rhine rivers.

The basic Soviet demand at Potsdam was for the immediate and unconditional recognition of the Soviet-dominated regimes in Hungary, Rumania and Bulgaria. Obviously, if accepted, this meant abandoning all the Yalta promises of free elections and representative governments, and Truman and Byrnes insisted again and again that they would not recognize governments in these countries until they had a "free government established by themselves without pressure from beyond their borders." Stalin made the Soviet position clear when he stated that "any freely elected government would be anti-Soviet and that we cannot permit."

After the vigorous assertion of the American policy of promoting free and representative governments in East Central Europe, Stalin and Molotov must have been somewhat confused by Secretary Byrnes' sudden suggestion that "the United States would approve of any arrangement that was accepted by the United Kingdom and the Soviet Government" concerning the recognition of the three satellite regimes. This was a last echo of the wartime assumption that East Central Europe was more a British than an American area of concern. After Potsdam it was clear that whatever pressure Britain and America could muster in support of the Yalta Declaration would be determined primarily by American determination and political skill.

The new and stubborn American stand at Potsdam had some significant repercussions within East Central Europe. In Rumania King Michael refused to sign the decrees of the illegal Groza government. In Bulgaria the elections, which were being "prepared" by the Communists with great ruthlessness, were postponed at the last moment. In Hungary the non-Communist parties rejected the Soviet demand for a single-list election, though they agreed to continue the coalition with the Communists regardless of the outcome of the election. Thus, Potsdam encouraged a courageous posture by the non-Communist political forces, while the postponement of the evacuation of American forces from western Czechoslovakia enabled the coalition government to negotiate the simultaneous withdrawal of the Soviet forces. Potsdam also ratified a major reshuffling of ethnic distributions, through its approval for removing the German populations not only from Poland, Czechoslovakia and Hungary, but also from the "Polish-administered" areas east of the Oder-Neisse line.

The first meeting of the council of Foreign Ministers, held at London in September 1945, made clear the deadlock which had developed between Soviet and American aims in East Central Europe. Molotov made it plain that his government insisted on having its way in the settlements with Hungary, Rumania and Bulgaria, and in support of Yugoslav claims against Italy. He insisted over and over on immediate and unconditional recognition of the Soviet-dominated regimes in the satellites. As at Potsdam, he denounced Secretary Byrnes' insistence on free elections as a desire to establish "anti-Soviet regimes" in these countries and to re-create the *cordon sanitaire* against the Soviet Union. To illustrate the absence of hostile intention on the American side and to make clear the American definition of free elections, Byrnes offered then and there to extend recognition to the Hungarian Government, provided it assured a relatively free and unimpeded vote. Following a complete deadlock between the two positions, on September 22 Molotov injected the Soviet demand for equal participation in the control of Japan, and when the American representatives were unwilling even to discuss this Soviet incursion into an American "sphere of responsibility," Molotov broke up the conference.

The strong American stand at Potsdam and London in favor of free elections in East Central Europe threw a few handfuls of grit into the grinding wheels of the Soviet power-machine, but it could not stop their turning. Meanwhile, a similar tug-of-war, this time in favor of the American position, was taking place between Moscow and Washington over the postwar control of Japan. At the Moscow Conference of Foreign Ministers, in December 1945, the United States received Soviet acquiescence in the substance of its claims to sole control over occupied Japan, and the Soviet Government gained the substance of American acquiescence in the policies which it was following in East Central Europe, making only a few concessions of form by allowing Western-nominated ministers to sit in the Rumanian cabinet. A similar Soviet promise to "suggest" to the Bulgarian Government the inclusion of Western-recommended ministers was promptly vitiated in Sofia by Vyshinsky's "suggesting" the opposite. The defeat of the American effort to assure to the nations of East Central Europe the enjoyment, in some degree, of the right of self-determination—an effort begun belatedly at Yalta—was sealed within the same year at Moscow.

What could American policy do henceforth to help the peoples of East Central Europe to escape the yoke which was being pressed down upon their shoulders? One hope was to use the offer of American economic aid to strengthen their ties with the West. Through the sale of surplus supplies and the timing of the restitution of stolen property and shipping, some efforts were made in this direction, but there was no consistent plan and no popular understanding of the need for one. Another, and somewhat contradictory, line of action was to press for the protection of American property rights. This was a feeble and two-edged sword, for it fed the Communist propaganda against the "imperialists" at the same time that the United States was committed in principle to accepting the nationalization of foreign owned properties provided the principles of non-discrimination and compensation were observed.

A more substantial hope was that the speedy conclusion of the peace treaties and the withdrawal of Soviet troops would allow the non-Communist forces to recover control of their national destinies. To hasten the conclusions of the treaties the American Government accepted many unfavorable provisions, including those for establishing the Free Territory of Trieste and for submitting the future status of the Danube to decision by a Soviet-packed conference. The Soviet negotiators made haste slowly. Agreed to in December 1946, the treaties were signed in February and entered into force in September 1947. In Hungary complete Communist domination had been established in May 1947, the Communist grip on Bulgaria and Rumania was unshakable, and the Polish "elections" of January 1947 set the seal on Communist control. In all these countries, except Albania, Soviet-dominated regimes had received American recognition, despite flagrant violations of the Yalta agreements. Soviet forces also remained stationed in Hungary, Rumania, and Poland.

During the war of 1941–1945 the United States moved from a parochially continental concept of its responsibilities to the exercise of leadership over the more productive half of Europe and over Japan, and to the development of new policies toward the British Commonwealth and the Middle East. The two areas where its new concept of responsibilities failed were China and East Central Europe. The expansion of American interests and responsibilities had been unforeseen and unplanned. As late as 1946 American policy-making assumed that, having defeated the aggressors, the United States would be free, once again, to limit drastically its commitments in other continents, leaving the United Nations to take care of what minor troubles and conflicts might arise.

Between 1941 and 1947 American hopes for a democratic and liberal future for the one hundred million people of East Central Europe rose and fell. Hopes were high so long as American opinion failed to realize that in East Central Europe Soviet aims and American aspirations ran directly counter to each other. Here two separate wars were being waged, but Washington failed during the war to assure power positions from which it could achieve its hopes after the war. The location of forces at the close of hostilities was to be, more than was realized at the time, the decisive factor in the divergent fates of East Central and Western Europe. Wartime strategy, in the event, determined the shape of postwar diplomacy. The strategy of coalition called for the assignment of military "spheres of responsibility," and these, as the Cassandras of the State Department warned over and

over, were likely to harden into postwar "spheres of influence" and into competition and conflict between them.

Despite gnawing doubts as to how far the administration in power could commit the United States to the enforcement of specific postwar settlements anywhere in Europe, Roosevelt and Truman found strong support at home for the hopes which were expressed in the Yalta Declaration on Liberated Europe. But the new and active course was begun with a whole necklace of incubuses hung around its neck. Not least of these was the continuing failure to co-ordinate the use of political, military and economic power within American policy-making. By the end of 1946, against unyielding Soviet insistence on transforming East Central Europe into a closed preserve, the American Government had a heap of broken Soviet promises to point to as a reminder that hope, divorced from power, is not a policy.

James F. Byrnes

THE YALTA SETTLEMENT

Unable to make their power felt in the East European theatre, the United States and Britain placed unwarranted hopes in the Declaration on Liberated Europe, which soon turned out to be a mere scrap of paper, like so many other noble documents that litter the paths of history. Writing after the event, Byrnes, appointed United States Secretary of State soon after the Yalta meeting, still clung forlornly to this scrap.

The day we arrived at Yalta I learned for the first time of a draft declaration of policy on the liberated areas that had been prepared by the State Department. The President did not like the declaration as drafted, but it greatly impressed me and I under-

took to see if it could be revised to meet his objections. After conferences with Secretary Stettinius and other State Department officials a draft was prepared which received the President's approval.

When Secretary Stettinius presented the

From James F. Byrnes, *Speaking Frankly* (New York, 1947), pp. 32–34. Copyright 1947 by Donald S. Russell, Trustee of the James F. Byrnes Foundation. Reprinted with the permission of Harper & Row, Publishers, and William Heinemann, Ltd.

paper, several amendments were suggested by Foreign Secretary Eden and Foreign Minister Molotov. These were accepted and the paper was placed before the Big Three.

The declaration referred to "a principle of the Atlantic Charter—the right of all peoples to choose the form of government under which they will live—the restoration of sovereign rights and self-government to those people who have been forcibly deprived of them by the aggressor nations."

It then asserted:

"To foster the conditions in which the liberated peoples may exercise these rights, the three governments will jointly assist the people in any European liberated state or former Axis satellite state in Europe where in their judgement conditions require (a) to establish conditions of internal peace; (b) to carry out emergency measures for the relief of distressed peoples; (c) to form interim governmental authorities broadly representative of all democratic elements in the population and pledged to the earliest possible establishment through free elections of governments responsive to the will of the people; and (d) to facilitate where necessary the holding of elections."

Agreement was quickly reached among the Big Three. At least, we thought there had been a meeting of minds, but, ever since, there has been continual disagreement between the Soviets and ourselves as to its proper interpretation.

The discussion of the proposal was brief. Stalin opened it by saying, "On the whole, I approve of the declaration."

The President called attention to the paragraph containing the agreement to "facilitate if necessary the holding of elections," and Stalin quickly replied: "I accept that."

"Poland will be the first example of operating under this declaration," the President said . . . "I want the election in Poland to be beyond question, like Caesar's wife. I did not know Caesar's wife, but she was believed to have been pure."

Stalin smilingly replied:

"It was said so about Caesar's wife, but, in fact, she had certain sins."

I only hope the lady had fewer sins than, in our view, this declaration has had violations. It seems to me there is no question as to the intention of the parties to the agreement. We thought it was a step forward. But it proved to be a very faltering step.

When the draftsmen assisting the Foreign Ministers agreed to include in the declaration a statement that certain things would be done by the three governments "where in their judgement conditions require," the Soviets were able to say—as they so often did—whenever they disliked to act, that in their judgement conditions did not require action.

The American public greeted the publication of this declaration with enthusiasm. Editorial writers commented on it favourably. From the close of the Yalta Conference to the present day it has been a source of conflict between the Soviet Union and ourselves. But it is the basis on which we have shown the world that Russian actions in eastern Europe have been in violation of Russia's pledged word. In that respect it has been useful.

INTER-ALLIED NEGOTIATIONS ON POLAND

In the East European sphere the Polish problem provided the *leitmotiv* of inter-allied diplomacy from Teheran to Potsdam. Russia had established relations with the Polish government in exile after the German invasion, but these relations deteriorated rapidly, since the Soviets continued to press for recognition of the Polish eastern frontier set up in 1939 after the fall of Poland. When in the spring of 1943 the Polish government in exile tactlessly, though understandably, demanded an investigation of the Katyn massacre of thousands of Polish officers who had been taken prisoner by the Russians in 1939, the Russian government broke off relations and thereafter supported the Union of Polish Patriots established on Russian soil earlier in the war.

At the time of the Teheran meeting the Polish question was the only sign of the rift that was to grow between Russia and the Anglo-Saxon powers. At Yalta Stalin stressed the supreme importance of establishing a strong Poland to act as a barrier to possible future German aggression. The length and vehemence of his speeches on Poland indicated his interest and also reflected the growing tension between the victors. Indeed the failure to achieve a peaceable settlement of the Polish question represented a major turning point in the relations between the wartime allies.

The quarrel over Poland centered on the delineation of her postwar boundaries and above all on the composition of her government. It was agreed at Yalta that Russia should receive that part of Poland lying east of the Curzon line, so called after the British foreign secretary on behalf of whom it had been prepared in 1920, and that Poland should be compensated with land from eastern Germany. A decision was also reached with regard to the government: Stalin agreed to admit representatives of the government-in-exile, headed by Stanislaw Mikolajczyk, and of other Polish groups to the Communist régime set up by the Soviets on Polish soil.

Roosevelt and Churchill were inviting Poland to put herself under Soviet protection by dislocating her borders and population to the extent they did. Communist domination of the provisional government in Poland in fact survived the efforts of the Western allies to tinker with it. Although the western frontier of Poland was left undefined at Yalta, Russia ceded to the Poles former German lands up to the Oder and western Neisse rivers without waiting for America and Britain to agree. At the Potsdam Conference Byrnes, the American Secretary of State, agreed to leave to the Poles the territory that had been assigned to them by Russia, but kept pending the final decision regarding the frontiers till the signing of the German peace treaty: the treaty has yet to be signed.

Poland was the test case in the tug-of-war between the allies. Stalin was so concerned for the security of Russia in Eastern Europe that he was willing to alienate his partners in the war over this question. Better than any other example, it illustrated how the United States and Britain were unable to enforce their point of view concerning a country which lay under Soviet occupation. Russian military might counted for far more than Stalin's subtlest diplomacy. The United States was the economic giant of the immediate postwar world, but Russian armies stayed in the heart of Europe, while American armies prepared to withdraw as soon as the war ended. The only European power remaining was Britain, crippled by the struggle against Germany and no match for Soviet arms.

SOVIET TREATMENT OF THE BALTIC STATES

Soviet relations with the three Baltic republics of Estonia, Latvia and Lithuania were on a special basis at the close of the war, since Russia had already engulfed these states once under the terms of the Nazi-Soviet pact of 1939. In 1944 they again fell into the grip of Soviet communism with the arrival of the Soviet armies. Their treatment at the hands of the Russians was an ill omen for the future of the other Eastern European countries that were occupied at the same time.

C. Manning

THE FORGOTTEN REPUBLICS

The occupation of the three Republics in 1940 was so clearly an act of aggression that the United States and Great Britain both refused to recognize it and they retained in their capitals the diplomatic representatives of the states, despite the Soviet assertions that the pseudo-elections of 1940 had expressed the will of the people for absorption in the Soviet prison of nations. Baltic representatives continued to keep their seats in the League of Nations from which the Soviet Union had been expelled at the end of 1939 for its attack on Finland.

On the other hand the position of the Baltic diplomats even in Washington and London was very often difficult, for pressure was put on both the American and British governments to reverse their policy not only by the representatives of groups favorable to the Soviets and opposed to Fascism but by Russian liberals and reactionaries who could not forget that they had once formed part of the Russian Empire.

With the Nazi attack upon the Soviet Union in 1941, this pressure was increased, as there came a wave of pro-Soviet sympathy. Stalin instructed his diplomats to sign the Atlantic Charter on September 24, 1941. Under this all the powers agreed to seek no territorial aggrandizement, to tolerate no territorial changes not approved by the people of the area affected and to allow the peoples of the several countries that had been overwhelmed to recover their liberty. On paper this involved the liberation of the Baltic Republics in 1940 as free and democratic choices and as occurring before the date of the Soviet acceptance of the principles. By this device, he completely perverted the sense of the document but at the moment Great Britain and the United States wanted the aid of the Soviets against Nazi Germany and President Roosevelt had hopes of bringing Stalin into a partnership with the free world. As a result the case of the three Baltic republics was not brought up during the War and their governments in exile were not allowed to sign the charter of the United Nations, when it was formed in San Francisco. Thus non-recognition of the Soviet occupation remained in a sense largely theoretical and no steps were taken to give it practical effect any more than practical steps were taken in the other countries of eastern Europe to back up the allied members of the joint commissions responsible for governing the liberated countries as Poland, Hungary, and the lands of the Balkans.

Under these circumstances the Soviet

From *The Forgotten Republics* (New York, 1952), pp. 230–238. Reprinted by permission of the Philosophical Library.

armies had a free hand in the Baltic. As the Germans in 1941, the Soviet forces advanced west and southwest and left Estonia for later reconquest. Riga fell into Soviet hands, on August 8, 1944, Vilnius on July 13, 1944, and Kaunas on August 1, whereas Tallinn was not "liberated" until September 22.

The lands were completely ruined by the movements of the armies and the bombing which they had undergone. Thus 95 per cent of the dwellings in Tartu had been destroyed or damaged and the proportion in the other cities was well over 50 per cent. The number of livestock had been reduced by over one half, there were practically no grain supplies, the factories were destroyed, and the Soviet army burst out of control as undisciplined barbaric hordes, killing and raping and plundering at will with no attempts by the officers to control them.

Yet everywhere the world was told of the liberal gifts made by the overjoyed population to the Russians and their great leader Stalin. It was only a euphemistic expression for the complete plundering of the land by the NKVD after the soldiers had finished their own personal work.

In the early weeks, the new Soviet regime which had been established largely under the same men who had been put in charge in 1940 issued statements of amnesty and proclaimed that with the end of Nazism and Fascism the Soviet Union had changed and that a more normal life would be lived in the future. A few selected foreign journalists were even taken around the country to see the ruined cities but the authorities very soon clamped down on their dispatches and did not allow the trip to be repeated.

Enough has come out of this period to show that the masses of the population had no illusions as to what would be their fate. They were not mistaken for in a very few weeks the NKVD moved in in full strength and commenced to question the population, to present them with questionnaires and to hold that all who had not retired to

the east before the German advance were very definitely enemies of the Soviet Union who deserved exemplary punishment. The questions put to the people individually were such as:

"Why did you not retreat with the Soviet Army in 1941?

"What employment did you pursue during the German occupation?

"What anti-German sabotage have you done?

"Name three accomplices.

"Name three collaborators of the Germans."

Men were given red tickets for military service, green calling them for labor service and white, calling for deportation. People's courts meeting without the presence of the accused condemned them to long terms of prison or to deportation, while their families were picked up, separated at the entrainment points and moved off to parts unknown. The majority wound up in the labor camps in or near the Arctic Circle, whether in Europe or Siberia. Here the living conditions were impossible and from the few persons who by chance succeeded in escaping it is known that from 60 to 65 per cent perished in a short time from cold, overwork, and starvation.

For a while the government delayed in introducing collective farms which made even less appeal to the people of the Baltic states than to the Slavs who were accustomed to village life. This was no act of kindness or of toleration for the machinery of the government was able to ruin the individual farmers even more easily than they could a village and by applying rules against hired labor and the other early stages of Soviet administration rigidly they hoped to force a situation where the people would accept peaceably all the weight and rigor of the new order.

The religious life of the people was totally disrupted. It goes quite without saying that the Orthodox congregations in the three republics were rapidly brought under the direct control of the Patriarch of Moscow and those priests who hesitated were handled through the machinery of the Church and the NKVD. It was easy to remove most of the Lutheran pastors and impoverish the churches by resorting to the traditional Soviet devices of confiscating the buildings and then leasing them at exorbitant rentals to the congregations.

The situation in Lithuania which was primarily Roman Catholic was more difficult. The Kremlin was a bitter foe of Roman Catholicism in all its manifestations and while it announced that the Church was functioning as usual, practically all the bishops were arrested on one charge or another together with the leading priests. The operations of the Church were sadly disrupted, the Church institutions were closed, and all kinds of indirect pressure was exerted to hamper the life and work of the churches, while many buildings for nonpayment of rent, etc. were transformed into state institutions.

The same thing happened with the intellectual and educational life. The universities were thoroughly russified and sovietized. This had been done in 1940 during the first occupation but a certain number of the old faculty had been able to retain their posts and to function in part even under the Nazi occupation. Most of the older men had succeeded in escaping. The new appointees did most of their lecturing in Russian and they followed strictly the lines of Soviet educational and intellectual theory, under which a proper understanding of the general line of the Party is more important than any other quality. Even so they like the writers were constantly called to account for indulging in dangerous nationalistic vagaries.

The press of all three countries was likewise standardized and as early as 1945 the ostensibly national newspapers had begun to print the great bulk of their notices and their communications in Russian.

A still more serious result of the second occupation was the introduction into the territory of large masses of Great Russians and individuals from the other Asiatic Soviet Republics to take the place of the departed population. Very early the Soviet government paid especial attention to the population of the islands of Saaremaa and Hiiumaa, which controlled the east coast of the Baltic Sea. Within the first year ten per cent of the population was deported from some of the communities on these islands and with the strengthening of the military garrisons, the number of persons removed was vastly increased, until now there are probably very few of the original population left on them. The Soviet Union has arbitrarily extended its domestic waters to a distance of twenty miles from shore and has shot down at least one American plane flying outside of this area. Soviet patrol boats guard this outer stretch and the fishermen from the shore are not allowed to go beyond the appointed line, and when they are on shore, their boats are carefully guarded to prevent any from escaping into the open Baltic and possibly reaching Sweden, exactly the same regulation as the Knights applied to the Kurs.

It is often overlooked that these republics are hermetically sealed off not only from the outside world but also from the Russian Soviet-Republic itself. Travel even within the Soviet Union is allowed only by special permission of the NKVD and the strict execution of the laws which prevent the workman from changing his place of abode has resulted in an even worse enslavement of the population than in the darkest days of the Middle Ages, when the regime was concerned only with the external life of the slave and paid no attention to his thoughts, his folksongs or his local customs.

This has not been without the opposition of the people. During the first Soviet occupation and then under the Nazis, a large number of the more active and patriotic took refuge in the forests and the swamps and organized themselves into armed bands to prey upon the invaders. The return of the Soviets accelerated this movement and during the first years after the

19

occupation, enough news leaked out to show that there was an organized guerilla force still carrying on a desperate resistance. While Poland was still semi-independent, armed bands of Lithuanian fighters on several occasions shot their way across the closely guarded borders and succeeded in arriving in lands under Allied control. They have revealed some of the exploits of these men who made common cause in the neighborhood of Byelorussia with the fighters from there and with representatives of the Ukrainian Insurgent Army which is still keeping up the hopeless struggle in various regions, especially in the Carpathian Mountains.

They have confirmed the rumors of the elaborate clearing of the borders, the many lines of frontier guards that are thrown around the land, the use of electrified wires, of trained dogs, and of torture patrols that roam day and night to justify and prove the devotion of the people to the great Stalin and the Soviet fatherland, the Russian Empire.

For the suppression of these "bandits" the Soviets employed not only troops of the NKVD but also regular military units. In areas where they appeared, they have burned villages, killed and tortured or deported the bulk of the population, and now and then they have let slip certain details in their attacks on the democracies which they

pour out so steadily in their press and at the United Nations meetings.

Within the three Baltic Republics since World War II life has continued to go on, but in a very real sense history has ceased to exist. There are still the periodic elections to the various Soviets in Moscow, but the names of the successful competitors in the Soviet elections are rarely announced and when they are, they are either well-known Russians or persons completely unknown, for all the outstanding men in the three countries who fell into the hands of the Soviets on their return have vanished as if they had never lived. Even most of the Communists who took part in the occupation of 1940 and had some previous connection with these lands have disappeared behind the same impenetrable veil. Of a few we know that they have been liquidated for "bourgeois nationalism." For the majority we can only guess but it is abundantly clear that they have not received the rewards and the prominent positions they expected for their betrayal of their own people.

Life is good only for the higher ranks of the Soviet hierarchy, for those people who receive large salaries and special ration cards and special facilities for purchasing in the special stores opened for their own benefit.

SOVIET TACTICS IN THE OCCUPIED COUNTRIES

In general Soviet policy in occupied Eastern Europe appeared to be motivated by several aims. Short-term objectives, which were the most prominent in the immediate postwar years, included the urgent need to deny the area to Germany, not only for the present, but for the future as well. Soviet national security was the predominant factor in the minds of those who fashioned Russian foreign policy. This obsession resulted in two subsidiary aims—the establishment of domestic governments in Eastern Europe which would be friendly to the Soviet Union, and a campaign to use the area as an economic mine from which materials and capital could be extracted for the benefit of crippled Soviet industry. There is no doubt that Stalin feared that world capitalism would eventually attempt to wrest Eastern Europe from the Soviet sphere of influence. The hardening of international relations in the years 1946–1947 confirmed him in this belief, as did growing signs of independence within Eastern Europe at the same time.

Stalin's answer to the problem was to impose rigid totalitarian patterns on all the East European countries under his control. This involved another long-term aim, which, although it had been present from the start, only gained positive impulse some time after the end of the war—the communization of Eastern Europe. Politically this was achieved throughout the area by 1947 except in Czechoslovakia, but the enormous social and economic revolutions which alone spelled fully-fledged communism in conformity with the Soviet pattern were put through after 1947 only.

The process of political alignment with the Soviet Union, which was already underway before the end of hostilities in some countries of Eastern Europe, proceeded along similar lines in Hungary, Rumania, Bulgaria and Czechoslovakia. In Yugoslavia and Albania civil wars had swept away the old political and social structure; in Poland the Nazis uprooted the existing regime, and on its entry into the country the Red Army effectively stamped out the remnants of the old political structure in the form of the Polish resistance movement. Professor Hugh Seton-Watson, in his book *The East European Revolution*, has given us a clear picture of the process of sovietization in the countries which still conserved most of their prewar class patterns in 1945.

Hugh Seton-Watson

SOVIET TAKEOVER METHODS

The prefabricated revolutions which between 1945 and 1948 brought nearly a hundred million Europeans under Stalinist rule were the first considerable triumph that could be claimed for the communist cause since the Bolsheviks seized power in Russia. Native communist forces obtained power mainly by their own efforts in Yugoslavia and Albania, but were defeated by foreign intervention in Greece, while in Poland the native revolutionary movement, which was not led by communists, was also suppressed by foreign intervention. By the summer of 1945 Soviet Russian military forces occupied all Poland, Roumania, Bulgaria, Hungary and Czechoslovakia, and the eastern half of Germany. In these territories, and for some years also in Yugoslavia, a similar type of regime emerged, which was officially described as "popular democracy."

Three distinct phases may be traced in the

From *The Pattern of the Communist Revolution* (London, 1953), pp. 248–256. Published in the United States under the title *From Lenin to Khrushchev*. Reprinted by permission of Methuen & Co., Ltd., and Frederick A. Praeger, Inc.

establishment of this regime. Not all countries passed through all phases, and the timing of each phase was different in each country.

In the first phase government was by a genuine coalition of parties of left and left centre. The coalitions in all cases included communist and socialist parties. In Hungary, Roumania and Bulgaria they included peasant parties; in Czechoslovakia, where there was no specific peasant party, its place was taken by nonsocialist democratic parties which drew their support partly from peasants and partly from the urban middle class. Yugoslavia, Albania, Poland and East Germany never passed through this stage at all. In Roumania and Bulgaria it existed from the autumn of 1944 to the spring of 1945. In Hungary it lasted until the spring of 1947, and in Czechoslovakia until February 1948.

In the second phase government was by bogus coalition. Several parties still nominally shared power and possessed independent organisations: but their leaders were in fact chosen not by them but by the communist leaders, and the policies of the coalitions were determined by the communists. Political opposition was however still tolerated, although attended with physical risks for those who practised it. Yugoslavia and Albania never passed through this stage. Poland and East Germany began their postwar history in it.

In the third phase the bogus coalitions were transformed into what the communists like to call a "monolithic block." The communist leaders not only laid down the lines of policy, but centrally controlled the organisation and discipline of the noncommunist groups that were still left in the governments. Socialist parties were forced to "fuse" with communist parties. No more political opposition was tolerated in parliament, press or public meeting. In Poland, Roumania and Bulgaria the transition from the second to the third phase began in the autumn of 1947, and was marked by the flight of Mikolajczyk to the West and the trials for treason of Maniu and Petkov—that is, by the political destruction of the leading noncommunist statesman of each of these three countries. In Hungary the transition began in the spring of 1948, with the flight or arrest of those socialist leaders who opposed "fusion." In Czechoslovakia the second and third phases were merged into one, and both were complete by the end of 1948. In East Germany the third phase was completed in 1949, if not even earlier.

Yugoslavia and Albania passed directly to the third stage in 1945 without ever experiencing the first two. Poland omitted the first stage and slipped into the final gear in the autumn of 1947, after the flight of Mikolajczyk, the sole remaining force amongst the Polish democrats. The first stage in Bulgaria and Rumania came to an end in the spring of 1945; by the autumn of 1947 these two countries were in the grips of the last stage. Hungary and especially Czechoslovakia were the laggards in this evolutionary process. The first country remained in the initial stage until May 1947, the second right up to the coup by Moscow's puppet, Gottwald, in February 1948.

The timing of the changes in the various countries was closely tied to the military position. For example in Hungary, which the Red Army was due to leave in 1947 on account of the impending peace treaty between Hungary and the Soviet Union, political terrorism was stepped up as of December 1946, since the Soviets feared that without Russian military influence inside the country the

Moscow-controlled communists would lose their hold over political life. The parliamentary regime in Hungary fell just four weeks before the Soviet troops had to leave the country. Subsequently fake elections were held after the Rumanian and Polish models.

We may turn to Professor Seton-Watson once again for a perceptive account of the details of Soviet takeover methods.

This is no place to recount the story of Stalinisation. It is however important to mention certain aspects of the process. These are the attitude of the communists to the peasant parties and socialist parties; the role of Soviet Russian military, political and economic intervention; the levers of power used by the communists. . . .

Peasant and Socialist Parties

The peasant parties were the first objects of communist attack. They represented, in reality or potentially, the majority of each nation. They must therefore be discredited and split. Some of the things that the communists said against them were true. It was true that in the past the peasant parties had devoted more energy to national than to social issues. It was true that urban middle-class elements were very influential in the Hungarian Small Farmers' Party and the Roumanian National Peasant Party. It was true that those peasant parties which had had power during the inter-war period had used it to the advantage of the wealthier minority of the peasants rather than of the peasants as a whole. But these defects were not the reason for the communist attack on the peasant parties: the communists were concerned not with the rights of the poor peasants but with their own lust for power.

In Roumania there was for a time a genuine reaction against the National Peasant Party. The Ploughmen's Front, a left peasant group that had been founded in 1934 but whose influence had been confined to a few counties of Transylvania, gained mass support in a large part of the country. But when it became clear that the Ploughmen's Front was being used by the communists to split the peasantry, and indeed that through its subservient leader Petru Groza it was controlled by the Communist Party, it lost support, and the old National Peasant Party and its veteran leader Maniu became more popular than ever. A similar group in Hungary, the National Peasant Party, played a less important part, as its leaders were not willing to be used by the communists, and the communists thus had little incentive to publicize or support it.

Communist manoeuvres against the peasant parties in Eastern Europe recall Lenin's trick in producing an artificial split in the Socialist Revolutionary Party in 1917. But the East European communists were less successful: the East European peasants were politically more experienced, and more loyal to their leaders, than the Russian peasants had been. The official communist version of the splits that were eventually engineered is that the left wings, the truly peasant elements as opposed to the urban bourgeois elements, those who sincerely believed in the revolutionary alliance of the toiling masses of town and country, followed the leadership of the communists; while the right wings, the bourgeois, the *kulaks* and the traitors to peasant interests opposed the will of the people. This is even less true of the East European peasant parties than it had been of the Russian Socialist Revolutionaries. In Hungary in the spring of 1947 it was precisely the genuine peasants among the parliamentary representatives of the Small Farmers' Party who opposed the commu-

23

nists, and a section of the party's intellectuals who supported them. In Bulgaria in 1945 it was from the compromised right wing of the Old Agrarian movement that the communists recruited their stooges, while the peasant masses remained loyal to Petkov. In Poland a heterogeneous clique of disgruntled persons collaborated with the communists, while the peasants, as long as they had any opportunity to express their feelings, showed their devotion to Mikolajczyk. In Roumania only insignificant groups could be detached from Maniu's party, and even in the Ploughmen's Front the true peasant leaders were purged in favour of intellectuals bribed or terrorised into obedience to Moscow. The turning-point in the development of the Bulgarian and Hungarian peasant parties was marked by direct Soviet military intervention: in February 1945 the Soviet general demanded the removal of Dr. G. M. Dimitrov from office in the Bulgarian Agrarian Union, and in February 1947 the Soviet military police arrested the General Secretary of the Hungarian Small Farmers' Party, Béla Kovács. The difference between the pro-communist minorities and anti-communist majorities in the East European peasant parties was not social but political. The theory of a class struggle in the villages between poor peasants allied with the workers and the communists, and rich peasants allied with the bourgeoisie was, as in Russia in 1918 and 1929, nothing but a myth. The only real difference was between those who would accept Moscow's orders and those who would not.

In the relationship between communists and socialists too, there is a communist myth and a quite different reality. The myth is that the proletarian masses, aware of the harm done in the past by workers' disunity, imposed unity against the wishes of the small clique of right-wing traitors to socialism and lackeys of the international bourgeoisie in general and of its British Labour agents in particular. All that is true

in this is that the workers were eager for unity: the horrors of Nazism were too fresh in their minds for them to feel otherwise. But the workers remembered that the old disunity had been at least as much due to communist as to socialist errors. Unity to them did not mean capitulation. But that was all it meant to the communists, who were impatient to lay their hands on the relatively efficient machinery of the socialist parties and socialist-dominated trade unions. For Moscow the only aim was to create a reliable instrument of its policy.

This first became obvious in Poland. Already in 1944 the socialist party, which had played an honourable part in the Home Army and the civil resistance to the Germans, was heavily purged of persons regarded by Moscow as "anti-Soviet," and key positions were given to people whom Moscow hoped that it could trust. But even the purged party strongly resisted communist — which meant direct Soviet Russian — pressure. The demand for "fusion" was evaded. Only in March 1948 did the malleable Cyrankiewicz suddenly announce, without previously consulting the party's central committee, that fusion would take place. Even after this, further mass purges were necessary, including, for example, the removal of the whole committee of the party for Lódz, Poland's largest industrial city, before the ceremony was performed, at a "congress of unification" held in Warsaw in December 1948.

If the Polish "fusion" was the result of four years of terror and blackmail, in East Germany "fusion" was suddenly decided in Moscow, and was imposed, by a combination of threats, blackmail and lies, in a few weeks, in April 1946. The new party was named Socialist Unity Party (S.E.D.). The most eminent Social Democrat who joined S.E.D. was Otto Grotewohl, joint chairman with Dr. Kurt Schumacher (resident in the British zone) of the S.P.D. for the whole of Germany. The formation of S.E.D. split German socialism, for the

S.P.D. not only in the western zones but also in the western sectors of Berlin retained its separate existence. Many socialists of the Soviet zone had been persuaded that in the new party socialist influence would predominate, and that by forming S.E.D. they were striking a blow against communist influence. The contrary however proved to be the case. Supported by the might of the occupying army, the communists were able to concentrate in their hands all key positions in the party. The process, accompanied by purges throughout the zone, took several years to complete. By 1952 though Grotewohl himself remained nominally prominent, socialist leaders had been removed from the upper and medium levels of the party, and former membership of S.P.D. was a black mark against a party member. S.E.D. was in practice a well-Stalinised communist party.

In Hungary the right wing of the prewar socialist party was purged in 1945, and the leadership was divided between a "left" which obeyed communist orders and a centre which, while socially very radical, wished to preserve the independence of both the party and the country. In February 1948 the leaders of the centre, Antal Bán and Anna Kéthly, were expelled from the party, and in June 1948 the ceremony of "fusion" took place. Only two years later the "left" socialists suffered the same fate as had overtaken the centre: some were merely removed from their posts in the party, others were also arrested.

In Czechoslovakia the Social Democrat Party, which before 1938 had been stronger than the Communist Party, was far surpassed by it: at the parliamentary election it won only 13 per cent of the votes in the Czech lands, to 40 per cent for the communists. This much-reduced party was divided between those who wanted an independent party and those who bowed before the communists. The subservient wing, led by Zdeněk Fierlinger, was at first

dominant, but at the Brno congress of the party in November 1947 he was overthrown by the party's right and centre. In the "revolution" of February 1948 Fierlinger was reinstated by communist force, and in the summer he duly led the rump party into "fusion."

The Roumanian socialist party had always been very small and weak: it won some importance in 1945 only because it was less disliked by the Roumanian workers than was the Communist Party. But communist pressure, reinforced by Soviet military power, quickly brought it to heel. At a congress held in March 1946 the party split, the opponents of· the communists forming a separate party which had but a short life. In November 1947 "fusion" took place. The Bulgarian socialists were also not numerous, but they were tougher than their Roumanian comrades. In the summer of 1945 the subservient wing, the communist physical support, seized the party's newspaper and co-operatives, but the majority, bravely led by the elderly Kosta Lulchev, opposed the government until forcibly suppressed at the end of 1948.

Soviet Intervention

Soviet intervention in East European affairs has been of three types—direct political action based on the threat of military force, indirect political action, and economic action. Hitherto, however, it has stopped short of the formal incorporation in the Soviet Union which was the fate of the Baltic states in 1940.

East Germany has been more subject and for longer to the first type of intervention than the other countries. The whole political life of the Soviet zone has been determined by Soviet policy. The Soviet authorities decided when to set up *Länder* governments, when to create zonal authorities, and when to set up a separate East German state. These decisions were, it is true, affected by the policy of the Western Powers in their zones of occupation, but from the beginning the initiative has been rather with the Soviet than with the Western governments, and of the Soviet intention from the first to Stalinise the eastern zone there can be no doubt. In Poland direct intervention has been very important, from the creation of the Lublin committee in 1944 to the nomination of the Soviet Marshal Rokossovski as Commander-in-Chief of the Polish Army in 1949. In Roumania Soviet intervention was decisive in February 1945 when Vyshinski flew from Moscow to Bucharest to order King Michael to appoint Groza Premier and so hand over power to the communist-controlled "National Democratic Front."

In Bulgaria and Hungary Soviet action was usually more discreet, though the removal of Dimitrov and Kovács, already mentioned, were acts of direct menace. In Czechoslovakia Soviet action was still more discreet. The presence of Soviet troops in 1945 enabled the communists to seize important positions in the local administration and police, but the withdrawal of all Soviet units in December 1945 removed the main source of intimidation. It seems probable however that the presence of the Soviet Vice-Minister of Foreign Affairs, Zorin, in Prague in February 1948 was not unconnected with the technique of Gottwald's "revolution."

Soviet economic pressure was an extremely important weapon. In Roumania and Hungary reparations were not only designed to compensate the Russian state for part of its war losses, but were also used to crush national opposition to Soviet and communist political aims. A special device were the so-called "joint companies" set up in Roumania and Hungary, in which Moscow nominally had an equal share with the Roumanian or Hungarian government, but which in fact were controlled by Moscow. Joint companies possessed a monopoly of air, river and maritime transport in both countries, besides owning substantial shares of such important resources as Roumanian oil and timber and Hungarian bauxite. In East Germany the Soviet government acquired enormous industrial interests, confiscated from the German state, the Nazi Party and other illegal organisations, and from German's wartime allies. These were organised as "Soviet corporations" (S.A.G.). It is estimated that in 1947 they accounted for 25 per cent of the total industrial output of the Soviet zone, and that in the period from January 1946 to June 1948 they deprived the German economy of goods to the value of two milliard *Reichsmark* valued in 1936 prices. Even in allied Czechoslovakia the Soviet government acquired a valuable economic interest, the Jachymov Uranium mines. The Soviet government was also able to put pressure on the East European governments by its trade policy, imposing unfavourable prices on governments which it was working to disrupt or to subject. An important example is the agreement with Poland of September 1945 by which Polish coal was to be sold to Russia at a price one-tenth of that offered by Denmark. Perhaps the most striking of all cases of Soviet economic pressure for political purposes is the order given to the Czechoslovak government to refuse the invitation to the preliminary conference in Paris on the Marshall Plan in July 1947, though the government had already accepted the invitation, with the consent of Gottwald himself.

Levers of Power

Already in the first phase of Stalinisation the communists seized certain key positions. The most important of these was the Ministry of Interior, which controlled the police. This post was held by a communist already in 1945 in all these countries except Poland and Hungary, and there too control of the security police was in communist hands. The Ministry of Justice, controlling the formal judicial machinery, was considered less important, but was held by communists in certain cases. Control of broadcasting was seized at an early date. Great efforts were made to control and to create youth and women's organisations. In industry, communists were placed in key positions in the management of nationalised factories and in trade unions.

Land reform was made an instrument of communist power. In Hungary, where redistribution of the landlords' estates was long overdue, and was desired by all the democratic parties, the Ministry of Agriculture, and so the supervision of the land reform, was put in communist hands. In Czechoslovakia and Poland land reform consisted of the expropriation of German peasants in the western borderlands. The confiscated lands provided an invaluable fund of patronage to the communists: Czech or Polish peasants who received such land were expected to support the communists, and to a large extent did. Already long before the third stage of Stalinisation had been completed in either country, the western borderlands were communist-ruled states within the state.

Finally, the communists attempted to remodel local government on Soviet lines. The local authorities were to be "people's committees" representing the broad masses but controlled by the communists. In this aim the communists were not successful. The committees did not resemble the bodies of the same name in Yugoslavia, or the Soviets in Russia in 1917. The attempt to capture the masses through new local organisations, which had been so successful in the rise to power of Lenin, Mao Tse-tung and Tito, failed in Eastern Europe. The East European communists got control of local government only after, with Soviet support, they had seized power at the centre. The remodelling of local authorities on Soviet lines was the result, not the cause, of their triumph.

Barry Brannen

THE SOVIET COUP IN RUMANIA

The communist takeover could afford to show its Soviet backing even more clearly in Rumania, an ex-enemy state. This is how the communist coup was described by an outside observer—Barry Brannen, an American representative on the Allied Control Commission.

Unlike the neighboring states of Bulgaria and Jugoslavia, Rumania is not Slavic in race or language. Unlike Bulgaria, her foreign policy has never been oriented toward Russia. There has never been the slightest disposition on the part of the great majority of Rumanians to collaborate with Russia on a military, economic or political plane. Accordingly, what we witness in the country today is the direct imposition of Soviet controls on a people whose race, language and previous politics give no indication that such controls are desirable or acceptable. It was accomplished, moreover, under an Armistice Convention, i.e., a negotiated settlement, the expressed purpose of which

From "The Soviet Conquest of Rumania," *Foreign Affairs*, (April 1952), pp. 466–472. Copyright © by the Council on Foreign Relations, Inc., New York. Reprinted by permission of *Foreign Affairs*.

was to safeguard the "independence and sovereignty" of the country. The experience is a warning to all free peoples against trusting in pacts with the Soviets.

Any attempt to analyze the Rumanian debacle must commence with the events of August 23, 1944. On that date King Michael, in conjunction with a number of Rumanian military leaders and the support of the leaders of the National Peasant and Liberal Parties, effected a successful coup d'état. The King acted forcefully and bravely, outfaced Marshal Antonescu, and ended by imprisoning him in the Palace. The army followed the King to a man. The not inconsiderable German forces in the Bucharest area were taken by surprise, and in a brief but spirited campaign were driven to the Hungarian frontier.

The Antonescu régime was succeeded by a government headed by General Sanatescu, who had served before the war as military attaché in London. Though this government was hastily established, it nevertheless contained representatives of all political parties. It lasted until shortly after the execution of the Armistice Convention on September 21, 1944.

It was at this stage that, in company with other American representatives on the Allied Control Commission, I first arrived in Rumania. We flew in from Athens, and landed at Baneasa Airport, just north of Bucharest, on October 25, 1944. Our Russian and British colleagues were already on the scene.

General Sanatescu had succeeded meanwhile in forming a second coalition government, in which all political elements of the Rumanian electorate were represented. Undoubtedly he intended well, but the Communist opposition was strong, and he had little personal support throughout the country. No one expected his second government to last long. A crisis developed in the latter part of November, and on December 2, 1944, the King called upon General Nicolae Radescu, an old soldier and an uncompromising anti-Fascist, to form a new government.

Prior to General Radescu's term of office, all left-wing elements had been engaged in a vigorous attack on the Sanatescu régime. The cabinet meetings were torn with dissension. Proposals made by the National Peasant and National Liberal leaders were criticized by the Communist Ministers in the most intemperate terms. Accordingly, when the Government fell there seemed no possibility of forming a coalition government in which Communists would be willing to participate. Nevertheless, to the surprise of some observers, the Communists again accepted portfolios in the Government and endorsed Radescu's program. A cardinal principle of this program required all Ministers "to co-operate in order and discipline with the Prime Minister."

The term of the Radescu Government may be divided into two periods. The first lasted from his appointment as Prime Minister until January 24, 1945, when the Communist leader and Minister of Communications, Gheorghiu-Dej, returned from an official visit to Moscow. Until then the political cauldron had been quiet. Communist press attacks against the Government had almost entirely ceased, and there was little criticism even of the leaders of the traditional (National Peasant and National Liberal) parties. General Radescu had used a firm hand against radicals who were attempting to usurp administrative powers in the provinces, and his administration appeared to grow stronger every day.

Upon returning to Bucharest, however, Gheorghiu-Dej issued a scathing statement attacking what he called the "anti-democratic" elements in the country. He repeated his charges a few days later in a speech before the Union of Railroad Workmen. At the same time a coalition of left-wing parties, called the National Democratic Front (F.N.D.), appeared to swing, surprisingly enough, to the Right. The National Democratic Front published a new party platform and appealed vigorously for public support. On its face, the new program seemed far less radical than a previous platform, published three months before. In particular, the National Democratic Front no longer proposed the nationalisation of banks or large industries. In an unpublished address to the railway workers, Gheorghiu-Dej stated expressly that the National Democratic Front expected to cooperate with all industrialists who would make their capital available for the reconstruction of Rumania; left-wing elements were apparently seeking conservative support.

The publication of the new platform was the signal for renewed criticism of the Government by the Communist press, and the period of political serenity came abruptly to an end. The Communist leader, Teohari Georgescu, attacked not only the "anti-democratic" elements in the country but the policies of the Government itself. His action was significant since he occupied the post of Undersecretary of the Interior, and his attack was patently contrary to the understanding which all Ministers had entered into at the time the Radescu Government took office. The traditional parties came actively to the support of the Government and attempted to publish manifestoes of their own. They were prevented from doing so, however, by the Communist-controlled printers' unions which refused to print any newspapers carrying the texts. *Viitorul*, the official newspaper of the National Liberal Party, continued to appear, but, perforce, without the program of the Liberal Party. The official newspaper of the National Peasant Party, *Dreptatea*, suspended publication rather than accede to the printers' demands.

In this state of affairs General Radescu announced that he would make a public address at the Scala Theater in Bucharest on February 11, 1945. When I arrived at the theater, the Communists were already in full control. They had, in fact, occupied the building the previous night and refused to leave. To avoid public disturbance, the Prime Minister chose to deliver his address at the Aro Theater nearby.

In it he severely criticized the action of the printers' unions, charging that their attempt to censor political publications amounted to a denial of freedom of the press. He considered the question of land reform at length, and announced that the Government would take no action with reference to the division of large estates at that time. He gave two reasons: first, that the contemplated land reform would interfere with the maximum production of wheat and corn, required of Rumania under the Armistice Agreement, and secondly, that soldiers then at the front had the right to be consulted and to participate in any measures designed to redistribute the land.

The National Democratic Front joined issue on the question of immediate land reform and called for a mass street demonstration against the Radescu Government on February 13, 1945. This was the first of a series of such demonstrations organized by the Communists. I saw them all, and the pattern was always the same. The labor unions attended in force, being marshalled to their places by organizers of the National Democratic Front. It seemed to many of us that approximately 25,000 people participated in this particular demonstration. They paraded down the Calea Victoriei to the King's Palace, and dispersed without disorder. Though there was no untoward incident, political and social unrest evidently was increasing sharply throughout the country. Shortly thereafter, the Communists made a number of abortive attempts to seize the governmental prefectures in the provinces. In Bucharest a series of disorders culminated in an armed attack on the Malaxa Steel and Locomotive Plant on February 20, 1945.

This plant had been under the direction of self-installed Communist elements for several months, as had other industrial es-

29

tablishments. To combat these tactics, the National Peasant Party had commenced a campaign to enlist industrial workers among its own members, and its efforts in this regard had extended to the Malaxa plant.

On February 20, the workers at the plant attempted to hold an election to designate their bargaining representatives. When it appeared that left-wing leaders would be defeated, a group of several hundred armed workers from adjoining industrial establishments demonstrated in front of the gates. Soon they attempted to enter, and shots were exchanged with workers within the plant, who meanwhile had possessed themselves of arms. During the course of the melee the labor leader Apostol, who had led the demonstration, was wounded by rifle fire.

The Communist press seized upon the disorders as the work of "Fascists" and "saboteurs of the Armistice," and called for a second mass demonstration to be held in Bucharest on February 24. This time approximately 50,000 people, assembling as before, paraded down the Calea Victoriei. The parade was without incident until the first marchers reached the building housing the Ministry of the Interior, directly across the square from the King's Palace. At this stage, a group of approximately 500 men detached themselves from the marchers, advanced against the building and attempted to force an entrance. Soldiers posted near the entrance repelled the men with rifle fire. While the soldiers appeared to be firing over the heads of the crowd, bullets ricocheted from adjoining structures and a number of casualties resulted. Meanwhile the demonstrators had fled in panic.

That night the disorders continued. Members of the National Liberal Party attempted to demonstrate in front of the Ministry of the Interior on behalf of Premier Radescu, but were fired upon without warning by unidentified assailants. The next morning the Communist press charged that the Radescu Government, by provocative action, had created the disturbances and had utilized them as an excuse to fire upon the populace. The sequence of events and the happenings of the day were completely misrepresented and the Government was viciously attacked. General Radescu in turn spoke out hotly against the Communist leaders.

Russian support of the National Democratic Front, heretofore passive, now became active and direct. From Moscow, by press and radio, came a completely distorted picture of the events of February 24. The Russian dispatches strongly attacked the traditional parties and openly demanded the ouster of the Government. By direction of the Russian military, a number of measures were taken to disarm the Bucharest garrison. The Russians insisted that the Rumanian forces in rear areas greatly exceeded the requirements of security and constituted a threat to the Russian armies at the front.

Still another mass demonstration was called by the National Democratic Front to be held in Piata Natiunei, in Bucharest, on March 8, 1945. Reliable reports at this time indicated that workmen were being armed, particularly by the militant Communist organization, *Apararea Patriotica*. It was evident that the security of the Government was directly threatened, for (as a result of the Soviet measures) no armed forces were available to prevent the occupancy of public buildings. To many of us it seemed that the possibility of a Communist coup d'état was very great indeed.

At this juncture Andrei Vishinsky, then Soviet Deputy Commissar for Foreign Affairs, and Marshal Malinovsky, Chairman of the Allied Control Commission, arrived in Bucharest. In the most militant terms Vishinsky demanded that the King dismiss General Radescu. Otherwise, he said, he would not be responsible for the continued independence of Rumania. He terminated the audience abruptly, and on leaving slammed the door with the greatest violence. I remember that the King later pointed out, somewhat ruefully, the resulting damage to the plaster on the wall.

The King yielded to the show of force. A mandate was first tendered Prince Barbu Stirbey, elder statesman and former Premier, who proved unable to form a government. At Vishinsky's suggestion, a limited mandate was then given to Dr. Petru Groza authorizing the formation of a coalition government only. It appeared almost at once that Groza could not obtain the support of either the Liberal Party or the National Peasant Party and that coalition under Groza of all political elements in the country was not feasible.

Nevertheless Groza did not return his mandate but presented to the King a list of Ministers which contained no representatives of the traditional parties. Again the King protested, and again Vishinsky intervened. The King's approval was given reluctantly during the late afternoon of March 6. The Government thus formed was not a coalition government but was composed entirely of left-wing elements. The Prime Minister, Groza, did not call himself a communist, but the leader of a small political party termed the Ploughmen's Front. But both before and after his designation as Prime Minister, Groza and his followers consistently followed the Communist Party line.

J. Nettl

TAKEOVER IN EASTERN GERMANY

Russian occupation was an established fact; an occupation, moreover, sanctioned by international agreement and undisguised. Nowhere outside Soviet Russia, except for the Soviet zone of Korea, had the Russians such vast legal powers as in the Eastern zone of Germany. The theoretical possibilities were also highly favourable for Communism. The collapse of Nazi Germany provided an almost perfect example of the collapse of capitalist society in its final monopolistic form, from sheer inability to cope with its task. This, according to Marx, was an historic inevitability, and provided the necessary situation for the institution of Socialism. . . .

The Communists took full advantage of their position. They were the first to reorganize local action committees in the Soviet zone, in order to keep essential services going. By the time the Russians started to reorganize a system of administration they already found the Communists and Socialists installed in positions of responsibility. From the very beginning, however, two main problems had to be decided by the Russians in Germany.

On what grounds should the measures long prepared in Moscow be put into effect? With the exception of the land reform, they were all in accordance with the basic principles of Marxist theory. The programme included nationalization of the means of production, except land, of commercial undertakings of any size, of banks, transport, insurance, and medical services. It called for State control of education, law, labour, and the arts, a centralized police force, a predominant Communist party, a centralized civil administration, and the

From J. Nettl, *The Eastern Zone and Soviet Policy in Germany, 1945–1950* (New York, 1951), pp. 297–311. Reprinted by permission of Oxford University Press.

ruthless destruction of potential as well as real opponents. In Russia these measures had been carried out early under Communist rule. The process had been complete, and, in spite of backward conditions, rapid. Under the favourable conditions in Germany the process could have been even more rapid. But haste and thoroughness cut out explanations, proposals, and compromises, the normal apparatus of democracy. The only moral support for complete and rapid action in Germany along the lines of early Soviet Russia was the same now as then, the conviction of absolute right, based on the theories of Marx. The coffin of capitalist Germany could only be fastened rapidly with the naked tools of Communism.

There could be no question of Russian inability to carry out this task. Their power in the Soviet zone was undisputed and complete. Fear of disrupting the Allied Control Council with unilateral measures was at best only a partial deterrent. To make four-power government in Germany a reality would have meant that only important measures which had previously been agreed by the four powers could be brought into effect in any zone. This proviso was very soon broken; Russian reparations, the most important reason for their presence in Germany, destroyed quadripartite unanimity as soon as the first reparations train left the Eastern zone for the Soviet Union. Within six months measures had been taken in all four zones which were plainly unilateral. It is improbable that Russian respect for the importance of four-power government was a strong reason for not adopting a whole-hearted Communist policy in the East.

In the event, most of the measures, particularly before summer 1947, were put through with an almost comic effort to avoid any breath of suspicion that they might be promoted by the exigencies of Communist theory. The land reform, it was claimed, was destined chiefly to break the power of the Junkers, and secondly to provide land, and with it a means of existence, for the two million or so German refugees from other countries. Not even the most radical member of the KPD (Communist Party of Germany) was allowed to see in the reform the beginnings of a Communist system. The utilitarian purpose of the measure was enhanced by the public announcement that, while co-operatives would be encouraged, the property of the new farmers was sacred and that collectivization was not intended. One KPD functionary who stated that "collectivization would follow automatically" was sharply and openly rebuked. The socialization of factories was painstakingly carried through piecemeal. The identification of the owners as Nazis or militarists was formally carried out even if the relevant evidence available was negligible. As prominent members of the SED (Socialist Unity Party of Germany) did not fail to point out to visiting journalists: "the basic factor for determining the economic development of the Soviet zone was the conviction and penalties falling on the war criminals and war profiteers . . . whose undertakings were taken over as the result of a plebiscite of June 1946 [in Saxony] with a majority of nearly 80 per cent. This would mean that all nationalized industries were seized from Nazis or war criminals and only nationalized after a period of trusteeship, during which their eventual disposal was an open question. In fact no 'nationalization' took place at all, but certain factories had to be taken out of the hands of Nazis and war criminals, and after due consideration it was felt that they would be best preserved in the hands of the State."

The advantages of disguising Communist intentions as long as there was no Communist supremacy have been mentioned. Their moderation enabled the Russians to obtain the services of men who might never have agreed to serve under a purely Communist régime; it provided a measure of popular support for the SED in the early days; and it helped to convince a considerable number of people both inside and outside Germany of the good intentions of the Russians. On the other hand, it ran counter to the most sacred principles of Communism and to the established practice of the Soviet government during its twenty-eight years of existence. The question of co-operation with bourgeois parties in office before the conquest of supreme power had constituted an insurmountable obstacle to the unity of the Second International as early as 1903; the majority, the *bolsheviki,* taking the view that even in the circumstances of the time such co-operation in forming a government was inexcusable, that historically the time for it had passed. Yet after 1945 a bloc policy of co-operation with bourgeois parties was an accepted principle of government in the Soviet zone, indeed throughout Eastern Europe.

We see a Soviet occupation, run by Russian Communists, instituting measures which seem Communist in tendency, but which these same Russians, and the Germans under them, were at great pains to prove to have been inspired only by the immediate needs of the situation. Marx and Engels envisaged, as part of the inevitable development of the Socialist situation, that the bourgeoisie in its last stages might take action which would unconsciously accelerate their own downfall. But the founders of historical materialism in its modern sense would have been astounded to find a Communist government *in plena potestate* adopting the reactionary expedient of explaining its actions in terms of bourgeois necessity. The dialectic, after years of struggle against its blind opponents, was discarded at the moment of vindication in favour of the tattered shreds of empirical legislation! What explanation can be given for this fundamental contradiction between theory and practice?

The possibility of Russia's abandoning her fundamental aims of introducing a Communist government in Germany must be ruled out. Political and economic developments since 1946 have made this all too clear. The use of empirical-looking legislation and the disclaimer of Communist intentions was a means rather than an end; strategy, not principle. Were the means used by the Russians more effective in gaining the ultimate ends of a Communist system than would have been an open avowal of Communist intentions from the first day of occupation? If they were, we have a possible explanation for Soviet actions.

The basic conditions for Communism were, as we have seen , highly favourable in May 1945. The very fact that Russia had been victorious gave Russian actions a certain *de facto* justification. Popular resistance in 1945 to even a radical Communist programme in Eastern Germany would have been impossible. The Western Allies were favourably disposed to Russia, and even if the governments of Britain and the United States had protested against a vigorous Communist policy in Germany from the start, public opinion in these countries would have taken a considerable time to turn against Russia. It was not wholly anti-Russian even in 1950. If fundamental discord over Germany was inevitable, the advantage to be gained by rushing things in 1945 was greater than that of attempting to make the change to an openly Communist policy two years later, by which time world events would in any case have stiffened the attitude of the Western Allies. Communist policy in Eastern Germany would have had to be much the same as that adopted by the Communist governments in Rumania, Bulgaria, and Hungary, a policy of taking the public by surprise and crushing opposition before it could be organized effectively. Such a policy in Germany would probably have achieved considerable success. Clearly this cannot be the explanation of the course of Soviet action.

In many recent discussions of Russian

post-war policy the conflict between Communist theory and Russian interests has been stressed to underline contradictory and puzzling Soviet actions. In Germany this conflict is particularly marked. Once its underlying causes are understood it is possible to explain the contradiction between theory and practice whose existence we have tried to establish.

Communist theory takes it for granted that the final dialectic will result in an improvement of conditions "in the operation of the means of production, after the breakdown of bourgeois society" as Marx himself put it. If a nation undergoing the last social struggle is fortunate enough to have the presence of a Socialist power at hand, it would be the role of the latter to smooth the path for its neighbour and to help to make the period of transition as easy and rapid as possible. Such certainly was the view of Lenin, Radek and all those Russians who supported the Rapallo policy, as well as of Lauffenberg, the "inventor" of National Bolshevism, in 1920; no new Communist state could be held responsible for the misdeeds of its bourgeois predecessor. The same principle had been tentatively expressed by the Soviet government during the last war. Strict adherence to theory demanded that Communism in Germany should be assisted into power by the Russians, and that the war guilt slate would then be wiped clean, reparations waived, punishment confined to bourgeois imperialists, and both moral and physical assistance given to the Germans. Inside the Soviet Union the hatred of Germany inevitably fostered by the invasion and the resultant atrocities would have to be combated by means of an acrobatic somersault of propaganda.

But this was not and could not be the case. It is doubtful whether even the Soviet propaganda machine could carry such a campaign in the teeth of a population whose national fervour had been roused. It is easy to exaggerate national feelings, and

difficult to estimate their influence, but a perusal of *Pravda* or *Izvestia* during the war shows that the Soviet government at any rate was consciously playing on the patriotism of its citizens, and such feelings once aroused, are difficult to quench at will. Reparations were, as we have seen, one of the three main reasons why the Soviet government considered the occupation of Germany to be essential. Enormous damage had to be made good, and both necessity and prestige demanded the exploitation of Germany for the benefit of Russia. The Yalta agreement shows that the demand for reparations then already formed one of the chief bases of Russian policy. As soon as Germany was occupied the detailed reparations programme was put into operation with speed and efficiency, directly supervised from Moscow.

Thus the role of "benevolent Socialist neighbour" went unperformed. While the Germans were inevitably prepared to see a considerable part of their industrial potential, their labour, and even their current production, go to Russia as reparations, they resented the fact that what had seemed and had been made to seem a genuine revival in the East was ultimately designed only to further reparations in different guises. The German administration laboured under difficult conditions to fulfil the SMA (Soviet Military Administration) plans for rehabilitation, only to find their work exploited and diverted by another, superior, Soviet agency. There was a chronic uncertainty in Soviet reparation demands which interfered with all planning. Moreover, the reparations scheme was arbitrary in the extreme; the SMA and control administration often received notice of dismantlings only when the German "Pilgrimage of Grace" arrived to bemoan the disappearance of a factory. The great Russian object was to keep the Germans ignorant of the state of reparations and dismantlings, and the Germans resented it.

Even more opposed to a friendly relationship between post-war Germany and Russia were the Soviet-owned Trusts within the German economy, the SAG. While the principle of reparation was admitted, if reluctantly, by nearly every German, even though the degree was considered excessive, this Russian interference in German domestic property-holding could only be the action of a victorious power over an enemy to be exploited at will. The purchase of real estate, the officially operated black market in scarce goods, and the use of German reparations for Russian re-export, all facts of which the Germans were mistily aware, increased the tension. It is notable that even the most ardent Communist, who was prepared to explain every action of the Russians in terms of genuine Soviet interest in the rebuilding of a progressive Germany, found it impossible to digest the question of reparations altogether. The explanation that Russia had after all been victorious, and that the damage done by Germany gave the Russians moral *carte blanche* to take what they liked (which became the official SED thesis when the question could no longer be ignored in public) was utterly irreconcilable with the usual picture presented by the SED of the benevolence of the Soviet Union towards Germany. The same was true of Soviet support for the permanence of Germany's Eastern frontier.

The Russians were fully aware that their reparation policy, which they intended to carry out at all costs, involved permanent disagreement with the Western Allies, and would tend to nullify all their other actions in Germany capable of presentation in a favourable light. It is partly for this reason that the question of reparations was kept so completely out of German hands, and entirely separate from their general administrative policy in Germany. The separation existed even in the philosophical sphere. An openly Communist policy in Eastern Germany would have been in such glaring contrast to the facts of reparation payments,

and would have so discredited Communist policy, that it was considered best, since a choice between the two had to be made, to drop the pursuit of Communism rather than the pursuit of reparations. In the initial period of May 1945 to May 1946 it was hoped that the Germans would come to accept a picture of Russia taking her reparations on the one hand, and on the other attempting to ameliorate the lot of the population by a series of progressive measures which were not intended to culminate in a purely Communist regime. A measure of political liberty was offered in return for economic exploitation. But the relative prosperity of the Soviet zone at this time, and the efforts of the political parties to obtain popular support, were strengthening parties which, once they had obtained sufficient popular strength, were likely to attack Russian reparation policy, in much the same way as the political parties in the West already atacked the far smaller demands of the Western Allies. This was an intrusion on the policy in which the Soviet Union was above all interested in Eastern Germany, and it had to be prevented at all costs, even if the Communist government, now to be instituted by force, suffered the odium of being a Russian tool undemocratically elected and supported only by force.

The new system of government after April 1946 was above all intended to ensure the safety of the Occupation while unhampered reparations continued to flow eastward. There was no real government, but only an administration. A German copy of the Supreme Soviet was dispensed with, but the Politburo and the executive departments of the U.S.S.R. were faithfully reproduced. Wherever possible, the shreds of the anti-Nazi system were retained, but they were never allowed to interfere in any way with the unhampered activities of the Russian reparation agencies and the Russian-owned industrial combines and trading companies. This was the middle period, characterized by maximum reparations and a system of administration designed to facilitate them.

By the summer of 1947 it was clear that Communism in Germany must be based on Russian power and could never have the strength of popular support sufficient to enable it to stand on its own democratic feet. Spasmodic attempts were still made by the political department of the SMA and by the SED to obtain popular support for specific measures, and to recruit members for the SED, but no great success was expected from these half-hearted gestures, and little was achieved. By the end of 1947 the continued flow of reparations to the east as well as the political power of the SED were seen by the Germans to be entirely dependent on the armed presence of the Russians. Both would disappear at the moment when the Russians left. The institution of Communism on a firm basis had become an impossibility. Even in the most extreme Leninist interpretation of Communism, with the "cadre-party" reduced to an absolute minimum in relation to the size of the population, it is still necessary that this party should, whether by popular support or by its own hold on government, be enabled to stand on its own feet. This the SED was never, and seems unlikely ever, to be able to do. The very fact that Communism was not introduced in its entirety in the early days of the Occupation means that a Communist party backed by Russian bayonets is even now running a predominantly bourgeois society. On the other hand it was impossible to institute Communism completely as long as large parts of the prerogative of the dictatorship of the German proletariat continued to be reserved and used by the Russians themselves for their own immediate purposes. The Communist apparatus was there, but it was built on sand, and supported by foreign props. Its existence did not serve German political development, but Russian economic expansion.

The difference between Eastern Germany and the Communist states of Eastern Europe is clear. In the latter countries Soviet demands for goods and services, though often irksome, were never the main object of Russian presence or control. In all these countries the strength of the local Communist governments arose out of their control of an armed movement fighting the Germans during the war. The step from there to control of the State was easy in the confused situation following the expulsion of the Germans. In Germany, however, reparations formed the basis of Russian occupation and all other measures were subordinate; the German Communists were treated as members of a defeated nation and their power came not from their own efforts but by command of the occupying power. Had the Russians been willing, the power of the German Communists in Germany could have been as great as that of their comrades in the Eastern countries, but as long as reparations were the chief object of Russian policy the Communists in Eastern Germany were merely a means for their easy extraction.

In 1948 the initiative passed to Western Germany. The absence of a dynamic policy in the East, the absorption in economic destruction instead of political fortification, enabled the Western powers, once they had cut themselves loose from the inhibitions of an out-of-date Potsdam Agreement, to embark on a constructive policy undisturbed by the resultant breakdown of the last political ties binding East and West Germany. The risks involved in this forward movement were greatly reduced by the fact that there was no constructive policy in the Soviet zone. Instead of being able to rely on the political momentum of Communism in Germany to counteract the Western currency reform and the concomitant reduction of Allied control, the Russians were forced to intervene directly, and mount a military blockade of Berlin. Even this failed dismally to arrest the Western movement towards independence from restraint by the Russians, and in 1950 the Russians had to resort to an *ultima ratio*, a direct threat of military action against a resuscitated Western Germany. Thus it became clear that the reparations policy had involved the sacrifice of the most elementary political weapon of Communism, its initiative of political action. Instead of being able to call its own tune, the SED now found itself in the role normally assigned to its opponents; it had to adapt itself to a series of *faits accomplis* and to show cause why it had failed to achieve similar success in the East.

This situation was peculiar to Germany. The people's democracies of the East had been sufficiently sealed off by this time to enable the ruling Communist party to operate in a politically uncompetitive atmosphere. Moreover, Soviet exploitation had not been on a sufficient scale to attract the attention of the entire population. Communism in these countries was in power and could behave with the insouciance of unchallengeable supremacy. In Germany the Communist party, though technically in almost complete control, had the uphill task of defending Soviet measures against a hostile population encouraged by the recovery of more than half their fellow countrymen. If the Russians had been prepared to extract their reparations and then abandon, for all constructive political purposes, the shell of Eastern Germany, this situation would not have mattered greatly. It was frequently believed in the West at this time that Russian plans were along these lines, and that an impoverished Eastern Germany would be left as an added burden for the struggling economy of Western Germany. But it was apparently decided otherwise. Possibly because the Russians were unwilling to abandon any territory once under their control; perhaps, encouraged by their successes since the war and the predictions of economic collapse in the West, they prepared for an experiment in a unique situation. Reparations were to be reduced to a level compatible with a measure of economic recovery in Eastern Germany. With the exception of the export of special consumer-goods on reparations account, the reparations potential of the zone had been reduced to a stark alternative of considerable reduction in removals or speedy economic collapse. An utterly bankrupt Eastern Germany could do nothing to further Russian plans of consolidation in Eastern Europe or for a political and economic attack against the West. If the economy of Eastern Europe could, by a series of long-term plans, be made to recover sufficiently, the division of Germany could still be used to serve Russian ends. From behind the East-West frontier of Germany, the initiative might be wrested from the West and the SED might become the means of bringing about the unification of Germany under Russian control.

Soviet diplomacy had always been, and was still, prepared to help with all the means at its disposal. As long as reparations hampered the Soviet representative at the Council of Foreign Ministers, his tactics were, in spite of all efforts, unlikely to succeed. But now that the demand for a United Germany could be put at the forefront of the German political scene, the Soviet diplomats and the Communist puppets of Eastern Germany were, for the first time since the war, talking the same language for the same ends. The demand for a share in the control of the Ruhr, based on the return to Potsdam, and the East German threat to the independence of the Bonn Republic, became part and parcel of the same objective, the extension of Soviet control to Western Germany—even though the Russians might be thinking of extending their reparations policy to Western Germany as well as the blessings of Communist domination.

The task of running the Unity campaign produced an unprecedented role for a Communist party in power, that of hiding be-

hind a bourgeois-nationalist facade. In undisputed control of Eastern Germany, the
SED had on the one hand to control a partly
Communist-type economy, on the other to
adopt the opportunist tactics of the Communist parties in bourgeois countries. This
led to all sorts of crass ideological para-
doxes. In Western Germany workers were
encouraged to strike against dismantling,
and the SED press in Berlin carried such slogans as: "Workers strike in protest against
British monopolistic dismantling." In the
East the Party press announced that "deliberate failure to fulfil production norms
can only be treated as economic sabotage."
On the question of rearmament, *Neues
Deutschland* said in a single issue that
"German rearmament can only lead to the
resurgence of Fascist aggressiveness under
the direction of American monopoly capitalism," and on another page that "the
well-equipped People's Police is a solid
bulwark against reactions . . . seeking to
interfere with the legitimate demands of all
Germans for a single strong and united
Fatherland." The SED leadership journal, in
defining the party's attitude to reparations,
prescribed that "Germany must, for a long
time, pay towards the restitution of the
enormous damage wantonly inflicted on
the U.S.S.R." The official newspapers, on
the other hand, stated that the export efforts of Western Germany had shown British business that only the continued dismantling of German industry could prevent
the replacement of British goods by goods
made in Germany. The best example of
all is probably the mildness, almost con-
ciliatory benevolence, with which the East
German government dealt with the accusations of intolerance and repression which
both Catholic and Protestant bishops suddenly unleashed in May 1950. Grotewohl
promised freedom to the church as guaranteed under the constitution, did not answer
with menaces — as did his colleagues in
Czechoslovakia and Hungary — indeed did
not answer the more violent protests at all,

and apparently took no measures of personal reprisal against the clergy. No doubt
his restraint was due to care not to offend
his imagined bourgeois sympathizers, like
Noack, in the West. Yet the SED press was
full of orthodox fulminations against political priests, (an attitude as acceptable to the
Communists of Eastern Europe as to the
bourgeois "priest-eaters" of the Third Republic.) Thus, instead of being able to
profit from its supremacy in Eastern Germany by coming out openly as a Communist party, the SED had to run two simultaneous and contradictory lines of policy
and perform unheard-of masterpieces of
illogicality.

At first sight the SED unity campaign
resembles the so-called doctrine of National
Bolshevism, linked with the name of Radek, the one-time envoy of the Comintern
in Germany. He had been acutely conscious of the need for the Communist party
to rally the German proletariat behind it,
and believed that this could be achieved by
an appeal to nationalist feelings. In both
cases it was necessary to wrest a valuable
means of popular appeal from the bourgeois parties, and in both cases the basis of
the appeal was the same. But in one case
the Communist party was following the
Leninist tradition of flexibility in order to
gain power by obtaining overwhelming
working-class support, while in the present
case a Communist party in power, having
carried out a large part of the "orthodox"
Communist programme, was appealing to
the bourgeois classes of Germany. Between
1921 and 1933 the Communists, and particularly the German Communists, envisaged
a mass proletarian movement. In 1950 the
SED relied on a police army whose leadership was composed mostly of non-prole-
tarians cooperating with nationalistic elements in the West to achieve its aims. Until
the expected economic crisis in the West
produced the necessary unemployment, an
appeal to the workers there had been
shown to be in vain, partly because the

Communists were in a minority among them) but chiefly because the iron curtain in Germany was sufficiently transparent for all to see precisely what they could expect from the Russians. In fact the SED unity campaign went to unprecedented lengths in discarding the most elementary tenets of Communism.

The philosophy of Communism, however, remained unchanged in Eastern Germany, as elsewhere. The teachings of the Marxist authorities were not, and could not be, adjusted to the existing situation. What happened was that the last restraints imposed by theory on practice disappeared. In this respect the SED was in advance of other Communist parties. Irrespective of their tactics before taking over the government completely, the Communists of Eastern Europe once in power, followed a pattern of policy which held good in every case except one, where differences arose over subordination to Russia. In Eastern Germany tactical adjustments to policy continued long after the advent of the party to power, and exceeded the limits imposed by class division. The cause may be found in the artificial division of Germany, which the Communists helped to complete in order to further the national interests of Russia, and in the absence of responsibility under Russian occupation, of which the SED unconsciously availed itself. Without the need to build up its own strength for its own permanent protection, the Party could devote itself to the task of furthering Russian aims throughout Germany. It is perhaps fitting that the depth of political irresponsibility and dishonesty should again have been reached in Germany.

Ultimately the responsibility lay with the Russians. If a country is occupied by us, they seemed to argue, an independent local Communist party has no useful functions to fulfil, for its normal function, that of ruling, is taken over by ourselves. While we continue to rule, it must attempt to make everything we do palatable to the population, and, since we are disciples of Marx, Lenin, and Stalin, they must be disciples too. Therefore even this task can only be carried out by a Communist-dominated party. If in time the Party succeeds in establishing itself firmly in the political and administrative power we allow to it, it will gradually be permitted to take over an increasing share in the government of the occupied area. It will not be allowed, however, to sit back and consolidate this power, for we control only part of the country, and once the first flow of reparations has been taken, we may concentrate on taking control of the rest of the country. This has become a more difficult and urgent task as the portion of the country outside our control has cut itself loose from the restrictive agreement previously negotiated with the Western powers, and since its recovery is undermining the safety of our strategic frontier. Moreover, the attempt to separate the two parts of the country has failed. Therefore it is now the task of our local Communists to devote themselves to the destruction of the government created on the other side of the frontier by every means at their disposal, and, since Germans are not Koreans, this may involve an appeal to bourgeois nationalist sentiment. In return, if the object is achieved, we will take our share in economic value, and the SED will obtain the measure of independent control over the whole of Germany which Communist governments have in Eastern Europe, subject to the demands of Soviet policy.

An examination of Russian policy in Eastern Germany cannot therefore be made at all in terms of Marxist, Leninist, or Stalinist theory. For those who follow its beliefs and translate its theories into actions, Marxism is the prime reason for their political existence. The moment Communist theory is subordinated to other interests it ceases by its very nature to be Communist. We are forced to come to the conclusion that the government in Eastern

Germany was not a Communist government at all, but a makeshift arrangement designed to fulfil certain immediate Russian needs, and therefore liable to be changed as the demands made on it changed. Those who measure Eastern Germany by Marxist standards apply a yard measure to a metric scale, whether they are observers outside Germany or Soviet-zone Communists. If the latter believed in their own Marxist orthodoxy, they were the biggest dupes of Russian policy.

Many of the institutions and measures in the Soviet zone undoubtedly originated in Communist theory, and while the method of government bore strong traces of Communist technique, these things were incidental and of secondary importance. They were mostly due to the routine of Soviet methods which imposed a pattern of their own on all actions and institutions under Russian control. The resemblances of Eastern Germany to a state methodically organized on deliberate Communist lines in order to achieve, as quickly as possible, a Communist society, was purely accidental. The completion of such a state and society, including nationalization of the land, local government by Soviets, and sensational spy trials of those with contacts in the West, would have made the success of the political unity campaign impossible.

SOVIET POLICY IN EASTERN EUROPE
AND THE ONSET OF THE COLD WAR

The cold war increased in intensity after 1945 as the result of two sets of factors, the first of distant origin, the second arising from events which occurred after the war. The legacy from the prewar period which has been discussed in connection with the coining of the phrase, "cold war," remained to cloud the international political scene. Neither Soviet suspicion nor communist hatred of the West, nor Russian nationalist territorial ambition was altered one jot by the war, any more than was Stalin's character. If anything, the Soviet leader became even more xenophobic and security-minded than before. The component roots of deep-seated mistrust were amply nourished after 1945 through a series of events which convinced each side that it could not afford to maintain any confidence in the other.

On the Western side, the early quarrel over the future of Poland was quickly followed by other instances, such as the relentless Soviet pressure in Bulgaria and Rumania, the interpretation of democratic rule in these countries and the general trend of events in Eastern Europe outlined above, which heightened Western suspicion of Soviet motives. As for the Russians, they in turn viewed the disclosure of America's monopoly possession of the atom bomb, the abrupt ending in August 1945 of lend-lease aid and their virtual exclusion from any influence over the future of Japan or Italy as omens of renewed capitalist threats directed against the weakened defenses of socialism.

One of the main symptoms of the international unrest was psychological in nature. Past memories and contemporary experience awakened a common neurosis, expressed in phenomena like the *Zhdanovshchina*[1] in Russia and, at a later date, McCarthyism in the United States. On the Russian side constant fear was no doubt heightened by the inferiority complex from which the U.S.S.R. had suffered since 1917 in her relations with the West. The fruit of this mutual fear was to be found in two speeches made by Stalin and Churchill on February 9 and March 5, 1946, respectively. They reflected the growing tension in the international arena and perhaps more than anything else drew the attention of statesmen throughout the world to the serious nature of the situation.

Stalin's pre-election speech was uttered in the same tone that characterized the *Zhdanovshchina*, except that it also included a reassertion of Lenin's theory that the uneven development of capitalism leads to war. Stalin's pessimistic view of future relations with the West was probably artificially enhanced by the consideration that this vision of a hostile world would act as a stimulant on the Russian people to rebuild their shattered state with added vigor. Churchill's speech at Fulton, Missouri, was likewise inspired by mistrust and fear. Calling the attention of his distinguished audience (which included the President of the United States) to the fact that "from Stettin in the Baltic to Trieste in the Adriatic, an iron curtain has descended across the Continent," Churchill urged American statesmen to join with the British Commonwealth in a joint effort to ward off the threat of communist aggression. At the time many of his listeners thought that his appeal was premature and would only serve to increase Soviet suspicions. The British loan proposed in the American Congress on December 6, 1945, was considered to be sufficient evidence of Anglo-American political solidarity, and there seemed to be no necessity for using the fear of Russia as an additional welding force.

In the light of later events, Churchill's comments on Soviet moves in Eastern Europe appear to be relatively mild in nature, but at the time they came as a shock to some of his listeners. The reaction of some members of Truman's government was perhaps warranted. In March 1946, outside of Poland, concrete evidence of open Soviet pressure existed in Bulgaria and Rumania only: both these countries were ex-enemy powers. On the subject of Poland, Stalin had admitted to Churchill and Roosevelt at Yalta that Russia could not afford to allow a government hostile to herself to be established in an area of such vital strategic importance.

From the Soviet point of view a parallel might have been drawn between methods used in ex-enemy countries occupied by U.S.S.R. and those used in Japan, where MacArthur had a strong military control over Japanese politics and industry. Although MacArthur did not in fact resort to such heavy-handed methods as were used in the European ex-Axis countries, his authority was such that he might have acted in a similar manner, and Japanese government and industry were actually reorganized after the war solely according to American designs. This parallel has been expressed in terms of the Soviet viewpoint in order to estimate the effect of Churchill's Fulton speech on the Russian leaders.

[1] A Stalinist campaign begun in 1946 to eliminate Western influences and restore ideological conformity in the arts and sciences, named after Andrei Zhdanov, third-ranking leader.

Another galling element in Churchill's speech was his scarcely veiled comparison of communist to fascist rule and political techniques. His catching phrase "the iron curtain" came from Goebbel's repertoire, according to the Russians, and must have stung the nation which had borne the brunt of the fascist whip. Stalin returned the insult in kind by referring in his speech to the "resemblance" of "Mr. Churchill and his friends" to "Hitler and his friends." The content of Churchill's appeal provided a heaven-sent opportunity for Stalin to justify his exaggerated theory that the capitalist powers were intent on invading Russia again, as they had done after 1917 and in 1941. He told the American ambassador in Moscow that he expected another intervention.

In the long run, however, most of Churchill's forebodings were proved right. From the West's point of view, the speech had the beneficial effect of drawing the United States into the growing international contest, for if Churchill was apt to dramatize the Soviet menace, some of the American leaders in 1946 tended to play it down or to ignore it. In the tense atmosphere of the postwar world both attitudes were dangerous: an amalgam of the two eventually proved to be the most effective weapon against Soviet aggression. Both the English and the Americans were conditioned by their previous experience, or lack of it. Churchill was a member of the English aristocracy and an old foe of the Bolsheviks since 1917. His close ties with the East European governments in exile in London during the Second World War and his wrangles over the future of Poland only reaffirmed his suspicions. In 1946 American isolationism was still unspent, as was the general mood of ideological radicalism which stemmed from the years of the New Deal. Not until September 1946 did the Russophile Henry Wallace resign from the American cabinet.

II.   *The Consolidation of Soviet Influence in Eastern Europe and Asia, 1947-1953*

SOVIET REACTION TO THE MARSHALL PLAN

The entry of the United States onto the European political scene was slow even after Churchill's Fulton speech. In 1946 the number of British forces overseas was only just below the United States figure, in spite of England's sorry economic plight. For September 13, 1946, the diary of the American Secretary of Defense, J. V. Forrestal, mentioned a plan for the quick removal of U.S. troops from Germany in the event of Russian aggression; there was little thought of defending Europe. But the situation changed after England's severe economic crisis in the winter of 1946 and her plea of February 1947 for American support in the armed struggle against communist guerrillas in Greece.

President Truman's Message to Congress in March 1947 called for American military aid to Greece and Turkey. The Truman Doctrine marked the adoption of George Kennan's containment policy toward Russia; it was also the prelude to a speech made in June 1947 by the American Secretary of State, General Marshall, in which economic aid was offered to Europe. Although Marshall let it be known that his proposals might also apply to Russia, Dean Acheson revealed that the professed aim of the Marshall Plan was to "preserve democratic institutions and human freedoms from totalitarian pressures." The Plan was formulated in the belief that communism would thrive if European economic chaos were allowed to continue.

In Eastern Europe the Polish and Czech political leaders expressed an interest in the American offer, but were ordered by Stalin to reject it outright. In her crippled condition Russia would find it difficult to rival the economic influence of the richest country in the world; the ideology by which the Soviets lived clearly taught them the eloquence of economic persuasion. Even if American dollars did not succeed in undermining Soviet influence in Eastern Europe, Marshall's scheme for integrating American aid into a single plan meant that each nation would have to produce what it was best fitted for. The effect of this might be to retain Eastern Europe as the traditional granary of the West and thus bypass Soviet plans for industrialization in the area. Furthermore American aid was repulsed for the same reason that international control of atomic stockpiles was later refused by the Soviets; both schemes would entail some measure of intrusion behind the veils of Russian security, which was a very powerful weapon in the cold war.

The Czech and Polish attempts to follow an independent line over the question of Marshall Aid were signs of an increasing preoccupation on the part of East European communists with the consolidation of their power within national borders. At this time relations were strained between the Hungarian and Rumanian parties over the territorial issue of Transylvania; this was also true of relations between Poland and Czechoslovakia regarding areas on their adjoining frontiers. The most blatant example of national selfishness (as opposed to devotion to the communist and Soviet cause) came significantly from Yugoslavia, who seemed to think that the communist camp should be ready to fight the West over the question of the city of Trieste, which Tito coveted.

The increased vigor of "domesticism" of this kind, coinciding with the direct entry of the United States onto the European stage, led Stalin to harden his policy with regard to Eastern Europe. The change was illustrated in the creation of the Cominform (Communist Information Bureau) in September 1947, the Czech political coup in February 1948, the Soviet rift with Yugoslavia in June 1948, and the dispute with the Western Allies over Berlin which began in the same month. By the end of 1947 the return to communist orthodoxy inside Russia itself had progressed sufficiently to provide a convenient model for enforcement on the countries of Eastern Europe. Stalin's creation of the Berlin crisis of 1948 was the last twist of the knife in the soft European stomach. Soviet failure on this occasion led to the abandonment of aspirations in the West and the subsequent removal of the velvet glove in Eastern Europe. The next time Stalin showed the mailed fist outside the communist zone in the East, it was in Asia, not Europe.

THE FOUNDING OF THE COMINFORM

The Cominform was the ideological spearhead of the new line. Its headquarters were placed in Belgrade, which for reasons given below was rapidly becoming the center of nationalist opposition to Soviet domination, although ironically enough it was the Yugoslavs who in 1945 had proposed the reestablishment of some sort of international communist organization to promote the exchange of views between the various parties. At the opening session of the Cominform in southwest Poland in September 1947 it was again the Yugoslavs who were the most persistent in asserting their ideological orthodoxy.

The chief Soviet spokesman was Andrei Zhdanov. This was significant, since it might have been supposed that Molotov or some other member of the Politburo more familiar with questions of foreign policy would be the one to pronounce the diatribe against American aggression and the call to communist unity. But the imposition of Soviet practice in Eastern Europe after 1947, not only in politics but in the economic and social spheres as well, was merely an extension of the domestic campaign for conformity headed by Zhdanov.

The main activities of the Communist Information Bureau centered on the publication of its organ *For a Lasting Peace,* which laid down the broad lines of policy to be followed by the People's Democracies in all spheres of national life.

Adam Ulam

THE COMINFORM AND THE PEOPLE'S DEMOCRACIES

The creation of the Cominform in the summer of 1947 marked an important stage in the development of communism in Europe. The precise reasons that led the leaders of Soviet Communism to revive a public form of co-operation between several Communist parties remain to this day uncertain. What is obvious is the use to which the Cominform has been put during its brief existence up to now. It has acted as an added catalyst of social and political change in the satellite countries. Its resolutions, like the one on the occasion of the expulsion of Yugoslavia from that body, have laid down the broad lines of policy to be pursued by the People's Democracies on such vital issues as the question of collectivization of agriculture, the "nationalist deviation," etc. The original concept of the Cominform included, undoubtedly, creation of the appearance of complete autonomy of the Communist parties in Eastern Europe. The language of the speeches at the founding meeting and the choice of the seat for the new organization, outside of the Soviet Union, testify as to the serious attempt to present the collaboration between the Soviet Union and her Communist allies under a veneer of equality. If the picture thus presented seemed to lack realism to the Communist leaders from Poland or Yugoslavia it is unreasonable to assume that the

propaganda effect of the establishment of the Cominform was entirely lost upon the masses who had, since the end of the war, joined the ranks of the ruling parties in the satellite states.

At the same time as the notion of equality of the participating parties was being proclaimed, the assembled Communist leaders were being treated to a demonstration of Leninist self-criticism. The representatives of the Italian and French parties freely admitted the tactical and ideological "errors" they committed in the wake of the liberation of their countries from German occupation. The new attitude of the Western Communists represented compliance with the new Russian line toward the West. The new line of Soviet policy, the reaction of Soviet leaders to the Marshall Plan and to the stabilization of the political situation in Europe, was being presented not so much by a series of political statements as by a presentation of a political drama in which parts were spoken by others besides the Russian representatives. The Cominform was created to give an opportunity for that public guidance and instruction to world communism, which, for all the less public contacts and connections, remains in the eyes of Soviet leaders a vital necessity. The very name of the organ of the Cominform—*For a Lasting Peace*—was to symbol-

---

From A. Ulam, "The Cominform and the People's Democracies," *World Politics,* (January 1951), pp. 200–202. Reprinted by permission of *World Politics.*

ize the recurrent motive in Soviet foreign policy and propaganda. The Western powers were to be pictured as bent upon a new war and the American plan of help to Europe was adjudged to be a subtle imperialistic scheme to extend the grip of American big business in Western Europe. In view of this danger, the People's Democracies were to close ranks, to cut down the remaining political ties with the West, and possibly to speed up and synchronize the process of social and political transformation which would eventually turn them into copies of the U.S.S.R., and thus destroy any popular basis for an anticommunist intrigue. On the other hand, now that the prospect of their seizing power legally appeared at best distant, Communist parties in the West, and especially the Italian and French ones, were to strengthen themselves organizationally and ideologically, to shake off the unreliable element in the membership swollen by the war, and to become an efficient instrument and vanguard of the movement designed to thwart American imperialist designs upon their countries.

Hugh Seton-Watson

THE CZECH COUP OF FEBRUARY 1948

Czechoslovakia alone among the East European states was a predominantly industrial country. In the Czech lands, if not in Slovakia, the social structure resembled that of a western country. The urban middle class was numerous and influential, the skilled formed a high proportion among the workers, and the peasants were as prosperous and as skilled as those of western lands. The level of education approximated to that of the West, and the intelligentsia found employment for its talents and an honourable place in society. The practice of parliamentary democracy was firmly rooted. The electoral success of the communists in 1946 was due to the same causes as in France—belief that the communists stood for the material interests of the workers, and enthusiasm for Russia. It was not due to bitter revolutionary feeling. Between 1945 and 1947 the old methods of government largely reasserted themselves against communist lawlessness. Yet when the crisis came in February 1948 the resistance of the democrats collapsed.

Some reasons for this include previous infiltration by the communists into the police and local administration, communist control of the western borderlands, communist exploitation of hatred between Czechs and Germans and of friction between Czechs and Slovaks. To these may be added the tactical mistakes of the democrats. The cabinet ministers representing the Czech People's, Czech Socialist and Slovak Democrat parties resigned in February 1948 in protest against the failure of the communist Minister of Interior, Vaclav Nosek, to carry out the cabinet's directive to him to stop packing the police with communists. But they resigned before they had made sure of the support of either the social democrats—which was necessary in order to have a majority against the communists in parliament—or of President Benes. They also made no attempt to contact the oppo-

From Hugh Seton-Watson, *The Pattern of Communist Revolution* (London, 1953), pp. 258–260. Published in the United States as *From Lenin to Khruschev*. Reprinted by permission of Methuen & Co., Ltd., and Frederick A. Praeger, Inc.

nents of the communists in army or police. The communists defended themselves with both constitutional and extra-constitutional means. They induced the social democrats to support them and bullied the President into accepting the resignations of the democratic ministers. They seized the radio and the newspaper offices, paraded armed detachments of workers through the streets of Prague, and set up "Action Committees" of communists and stooges which took over the powers of the local authorities. Neither the resigning ministers nor the president could address the people. Generals subservient to the communists kept the army immobile. There was no resistance. Gottwald's "revolution" was made with the help of the police: it resembles Mussolini's march on Rome by sleeping-car or Hitler's acceptance of office from President Hindenburg rather than any genuine revolution. Indeed there is a certain tragic similarity between the roles in these two crises of the aging Hindenburg and the ailing Benes — two men whose careers have otherwise nothing in common.

The international background to the Prague "revolution" is most important. Soviet Assistant-Foreign Minister Zorin was in Prague, and Soviet troops surrounded four-fifths of the Republic's frontiers. The willingness or ability of the United States to help the Czechs resist was highly doubtful. Whether, if Benes and the noncommunist ministers had stuck together and had prepared their action in consultation with the army leaders, the communists would have secured power, and whether, if the communists had been defeated, Soviet forces would have invaded Czechoslovakia, is also doubtful. But neither Benes nor the Czech politicians were in a mood to take these risks. The catastrophe of Munich had left its mark on them. They had the habit of surrender and they were accustomed to regard the Western Powers as unreliable friends. Britain's war record had not wiped out the "Munich legend," sedulously fostered by the communists and swallowed in good faith by millions of Czechs who were not communists. Nor had the extremely modest achievements of wartime Czech resistance increased the Czechs' confidence in themselves. Perhaps most important of all was the fact that the Czechs did not wish to oppose Russian wishes. The Czechs still regarded Germany as the enemy, Russia as a friend. It took some years of Gottwald's regime to show them that indirect Russian rule could be more unpleasant than direct Nazi rule. The uncritical admiration of most Czechs for all things Russian disarmed the Czech people in the moment of crisis. This is seen more clearly when events in Czechoslovakia are compared with events in Finland. The refusal of the Finns to accept even cultural influence from Russia protected them. Only three months after the Prague "revolution" the Finnish parliament forced the communist Leino to resign from the Ministry of the Interior. Shortly after this, free parliamentary elections were held, at which the communists' poll fell by one-quarter, and in the new government the communists were not represented. Finland was not less exposed to Russian armed intervention than was Czechoslovakia. But the Finns risked the danger which they clearly saw, and emerged unscathed.

As long as the communists had observed the constitutional rules and had remained loyal to the genuine coalition of the People's Front, the democrats had preserved their independence and Czechoslovakia had been a relatively free country. But when the communists forced a crisis, the various factors enumerated above operated to their advantage. These factors were however so peculiar to the Czechoslovak situation that they make it an unique event. Czechoslovakia is the only western industrial state that communists have captured, but its experience does not provide any general conclusions on the ability of communists to capture industrial states.

Hubert Ripka

CZECHOSLOVAKIA ENSLAVED

Hubert Ripka was one of the Czech cabinet ministers who resigned in February 1948 in protest against the communists. In the following passage from his memoirs he surveys, with the benefit of hindsight, the nature of Soviet intervention during the Czech coup.

During the days of solitude and complete inactivity which followed the *coup d'état* I had time to think over at length the causes of the catastrophe which we had just suffered. The more I reflected, the more it appeared to me that the decisive factor in our defeat had been the intervention of Moscow.

I had been one of the most ardent and most sincere defenders of a loyal co-operation between our country and the Soviet Union. Given our geographic position between Germany and Russia, and in view of the fact that the U.S.S.R., emerging victorious from the war, was the dominant Power in central and eastern Europe, I judged that this was the only policy which could guarantee our national independence, on condition, of course, that our traditional policy of co-operation with the Western Powers was not affected. I did not cease to recommend a friendly and loyal attitude towards the Soviets, in order not to give them a pretext for meddling in our affairs. The development of the situation in the first two years following the war seemed to prove me right: it must be said that up to 1947 the Soviets, after the departure of the Red Army, behaved themselves "correctly" towards us, in contrast to what was happening to certain of our neighbours.

Since Stalin's ultimatum concerning the Marshall Plan, the position had changed completely: his intervention constituted a flagrant violation of our treaty of alliance, according to whose terms the U.S.S.R. had engaged itself not to intervene in our affairs. It was a grave blow to our national sovereignty. Even the man in the street, who spoke of a new Munich, understood perfectly.

Our policy of co-operation with Russia had therefore failed. The rest followed as a natural consequence. A small country like ours obviously had no means of carrying on a struggle against a great Power on the scale of Soviet Russia. But knowing that as long as there was no world conflagration Russia would continue to subject us by using the Communist fifth column, we concluded that the only means of saving our independence was to defend the democratic regime by barring the way to those who were trying to bolshevize the State. The Russians realized that as well as we did, so that when our attitude in regard to the Communist Party stiffened and the Muscovite plans risked being defeated, they hurried to the rescue.

Beginning with the intervention of the Kremlin in the matter of the Marshall Plan, the Communist Party, sure of being able to count on the support of Moscow, displayed a more and more intense activity with the aim of gaining power. The Slovak crisis was the most outstanding episode of this cold war. The progressive communization of the police and the Army was only another aspect of the same struggle.

But while they were strengthening their

From Hubert, Ripka, *Czechoslovakia Enslaved* (London: Victor Gollancz, 1950), 304 – 311. Reprinted by permission of Opera Mundi, Paris position by degrees, the Communists did not feel themselves strong enough before our desperate resistance to stifle democracy in a country where it had such deep roots. They saw themselves obliged, in the end, to have recourse to extreme measures. Now, the decision to execute a coup d'état could not have been taken without the consent of Moscow. Besides, the project could only be successful with the help of the U.S.S.R.

In 1945 the Communists would have been able to bolshevize Czechoslovakia without running into serious difficulties. At this time, with the exception of a small section given over to the American Army, the national territory was occupied by the Red Army, and no organized force existed in the country capable of opposing effective resistance to it. In 1946 the Communist Party was infinitely stronger than in 1948. If it hesitated to institute a totalitarian regime at a time when the circumstances were favourable, it was because it was necessary to take into account the international situation. In 1945 and 1946 Moscow did not want to compromise her relations with the Western Powers, particularly with the United States, by bringing Czechoslovakia to heel, the love of this country for democratic principles being notorious. It was the period when Soviet Russia was agreeing to compromises: she had agreed that Poland should be governed by a coalition Cabinet of which Mikolajczyk, leader of the Peasant Party, was a member. In Hungary she had permitted comparatively free elections to take place, which had brought a great victory to the Small Landholders Party. Even in Bulgaria and Roumania coalition governments had been tolerated. It was only in Yugoslavia, where a totalitarian regime had been set up by Tito, that the last traces of democracy had already disappeared.

During the Slovak crisis in the autumn of 1947 the Communists had means of action no less powerful than in February 1948.

They proceeded according to a plan which they applied four months later in Prague without changing an iota. But at the moment of moving into action they drew back, doubtless because Moscow thought the time had not yet come.

If in February 1948, in Prague, the Communists went the limit, it was because Moscow had given them the go-ahead signal. There are no written documents proving this interference of Moscow in our affairs, but there exists a series of facts which are significant in the highest degree.

The unexpected arrival, at the height of the crisis, of Zorin, Vice-Commissar of Foreign Affairs and former Ambassador of the U.S.S.R. to Prague, indicated clearly that the Soviets had a hand in the matter. No one had been forewarned of his coming, neither Masaryk nor even Clementis, who was told at the last moment, so tardily that he had to suddenly leave a lunch in which he was participating to reach the airfield in time. No one knew the real motive for this visit. The official communiqué, according to which Zorin had considered it advisable to come to Prague to check on the deliveries of Russian wheat, could not be taken seriously. Everyone was convinced that his visit was connected with our internal political affairs.

But why had the Soviet Government sent an official personage, when there was certainly no lack of secret agents of the Cominform, not to mention its famous political police, which had installed itself in Prague some weeks before the coup d'état? The Russians could have only one motive: by this spectacular gesture they were bent on showing that they approved the actions of the Communists. Thus all those who evinced the least inclination to resistance were to be intimidated. The Soviets, whom the progress made by the democratic forces in Czechoslovakia had not escaped, knew that the Communist Party was not strong enough to accomplish the task imposed upon it by the Cominform. Hence the ne-

49

cessity for a concrete act on Moscow's part. The Soviet Press and radio did not limit themselves to reproducing the arguments which the Czechoslovak Communists used against their adversaries during the crisis; they vied with one another in proclaiming that it was necessary to liquidate the "anti-Soviet agents of domestic and foreign reaction" in Czechoslovakia, presenting this slogan as the point of view of the Soviet Government. The Czechoslovak Communist Press did not fail to reprint these articles and declarations, emphasizing that the official opinion of Moscow must be seen in them.

During the crisis Gottwald did not take a single step without justifying it by the necessity of liquidating the enemies of the Soviet Union and the adversaries of the Communists, whom he put on the same plane. The Communists, among others the Minister of Information, Kopecky, tried to impress public opinion by declaring that the Red Army, massed on the Czechoslovak frontiers, was ready to intervene in favour of the Communists against the "reaction." Not only did the Soviet authorities never deny this purposely ambiguous news, but their propaganda did everything to give the impression that the Communists could count on the help of Moscow.

According to trustworthy information, some of which was reproduced in foreign papers, like the Zurich *Volksrecht* of February 20, new Soviet units were brought into Austria during the crisis and were garrisoned not far from the Czechoslovak frontier. Troop movements in Saxony were also reported.

The Hungarian Communists had known since February 9 that a change of regime in favour of the Communists would take place in Czechoslovakia before the end of the month. The Yugoslav and Roumanian Communists had spread similar rumours. Without doubt they had knowledge of the Cominform plan.

On February 23 I had learned that eight days earlier—that is, before our resignations—new members of the Russian Secret Police had arrived in Prague.

On February 27 a high official of the Communist Party declared during the course of a private conversation, "Our friends have given us guarantees against any eventuality." When the person to whom he was talking asked him if by "our friends" he was alluding to the Soviets, he answered without hesitation, "Who, if not the Soviets, could be our friends?"

On March 15 the new Minister of Foreign Trade affirmed: "It is to our Slavic allies, and above all to the Soviet Union, that we owe our success in surmounting the obstacles which barred the way before us, which could have prevented us from inflicting defeat upon the reaction!"

This phrase—the fact is worth noting—disappeared from the accounts reporting the declaration of my successor, who, it seemed, still lacked political experience.

Do not the few facts I have just cited demonstrate undeniably that the Communist coup d'état was realized with the consent and political support of the U.S.S.R? It is to be expected that other additional proofs will supervene to establish the fact that Soviet intervention played a directing role in the crisis.

Finally there is an argument which seems to me decisive: no Communist Party in the world is authorized to take an initiative of any importance without the consent of Moscow. That should settle once and for all the question of Soviet interference in our domestic affairs.

On March 22, 1948, the Communist coup d'état in Czechoslovakia was the subject of a debate in the Security Council of Lake Success. Ambassador Papanek, who up to February had headed the Czechoslovak delegation to the United Nations, made a report on the events which had occurred in Czechoslovakia, and concluded: "All this proves that Czechoslovakia has been the victim of political infiltration and indirect aggression on the part of the Soviet Union, of that indirect aggression which, in 1938 Mr. Molotov recognized as just as dangerous as direct aggression. During negotiations concerning an alliance with Great Britain and France, did not Mr. Molotov declare that the treaty in question should be valid both in the case of direct aggression and of indirect aggression, that is to say of an internal coup d'état or an internal political change in favour of the aggressor?"

If Soviet intervention is doubted by no one, it may still be wondered why the Soviets suddenly changed their attitude towards us, beginning with the summer of 1947. In my opinion it was because the Soviets were determined above all to consolidate their "Eastern bloc" and strengthen their bastion to improve their strategic position in respect of the Western Powers. The coup d'état of Prague was in a large measure a military operation.

There are other very complex reasons, which may have determined and hastened the Soviet intervention.

The Russians knew that they could count on the Czechoslovaks of all parties and all social classes to bar the road to a new *Drang nach Osten* of Germany. They were not unaware, on the other hand, of the fact that if they carried on a policy directed against the Western Powers, they would not be able to rally to them anyone except the Communist minority, and that in case of war between the Soviets and the Western democracies the majority of the population would make common cause with the latter.

Moscow did not feel the need of taking special precautions in Prague as long as the Soviet policy was distinctly anti-German.

But if during the war Stalin had called for the carving up of Germany (he had pronounced himself in favour of this solution in his conversation with Benes in December 1943), after the war Soviet policy, to oppose the Western Powers, changed direction and defended the thesis of a unified Germany, a centralized Reich being more likely to "turn Red."

From the end of 1946 signs indicative of a return of Russia to the Rapallo policy, whose culminating point was the Molotov-Ribbentrop pact, multiplied. The new tendencies did not fail to arouse grave anxiety in Czechoslovakia and Poland, even in certain Communist circles. People began to wonder whether some day Moscow would not find some advantage in satisfying German nationalism by consenting to a revision of the western frontiers of Poland in favour of the Germans and to the return of the Sudeten Germans to Czechoslovakia. In December 1947 I stopped in Warsaw for a few days on my way back from Moscow, and learned that Gomulka, Secretary-General of the Polish Communist Party, was in disgrace with Moscow because of his pronounced anti-German nationalism. During the summer of 1948 Gomulka was liquidated.

It is understandable, then, that if the Soviets intended to carry on a pro-German policy, it would be necessary for them to install a regime completely devoted to them in Prague, as in Warsaw.

For the rest, the existence of an independent democracy in Czechoslovakia was enough of itself to be embarrassing for Moscow. Passionately attached to our traditional policy of co-operation with the East and the West, we were seeking by every means to avoid being shut up within the Soviet bloc. Now the U.S.S.R. could not admit that Czechoslovakia, the only country in Central Europe which had a common frontier with the American zone of Germany, should be a centre for the expansion of Western influence in a sector which she considered as her fief. The most simple means of parrying this danger was, of course, to suppress Czechoslovak democracy and to install in Prague a puppet government ready to obey the Kremlin's every beck and call.

The Communists of the other States of Central Europe desired the disappearance of our democracy as much as did the Russians. So long as Czechoslovakia was not transformed after the image of the other "popular democracies," of which the most perfect model (it is that no longer) was the Yugoslavia of Tito, the Czechoslovak democracy risked contaminating the neighbouring nations, all subjected to a Communist minority, all discontented with the new regime.

What we had been trying to bring about was a synthesis of the fundamental principles of political liberalism and of certain elements of collective socialism. If this political experiment, which was not without audacity, had succeeded, the expansion of Communism in Europe would have been threatened. The direction we had taken already permitted us to win several successes which indicated that it would be possible to realize the principal aims of Socialism without suppressing individual liberty. This mixed system, based on the coexistence, in the economic domain, of private businesses and, in the political domain, of civil liberties and a strengthened governmental authority, was incompatible with the totalitarian regime of a single party. The Cominform, realizing the growing danger the first successes of this system in Czechoslovakia represented for the satellite States, decided to put an end to it. It was necessary to act quickly, for if the elections fixed for May 1948 had taken place under normal conditions the democratic parties would have emerged from them considerably strengthened. At the moment when the Kremlin was reincarnating the Comintern from its ashes to crack the whip for Communism in other countries and support Russian political expansionism, it could not admit that the Communist Party should be weakened in Czechoslovakia—that is to say, in a vital region of the Russian sphere—from the triple point of view of politics, economics and strategy.

The Czechoslovak crisis was provoked shortly after the defeat suffered by the French Communists when the general strike of 1947 collapsed. The coincidence is significant. Elsewhere the Italian elections were to take place in April 1948, and a Communist success appeared scarcely probable. At the same time, a certain tension was already characterizing the relations between Moscow and Tito, although the affair had not yet become public. In Poland it had been judged necessary not only to liquidate the peasant and Catholic opposition, but also to purge the Communist Party by expelling its "nationalist" elements. In these conditions an intervention against the Czechoslovak democracy seemed to impose itself.

Moscow was well aware that the installation of a Communist regime in Prague would be followed at most only by diplomatic protests, while the Communists were sure of the complete and effective support of the Kremlin. Even in the economic field we had from our Western friends only very limited help; while Stalin was sending to Czechoslovakia more wheat than Gottwald had ever asked for, I did not even succeed in obtaining commercial credits from the United States, although American Ambassador Laurence Steinhardt, realizing the political importance of such a gesture, intervened urgently in our favour with the highest authorities of Washington.

Even inside the country we were far from having at our disposal means of action as powerful as those of our opponents, since they occupied all the key positions. In the international domain we were practically isolated, while the Communists enjoyed the support of a great Power. The fight was uneven, and we knew it. Were we wrong, in these conditions, to refuse to submit to an enemy infinitely stronger?

I have thought over this question at length, all the more since I am conscious of the responsibility which I incurred in the recent developments in my country. I think today, as I thought at the time of the crisis, that we could not have acted otherwise.

THE SOVIET-YUGOSLAV QUARREL

The Cominform's denunciation of Tito in June 1948 represented the climax of a deep-seated maladjustment between Yugoslavia and Russia. More clearly than any other event in the period from 1945 to 1953, the Soviet-Yugoslav quarrel revealed the true nature of long-term Soviet designs in Eastern Europe, at least as they had been molded by the end of 1947. The dispute coincided with the high tide of Russian nationalism as opposed to Soviet communism, and although the quarrel, like that between Henry VIII and the Pope, was clothed in ideological language and dwelt on theoretical subjects, the real core of the struggle lay in the clash over national ambitions.

This does not mean to say that the Soviet leaders were hypocritical. They were like the French Republicans engaged in exporting the benefits of revolution abroad, who

> believed themselves to be cosmopolitans, they were that only in their speeches; they felt, they thought, they acted, they interpreted their universal ideas and their abstract principles in accordance with the traditions of a conquering monarchy. . . . They identified humanity with their homeland, their national cause with the cause of all the nations. Consequently and entirely naturally, they confused the propagation of new doctrines with the extension of French power, the emancipation of humanity with the grandeur of the Republic, the reign of reason with that of France, the liberation of peoples with the conquest of states, the European revolution with the domination of the French Revolution in Europe . . . they established subservient and subordinate republics which they held in a sort of tutelage. . . . The Revolution degenerated into an armed propaganda, then into conquest. . . .[1]

In 1945 the Yugoslav regime was more pro-Russian and more prepared to adopt Soviet communist methods than any other communist-infiltrated government in Eastern Europe. It was Yugoslavia who first suggested the resurrection of the Comintern or a similar organization. It was also Yugoslavia that collectivized her agriculture at a faster rate than any other People's Democracy except Bulgaria in the period from 1945 to 1948. The ideological purity of Tito's regime was marred in Soviet eyes, however, by the fact that the Yugoslav communist partisans had won control over their country on their own initiative and had managed to build up a political hierarchy independent of Soviet influence. In the other East European states the communist regimes were composed of a motley collection of leaders; some of them had been sent from Moscow, others had risen through the underground movements. The amazing solidarity of the Yugoslav band of partisans was without parallel. The career of the famous rebel Djilas was a good instance of this. In 1945 he criticized the behaviour of Russian troops in Yugoslavia and provoked Stalin into demanding an apology, but Tito left his wartime comrade in a position of power. Even after Djilas' break with

[1] Albert Sorel, *L'Europe et la Revolution Francaise*, 3rd ed. (Paris, 1893), I, pp. 541–542.

53

Tito much later and the publication in the United States of his critique of communism, *The New Class*, Tito mitigated his old friend's prison sentence until the appearance of a new manuscript, *Conversations with Stalin*, made him change his mind.

Regardless of whether their directives were obeyed or not by Tito, the Soviet leaders in 1948 could no longer tolerate a system in Eastern Europe which they were unable to supervise from the inside, and in which the army, the police and the party cadres were all in the hands of Tito's own men. The mainspring of the new conformity that was imposed after 1947 lay in a rigid hierarchy whose centre was Moscow.

Significantly the Soviet-Yugoslav quarrel grew over issues of power, not of ideology. In 1948 *Pravda* attacked Tito's scheme for a Balkan federation, not primarily on ideological grounds, since Stalin at first egged Tito on in his plans, but because Tito's hold over the reins of power inside Yugoslavia could not be weakened despite the attempts of Soviet agents. If Tito could manage both to prevent the Soviet military and economic missions in Yugoslavia from infiltrating into Yugoslav domestic affairs and to dominate a Yugoslav-Bulgarian federation which eventually aimed at including Rumania, Albania and Hungary, a new independent nexus might be created in southeast Europe that could elude Soviet domination. The Soviet propaganda war against Tito was accompanied by more practical measures. Soviet agents in the Belgrade Cominform office attempted to establish a Stalinist group within the Yugoslav party, while other East European communist parties were ordered to isolate Tito.

Efforts to contain the quarrel broke down after the failure of Kardelj, the Yugoslav Deputy Premier, to appease the Soviets during a visit to Moscow. A rift followed immediately in March 1948 when the Soviets withdrew their military mission from Belgrade.

The Soviet party complained that the Yugoslavs were holding back information regarding their internal affairs. Much of the dispute continued along these petty lines, touching on Soviet control in a joint Soviet-Yugoslav trading company or Yugoslav reluctance to dismiss an official who was not liked by the Russians.

This section of the debate may seem of trifling importance, but in fact it dealt with the many hinges on which Soviet power rested in the other East European countries. The quarrel was peppered with Soviet complaints of an ideological nature also, but their very hollowness demonstrated that they did not form the basis of Soviet grudges. Tito was accused of running his party on dictatorial lines, of concentrating key positions in the hands of a few favorites and of choosing new members for the Central Committee instead of electing them—this from a ruler who held the whole of the Soviet government and the party in his grasp and had not called a Party Congress for nine years.

Stalin's final blow fell at the end of June, when Yugoslavia was expelled from the Soviet communist camp by the Cominform. Since the Cominform officially voiced the opinion of all the East European communist parties, Tito's isolation was complete. The headquarters of the Cominform was transferred to Bucharest.

The polite debate between Yugoslavia and Russia had deteriorated into an open clash of power. At first the opponents argued through diplomatic notes, . . . Stalin took practical steps at the beginning of 1948, which were countered by Tito. The final break seemingly left Yugoslavia without a genuine political ally in the world. Russia appeared to be on the brink of employing armed force against her. Tito parried once again, this time by an even more daring move: he re-established contact with the capitalist West. Tito resolved to hold fast. If he had not, he would surely have suffered the fate of other East European leaders who were purged in the wake of the Yugoslav quarrel. His party would have dissolved at the touch of Soviet intrusion. Apart from Hebrang and one or two other party leaders, the Yugoslavs once again demonstrated their solidarity by backing up their leader in what appeared to be a foolhardy gesture. Luckily for Tito the spine of his supporters was composed of young idealists and nationalists who had followed him through the war, and whose views on political affairs, and in particular on foreign affairs, were too naïve and narrow-minded to allow for any second thoughts.

Adam Ulam

DETAILS OF THE FINAL DISPUTE

The crux of the dispute from the Soviet viewpoint in 1948, when it had not yet been "discovered" that Tito was an agent of the Gestapo and the imperialist powers, consisted in three classes of grievances. There was, first of all, the feeling that the Yugoslavs refused to divulge to the representatives of the Soviet Union economic and other information to which the Russians felt they were entitled. Connected with this complaint were the facts that Soviet experts and representatives in Yugoslavia were surrounded by spies and informers, and that the Yugoslav regime did not treat Soviet Russia deferentially but seemed to consider it a "bourgeois power" rather than the "friendly power which had liberated Yugoslavia from the German occupation." That the Soviet experts, military specialists, and so forth merited the privilege of being maintained by a fellow socialist country at a great cost, and that they had the unquestioned right to go snooping around and attempting to subvert the regime, appeared to the Russians as the most natural thing in the world. The Soviet ambassador "not only has the right but is obliged from time to time to discuss with the Communists in Yugoslavia all questions which interest them." The Russians also had the right to choose the officials they had to deal with in Yugoslavia. Thus Tito and Kardelj failed in their duty when they did not remove Vladimir Velebit,

Reprinted by permission of the publishers from Adam Ulam, *Titoism and the Cominform* (Cambridge, Mass.: Harvard University Press), pp. 117–125. Copyright © 1952 by the President and Fellows of Harvard College.

Deputy Minister of Foreign Affairs, despite Molotov's statement that Velebit was an English spy. The same was true of the Yugoslav ambassador in London, Leontich.

The first and most obvious series of Russian grievances is far from being unimportant despite the petty character of the complaints. They disclose, in fact, the initial reason for Soviet dissatisfaction with Tito's regime, and those writers who have chosen to look much deeper for the "real" causes of the Soviet-Yugoslav crisis have unwittingly fallen into a trap of their own making. The Yugoslav regime in 1945 was more pro-Russian than any other Communist-dominated government in Eastern Europe. None of the complexities which the Russians encountered in strengthening their hold in Poland or Czechoslovakia seemed to exist in Yugoslavia. On all the major issues the Yugoslavs were behind them. But when it came to the small things—arranging a "joint" Russo-Yugoslav trading or industrial company, or getting rid of an official personally obnoxious to them—the Russians encountered difficulties. The difficulties were not due solely to the Yugoslavs' pride in their sovereignty. The Yugoslav leaders, hardened revolutionary fighters and conspirators that they were, were remarkably innocent of the facts of life when it came to international politics and economics. When the issue was an economic deal with Russia which would put them at a disadvantage, or when they were asked to destroy a deserving official because the Russians insisted upon it, the Yugoslavs were likely to ask themselves: "But what does it have to do with Marxism or our love for the Soviet Union?" Their innocence, as is often the case, was interpreted by the Russians as a sign of perversion, and it was soon easy for them to feel that Tito must be engaged in some horrendous anti-Russian intrigues.

One specific Russian charge requires some comment. Vladimir (Vlatko) Velebit had been continually accused by them of being an English spy. The Yugoslavs finally did remove Velebit from the Ministry of Foreign Affairs, but they kept asking—an unheard-of thing—for definite proofs of Velebit's guilt. The answer they got was characteristic: "Why so much consideration for an English spy, who at the same time is so uncompromisingly hostile toward the Soviet Union?" Velebit was a man of no political consequence in Yugoslavia. He was, however, in 1948 one of the very few men in Tito's entourage who seems to have known and understood the West. A lawyer by profession, he had during the war performed a variety of confidential and diplomatic missions for the Partisans. Such a man was, from the Russian point of view, most undesirable as an official of the Yugoslav government. He had visited London during the war and had made a good impression on the British. That was his treason, and no further proof was required.

In a letter of May 4, 1948, the Central Committee of the Communist Party of the Soviet Union (C.P.S.U.) undertook another line of attack upon the Yugoslavs. This line has been most emphasized by those analysts who believe that there must be something deeper in the dispute than the question of political power and personalities—that there must be an "ideological" explanation. The letter, written under the heading, "On the incorrect political line of the Politburo of the Central Committee of the Communist Party of Yugoslavia (C.P.Y.) struggle in Yugoslavia," proceeds to castigate social policies of Tito's Yugoslavia. The issue turns largely on the extent and character of the collectivization drive in Yugoslavia and its real or feigned meaning as the reason for Russia's displeasure with Tito. A historian or social scientist abhors very often a simple solution, and it has been easy for many even non-Communist commentators and writers on the Yugoslav problem to envisage Soviet Russia—the guardian of Communist morality and ideology—turning its solicitous

gaze upon Yugoslavia where "the capitalist elements are increasing in the cities and
the villages" and demanding a radical
change in the policy of the regime. What
are the facts?

The Russian charge was summarized in
the communiqué of the Cominform of June
28, 1948, which stated that in Yugoslavia,
where "individual peasant farming predominates . . . [where] the land is not
nationalized, where there is private property in land and where land can be bought
or sold, where much of the land is concentrated in the hands of the kulaks . . . there
could be no question of correct Marxist
policies being applied." But the question
obviously cannot be judged in absolute
terms; it must be considered from two separate angles. First, was the extent and nature of collectivization considered by the
Russians as the main criterion of their satellites' loyalty and Marxist "correctness" in
the period from 1945 to 1948? And, secondly, was Yugoslavia's stand on collectivization less Marxist than that of the other satellites? The answer to the first question
must be emphatically in the negative. As
we have already seen, Soviet Russia's interest during the years from 1945 to 1948
consisted in building up strong pro-Soviet
regimes in the satellite countries, governments which were allowed and encouraged
to develop considerable flexibility in their
social policies in order not to alienate the
support of the peasants and lower middle
classes. The Russians, with the terrible experience of their enforced collectivization
of the early thirties in mind, were not likely
to insist, prior to the crisis of 1948, on a
rigorous policy of collectivization in their
satellites, for such a course would have
threatened their economic recovery and the
progress of political consolidation by the
Communists.

As to the second question, there is ample
ground to believe that the rulers of Yugoslavia, out of their Communist fanaticism
and economic naïveté, before 1948 pursued
a faster pace in the collectivization of agriculture than any other country in the satellite area except, perhaps, Bulgaria, where
the same characteristics motivated its Communist government. It is very difficult to
see a genuine reason in the Cominform's
accusation of Tito's agricultural policy as
antirevolutionary and helpful to the growth
of capitalism in the villages, when he in
effect had been doing before 1948 what
most of his accusers were ready to undertake, and on a less ambitious scale (largely
because they viewed more realistically the
economic and social aspects of collectivization), only after 1948. The whole line of al-
legations that the Soviet offensive against
Tito's Yugoslavia has been caused by the
social and economic policy of the regime
cannot confront the facts of the case.

Has then the displeasure of Soviet Russia
and the Cominform been incurred by the
incautious character of Yugoslavia's economy and by the extra-leftist character of its
economic laws? It is very difficult to see
how this criticism, which appears to be
perfectly sensible, fits in with the accusation that the Yugoslav leaders have not
gone far enough in socializing their country and in paying attention to Russia's ad-
vices. Tito and his group cannot be both
lacking in the Marxist fervor and perpetuating capitalism and ruining the economy
of their country through a variety of doctrinaire Marxist measures. The Cominform's criticism of Yugoslavia's economic
plans brings out very clearly that the Yugoslav Communists have erred in their economic policy. Their errors found their
source in the uncritical acceptance of the
most naïve premises of Communism and
could not, originally, figure one way or another as the basis of the Soviet-Yugoslav
dispute.

It must not be thought, however, that the
economic and social part of the Soviet accusation against Tito is insincere. As the
tone of these accusations suggests, and as
the sequence of events in the Cominform

countries confirms, the Russians managed to convince themselves that Tito's reputed intransigence was not merely an act of personal treachery but that it was deeply connected with a basic anti-Marxist tendency of his social and economic policy. Perhaps the most frightening and significant feature of the correspondence is that it reveals the ease with which doctrinal considerations can often color and distort the analysis of a political situation. Russian Communism stands revealed as being influenced by the habits of thought and speech, if not properly speaking the ideology, of its creed.

"We are disturbed by the present condition of the C.P.Y." Here is the third line of attack pursued by the Russians against the Tito regime. The Yugoslav Communist Party is run dictatorially. New members for its Central Committee are coöpted instead of being elected. The Party itself is content to remain hidden behind the facade of the People's Front. Its lack of intra-Party democracy is underlined by the fact that one of the secretaries of the Central Committee (Alexander Rankovich) is not only the Minister of State Security but also the Personnel Secretary of the Party. In short, according to the Russian charge, the Party, instead of being a democratic organization run by the rank and file of its membership, is a closed private preserve of a few leaders who constitute its Politburo and is in fact run dictatorially by its Big Four: Tito, Kardelj, Djilas, and Rankovich. That such a charge could be raised by the leaders of a Party which, at the time the accusations were being presented, had not had a Party Congress for nine years, whose highest officials had been purged at the orders of a dictator and in a manner which makes the purging of Hebrang and Zhujovich mild by comparison, and whose history for the past twenty years had been one long record of complete denial of its basic organizational tenets, is testimony to the extent to which self-indoctrination and absolute power may lead in the destruction of all sense of proportion and capacity for introspection. The Communist Party of Yugoslavia was thus accused of having imitated successfully the main organizational and personal features of the Communist Party of the Soviet Union.

There must have been many reasons why the Russians, even before 1948, were disturbed about the situation in the C.P.Y. It was a Party which exhibited all the characteristics that make its successful manipulation from the outside quite difficult. The Russians prefer a situation in which no single leader or group of leaders, no matter how great their attachment to the Soviet Union and Communist fanaticism, are in the position of complete authority. Tito's position was different from that of Gomulka in Poland, or Gheorgiu-Dej in Rumania, or even Rakosi in Hungary, in that he was the undoubted master of both the state and the Party. Unlike Rakosi or Dimitrov, he was furthermore a man covered with a panoply of military honors, the national hero to many of his countrymen, and, alone among the Communist Party leaders of Eastern Europe, in complete command of his army. Such a combination of attributes would have made even the most humble and devoted servant of Communism a very difficult man to deal with, and the dictator's personality is not marked by an excess of humility. It is not difficult to perceive in the letter of the Russian Central Committee a note of scorn and exasperation; the Russians had not really accustomed themselves to the idea that Tito was no longer a rather inferior agent of the Comintern and that the "Comrade Walter" who used to report dutifully to the Comintern was now the leader of his state and a man to be argued with.

The solidarity of the high command of the C.P.Y. must have also worried the Russians right from the beginning. Early in 1945 Milovan Djilas made some disparaging remarks about the behavior of the Russian troops in Yugoslavia, contrasting unfavorably some actions of the Soviet officers with the behavior of the British officers attached to the Partisans. Djilas' remarks were made at a session of the Central Committee of the C.P.Y., yet they became known immediately to the Russians and provoked a telegram from Stalin to Tito. Djilas personally apologized to Stalin, but the fact that he was allowed by Tito to remain in a position of high importance and power was an unpleasant lesson to the Russians. That the Minister of Propaganda was, until the Soviet-Yugoslav break, the person most renowned in Tito's entourage for his violent anti-West tendencies and his fanatical Communism was evidently of little consequence in comparison with his one outburst of bad temper. He became, in fact, a marked man to the Russians, and three years afterwards they were to see in that rather trifling incident a significant proof of the anti-Soviet tendency of the regime. But Djilas's case is a fine example of the working of the despotic mind, which balances the lifetime of devoted service against one incautious remark.

Within the Communist Party of Yugoslavia the Russians encountered, in brief, a strong and united nucleus of leadership. These leaders had stood the test of the postwar years, and official honors had been heaped upon them. Taught by their own Party history, the Russian Communists may well have expected dissension to arise within the central organs of the Yugoslav Party and state. Yet aside from Hebrang and Zhujovich the Russians obviously failed to recruit any Communist leaders of the first rank in Yugoslavia. The ideological tie which bound together the Yugoslav hierarchy was reinforced by an extraordinary feeling of solidarity, born of the war, and a most common-sense notion of self-interest. The Russian Communist Party after the Bolshevik Revolution had had as its elite a group of "prima donnas," people who intellectually and temperamentally had often very little in common, and who had been harnessed to the common task only through the extraordinary personality of Lenin. To some extent the same situation was reproduced after World War II in Eastern Europe, where the Communist Parties found among their leaders people of the most diverse backgrounds and temperaments: old revolutionaries and underground fighters confronted the intellectual type of Communist who had spent his war years in Moscow. It was only in Yugoslavia that the hard core of leadership consisted of a veritable "band of brothers" who, having survived the common danger, were now securing their hold upon the country with the mixture of implacable fanaticism, naïveté, and cunning which had characterized them during the war.

Against that background the Soviet agents were busily employed, but with little success, in trying to subvert this or that general or Party official. It is perhaps a tribute to General Rankovich's secret police that the Soviet efforts were to yield such a meager result. It is also significant, and a rather unusual circumstance, that most of the wooing had to be done by the Soviet ambassador, since he was the only man who could meet Yugoslav ministers and high officials without arousing too much suspicion. This combination of the solidarity of the top leaders and the supervision of every official not within the charmed circle yields, of course, a great deal of credence to the Soviet assertion that the Yugoslav Party was not run democratically. The Central Committee of the Party had, at the time of the exchange of letters with Moscow, twenty-six members, a surprisingly small number for a Communist Party in power. The Yugoslav Party had not held a Congress since the war, not, as a matter of fact, since 1928. In this, of course, it was in a sense following the example of the Communist Party of the Soviet Union, which has not held a Party Congress since 1939. All the important and key Party posts were held by handpicked nominees of Tito and his group.

THE BERLIN CRISIS

Western suspicions aroused by the Czech coup of February 1948 were galvanized by the Soviet imposition in June 1948 of a blockade on the non-Russian sectors of Berlin which lay far inside the Soviet zone of Germany. Stalin's first act of overt aggression against the West was motivated by an old malady of his, a deep-seated fear of German power. At this time the western Allies were intending to bring Western Germany into their group, thus anchoring great industrial potential on their side. The introduction of a reformed currency in the western zones of Gemany and also in the Allied sectors in Berlin provided the Soviets with an argument similar to the one they had used against the Marshall Plan; economic pressure was being put on the western part of Germany, while the reform could only create monetary troubles in the Soviet zone.

There may have been some sense in Stalin's reasoning, but there was little in the steps he took to act on it. No doubt he counted on both previous Western softness and noninterference in East European affairs (Czechoslovakia had provided a very recent instance of this) and on Berlin's delicate geographical position. He was disappointed. The Western Allies organized an airlift of vital supplies from western Germany into Berlin. A peaceful settlement was not reached until May 1949. The immediate result of Stalin's aggressive action was the formation of the West German Federal Republic on May 23, 1949. This was preceded by the definitive establishment of American forces in Europe through the instrument of the North Atlantic Treaty Organization, signed in March 1949, Stalin retaliated in October of the same year by setting up a German Democratic Republic in the Soviet zone, although the communist equivalent of NATO, the Warsaw Pact, was not agreed upon until 1955.

In a message to Washington of April 16, 1948, General Clay, the United States military governor in Germany, dramatically pointed out the significance of the Soviet thrust in Berlin as it appeared to the noncommunist world.[1]

> We have lost Czechoslovakia. Norway is threatened. We retreat from Berlin. When Berlin falls, western Germany will be next. If we mean . . . to hold Europe against communism, we must not budge. We can take humiliation and pressure short of war in Berlin without losing face. If we withdraw, our position in Europe is threatened. If America does not understand this now, does not know that the issue is cast, then it never will and communism will run rampant. I believe that the future of democracy requires us to stay. . . .

[1] Quoted in *Berlin—Pivot of Destiny*, ed. C. Robson (Chapel Hill, 1960), p. 48.

C. Robson

BACKGROUND OF THE BERLIN CRISIS

In the relationships among the victor powers, the controlling factor was that the Russians arrived on the scene first, and had had more than three months, from May to August 1945 to establish the foundation for their influence in all parts of Berlin. They set up the first civil authority, they specified the form of organization of the city administration, and they exercised influence in the establishment of the political parties, which they licensed. It was a fact of great importance that every one of these parties was compelled by the sharpest kind of pressure to locate its headquarters in the Eastern sector. The same kind of maneuvering was systematically applied to the Berlin press. The creation of a network of confidential agents by means of a renewal of the National Socialist system of the block- and house-spies was another precautionary measure which assured the Russians a method for the exertion of influence.

The Western powers had the greatest difficulty in combatting the consequences of these initial Russian measures, even in matters in which, in the name of genuine democracy, they began very soon after arrival on the scene to counter the established Russian policies. At the beginning of the Four Power administration of Berlin, the Allies had recognized the continuing legal validity of the organizations and regulations which had been established by the Russians. Thereafter, being in possession of the veto-power which was the basic assumption of all the agreements that described the authority of the Allied Kommandatura in Berlin as well as the authority of the Control Council for Germany, Russia could make the repeal of any established practice at least the subject of a protracted struggle.

Even in the drafting of the Temporary Constitution of 1946, though the Western powers made strenuous opposition to Russian demands, they were finally persuaded to include a fateful "rubber clause." According to this article, not only the choice of the Chief Mayor and the city councilors, but appointment and dismissal of all "leading officials" of the city administration, had to receive the approval of the Kommandatura. The Russians were thereby enabled to extend their own conception of "leading officials" to every branch of the administration of the city. As a result, they were in a position to make an issue of every personnel action and thus to obstruct indefinitely the development and operation of the civil government in the city.

The classic case in this "struggle of the veto" was the Russian opposition against the choice of Ernest Reuter as Chief Mayor. Although the Western powers protested from the outset against this abitrary action, it prevented the people of Berlin, right up to the beginning of the blockade in 1948, from being led, even in their external affairs, by a man in whom they really had confidence. Even the Allied Control Council had to submit to the obstinacy with which the Russians maintained their opposition in this instance.

Thanks to this position of power, which was impregnable by any means short of armed conflict, the Russian occupation authorities systematically excluded their allies from any influence at all in the Eastern sector of the city, while, by means of their

From *Berlin—Pivot of Destiny*, ed. C. Robson (Chapel Hill, 1960), pp. 56–66. Reprinted by permission of University of North Carolina Press.

veto-power, they clung tenaciously to every position of advantage which they had established in the Western sectors in 1945. The continuation of this situation could only result in the capitulation of the Western powers, the surrender of all of Berlin to the Russians and the eventual absorption of the entire city into the Soviet Occupation Zone—or if the Western powers offered any resistance, in the splitting of the capital city. Both of these solutions stood in irreconcilable contradiction to the spirit and the letter of the agreements made at the end of the war. Nevertheless, the politics of schism spread gradually to all phases of life in Berlin.

In this local "cold war," which set in long before the cold war in world politics became apparent, the Russians exploited most relentlessly and unscrupulously the economic weapons at their disposal. Here, without a doubt, they had the advantage, because the city of Berlin was entirely surrounded by their occupation zone. The very fact that each occupying power had to feed and otherwise supply its own sector put that power which had the hinterland of the Eastern zone at its disposal at a great advantage over the others in Berlin and elsewhere; on the other hand, a power with a quite limited and economically not self-sufficient zone—as was the case with France, for instance—was put in an undeniably difficult position, and indeed in an almost insupportable one.

The Russians could make the normal dependence of Berlin upon deliveries of foodstuff from the surrounding region an instrument of pressure, a lever, in an interminable "carrot-and-whip" policy. Since the Russians made the delivery of potatoes and grains, the provision of fruit and vegetables, indeed even the supply of milk for children, a tool in the political struggle, and applied it with unhesitating purposefulness, especially in election periods, they were able to keep the people in the Western sectors in a constant state of apprehension. There were actually cases of direct political blackmail in this matter of food. In the fall of 1947, for instance when, after a severe winter and spring, the harvests held out hope of somewhat better times, the Russians announced that the agricultural surplus of the province of Brandenburg would be used to supply Berlin only when the outstanding balance of payments for the delivery of agricultural products had been fully paid.

This kind of politics was only brought to its culmination with the beginning of the outright blockade in 1948 when the attempt to shut off the supplies from West Germany at the beginning of July was accompanied by an offer to give people from the Western sectors the opportunity to secure ration cards in the Eastern sector. In every period of human history there have been instances of submission to treacherous and dishonorable blandishments. It is notable, then, that at the outset only 21,000 West Berliners out of a population of over 2 million (1.5 per cent of the total) availed themselves of this opportunity to enter into a kind of reinsurance arrangement in East Berlin. This is a fact which the Berlin public rightfully holds in honorable memory to the present day. If this number reached a peak of 70,000 before the end of the blockade, this is understandable, for not until the late fall of 1948 was it possible to provide the people in the three Western sectors with rations which were equal to those supplied to the population of East Berlin, at least according to the figures that appeared on the ration cards.

Still another important fact in the economic sphere must be mentioned. In June 1948—that is, immediately before the break, the final decision to impose the blockade—the general regulation of the pay scales of all the industrial and transport workers in Berlin was taken over by central offices which were controlled by the Soviet administration. Thus the most numerous and the most important group of workers in Berlin would have been forced into economic dependence on the East, had not the struggle over the blockade begun at this very moment.

While all these events were taking place, it was by no means easy to recognize in any one of them by itself the consequences inherent in the total pattern which was being established. But this almost unbelievably complex combination of events was leading toward a situation in which either permanent separation on the one hand, or total subjugation on the other, would be inevitable. Historically, however, perhaps the most significant area of interaction between East and West in Berlin may have been currency. In this question, the nature of the advantages the Russians possessed stood out very clearly. And this was also a question in which the decision to allow the break to occur was the most difficult for all participating groups, both within Berlin and outside it.

Even after the Western powers had decided to carry through the currency reform of June 1948—a step that is said by the Russians to have caused the blockade—they were still willing to exclude Berlin from the sphere of operation of Western currency, in case the introduction of the new currency could not be accomplished in conjunction with the Soviet Union. Fundamentally, they had wished to carry through the currency reform in cooperation with the Russians, with only one modest condition—that the currency printing establishment, which was in Leipzig under Russian control, be subjected to quadripartite control. This control limitation was intended to prevent the reformed currency from immediately becoming a plaything in the struggle between the East and West.

Only a small group of leaders in Berlin was fully conscious of the seriousness of the situation—Ernst Reuter, whose observation that whoever controlled the currency had the real power in his hands was an accurate summary of the problem, Gustav

Klingelhöfer, and Frau Luise Schröder, who supported both of these men loyally. These leaders realized that if the moves towards a solution of the currency issue took a false direction, the struggle for the realities of power in Berlin would be lost. In their warning to the Allied powers, they were successful only to the point that the American military government prepared an alternative plan for the limited introduction of West German marks in Berlin, in case the discussion with the Russians might lead to a rupture—something that did in fact take place.

At the outset, official opinion in West Germany remained just as cool and hesitant as the Allied views toward the bold suggestion to couple Berlin now, once and for all, to the West German economy. Regardless of party affiliation, even the overwhelming majority of the political leaders in Berlin itself shrank from the radical proposal to bind the city for better or worse to West Germany, which was just at the time in the act of forming itself into a state. The idea of a "Bären mark," a special Berlin currency existing between the currencies of East and West, was seriously discussed for several weeks at that time out of sheer dismay at the idea of separation and the dangers that it would entail.

If one brings all of this background together, it becomes a rather simple matter to find the key to the dramatic events of the blockade year of 1948, and the logic of all these preliminaries then becomes apparent. Today it seems possible to establish historically—and this is a very interesting and stimulating problem indeed—that the Russian decision to allow the struggle for the conquest of the entire city of Berlin to come to a head in 1948 probably was determined in the last analysis by the unconsolidated position of the SED (Socialist Unity Party of Germany) in the Soviet Occupation Zone. It is at least very noticeable that as early as September 1947 suggestions began to appear again and again in the East German press that Berlin was really a part of the Soviet Zone. The two themes that the struggle for exclusive possession of Berlin should be carried on as a logical rebuff for the consolidation of West Germany under the direction of the Western powers, and that the "thorn" of Berlin should be removed from the body of the Soviet Zone, began to emerge openly and conclusively in SED policy and propaganda. There is no doubt that the campaign to subjugate all of Berlin was being systematically prepared by the highest authorities and organs of the SED, and that they urged it upon the Russians with the greatest zeal.

With the role of the SED in mind, the relatively noncommittal personal attitude of Stalin toward the attack upon the soil of Berlin becomes more understandable. In 1948 he seemed generally to be acting in accordance with the formula that he had expressed quite candidly at the Moscow conference in 1947 when he said, "We are allies, and what we have here are only skirmishes, preliminary bouts over the differences which exist between us. That cannot prevent us from remaining friends."

All of this indicates that in 1948 the internal German aspect of the situation, i.e., the parochial interests of the satellite regime in East Berlin, played at least as important a role in the decision of the Russians to take the risk of the blockade (a maneuver that wasn't actually carried through to its ultimate consequences) as it does in the Russian policies that have resulted in the crisis we are living through today. Under this assumption, the whole history of the blockade year becomes quite simple and obvious, and all that remains is to examine the last stages of the blockade itself.

Each side had its resources. In the East there was the continuing effort to render the population of the Western sectors unreliable within its own ranks. On the other side, however, there was the entire sum of the experiences which the people of Berlin

had passed through since 1945, and these proved much more powerful. The events in Berlin itself, and what could be observed from the proximity of the Soviet Occupation Zone, left the West Berliners with no doubts. The Soviet Zone was ever more rapidly being forced to submit to total absorption by the East, and the movement of refugees to the West had already begun to set in unmistakably. It became quite clear to the West Berliners that all the freedom and independence of development for political parties and trade unions, for the organs of local self-government, and for the citizenry in general which had been gained in the strenuous struggle since 1946 would be lost in case the Russian policies were successful.

To prevent this, the people of West Berlin rallied again and again around the great leaders — Ernst Reuter, Otto Suhr, Franz Neumann, Ernst Lemmer and Hubert Schwennicke — who, with more and more support from the Allied headquarters, called upon them for determined resistance in the recurrent crisis of the year of the blockade. In the famous mass demonstrations of the summer and fall of 1948, they proclaimed anew their unshakable determination not to allow Berlin to become a second Prague. They proclaimed it on July 23 when for the first time the city Representative Assembly was threatened by organized force; on August 26 at the time of the debate over the winter relief program and in connection with the decision of the Assembly to hold new elections in the fall; on September 6, when it became necessary to transfer the Assembly to the Student House at Steinplatz in the British Sector; and on September 8 when the City Hall was surrounded, nineteen officials of the city government, Berlin policemen, were arrested, and access to their own meeting place was denied to the city representatives.

It was here in Berlin that that well-known Russian tactic of intimidation through systematic terror, which in all of the satellite states had paved the way for the final collapse of all resistance, was for the first time forced to recoil in the face of the resistance of representatives of the people and the broad masses of the people themselves. On September 9 there occurred, finally, that famous rally of 300,000 people in the Platz der Republik—in sight of the Brandenburg Gate and the ruins of the Reichstag Building—which summed up the people's determination to fight back.

Hand in hand with these attempts to intimidate the city Representative Assembly, there had been a systematic attempt to split the city administration between Eastern and Western zones. The high point of this process was the struggle against Colonel Markgraf, the Berlin Chief of Police. On July 26 he had to be dismissed by the city government for open and notorious mutiny, but this did not prevent him from continuing his command over the police in East Berlin. This incident, however, was the occasion of a clear indication of the attitude of most of the employees of the Berlin city administration. Within a few days, 70 per cent of the personnel of the police department responded to the call to place themselves under the direction of the new Chief of Police, Stumm, in the building on Friesen Street that is today the police headquarters in West Berlin.

The same process of splitting up took place at all levels of the city administration, from the most to the least important. The rationing office was compelled in July to move its principal divisions to West Berlin in order to continue to function. The postal service had to be divided and a central office for money orders set up in West Berlin. In contrast to Ernst Reuter and his friends, who knew from mid-summer on what the final result would be and desired to prepare for it systematically, Deputy Mayor Friedensburg, who had taken the place of the ailing Luise Schröder, maintained his office in the old East Berlin City Hall as long as possible, because he did not wish to recognize the compulsion that prevented the City Assembly from holding its meetings there as final. At last, however, the reality of split became so clear that on November 20 and 21 even the fire stations in the Eastern sector of Berlin were forbidden to answer calls to help in extinguishing fires in West Berlin.

The final step in the split of Berlin took place in a meeting in the Admiralpalast on November 30 that pretended to be a special session of the City Representative Assembly. Instead of the elected representatives, however, there were some 1600 participants present. In the midst of a carefully organized mass demonstration, this rally proceeded to elect a city government for East Berlin under the leadership of Friedrich Ebert. This turn of events, however, was only the logical conclusion to a long series of maneuvers extending over a period of years. It was not a response to a challenge from the West; it was in fact staved off by the West as long as that was possible. The decision to accept the split was forced upon the West and was completely unavoidable if all of the values which the people of Berlin had struggled for since 1945 were not to be surrendered.

THE EXTENSION OF SOVIET CONTROL IN EASTERN EUROPE

Stalin's double failure to force his opponents' hands either in Berlin or in Yugoslavia affected his policies in Eastern Europe. The solidarity of the Allies convinced him that he could go no further in Western Europe at that time, while Yugoslavia's stubborn resistance within the communist camp led him to wonder whether other national communist leaders would imitate Tito. The Soviet Union began to cement its hold in the rest of Eastern Europe: from this time on a quicker pace was set and more drastic methods were employed.

The purges in Eastern Europe following on Tito's excommunication were the clearest indication of the shock Moscow had received. Although the liquidation of some of the top leaders in Eastern Europe cannot be wholly explained by the phenomenon of Titoism, there is no doubt that Stalin's new apprehension and the convenience of labelling unwanted communists as Titoists speeded up the process. There were other reasons springing from changing conditions in the individual countries and on the world scene. Now that both protagonists in the cold war had thrown down the gauntlet it was necessary to steel themselves for open struggle. The last gap in the iron curtain had been closed by the communist coup in Czechoslovakia, but there was as yet little homogeneity within party ranks. After the war many opportunists and former members of pro-German parties had climbed onto the communist party bandwagon in Eastern Europe. Not a few reached very high positions in the state. It was obvious that some of them would have to go.

Less evident but equally important was the need to purge the type of person who had risen to influence during the war in the communist resistance movements and had subsequently inclined to national rather than purely, or rather pro-Soviet, communist policies. Finally the drive after 1948 to implement far-reaching economic and social plans on Soviet lines called for leaders of a new kind in Eastern Europe. Just as Stalin, the careful organizer and bureaucrat, had replaced Trotsky at the helm of the Soviet state in the 1920's, so now Moscow-trained administrators took precedence over the men who had led the communist cause to victory in the heroic early days.

Victims of these policies fell thick and fast in 1949: Koci Xoxe in Albania, Traicho Kostov in Bulgaria, and Laszlo Rajk in Hungary were executed for noncompliance with the Soviet line. In Poland the imprisonment of Wladyslaw Gomulka was an omen of the shift inside the People's Democracies from the domesticism described above to clear examples of national communism in opposition to the Soviet pattern. Gomulka had been the only East European leader to object to the formation of the Cominform. Again in 1949 he tried to stem the mounting tide of Soviet control over Polish affairs, but his protests, unlike those of Tito, were not founded on any solid power basis independent of Soviet manipulation. Also in contrast to Tito, the source of Gomulka's grievances was ideological in nature from the start. As a result, he was bound to lose against the country which had a monopoly of both power and Stalinist ideology.

The purges in the higher reaches of the states concerned were accompanied by the increasing use of terror at all levels. The secret police acquired more power in Eastern Europe and became largely independent of national party control while remaining subservient to Soviet designs. A regular system of concentration camps developed in the various countries and forced labor was recruited on the Soviet pattern. Especial blame was attached to persons convicted of crimes for negligence in the fulfillment of state economic plans. Highly placed members of the Roman Catholic Church became the target of frequent attacks.

THE POLITICAL BACKGROUND OF POSTWAR DEVELOPMENT

At this point in the postwar development of Eastern Europe, we may stand back from our consideration of events and take a look at the general character of the political, economic, and ideological background as it appeared in the years between the founding of the Cominform in 1947 and Stalin's death in 1953.

Hugh Seton-Watson

THE STATE MACHINE

Six of the East European countries have adopted constitutions closely modelled on the Soviet constitution of 1936. They are Yugoslavia, Albania, Bulgaria, Rumania, Czechoslovakia and Hungary. Poland has adopted a provisional constitution, a halfway stage between the democratic constitution of 1921 and the new constitution—no doubt of the Soviet type—which the present parliament will make.

All seven countries are republics. Their official description is "people's republic," a halfway stage between "bourgeois republic" and "soviet republic." The disappearance of the Coburg dynasty in Bulgaria was inevitable after the second unsuccessful war on the side of Germany. The Albanian monarchy of King Zog had not deep roots, for Ahmed Zogu had only been one of a number of notables in a land of turbulent beys and chieftains. The Yugoslav dynasty had a peculiar position. The Karadjordjević family was of Serbian origin, and had al-

ternately occupied and claimed the throne of Serbia since the early nineteenth century. It still enjoyed popularity among the peasants of Serbia in 1941, and doubtless has many well-wishers still. But outside the kingdom of Serbia its hold was slight. Even the Serbs of Bosnia and the Voivodina were lukewarm, while Croats, Slovenes, Macedonians and Montenegrins had little use for it. The reign of Alexander had associated the dynasty too closely with "Greater Serb" nationalism. Tito's partisans were justified in arguing that the dynasty had become a cause not of unity but of discord among the people of Yugoslavia. The Rumanian dynasty, though of German (Hohenzollern) origin, was the most genuinely popular of those of Eastern Europe. King Michael's overthrow of Antonescu in August 1944 had not only vitally affected the course of the Second World War, but had also won him increased popularity from his subjects. In the following years he became

---

From Hugh Seton-Watson, *The East European Revolution* (New York, 1950), pp. 296–304. Reprinted by permission of Frederick A. Praeger, Inc., and Methuen & Co., Ltd.

a symbol in the eyes of Rumanians of all classes of their country's independence. It was this which won him the hostility of the Soviet leaders and led to his forced abdication.

Clearly a sovietised political and economic system is not compatible with hereditary monarchy. But the overthrow of monarchy should not be considered simply a result of Soviet and communist force. It may be doubted whether the institution, which was taken from the West European model in the nineteenth century when the East European countries won their independence, is suited to them. They had not experienced the historical development from which the constitutional monarchies of Britain and Scandinavia arose. The monarchs sought to apply Western standards without understanding the different foundations of their kingdoms. They associated with the small number of their subjects who lived in a West European manner, not realising that these men had less in common with their own compatriots than with Westerners of their own class. The courts maintained a level of pomp and luxury approximating to those of the West. The contrast between this and the poverty of their countries was profound. The kings were far removed from the peasant hovels and workers' slums. This became true even of the Karadjordjević dynasty, whose founder was a Serbian peasant. The monarchies of Eastern Europe, despite the excellent motives and considerable achievements of many of the kings, and the patriotism of which they sometimes became a symbol, were alien growths. It is unlikely that they will be revived, or if they are revived that they will last.

The head of the state of Poland and Czechoslovakia is a President of the Republic. Both are elected for seven years by the parliament. The Polish President's powers are substantially the same as under the 1921 constitution. He is in effect bound to act as government and parliament wish.

The Czechoslovak President has greater powers. He may dissolve the Assembly, appoint both the Premier and individual ministers, preside over cabinet meetings, and require reports both from the government as a whole and from individual ministers. These powers are not, however, likely to cause difficulty as long as the presidency is held by Gottwald and the government is controlled by the Communist Party of which he is chairman. If the presidency should fall vacant, it is temporarily held in Poland by the Speaker, in Czechoslovakia by the cabinet as a whole, which may delegate specific powers to the Premier.

In Yugoslavia, Rumania, Bulgaria, Hungary, and Albania there is no single head of state. The function is collectively performed by the Presidium of the Assembly.

All seven countries have legislative assemblies elected by direct, equal, secret and universal suffrage. Yugoslavia is the only country with a bicameral legislature. The second chamber, like that of the U.S.S.R., is based on nationality. The six republics, the autonomous region Voivodina and the autonomous province Kosovo-Metohija, are represented respectively by thirty, twenty and fifteen members each in it. Its title is Council of Peoples. The principal chamber, the Federal Council, is elected in the usual manner by territorial constituencies. In Czechoslovakia there is only one central legislature, but there is also a subordinate regional legislature for Slovakia, elected directly by the Slovak voters. The Polish, Rumanian, Bulgarian, Hungarian, and Albanian legislatures are unicameral. In all seven countries the cabinet is formed from a majority in the legislature and is responsible to it.

The legislature also elects from its number a body called the Presidium, modelled on the institution of the same name in the Soviet constitution. It consists of a president, several vice-presidents, a secretary, and a number of members varying in different countries. It performs the functions of the legislature when the legislature is not in session. Since the sessions of the legislatures are, as in the U.S.S.R., only for a short period each year, the presidium enacts a large number of decrees. These later have to be ratified by the full assembly. Since the elimination by the summer of 1948 of all parliamentary opposition, the assemblies have become mere meeting-places at which prominent supporters of the regime have opportunities to try their hand at popular democratic rhetoric. What powers belong to them by the constitution are in fact exercised for the greater part of the year by the presidiums.

Apart from this, and in addition to the functions of head of state, the presidium also has powers of interpreting the constitutionality of laws. In the case of Yugoslavia, the presidium may dissolve parliament if there is a disagreement between the two chambers. It may also decide whether laws passed by the governments of the constituent republics are in conformity with federal laws and with the federal constitution, and whether institutions or economic enterprises should be administered by the republican or federal authorities. In Poland the powers of a presidium are held by the State Council. It is composed of the President of the Republic, the Speaker and Deputy-Speakers of the Assembly, the Chairman of the Supreme Auditing Board, and not more than three others elected by the Assembly at the unanimous request of the State Council itself. In time of war only, the commander-in-chief is also a member. The powers of the Czechoslovak presidium are more limited. It may not elect the President of the Republic or introduce constitutional amendments in any circumstances, and at times when the Assembly is not in session for normal reasons it may not extend military service, declare war, or create "permanent charges on the state finances."

Local government authorities — people's committees or people's councils — are also elected, at each administrative level. The pyramid of councils and committees corresponds to the pyramid of soviets in the constitution of the U.S.S.R. The Yugoslav committees are the only bodies whose origin resembles that of the Russian soviets. As we have seen, they were more or less democratic bodies created by the circumstances and needs of national and civil war. Only after the war was over were they emasculated and made subservient to the central government. The Czechoslovak committees, apart from abuses of power in certain areas, resembled local authorities in Western Europe until in February 1948 they were taken over by the communists. In the remaining five countries the committees or councils were born emasculated. They resemble the Russian soviets of the 1936 constitution, not the spontaneous and democratic soviets of 1905 or 1917. In this sense only, the statement of Rákosi that "people's democracy is dictatorship of the proletariat without the soviet form" is true.

Apart from providing the usual municipal or district services, the committees or councils are also the local executive authorities of central government departments. The executive committees of the local authorities, and the departments within them, are responsible not only to their own bodies and their electors, but also to the executives and departments of the authority at the next administrative level above them, and to the corresponding central ministries.

The judiciary is being brought steadily nearer to the Soviet model. In Yugoslavia judges are elected at each level, from the Supreme Court — elected by the federal legislature — down to the district courts — elected by the district people's committees. In Bulgaria and Rumania judges, who include professional judges and lay assessors, are elected partly by people's committees and partly directly by the voters. In Czechoslovakia, Poland and Hungary the process did not get so far in 1949, but the importance of lay assessors was increasing. They were in practice nominees of the Communist Party. Throughout the region there has been steady pressure against pre-war professional judges, who are accused of reactionary prejudices, and of failure to act according to the spirit of popular democratic justice. Some have been purged and others have been brought to heel. The whole legal profession has been reorganised. The activities of private lawyers have been ever more circumscribed. In Czechoslovakia district committees direct all lawyers, assign to them their clients, take from them their fees, and pay them a salary. In the other countries similar conditions exist.

An important office is that of Public Prosecutor. His task is to watch over the execution of the laws from the point of view of the government's interests. The Bulgarian public prosecutor has the "particular duty to attend to the prosecution and punishment of crimes which affect the state, national and economic interests of the People's Republic, and crimes and actions detrimental to independence and national sovereignty." The tendency throughout Europe is, as in the U.S.S.R., to stress the interests of the state. Offences against state property are more severely punished than offences against private property. Disputes between private individuals are of minor importance in the legal system, but there is no essential reason why they should not be fairly judged. In disputes between an individual and the state, the weight of the law is on the side of the state.

All the constitutions have wide guarantees of civil liberties — speech, religion, association, meeting, inviolability of the home, right to work and leisure. They also contain clauses on the punishment of racial or nationalist hatred, and guarantee the right of minorities to use their own languages. But they also contain "escape clauses" making these liberties inoperative if used against the government. For in-

stance, Article 43 of the Yugoslav Constitution declares: "It is illegal and punishable to use civil rights to change and infringe the constitutional order with an anti-democratic aim." The Polish Declaration of Rights and Liberties, a fundamental law passed together with the provisional constitution, declares: "Abuse of civil rights and liberties for the purpose of overthrowing the democratic form of government of the Republic of Poland shall be prevented by law." Similar provisions are found in Section 37 of the Czechoslovak, Article 32 of the Rumanian, and Article 87 of the Bulgarian constitutions. There are also special laws on "Defence of the People's Power" and on "espionage," which prescribe heavy penalties for a large variety of offences whose definition is conveniently elastic.

From the first days of "liberation" the Communist Parties paid great attention to the police. There were at first considerable local variations. In Poland, as in the U.S.S.R., a Ministry of Security was set up distinct from the Ministry of the Interior. In Rumania the communist under-secretary of the Premier's office, Bodnăraş, took over a special secret police organisation which had been created by King Carol II and managed it independently of the regular security police (Sigurantsa), which also had its own political section. In Hungary, a political department in the General Staff, led by Colonel Pálffy-Österreicher, performed political police duties in addition to the political department of police headquarters at No. 60 Andrássy Út. In Czechoslovakia the counter-espionage department of the General Staff, under Colonel Reičin, performed police duties side by side with the People's Security Corps controlled by the communist Minister of the Interior Nosek.

Only in Yugoslavia have the political police actually relinquished some of their power. In a speech to the Central Committee of the Communist Party in June 1951, Minister Ranković admitted that the police had seriously abused their powers. Of all arrests made in 1949, as many as 47 per cent had been unlawful. A new code of law was introduced in 1951. It contained measures against arbitrary arrest and excessive reliance by the law courts on confessions.

Of little less importance than the political and security sections of the police were the various forms of "economic police." Like their original model, the Russian Cheka, they specialised in the fight against "speculation and the black market." This fight was in practice used to catch out business men and shopkeepers in violation of some regulation, in order to confiscate their property without compensation and perhaps send them to forced labour. Great distinction was attained in this field by various "special commissions" in Poland which were directed by the communist Zambrowski.

By 1950 it seems that the various police organisations were more systematically organised. It would be surprising if the police leaders were not advised by experts from the Soviet M.V.D., but exact information on this point is not available to the layman. The key positions in the police are now held by more or less reliable communists. As long as purges continue in the parties, there will always of course be a danger of purges in the police. The Ministries of the Interior of Hungary and Albania were both purged after the disgrace of Rajk and Xoxe. If not always very intelligent, if suspicious to the point of inverted naïveté, the East European communist political policemen are without doubt industrious and persevering. Their technique of producing the right plots and the right confessions at the right time must have earned them fair marks from their Soviet masters. Their dossiers, if not always accurate, are probably extensive. And their peoples live in terror of them.

Communist penetration of the armies also began early. The pre-war officers of the Polish army were almost completely re-moved by the course of the war. The nucleus of the new Polish army was formed by the officers of the three divisions which served under General Berling in the Red Army. Many were Poles who had lived for years in the U.S.S.R. The senior officers were for the most part Russians. The pre-war Yugoslav officers, mostly Serbs, were either taken prisoner in 1941 or associated with the Chetnik movement of Nedić. Only a few joined the partisans. The post-war Yugoslav army was formed by the expansion of the National Liberation Army created by Tito. Its officers were the leaders who had come to the fore during the resistance.

The Czechoslovak army was composed of two sections, which had fought respectively in the British and Soviet armies. In the first three years after the war there was steady but quiet discrimination against those who had been in Britain. After February 1948 it became outright persecution. Air-Marshal Janoušek was sentenced to eighteen years in prison for trying to leave the country. The most flagrant case was the judicial murder of General Heliodor Pika, who had served the exiled government first in Istanbul and then as head of the military mission in Moscow. He had won the hatred of Gottwald, Nejedly and company when he refused their blandishments to betray his government (with which of course the Soviet government had formal diplomatic relations) and serve their rival group. They enjoyed an ignoble revenge after the February police revolution. General Pika was arrested in 1948, tried for treason and espionage in February 1949, condemned to death and executed in June 1949. One of the accusations against him was that he had passed to the British in 1940 information about the Red Army. At that time Britain was his country's only fighting ally, the U.S.S.R. was the good friend of the German oppressors of the Czechs, and Gottwald, Nějedly and company were urging their compatriots to ignore the anti-

German "provocations" of the "tool of the Western imperialist" Beneš.

An important stage in the communist penetration of the armies was the creation of "political departments," which formed a hierarchy of political commissars such as has existed under various names ever since the formation of the Red Army in the U.S.S.R. In Rumania special units, the Tudor Vladimirescu and the Horia Cloșca Crișan divisions, were formed from prisoners-of-war indoctrinated in special political training camps in Russia. Exiles who had served in the Red Army or in Spain returned to take important positions in their countries' new armies. Such were General Kinov in Bulgaria and General Świerczewski in Poland. The Yugoslav generals included several Spanish veterans, but they rose to their positions by four years' liberation war in their own country, not through the ranks of the Soviet army.

In Hungary, Rumania, and Bulgaria, the disarmament clauses of the peace treaties made it possible to purge selected officers, leaving behind those most reliable or malleable. By 1948, when purges and political commissars had done their work, it became possible once more to build up the armies. The leaders of the ex-enemy states began to speak of the need for strong armies. Though sure figures are not obtainable, the British and American governments believed, on the basis of information from their official sources, that the Bulgarian army in 1948 already exceeded the provisions of the peace treaties. It may be ex-

pected that the supply of trained Rumanian and Hungarian cannon-fodder will also be increased.

Taken at their face value, the constitutional documents do not show a despotic state. If applied in a different spirit, which would give reality to the civil liberties, and free elections, they could provide extremely democratic government. The reason why this is not the case is that all power is in fact held by the Communist Parties. At elections only communists and approved sympathisers have any chance of being elected. Key positions, not only in the cabinet and upper administration but also in the executive committees and departments of local government bodies, are held by communists. Through the local government bodies the communists appoint the judges. The Public Prosecutor jealously watches over the action of the courts, and he too is chosen by the communists. Another important instrument is the State Control Commission, also modelled on Soviet experience. Its task is to examine the efficiency and honesty of the administration and to investigate reports of abuses submitted to it by official bodies or individual citizens. In practice it shows less zeal for the defence of the citizen against bureaucratic abuse than for the interests of the government against both private individuals and subordinate officials. In it too the key positions are held by communists. If the state controls the citizen, the party controls the state.

R. Burks

PARTY STRUCTURE IN EASTERN EUROPE

The Communist masses in eastern Europe are not in any real sense of the term proletarian in character. In fact, all social classes are involved, and the single most important element, at least numerically, is not the proletariat but the peasantry. Of all the types of Communists it was, curiously enough, the opportunists flooding into the parties after the seizure of power who had the most proletarian complexion. Communist guerrillas and insurgents were overwhelmingly peasant and mountaineer in their composition. Communist voters were located largely in rural constituencies and industrial workers voted for the extreme right as well as for the center and the left. In an industrialized area like Bohemia-Moravia the workers voted primarily for the Socialists.

The hard core of the east European Communist movements represents a cross section of the class structure of the area, but with a strong urban bias. Both the middle class and the city workers are overrepresented among activists, while at the leading cadre level middle class professionals squeeze out the peasants altogether and leave only a small minority representation to the proletariat. Since worker cadres in effect receive on-the-job professional training, it would be accurate to say that at least the cutting edge of the movement consists of a professional elite group (what Djilas calls the "new class").

Communism in eastern Europe has many causes, but the notion that it represents, or is led by, the suffering proletariat is largely fictional. Those interested in the dynamics of the movement should study, not the distress of the proletariat, but two other less dramatic factors: the proclivity of certain ethnic groups for the Communist cause and the impact of the highly industrialized countries of the West on the more backward regions of eastern Europe.

The Ethnic Factor

We may erect almost as a principle the proposition that in eastern Europe numerically weak ethnic groups produce above-average numbers of Communists, providing these groups have a traditional or an ethnic tie to Russia. Other factors being equal, the weaker the ethnic group, the greater the proclivity. On the other hand, if there has been a strong traditional enmity toward Russia, a weak ethnic group reveals a lower than average susceptibility to the Communist appeal, and the traditional enmity can offset even an ethnic bond.

The most obvious and important instance of this principle is the typical distribution of Communist strength among the Slavic peoples. Within the multinational Soviet union it is the approximately 100 million Great Russians who are the paladin of Communism. The three Slavic peoples immediately adjacent to the Great Russians — 40 million Ukrainians, 8 million Belorussians, and 25 million Poles — all have Communist movements substantially below-average in strength. At least two of these peoples, the Ukrainians and the Poles, have centuries-old traditions of bitter conflict with the Russians. In the interwar period, however, oppressed Ukrainian and Belorussian minorities trapped in Pilsudski Poland produced remarkably strong and virile Communist parties. Moreover, among the 12 million Czechs and Slovaks (particularly the Czechs, who were virtually surrounded by German enemies), and among the 24 million Slovenes,

From R. Burks, *The Dynamics of Communism in Eastern Europe* (Princeton, 1961), pp. 187–195. Reprinted by permission of Princeton University Press.

Croats, Serbs, Montenegrins, Slavo-Macedonians, and Bulgars, supporters of Communism were very much more numerous than in eastern Europe generally.

The greater proclivity of the Slavs is matched by the greater immunity of the non-Slavic populations of the area. Of these the German minorities are a good example. Scattered in crazy-quilt fashion over eastern Europe, even as far to the east as the lower reaches of the Russian Volga, these German colonists persisted in looking to the German *Reich* for both political protection and ideological inspiration. As a kind of counter-point to their low Communist response we have the relative philo-communism of the Czech and Polish countercolonists settled in the territories from which German populations have been ejected.

The Turkish (Moslem) case was essentially the same as the German, but more complex. Not all Moslems were Turks, and any prospect of protection from the Ottoman empire had long since vanished. Nonetheless, the Turkish area, which stretched in a great crescent-like arc from the Bosniaks and the Albanians of the Dinaric Alps, through the Ottoman Turks in the highlands of Anatolia, to the Kasakhs in the shadow of the Tian Shan and the Bashkirs in the foothills of the Urals, was an area of far below average Communist activity. The Turkish Green Apple flourished only so long as the Greek invader clung to the rugged coasts of Anatolia, so long (that is) as Russian help was required. Even the Green Apple was, from its very inception, a movement of national deviation. And all along the Turkish confines there are peoples with both a traditional enmity for the Turks and a strong Communist movement: Bulgars and Greeks to the west, Syrians and Kurds to the south, Armenians and Georgians in the Caucasus, Great Russians to the Siberian north. Through conversion to Communism such non-Turkic Moslems as the Bosniaks tended to lose their Turkish identification and become Yugoslav.

A few non-Slavic peoples have a high susceptibility to Communism. The most prominent case in eastern Europe (and in Russia as well) is that of the Jews. But the Jewish story has its analogue in the history of the Armenians. The two peoples had much in common. Both were small in number. Both lived scattered over a wide territory among sovereignties frequently in conflict. Both were essentially commercial peoples. If the Jew lived in fear of the Russian pogrom, the Armenian dreaded the Turkish massacre. From the Bolsheviks the Armenians received a kind of homeland in the Armenian Socialist Soviet republic. The Jews offered, somewhat disdainfully, the autonomous territory of Birobidjan, half ethnic experiment, half prison colony. The foundation of a Jewish state in Palestine set off a persecution of Jews in the Soviet bloc precisely because it created an alternative to both conformity and assimilation and hence brought into question the basic loyalty, not only of Orthodox Jews, but even of Jewish cadres.

Thus there appear to be non-ideological communities of peoples — Slavic, Moslem-Turkish, Germanic — whose presence strongly affects the distribution of Communist strength in eastern Europe. This notion is not so startling if we consider the fact that Lutheranism in its spread was largely confined to the Germanic-speaking peoples, or that liberal Democracy has developed its most stable institutions among speakers of English. Language is, to be sure, only the most apparent common trait in such a complex of peoples.

The Cultural Factor

The ethnic factor thus does much to explain who in eastern Europe is a Communist and who is not. A second important factor is the impact of the influence of the most industrialized countries of the West.

This impact is transmitted in two ways, through the mechanism of international prices and through the cross-cultural education of the young.

Interwar eastern Europe was an exporter of raw materials—coal, copper, wheat, pork, oil, and tobacco. In exchange for these exports eastern Europe obtained manufactured goods produced in the West. (The Czech lands, with their exports of shoes, porcelain, and beer, constituted an exception to the general rule.) The prices of the commodities eastern Europe exported shifted sharply, sending economic shock waves throughout the area. The rhythmic alternation of prosperity and poverty, especially when it affected conversational trades or migrant groups, created deep-going discontent. Communist votes and Communist ideas tended to concentrate where the impact of these price changes was greatest, among, say, the wheat growers of Slovakia or the tobacco workers of Macedonia. The most backward areas and the poorest—e.g., those which continued to practice a more or less self-sufficient agriculture—were not really involved. It was the valley floors and their transportation hubs, not the isolated highlands, which became strongholds of Communism in the interwar period. The contrast between the Communism in southern Albania, a wheat-growing plain, and the anti-Communism of northern Albania, which was much poorer, but mountainous and economically self-sufficient, is characteristic.

While within any given area it was likely to be the economically more advanced parts which were affected, in the east European areas as a whole it was the more backward provinces, those which had lived long under Turkish rule, which in general developed the stronger Communist movements. As one moved east and south, the proportion of the total Marxist vote which went to the Communists increased sharply. As one moved east and south, the strength of trade unions dropped off, but the influence of Communism in trade unions increased. This progression we inferred to be the result of the contrast between conditions in eastern Europe and those prevailing in the most industrial nations of the West. This contrast achieved its social imprint through students and teachers who had received a Western education, either in schools of the area or abroad, and who found themselves overtrained and perhaps even unemployable in their native environment. From this situation followed the decisive role in the party of what the Russians would call the intelligentsia, the lawyers, teachers, doctors, and other professionals who provided three-fourths of the Communist leadership.

Thus we add a cultural factor to the ethnic. At times the two operated together, as when the Tosks of the south Albanian plain used Communism to overthrow the rule of the northern mountaineering Gegs, or when the cash-cropping Magyar minority of southern Slovakia turned to a Communism which stood for the reconstruction of the Hungarian empire. At other times, the two factors ran counter to each other, as when the Montenegrin mountaineers, just north of the Gegs, produced a high Communist vote as early as 1920, or when Romanian peasant plain-dwelling growers of wheat proved almost impervious to the appeal of Communism because it was associated with a traditional enemy. In general, we are inclined to believe that the ethnic factor takes precedence over the cultural factor, as these last two examples suggest. This precedence was also indicated by the multiple correlation exercise which measured the weight of the two factors when their influence ran parallel.

Both factors, the ethnic and the cultural, have an obvious influence on the formulation of Communist policy. The cultural factor is evidently connected with the marked tendency of east European Communist parties to industrialize their respective countries under forced draft and to modernize their agriculture; to create, so to speak, a society in which overtrained surplus professionals can find appropriate employment. The ethnic factor is certainly not unrelated to the powerful penchant of the Communists to push for the development of what, for want of a better term, we may call supranational states. Both policies are understandable in terms either of national interest or of Communist power. Since Communist industrialization has been widely studied we may confine our attention here to summarizing our findings concerning the supranational state.

The first instance of this empire-building, proclivity of the Communists of eastern Europe is provided by the Bela Kun regime, which showed signs of transforming Stephen's holy kingdom into a Union of Socialist Danubian Republics. The political vertebrae of this union would have been a Jewish-led, Magyar-dominated, multinational Communist party.

A second example is provided by the scheme for Balkan federation advanced interwar by the Bulgarian party. At that time, as we now can see, such a proposal was bound to remain a political chimera. But if the Bulgarian comrades could have had their way, the existing Balkan states would have been dissolved into smaller components and then all brought together again in a Balkan-wide state under the federal principle. The whole arrangement would have been held together by a multinational Communist party in which the Bulgarian element, backed by the might of Soviet Russia, would have predominated.

While both the Danubian and the Balkan federation schemes fizzled out, something analogous to them did take place within wartime Yugoslavia. Broken up more or less into its component ethnic parts by the Axis occupiers, the country was reconstituted on a federal basis by a multinational Communist party which was imbued with a true Yugoslav nationalism and in which all the Slavic nationalities of prewar Yugoslavia were represented. In the course of the civil war it was the *prechani* members of the traditional Serb ruling nation who played the decisive role in keeping Tito's cause afloat.

Towards the close of World War II, the Yugoslavs sought to extend the Communist principle of federation to the whole Balkan area, and create thus a constellation of Communist power second only to that represented by the U.S.S.R. In the years 1945–1948 the Yugoslavs came within an ace of absorbing Albania, whose Communist party they had founded and controlled. The Yugoslavs were probably the moving spirit in the second Greek civil war (1946–1949), one object of which was to solve the Macedonian problem at the expense of Greece and thus make possible the federation of Communist Yugoslavia and Communist Bulgaria. The Yugoslavs also had designs on Greece, Romania, and even Hungary. Needless to say, the Bulgarian party now *de facto* opposed federation, and in this it had the powerful, if covert, support of Moscow. In all probability these differences over federation constituted a major factor in producing the breach in the Cominform.

This brings to mind the concrete historical nexus between imperial and Soviet Russia. As a consequence of defeat in war the Russian empire was on the verge of disintegration. Independent Ukrainias, Polonias, Siberias, and Georgias were threatening to emerge on the peripheries of the empire. It was the Communist party under Lenin and Trotsky, operating from the Great Russian center, which, at the cost of a bloody civil war, put the tsarist humpty-dumpty back together again. The new Soviet Russia was a federation of many and diverse national units, held together by a monolithic multinational ruling party whose language, tradition, and outlook were Russian.

Nor is the Chinese population of Malaya, which produced the Malayan Communist Party unique. There are overseas Chinese in large numbers in other parts of southeast Asia, in Indonesia, Indochina, the Philippines, and so on. There are also indigenous populations — Burmese, Thais, Laotians, Vietnamese, and in the far north, Koreans — whose languages and cultures are closely related to those of China. It is not inconceivable that Communist elements in this complex of minorities and nations will some day become basic components in a reconstitution of the Chinese imperium in Asia.

It may of course be mere coincidence that so far only those supranational Communist entities which were predominantly Slavic in population have succeeded in establishing themselves on a more or less permanent basis. What is significant here is not that there are Croats or Ukrainians in opposition, or that Belorussians or Tadzhiks are greatly underrepresented in the party, but that Communism is able to assemble and retain Croatian, Ukrainian, Belorussian, and Tadzhik cadres. The key development is the ability of Communism to produce within its own ranks something akin to a Yugoslav or Soviet nationalism. Within its own ranks it produces new arrangements of ideology, ethnic group, and national awareness. In so doing, Communism demonstrates that an international ideology can serve as a fundamental component of national consciousness.

THE ECONOMIC BACKGROUND

The figure of Stalin dominated the Soviet and East European scene to such an extent that the ties between domestic and foreign policy were exceedingly close, even for a totalitarian regime that from 1948 onwards was treating other states under its supervision almost as if they formed part of the Russian national inheritance. The advent of more rapidly enforced collectivization and industrialization in Eastern Europe after 1948 was characterized by the application of methods that Stalin had himself put through in Russia in the late 1920's and 1930's.

The marked conservatism and reliance on past experience that we have noted in other spheres, and particularly in connection with the assertion of party control over Eastern Europe after the war, was again apparent in the Second Revolution in this area. In industry Five-Year Plans were carried out on the well-tried Soviet lines; the prototype was so slavishly copied that in this period no regard was paid to economic interdependence between the countries. Autarchy prevailed, and there was a dangerous repetition of almost identical schemes, overstressing the role of heavy industry within each country and leaving no room for interstate collaboration. The collectivization campaign likewise relied on such familiar Soviet procedures as high taxes, forced state deliveries, party pressure, and some measure of violence.

In order to get a clear picture of the postwar economic revolution in Eastern Europe, we must trace its beginnings in the years immediately after the war and then follow its course through the period of increasing sovietization.

Hugh Seton-Watson

ECONOMIC RECOVERY AND PLANNING

The economic development of Eastern Europe since the end of the war falls naturally into three periods. The first was post-war dislocation, when military operations, occupation in turn by the German and Soviet armies, and internal disorder reduced most countries in the region to a desperate plight. The second stage was planned recovery, whose aim was to reach as soon as possible a level of production and standard of living approximating to those on the eve of the war. The third stage is that of longer-term plans of construction, intended to transform and develop the economy for many years ahead. In each stage, and especially in the third, examples for the experience of the Soviet Union were closely followed.

The Aftermath of War

The experience of the seven countries in the last months of the war had common features and differences. All but Bulgaria had had considerable numbers of German troops on their territory. All had been economically exploited by the Germans. All but Bulgaria had been fought over. All but Albania had been liberated or occupied by the Red Army. The differences lay in the different attitudes of both Germans and Russians to different peoples, and in the different nature of the warfare conducted on their territory.

As we have seen, the Germans systematically exploited the countries they had defeated, showing a special ruthlessness in Poland. Their treatment of the countries allied to them, Hungary, Rumania, Bulgaria and Slovakia, was not entirely bad. It is true that they ran up enormous debts, which with the defeat of Germany finally became a complete loss. But they also assisted the development of industry in these countries. In 1943 industrial output was considerably higher than in 1939. Even the annexed Czech lands benefited from this. It is true that in 1944 supplies of raw materials and equipment broke down. But industrial capacity in the countries allied to the Axis was still greater than it had been before the war. When their allies abandoned them in 1944, the Germans of course changed their attitude. But military circumstances permitted reprisals only in the case of Hungary, whose wartime material gains were thus largely destroyed.

Military operations left deep marks in central Poland and in Silesia, but western Poland from Lódź to Poznan escaped comparatively lightly. Eastern Slovakia was thoroughly ravaged. Transylvania suffered some destruction. Fighting raged right across Hungary. Her capital was shattered by artillery and bombing. But regular operations are not necessarily more destructive than irregular. The destruction of Warsaw, defended by the Polish Home Army, was more complete than any other. Yugoslavia and Albania were sacked by guerrillas and by enemy reprisals. In both countries it was small towns and villages which suffered. The bigger cities, held by the enemy until the end, were hardly harmed. Even Belgrade, bombed by the Germans in 1941 and the Allies in 1944, and captured after a fairly fierce battle by combined Yugoslav, Soviet and Bulgarian forces, emerged surprisingly little damaged.

From H. Seton-Watson, *The East European Revolution* (New York, 1951), pp. 230–255. Reprinted by permission of Frederick A. Praeger, Inc., and Methuen & Co., Ltd.

The Soviet attitude to the "liberated" peoples differed considerably. Yugoslavs and Czechoslovaks were regarded as friends. Bulgarians, though former enemies, were Slavs traditionally friendly to Russia. Poles were allies, but as their friendliness was far from certain they were regarded with suspicion. Rumanians and Hungarians were plain enemies, and of the two the Hungarians were the worse, as they had gone on fighting on Hitler's side longer. This difference of attitude in the military and political command was reflected in the behaviour of the troops, who were presumably given directives corresponding to the differences. Everywhere the Red Army shocked the liberated populations by the barbarity and indiscipline of its soldiers. But in Rumania and Hungary an orgy took place such as Europe had not seen for centuries. Its effect should not be underestimated. It was not, as western apologists of the U.S.S.R. maintain, a regrettable incident partly excusable by the sufferings of the Soviet peoples under German occupation. It was the result of a deliberate hate campaign begun by the Soviet leaders at the time when the Soviet state was shaking, when a frenzy of racial hatred against the invaders seemed the surest way to rally the suffering Soviet peoples behind their government. As the Soviet soldiers advanced into Europe, they were encouraged to revenge themselves on the 'fascist and bourgeois hordes' whose lands they entered. It is true that the Germans and their allies had committed abominable outrages on Soviet territory. But this vengeance was wrought not on soldiers but on Hungarian and Rumanian, and to a lesser extent Polish and Bulgarian, civilians, of whom the vast majority were innocent of any crimes against Soviet subjects, and whom it was now supposed to be official Soviet policy to conciliate. Serbs and Czechs were better treated, but even they did not like what they saw of the Soviet soldiers. The millions of Europeans who personally experienced outrages will never forget the meaning of the word "liberation."

A brief catalogue of the losses sustained from the three main causes—warfare, German pillage and Soviet pillage—will give some impression of the degree of devastation. The worst human casualties were of course those of Poland and Yugoslavia. In Poland about 6,000,000 people perished, of whom at least half were Jews. In Yugoslavia, with rather less than half the population, losses were some 2,000,000. Rumania lost about 500,000 in her two wars on two sides. Hungary's military losses were only about 100,000, to which must be added 220,000 Jews massacred in 1944. Both Rumania and Hungary had large numbers of prisoners-of-war in Russia, not all of whom have come back after four years. The Hungarian prisoners included many pressganged by the Soviet troops after hostilities had ceased. Czechoslovakia lost 38,000 executed by the Gestapo, including a very high percentage of intellectuals, and 200,000 deportees who never returned from Germany. Albania lost 28,000 out of 1,000,000, and Bulgaria only 30,000 out of 7,000,000.

Estimates of material damage are of necessity unprecise. But the following figures, derived from U.N.R.R.A. reports, if not absolutely certain, at least give a correct general picture.

Losses of livestock were heaviest in Poland (43 per cent of horses, 60 per cent of cattle, 70 per cent of pigs); Hungary (39 per cent horses, 44 per cent cattle, 78 per cent pigs); Yugoslavia (60 per cent horses, 54 per cent cattle, 53 per cent pigs, 50 per cent sheep). Bulgarian and Rumanian losses were fairly light. In Czechoslovakia, a special case was eastern Slovakia, where some 80 per cent of all livestock was lost. Elsewhere in the country losses were much smaller.

Communications suffered heavily. In Hungary 90 per cent of the large bridges on the railways and 63 per cent of medium bridges were destroyed, and 69 per cent of locomotives and 86 per cent of freight cars were lost. In Yugoslavia half the total rail track and three-quarters of railway bridges were destroyed, and losses of rolling stock were on a similar scale. Czechoslovakia lost 11 per cent of locomotives and 28 per cent of freight cars. In Poland losses to transport were estimated at 3,500 million U.S. dollars.

In Yugoslavia the heaviest housing losses were in Bosnia, where 29 per cent of houses were utterly destroyed and a further 15 per cent seriously damaged. In eastern Slovakia nearly half the population were made homeless. Approximate estimates by official sources of damage to industry are for Poland 5,700 million U.S. dollars, for Czechoslovakia rather more than 1,000 million U.S. dollars. In Hungary losses in the engineering industry were estimated at 40 per cent, in textiles 13 per cent, and iron and steel 12 per cent. The total material loss to Hungary was estimated as 40 per cent of the national income. The estimate of total material loss in U.S. dollars for Poland was 18,200 million; for Albania (with a population more than twenty times smaller), 600 million.

Apart from these severe direct losses, great economic damage was done by the fact that the whole region was cut off from its old sources of raw materials and its markets. Particularly important was the collapse of the German market, towards which their trade had been increasingly directed even before the war. A further cause of impoverishment was the fact that large areas had not been sown in 1945.

The work of U.N.R.R.A. was of vital importance in 1945 and 1946 in Yugoslavia, Poland, Albania and Czechoslovakia. Hungary received a very small quantity of U.N.R.R.A. help in 1946, which was useful but not decisive. Bulgaria neither needed nor had any claim to U.N.R.R.A. help. Rumania had no claim, as a defeated country, but despite her natural wealth she was reduced by drought and devastation to mis-

ery by the winter of 1946–7. But by that time U.N.R.R.A. had ceased to operate. Some American help was sent but it too was not of decisive importance.

The total value of U.N.R.R.A. help to the four countries, in U.S. dollars, was as follows: Poland 481 million, Yugoslavia 420 million, Czechoslovakia 270 million, Albania 24 million. The main headings were food, clothing, medical supplies agricultural rehabilitation and industrial rehabilitation. The first three items in each case formed about one-half the total. The main items of industrial rehabilitation were transport and communications equipment, fuel and lubricants, textile and leather raw materials, and chemical and engineering materials. Agricultural rehabilitation consisted mainly of livestock, seeds and machinery. It is probably Yugoslavia which owes most to U.N.R.R.A. Large imports of food and of transport saved hundreds of thousands from starvation. Imports of machinery, though small, were also of great value. When the U.N.R.R.A. programme was completed Yugoslavia had more tractors than ever before the war.

The currencies were all greatly inflated when war ended. In Czechoslovakia and Yugoslavia more than one currency was in use (Reichsmark, Slovak crown and Hungarian pengö in the first and Reichsmark, Croatian kuna, Serbian dinar, Bulgarian lev, Hungarian pengö and Albanian lek in the second.) The Polish, Czechoslovak, Yugoslav and Bulgarian governments introduced currency reforms before the end of 1945. Bank deposits were blocked. Individuals were only allowed small amounts of the new currency, while businesses were supposed to have a minimum for current expenses. Capital levies and special taxes on war profits were introduced, which took the greater part of the blocked balances. In all four countries a strict credit and circulation policy was pursued. The revival of production and U.N.R.R.A. help, and in the case of Bulgaria the comparatively small scale of destruction, ensured the minimum quantity of goods. Thus inflation was avoided.

Hungary and Rumania were less fortunate. Neither received substantial assistance from the West, and both were subject to crushing Soviet demands. The peace treaties fixed for both the sum of 300 million U.S. dollars in reparations, of which Hungary paid two-thirds to the U.S.S.R. and one-third to Yugoslavia and Czechoslovakia, while Rumania paid the whole sum to the U.S.S.R. This sum was of course smaller than the total damage incurred in the portions of the Soviet Union where the two armies had fought. But it was larger than at first sight appeared, for the goods in which reparation payments were made were priced at 1938 price levels. This meant that the actual cost was from two and a half to three times greater than the nominal sum. But formal reparations by no means exhausted the Soviet bill. Under Article 23 of the Rumanian armistice, movable property seized from Soviet territory by Rumanians had to be restored in addition to reparations. This article was liberally interpreted and ruthlessly enforced. Ingenuity and manpower which might well have been devoted to more urgent purposes at a time when the war with Germany was still on, were spent in tracking down even minor objects. Far more important, however, for both countries was the obligation to maintain the Soviet forces in transit and occupation. This was used to extract not only the normal requirements of the troops but also very large quantities of food, civilian clothing and various luxuries which were exported from Rumania and Hungary. Thirdly there were the "unofficial" requisitions and loot, especially severe in the first months of "liberation." These three items together cost each country certainly no less than the sum total fixed for reparations — 300 million U.S. dollars. According to some estimates they may have been more than twice as costly. Finally there was the Soviet claim to German property in both countries, which was also liberally interpreted. The huge debt of Germany to her allies could not be recovered, but the U.S.S.R. claimed the full amount of debts owed by the satellite countries to Germany. Moreover in taking over German property the Soviet authorities refused all liabilities to third persons arising from them, though taking for themselves all assets.

Economic disaster came first in Hungary. Devastation, Soviet demands and dislocation of trade produced their effects. Some raw materials were imported from the Soviet Union, but reparations deliveries took up a large proportion of the goods produced therewith. Taxation receipts were negligible. The extreme shortage of manufactured goods made the peasants unwilling to give up their produce. Factories had to employ their workers and vehicles in food-hunting expeditions to the villages. The currency rapidly fell from the summer of 1945. Between June 1945 and January 1946 the note circulation increased sixteen times. A device known as the "tax pengö," introduced in January 1946, slowed up the decline for a few weeks only. By the summer of 1946 the sterling-pengö rate reached milliards of milliards. In July it had twenty-seven o's, the highest figure known in financial history. Attempts were made to pay workers in 'calories' (of food). Those who had goods to barter tried to bargain with the peasants. Almost the whole urban population lived in fear of hunger, none perhaps more than the professional class. In these circumstances the effort of the Budapest workers was truly heroic. Thanks to them, by the summer the factories were again turning out some goods. The harvest was moderately good. When it was in, and stocks of manufactured goods were at last available, and with the psychological gain of the return of the gold reserve of 32 million dollars from United States custody, the government on 1 August introduced the new currency. There followed a period of great money shortage, of restricted credits and low money incomes. Hardship continued, but at least money had a value. One important feature of the new price level, fixed together with the stabilisation, was that the relationship between agricultural and industrial prices was very much more unfavourable to agriculture than it had been in 1939.

Inflation came later to Rumania. The country was richer and had suffered less. The main cause of economic strain was the Soviet occupation, to which in the winter of 1946–7 was added a really disastrous drought, involving starvation in parts of Moldavia and great shortages in all but the western provinces. The currency fell throughout 1946 and the first half of 1947. A rough indication can be given by the unofficial rate at which the pound was exchanged into lei by the British Military Mission in Rumania. The rate was 32,000 at the end of 1945, 130,000 in the summer of 1946, 500,000 in early 1947, and over 1,-000,000 by the summer. Stabilisation was attempted on 15 August 1947. As in the other currency reforms, balances were blocked and extremely small amounts of the new currency were allowed to individuals. But a new decline set in in the autumn. The communists blamed the liberal leader Tătărescu, whose party held the Finance Ministry. When the ministry was taken by the prominent communist Luca, things improved. Whether this was due to communist wisdom, or to more ruthless taxation and the results of an improvement in industrial output which had begun earlier, is not clear. But by the summer of 1948 Rumania was at last well on the way to recovery.

Nationalisation

The first aim of all the communist-led coalitions was to control what Lenin once called the "commanding heights" of the economy, especially mines, power, communications and heavy industry. In all Eastern Europe the railways were already state-owned. So were certain other major enterprises such as the Pernik coal mines in Bulgaria or the M.A.V.A.G. locomotive works in Hungary. But the great majority of large enterprises, which were privately owned, were effectively controlled by the new governments at an early stage. Formal nationalisation came later and in different ways in each country.

Czechoslovakia and Poland were the first countries to pass far-reaching nationalisation laws. By the time of liberation all important enterprises in both countries were completely controlled, and most were also owned, by Germans. They could therefore be expropriated on patriotic grounds without compensation. Enterprises owned by Allied capital would require compensation, but the Czechoslovak and Polish governments, as allied Powers, could negotiate with them on equal terms.

Czechoslovakia's nationalisation law was passed on 24 October 1945 by the provisional parliament. It covered all banks, insurance, mines, armaments and munitions plants, and most of the iron and steel and chemical industry. In addition, all factories in any branch of industry which employed more than 400 persons were nationalised. Compensation was promised to owners innocent of "collaboration," but was in fact extremely small. Large "national enterprises" were formed, grouping a number of factories together. Regional and central boards of industries were set up, under the ministries of Industry and Food.

Immediately after the liberation enterprises belonging to Germans and Hungarians had been seized and placed under the direction of appointed "national administrators." The future of those ex-German enterprises which did not fall into any of the categories nationalised by the law was a source of controversy. The communists and social democrats wished them all to be nationalised, the other parties wished to dispose of them to private Czech business. A compromise of March 1947 provided that those which existing national enterprises considered necessary for the completion of their production process should be nationalised, the rest be privately owned.

For two years private enterprise survived in all parts of the country. Some privately owned factories were very successful, and increased their capacity even beyond the limit which in 1945 had qualified a factory for nationalisation in any branch—employment of 400 workers. The success of private enterprise was attributed by the communists to the unscrupulous methods and exploitation of workers by capitalists, by their opponents to greater efficiency than the allegedly cumbrous nationalised factories could attain. The communists demanded an extension of nationalisation. Their opponents claimed that all parties had agreed that the law of 1945 should be a maximum. This dispute was one of the contributory causes of the communist coup d'état of February 1948. After it a new nationalisation law was introduced, which took over all enterprises employing more than 50 persons. Even smaller businesses in fact became nationalised.

The Polish law was passed in January 1946 by the provisional parliament (K.R.N.). It covered all German-owned enterprises, of whatever size and in whatever branch, without compensation; all other enterprises, whoever their owners and whatever their size, in mining, power, communications, armaments, sugar, textiles, printing, flour-milling and brewing, with compensation; and all other factories, in whatever branch, employing more than 50 persons, also with compensation. In practice compensation was very small. The limit of 50 persons was later raised to 100 and in certain cases to 200. New private enterprises could be started, and could even exceed the maximum number of employees, but they required a licence, and could not be allowed in any of the branches

which had been wholly nationalised. Private business was taxed more heavily than nationalised enterprises. In practice private business did not flourish in Poland as in Czechoslovakia. By the end of 1948 only 6 per cent of Polish industry was in private hands.

In Yugoslavia most industry was taken by the state soon after liberation. But the government did not at first proceed to formal nationalisation. It preferred to seize businesses on the grounds that their owners had collaborated with the enemy. This notion was extremely widely interpreted. Simply to have continued production was in some cases considered proof of treason. Even men who had had no relations with the Germans, who could prove their patriotic attitude, who were begged by their workmen to keep them employed, and had even given secret money contributions to the partisan movement, found themselves deprived of their property as "collaborators." This procedure may have been chosen in order to save the government the expense of compensation. But the gain was small, because in fact the compensation paid by the governments which introduced nationalisation was negligible. On the other hand the Yugoslav policy created plenty of unnecessary bitterness. It was not until early 1947 that formal nationalisation of industry was introduced.

The situation was more delicate in the three ex-enemy states. German property had become Soviet by the armistice terms, and could only be controlled by the governments on whatever terms the Soviet authorities allowed. Allied property could not formally be nationalised by defeated enemies. It was in fact specifically protected in the peace treaty. Home capitalists could hardly be accused of "collaboration" when the country had been at war with the Allies. It was therefore found convenient for some time to leave the factories nominally under private ownership. In the economic crises of Hungary and Rumania the capitalists were a useful scapegoat. They were burdened with heavy obligations to provide for their workers. Rumanian factories had canteens and shops (Economate), which could only be stocked by expensive purchases on the black market but had to sell at low prices. The continuing hardships arising from the general economic situation were blamed by the communist agitators in the factories on the "unsocial behaviour" of the owners. In Hungary reparations were used as a means to drive private business to bankruptcy. The government was supposed to pay the factories for the goods which they delivered to the Soviet authorities as reparations. In fact the government simply did not pay, and the factories first exhausted their funds and then sought loans from the National Bank. This enabled the government, with brazen dishonesty, to accuse the owners of incompetence. Private ownership, the communist leaders argued, was ruining the Hungarian economy. Nationalisation was required for efficiency. Thus Hungarian and Rumanian policy was to make private business pay for the national economic disaster until it was ruined, and then take over without any obligation of compensation.

Nationalisation came piecemeal in Hungary. The mines were taken over early in 1946. At the end of the year the three great heavy industrial concerns Manfred Weiss, Ganz and Rimamurány were combined with two state concerns in a Heavy Industries Centre (N.I.K.). In January 1948 all the banks were nationalised. In March 1948 came the general nationalisation law, which covered all factories employing more than 100 persons. In Rumania the first stage was the creation, in the summer of 1947, of a number of industrial boards (sindicate), grouping factories together in their main industrial branches. The boards controlled the allocation of raw materials and machinery, and decided what types of goods should be produced and where they should be sold. Their directors were appointed by the Minister of National Economy. Formal nationalisation came in June 1948. It did not specify the size of firms to be nationalised, but simply affected all firms of national importance. Bulgaria's nationalisation law was passed in December 1947, and covered all industry and banks.

The position of Allied firms in both ex-Allied and ex-enemy countries provided a long series of disputes. Czechoslovakia and Poland offered small compensation. The position of the British firms in Yugoslavia was formally settled by the agreement of January 1949, but the provisions for the payment of the not very generous sums were still not entirely clear. The Rumanian oil industry in 1946 was mainly owned by Allied capital (51 per cent Anglo-Dutch, 11 per cent American, while 28 per cent belonged to the Soviet company Sovrompetrol). The British and American firms suffered endless difficulties. Most of their production went as reparations to the U.S.S.R., and the government did not repay them. Only 3 per cent of the output could be sold on the free market, which did not enable them to obtain foreign currency with which to buy urgently needed new equipment. They were forced into borrowing. In the summer of 1947 the Ministry of Mines appointed administrators to both British and American firms. The administrators interfered in details of organisation, and prepared accusations of inefficiency, corruption and profiteering during the war against the U.S.S.R. The firms' managers were accused of deliberately sabotaging production. In the face of these obstacles, a meeting of the shareholders of Astra, the Shell Company's branch in Rumania, decided in March 1948 to declare the company "forcibly dissolved." Similar methods of obstruction and accusation were used in Hungary against the American-owned oil company "Maort," which was effectively seized by the government in 1948. Finally the Hungarian government nationalised all allied firms in the autumn of 1949.

Not only industry and banking, but also trade was progressively nationalised. By the end of 1948 most of the wholesale trade of Eastern Europe was controlled either by state-owned shops or by state-controlled co-operatives. In Poland a struggle developed in May 1947 between the co-operative organisation Spolem, a stronghold of the Socialist Party, and state shops. The communists denounced the "harmful autonomy tendencies" of the co-operative movement. This "battle of trade" ended with the victory of the communist-sponsored state shops. By the end of 1948 only 2½ per cent of Poland's wholesale trade was privately owned, and the "state sector" was rapidly penetrating the retail trade. In Yugoslavia wholesale trade was taken over at an early stage. In the retail trade, private ownership accounted in 1945 for 85 per cent of the turnover, in 1946 for 48 per cent, and in 1947 for 12 per cent. In May 1948 a new law nationalised all remaining private retail businesses. In Bulgaria there was very little private trade left at the end of 1948, in Rumania slightly more. In Czechoslovakia the process was slower, but the end is the same.

Recovery Plans

Four countries introduced short-term recovery plans from the beginning of 1947. Czechoslovakia and Bulgaria had Two-Year Plans (1947–8), Poland and Hungary Three-Year Plans (1947–9). Rumania introduced in 1948 a single-year plan for 1949. The Yugoslav plan is in a separate category. It was for five years, and provides not only for recovery but for a great deal of new construction. It will therefore be considered later, together with the longer-term plans for the other countries, which were announced when their recovery plans were nearing completion. Albania's plan was at first dependent on Yugoslavia, and then had to be radically changed after the Cominform-Tito quarrel which led to a rupture of Albanian-Yugoslav economic relations. It will therefore be considered in connection with Yugoslavia.

The Czechoslovak Two-Year Plan provided for an investment of 70 milliard crowns. Of this sum 22 milliard crowns was to be devoted to Slovakia, a proportion higher than Slovakia's share in either the population or the wealth of the whole republic. Of the total investment 36 per cent was to go to industry and mining, 22 per cent to transport, 35 per cent to housing and public services, and 7 per cent to agriculture. The investment in housing included both factory and public building, the share of private dwellings being comparatively small. The general aim was a level of output 10 per cent above that of 1937, but in some industrial branches the target was much higher. The low figure for agriculture should not be taken to mean that this branch of the economy was neglected. A considerable part of the industrial production was for the needs of agriculture. For instance, output of tractors and fertilisers was to be substantially increased. In a speech in parliament in October 1948, Prime Minister Zápotocky stated that the industrial part of the plan had been satisfactorily fulfilled. The 1937 level had been surpassed by 18 per cent in mining, by 33 per cent in electric power, by 30 per cent in engineering and by 14 per cent in chemicals. The building target, however, had been reached only to the extent of 70 per cent, and private house building only 47 per cent. Agriculture had suffered severely from the drought of 1947. The grain harvest, and grain deliveries to the authorities, had been only two-thirds of the quantities planned. Output of beef and pork in the first half of 1948 had been slightly more than half, and milk five-eighths, of the targets.

The proposed investment of the Polish Three-Year Plan was 340 milliard zloty. Distribution of investment between branches of the economy was industry and mining 39 per cent, transport and communications 24 per cent, agriculture 13 per cent, housing and public services 18 per cent. Comparisons with the level of output of earlier years are very difficult owing to the changes in frontiers. The area at present contained within Poland had in 1938 (the year taken by the Polish planners for comparison) a very much greater industrial output than the area which in 1938 constituted the Polish state. The present population of Poland is considerably smaller than that either of pre-war Poland or of the present area of Poland before the war (24 million instead of 35 or 33).

The Three-Year Plan target for industry was 152 per cent of the 1938 level for old Poland, which was about 70 per cent of the 1938 level for the present area of Poland. Heavy industry was to be 250 per cent of the 1938 old Poland level, and consumers' goods industry only 125 per cent. Output of motor lorries was to be twenty-six times, locomotives eleven times, agricultural machinery three times and machine tools one-and-a-half times greater than the 1938 old Poland level. Output of fertilisers was to increase by 60 per cent, and textiles were to reach the 1938 level.

The target for agriculture was to be 80 per cent of the 1938 level for old Poland. As the new territories were less agricultural than those lost in the east, but their agriculture had been more efficient, the difference between the total agricultural output of 1938 in the old and the new area was much smaller than in the case of industry. The Three-Year Plan, like the other East European plans, gave much more attention to industry than to agriculture. But apart from general considerations of policy, this was justifiable by the fact that the territorial changes had considerably altered the relationship between the industrial and agricultural population. As moreover the whole population was smaller by one-third than before the war, the achievement of the plan would mean a higher income per head than in 1938.

The results of two years of the plan were summarised by Minc, the communist Minister of Industry, in a speech to the first congress of the "fused" United Workers' Party in December 1948. The proportionate share of industry and agriculture in national production had been 45.5 : 54.5 in 1937, and was 64 : 36 in 1948. The proportionate share of capital goods and consumers' goods in industrial production had been 47 : 53 in 1937, and was 54 : 46 in 1948. The industrial target for 1947 had been exceeded by 6 per cent, and in 1948 it was estimated that it would be exceeded by 10 per cent. In agriculture, the sowing and harvesting plans had been fulfilled, and the aims set for horse- and cattle-breeding had been achieved. Pig-breeding, however, was substantially behind. In 1945 almost half the cultivatable area had lain fallow, in 1948 90 per cent had been sown. Production of bread grains per head was 22 per cent higher than before the war. Production of meat and edible fats per head had been 21 per cent of the 1937 level in 1945, and had risen to 92 per cent in 1948. Minc also claimed that real wages at the end of 1948 were on the average 10 per cent higher than before the war. In November 1949 the State Planning Commission claimed that the Three-Year Plan had been completed in two years ten months.

The total investment proposed for the Hungarian Three-Year Plan was 6,585 million florint. Of this sum 32 per cent was to go to industry and mining, 27 per cent to transport and communications, 9 per cent to agriculture and 22 per cent to building and public services. The industrial level at the completion of the plan was to be 27 per cent higher than in 1938, while agriculture was to reach 91 per cent of the 1938 level. The output of iron, metallurgy and engineering was to be 54 per cent higher than 1938, of chemicals 40 per cent higher, of electric power 43 per cent higher, and of textiles 25 per cent higher. Industrial production of benefit to agriculture included the attainment by 1949 of a yearly output of 3,700 tractors, and greatly increased quantities of nitrogen fertilisers and superphosphates. The chief economic planner of the Communist Party, Gerö, declared in December 1949 that the plan targets had been fulfilled in two years and eight months. In particular, mining output and production of machine tools had surpassed the plan. Steel output was already higher than it had been in the peak period during the war. Investment had been 18 per cent greater than was originally planned. Gerö also claimed that in the three-year period the standard of living had risen by 38 per cent.

The proposed investment under the Bulgarian Two-Year Plan was 55,000 million leva. Of this sum 45 per cent was to go to industry and mining, 15 per cent to transport and communications, 6 per cent to agriculture and 28 per cent to building and public services. Special attention was given to electric power. A number of new dams, hydro-electric and thermo-electric centres were to be set up. The output of ores was to be increased nine times. Very large increases were to be made in industries which had hardly existed before the war, including chemicals and rubber (to increase by 142 per cent) and iron, metal and engineering (by 67 per cent). Building was to increase by 85 percent and textiles by 66 per cent. In a speech at the 5th Congress of the Bulgarian Communist Party in December 1948, the communist head of the Economic Council, Tarpeshev, stated that in 1947 the plan had been achieved in industry to the extent of 85 per cent, in 1948 to 99 per cent. Shortcomings were attributed to the drought, which had deprived the food industry of some of its raw materials, and, by making necessary larger imports of food than had been anticipated, had reduced the amount of industrial raw materials that could be imported. Coalmining output was expected to be 88 per cent of the two-year target, and electric power construction 69 per cent. The live-

stock programme had been fairly successfully carried out. Horses and sheep were nearly up to their pre-war numbers, while cattle were 8 per cent and pigs 26 per cent more numerous.

In Rumania 1948 was a year of industrial recovery, at the end of which output approached that of 1938. In iron and steel and in textiles, the 1938 level was surpassed. The yearly plan for 1949, introduced by the Minister of National Economy, Gheorghiu-Dej, in a speech in parliament on 27 December 1948, provided for an investment of 82 milliard lei: 36.8 per cent was to go to mining and heavy industry, 10.4 per cent to light industry, 9.4 per cent to agriculture. The general industrial output was to be raised to 140 per cent of the 1938 level. Particular branches were to increase by the following percentages above 1938: coal mining 15, oil 13.7, cast iron 35, steel 16, tractors 38, railway trucks 17, cement 37. Agricultural output was to increase by 40 per cent above the level of the preceding year (1948). Grain production was to increase by 14.5 per cent (wheat 12 per cent), vegetables by 74 per cent, and industrial plants by 80 per cent. Livestock was to increase by 15 per cent as a whole, but pigs and poultry were to be doubled.

In October 1949 it was announced that the targets for the third quarter of the year had been achieved to the extent of 109 per cent. The most successful industries were lead and copper mining, and some sections of machine-building and chemicals. The building trade was the least successful. A new One-Year Plan was drawn up for 1950. It laid down that crude oil output was to increase by 21 per cent in comparison with 1949, coal by 10 per cent, cast iron by 17 per cent, and steel by 19 per cent.

These plans were all ambitious, and demanded a heavy sacrifice from the population. The rate of investment, as a percentage of national income, was estimated to be 20 per cent for Poland, 16 per cent for Czechoslovakia, 9 per cent for Hungary and

7 per cent for Bulgaria, per year. Production of consumers' goods was sacrificed to capital construction. Even if the results achieved were really as stated by the leaders, the increase in output was not accompanied by an equal increase in standard of living. In all countries it was a matter of simple observation that consumers' goods were much scarcer than before the war. There is no independent means of estimating the accuracy of the official results. The use of percentages, and absence of quantitative figures, in the statements of results, greatly reduces their value. Even if the planned output was achieved to the extent officially claimed, it is probable that quality was sacrificed to quantity. Harassed managers and workers, constantly pressed to complete the demands of the planners, concentrated on numbers at the cost of lower standards. A good deal of the reconstruction of the early days consisted of improvisation and cannibalisation, often brilliant but of course not permanent. It is uncertain to what extent this was succeeded by real replacement. With these reservations it must be admitted that immense material progress was made. For this the main credit should go to the vitality and endurance of the workers and peasants.

The Long-Term Plans

The first of the long-term plans was the Yugoslav Five-Year Plan, introduced in 1947. The others were announced as the completion of the recovery plans drew near. Czechoslovakia and Bulgaria have Five-Year Plans beginning in 1949, Hungary a Five-Year Plan beginning in 1950, Rumania a Five-Year Plan beginning in 1951, and Poland a Six-Year Plan beginning in 1950.

In these plans, even more than in the recovery plans which preceded them, the emphasis is on industry rather than agriculture, and on capital goods industries rather than consumers' goods industries. Their purpose is stated to be, not to create socialism, but to "build the foundations of socialism." As in the Soviet Union, this purpose is to be achieved by industrialisation, and industrialisation is to be achieved by creating heavy industries. The development of already existing lighter industries, though not completely ignored, receives a low priority. Special emphasis is given to engineering and the production of machinery, not only in Czechoslovakia, Poland and Hungary, which had some experience in these fields, but also in Rumania, Bulgaria and Yugoslavia, which had little or none. Production of tractors is stressed in all plans except the Bulgarian, as these are needed in connection with the projected collectivisation of agriculture.

In the first half of 1951, the Polish, Czechoslovak and Hungarian plans were revised. New, and greatly increased, output targets were set. The change was explained, in the speeches of the communist leaders, by the great progress already made, which exceeded expectations and made possible more ambitious planning. Another interpretation is that these almost simultaneous changes in the three most advanced countries of the area were ordered from Moscow for political reasons. According to this view, the aim was a rapid growth of the industries of greatest potential military importance. The Rumanian Five-Year Plan, announced at the beginning of 1951, was on the scale of the revised plans. In Bulgaria increased emphasis was put on agricultural output, and especially on collectivisation of agriculture. It seems likely that the overall planners in Moscow, thinking in terms of immediate needs, were less interested in the ultimate industrialisation of this backward country than in the full exploitation of its agricultural and raw material wealth. The contention of Yugoslav propagandists, that Russia was making Bulgaria a colony, and retarding her industrialisation, may have some foundation. Meanwhile the Yugoslav plan had been badly disorganised by the Cominform blockade, instituted in 1949, and had to be substantially modified.

The figures available for the revised plans are incomplete. There may also be further changes before the end of the plan periods in 1953–1955. Nevertheless the following figures from official sources may give some impression of the planners' general aims.[1]

Certain specific features of each plan deserve brief mention.

The Polish plan originally aimed to increase industrial output to 158 per cent of the 1949 level: the revised plan raised this target to 195 per cent. The corresponding aim for agriculture was increased from 145 per cent to 163 per cent. On completion of the revised plan, the chemical industry is to be the first of Poland's industries, followed by coal mining. The share of capital goods

industries in total industrial production, which was 59 per cent in 1949, is to be 63.5 per cent in 1955. A new steel-mill with a capacity of 1,500,000 tons is to be completed within the plan period. The plant is to be imported from the U.S.S.R. Within the period the construction of a second great steel-mill is to begin in eastern Poland. The sugar industry, one of Poland's oldest branches, is to have in 1955 an output of 1.1 million tons. The number of workers in industry in 1955 is to be one million more than in 1949, and 690,000 of the new workers are to be skilled.[2] Polish agriculture is to be supplied with 61,000 tractors, from home or foreign production, during the plan period. In 1955 25 per cent of agricultural output is to be produced by state farms, and of the remaining 75 per cent more than half is to come from collective farms. Industry will also be geographically redistri-

TABLE I

Percentage of investments in main branches of economy[1]

	Czecho-slovakia[2]	Hungary	Rumania	Bulgaria	Yugo-slavia
Industry[3] ...	41	52	51	40	42
Agriculture ...	8	13	10	17.5	8
Communications	16	12	16	24	26
Building[4] ...	25 }	16	13	11.5	20
Social Services ...	8 }				

[1] Figures for Poland have not been available.
[2] Figures for the original plan. As revised in 1951, the percentage for industry will certainly be higher, probably about the same as for Hungary and Rumania.
[3] Including both mining and electrification schemes.
[4] This includes (except for Czechoslovakia) social services, and (in all cases) housing and various public works. Housing includes government buildings as well as private dwellings. Social services include not only education but all the various forms of propaganda and "public enlightenment."

[1] In addition to the sources quoted above (. . .) the following have also been used:—Doreen Warriner, *Revolution in Eastern Europe*, London, 1950; Hungarian law for the amendment of the Plan, introduced to the National Assembly by Gero on 15th May 1951; Speech by Minc to the Central Committee of the United Workers Party Polish on 15th July 1950; Article by V. Karra on the Rumanian Five-Year Plan in *Vnyeshnyaya Torgovlya*, Moscow, No. 2, 1951; Article by Dr. M. Zd'arsky in *Statisticky obzor*, Prague, June 1951, entitled "Zvysujeme ukoly petiletky" ("Let us raise the tasks of the Five-Year Plan"). As a comparison with the output figures in Table II, it may be useful to give here the coal and steel output in various countries outside Eastern Europe, together with the more advanced East European countries. They are taken from the *Economic Survey of Europe in 1950*, published by E.C.E. of U.N., and refer to 1950 output.

	Crude Steel	Hard Coal
	(millions of tons)	
Belgium-Luxemburg ...	6.2	27.3
France (with Saar) ...	10.6	65.9
Western Germany ...	12.1	112.3
United Kingdom	16.6	219.7
United States	87.7	504.6
Czechoslovakia	2.9	18.5
Hungary	1.0	–
Poland	2.5	77.8

[2] Statement by Nowak, a member of the Politburo of the Polish United Workers' Party, at a session of the Central Committee 15th July 1951.

TABLE II
Output Targets in Certain Industries

(Figures in brackets show the planned output in the last year of the plan as a percentage
of the output at the beginning of the plan period)

	Poland[1]	Czechoslovakia	Hungary	Rumania	Bulgaria	Yugoslavia[4]
Coal (millions of tons)	100 (133)	21 (118)[2]	–	–	–	–
Brown coal and lignite (millions of tons)	–	32 (135)[2]	27.5 (250)	8.5 (238)	6.5 (163)	16.5 (272)
Steel (millions of tons)	4.6 (201)	3.5 (133)[2]	2.2 (230)	1.25	–	0.76 (300)
Electric power (milliards of Kw)	19.3 (236)	11.2 (149)[2]	4.2 (191)[2]	4.7	1.8 (221)	4.4 (395)
Nitrogen fertilisers (thousand tons)	980 (240)[2]	214 (134)[2]	310 (462)[2]	–	40[3]	350 (481)
Superphosphate fertilisers (thousand tons)	878 (200)[2]	399 (103)[2]	330 (273)[2]	–	–	–
Tractors (units)	11,000 (400)	20,000 (222)[2]	4,600 (177)[2]	5,000[3]	–	1,500[3]

[1] Comparisons refer to present boundaries.
[2] Unrevised plan figures. Czechoslovak coal (black and brown together) is to increase by 20 per cent more than these figures. Czechoslovak chemicals (which include fertilisers) by 30 per cent more. The revised targets for electric power and chemicals in Hungary are about double the original targets.
[3] No production of these in the past.
[4] Comparisons are with the 1939 output.

buted. New factories will be set up in areas hitherto purely agricultural, and rebuilt Warsaw will be an important centre for the metal, electro-technical and clothing industries.

The chief feature of the Czechoslovak Five-Year Plan is enormous development of heavy industry, to the comparative neglect of the light industries and consumers' goods industries which were so important in pre-war Czechoslovakia. This may be explained partly by the fact that the workers in the latter industries were largely German, expelled after 1945, and still more by the fact that their products were previously sold in the West European and overseas markets. The new plan is intended deliberately to tie the Czechoslovak economy more closely to those of the Soviet Union and the "popular democracies" and to weaken economic ties with the West. This change may well be the main reason for the February 1948 communist police revolution. The non-communist parties were all prepared to co-operate closely in

foreign policy with the U.S.S.R., but they were sceptical about the wisdom of transforming the economy on the ground of a demand from the East for capital goods which might not be lasting. It was probably in order to overcome this opposition to their economic aims that the Soviet leaders approved a seizure of power by the communists which was not required merely by diplomatic considerations. This tendency of the Czechoslovak plan became still more apparent after the revision announced in February 1951.

Under the original plan, total investments were to have been 336 milliard crowns (4½ times those of the completed Two-Year Plan; under the revised plan they are to be 558 milliard. Under the revised plan the target for heavy industry was raised from 170 per cent of the 1948 level to 230 per cent. The new target for heavy engineering is 48 per cent higher than that originally planned, for coal 20 per cent higher and for chemicals 30 per cent higher. The industrial labour force is to increase by 550,000 — about twice the number originally planned. The development of Slovakia was emphasised in the original plan, and still more in the revised plan. The creation of heavy industrial plants in Slovakia, and the transfer eastwards of a part of Bohemian industry, can be justified rather by military than by economic considerations.

The investments under the Hungarian Five-Year Plan were originally to have been nearly 51 milliard florint, more than five times the amount invested in the completed Three-Year Plan: under the revised plan, announced in the early summer of 1951, the sum was raised to 85 milliard. The targets for chemicals and electric power were almost doubled, those for machine production were trebled. The industrial labour force was to increase not by 480,000 as originally proposed but by 650,000. At the same time it was claimed that the productivity of labour would rise not by 50 per cent as originally proposed but by 100 per cent. It was also claimed that the standard of living would rise by 50 per cent instead of 35 per cent.

The Rumanian Five-Year Plan, announced at the end of 1950, was equally ambitious. The industrial labour force was to rise during the plan period by 38 per cent to a total of 3 million. Productivity of labour in industry was to increase by 75 per cent and the standard of living by 80 per cent. The oil industry was to produce 10 million tons in 1955. Even if the most rapacious methods were used, to the irreparable harm of the industry in future, it seems doubtful whether this target can be achieved. At the end of the period, Rumania was to have become a predominantly industrial country. Special stress was laid on the industrialisation of regions hitherto almost lacking in industry — Moldavia Oltenia and Dobrudja, and the northern corner of Transylvania. The total investment under the plan is to be 1330 milliard lei.

The Bulgarian Five-Year Plan proposes a total investment of 425 milliard leva, more than seven times as much as under the completed Two-Year Plan. Its completion is intended to change the relationship of industrial to agricultural production from 30 : 70 in 1948 to 45 : 55 in 1953. The number of industrial workers is to increase by 138,000. Mining and electric power are stressed. New industrial enterprises are to include non-ferrous metallurgical works and the construction of machines never yet produced in the country. In agriculture special attention is paid to industrial crops. An important feature of the Plan was the intention to extend the area under collective farms so that these would produce in 1953 60 per cent of Bulgaria's agricultural output.

Starting from the ruins left by war and civil war, in a country where industry had made little progress before the war, the planners of Yugoslavia aimed to achieve by 1951 an industrial output more than three times that of 1939 and an agricultural output more than half as large again as in 1939. The share of industry in national production in 1939 was estimated by the planners, somewhat optimistically, as 45 per cent: in 1951 it was to be 64 per cent. To attain this result, 27 per cent of the national income would have to be invested every year. High priority was given to electric power, based on the country's great resources of water power. Ambitious public works include the irrigation of areas such as Lonsko Polje in Croatia, the draining of Lake Scutari and measures against flooding in the Danube, Tisza, Sava and Morava valleys.

This plan could hardly have been achieved even under the most favourable conditions. But conditions were not favourable. In 1946 and 1947 there were severe droughts. In 1949 the Cominform states blockaded Yugoslavia, depriving her of raw materials and machines on which vital parts of the plan depended. Not only were materials insufficient, but it was discovered that the planners' original estimates of the labour force available had been unduly optimistic. According to a competent observer the estimate of 350,000 skilled workers, made in 1946, should be divided by ten. The few skilled or semi-skilled workers had to be moved from place to place according to changing priorities, often leaving large-scale projects unfinished. The available machinery quickly deteriorated for lack of proper care. Successes were achieved in the manufacture by skilled craftsmen of prototypes of complicated modern machines, but there was no prospect of putting these into mass production within the foreseeable future. Even the mining industry, for which there was previous experience to guide, fared badly. According to Yugoslav press statements, the Bor copper mines at the end of 1949 were producing only 55–70 per cent of the plan target. That conditions in the timber industry were desperate, was admitted by Kidrič and Kardelj in speeches to the Executive Committee of the People's Front in January 1950. On 28th December 1950 Kidric told the parliament that it had been decided to prolong the plan period by one year, till the end of 1952, and thereafter to have no further five-year plan.

During 1951 there was much public discussion in Yugoslavia of the faults of the Soviet system of planning, which it was admitted had been uncritically imitated. Measures were introduced to decentralise economic control. Powers were devolved from the central to the republican governments, and from these to the managements of factories. Managers were to find their own raw materials, machines and spare parts, within the country or abroad. Prices of basic raw materials were still to be fixed by the central authorities, but the prices of the finished products would be left to supply and demand. Factory managements would be given production quotas in money value, not specific output targets. They would thus be able to decide between the claims of quality and quantity. They would have to sell their goods in competition with other firms. They would also be able to decide how to spend their profits between such rival claims as reinvestment, workers' houses and wage bonuses.

It still remained the avowed intention to complete the original plan in 1952. It appeared however that the plan had undergone silent but far-reaching revision. Some projects, such as large-scale manufacture of locomotives and bicycles, had been abandoned. Responsible officials admitted that there was no prospect of achieving the target of 450,000 tons of crude oil from the oilfield in Slavonia. On the other hand electrification targets were actually increased.

The plan had aimed at industrialising the backward regions. The most rapid rate was to be in Macedonia, which was to become an important centre of electric power and to have a large textile industry, an iron foundry and factories producing soap, concrete prefabricated products and tinned fruit and vegetables. Bosnia was to become a centre of metallurgy, based on coal and iron ore, of which it has some deposits. Mostar, the picturesque Turkish garrison town in Hercegovina, was to be the centre of a new aluminum industry. As steps towards these results, important railways have been constructed. The Bosnian iron ore district of Ljubija has been linked with the railway system. The first half of a standard gauge north-to-south line through Bosnia has been completed, from Samac to Sarajevo. It is hoped to connect Sarajevo by standard gauge line with the Adriatic by the end of 1951, and to electrify this whole line from a new power station at Jablanica, in the precipitous mountain valley of the river Neretva.

Albania's economy was for three years dependent on that of Yugoslavia. The Albanian-Yugoslav economic treaty of November 1946 provided for co-ordination of the economic plans of the two countries, adjustment of the currency values, circulation and price levels, and a Yugoslav guarantee that sufficient goods would be in circulation to maintain the purchasing power of the two currencies at the agreed rate of exchange. Albanian-Yugoslav joint companies were created, similar to the Soviet-Rumanian and Soviet-Hungarian companies. These joint companies covered railway building, diesel oil production, electrification, mining, shipping and an Albanian-Yugoslav bank. The capital contribution of each was to be equal, and each was to have an equal vote on the directing boards. For a year and a half Yugoslav-Albanian economic relations were outwardly excellent. Then the Tito-Cominform breach gave the Albanian government a chance to break an association that had evidently been irksome to it.

At the Albanian Communist Party congress in November 1948 a new Two-Year Plan was announced for 1949–50. According to the congress speaker Gogo Nushi, progress had been made since the war despite Yugoslav interference. Mining output in 1948 was 121 per cent of the 1938 level, and the cultivated area was 119 per cent. Under the new plan, cereal output was to be increased 68 per cent beyond the 1948 level. A new hydro-electric power station was to be built, and a sugar refinery, a large textile factory and a large tannery were to be set up. The cement output by 1950 was to be 160 per cent of 1948. The most important mining increases were to be in petrol (1950 output to five times that of 1948), copper ore (six times), chrome ore (thirty times) and brown coal (one hundred times). The output figures for 1948, which are not given in the report, were presumably very small. But the proposed pace of development is at least superficially impressive. Its achievement would be ensured, official spokesmen stressed, by the help of Soviet raw materials, machinery and technicians.

These far-reaching plans strike the imagination. Even a foreign observer cannot fail to be affected by the enthusiasm and optimism of the planners. Moreover it is certain that large-scale industrialisation, public works and mechanisation of agriculture are the right remedies for the rural over-population and poverty, and the lack of manufactured goods, which were so striking in the old Eastern Europe. It is also understandable that the new regimes should wish, from a general feeling of patriotism, to diminish their countries' economic dependence on foreign countries.

But it would be a grave mistake to assume that because these aims have been set down on paper they will necessarily be achieved. It is still less certain that they will be achieved in the best way. Two features call for brief comment here.

One is that all the plans aim to create similar industries. It is true that the south-eastern countries are so deficient in heavy industry that it will be a long time before their needs can be satisfied. It is also true that between the two most advanced countries, Czechoslovakia and Poland, attempts are being made to co-ordinate plans. In particular the power resources of the Silesian industrial basin are to be to some extent pooled. There are also major construction schemes of benefit to several countries such as the Oder-Danube canal in Czechoslovakia, and the Danube-Black Sea canal in Rumania. Both would facilitate trade throughout the whole area between the Baltic and Black Seas. As long as the Soviet leaders think in terms of military preparations against the West, and are able to impose their will in Eastern Europe, the demand for the products of heavy industry is likely to exceed the supply. But these conditions will not last for ever. The danger that the plans will ultimately lead to wasteful competition between the East European countries, and to over-production in heavy industry, though improbable in the immediate future, cannot be lightly dismissed for further ahead.

The second feature of the plans is the

comparative neglect of consumers' goods industries. It is of course true that a much sounder foundation of capital goods industries is needed than Eastern Europe possessed before the war, and that the region's natural resources can be far more thoroughly exploited for this purpose than hitherto. It is also true that the consumers' goods industries are to make considerable progress under the plans, and that the official statements declare that the standard of living will greatly increase. But estimates of standard of living are difficult and controversial. The experience of the short-term recovery plans already carried out, and of the successive Five-Year Plans in the U.S.S.R., suggest that in practice whenever adjustments have to be made it is the consumers' goods industries that are scrapped. The standard of living, as revealed in the observation by unbiased witnesses of obvious objects of everyday life, has not improved so notably as was promised. It is possible to attribute this to bad luck—to drought, or "capitalistic encirclement." But the fact remains that there have been and are likely to be disappointments, and that in the face of disappointments the planners will not sacrifice their capital construction plans but will ask for further sacrifices from the people.

The percentage figures of plan fulfilment, officially released at more or less regular intervals by the governments, are meaningless as there is no way of discovering on what the percentages are really based. But enough information is available to show that the waste of materials, machines, working time and skill, and the production of goods of miserable quality, well known features of Soviet planning, are occurring in Eastern Europe. The familiar dilemma of the Soviet planner—to be unmasked as a saboteur today for planning a target too low for the taste of the political bosses, or to be unmasked as a saboteur next year for not fulfilling the impossible target which he set in order to please the political bosses —increasingly confronts the planner in Eastern Europe. Only Yugoslavia has turned her back on this witches' sabbath, and where her retreat will end is not yet clear.

In any case, the fulfilment of the plans depends on the supply of labour, raw materials and industrial equipment. The first of these depends on the organisation of the peasants, workers and technicians, which will be considered in the next chapter. The second and third factors depend on the organisation of international trade.

L. A. D. Dellin

AGRICULTURAL POLICY IN EASTERN EUROPE

Pre-Communist Eastern Europe was known as the "agricultural half" of the continent, and more specifically as its "granary," for its population, with the exception of Czechoslovakia and present-day East Ger-

many, was overwhelmingly occupied in agriculture (between 50 per cent in Hungary and 95 per cent in Albania), and the area as a whole was a substantial exporter of foodstuffs, mainly grains, to Western

From *Eastern Europe in the Sixties*, ed. S. Fischer-Galati (New York, 1963), pp. 56–62. Reprinted by permission of Frederick A. Praeger, Inc.

Europe. The peasant-agricultural character of the area should not be taken as an indication that the socio-economic structure was necessarily healthy or that farming methods and surpluses were of the conventional Western type. In fact, the physical setting, with some exceptions, is none too favorable for agriculture, and rural overpopulation, primitive cultivation, and low living standards were widespread. But tradition and lack of capital and skills permitted only moderate and selective industrialization, except in Czechoslovakia and East Germany. Moreover, peasant farming was a way of life, and, in the absence of any threat of food shortages, it progressed only slowly.

A major feature, one that explains more than anything else the peasants' scale of values, often in conflict with economic efficiency, was the character of land tenure. Before the Communists took over, East European agriculture showed a marked preponderance of small family farms: About 70 per cent of the holdings were up to 12 acres in size, and another 20 per cent between 12 and 25 acres. The share of large estates (over 250 acres) in total acreage was most pronounced in Hungary (about 45 per cent) and parts of Poland, Czechoslovakia, and Albania, with Hungary registering the highest percentage (35) of landless peasants. The trend toward land concentration and capitalist farming prophesied by Marx failed to materialize; instead, repeated land reforms made excessive parceling a more serious economic problem. It was difficult to improve efficiency and increase marketable output, but the governments encouraged agglomeration and higher-value, labor-intensive crop farming and livestock-raising; more important, the peasants themselves saw merits in a growing cooperative movement that did not disturb private ownership.

In most of the countries, political parties expounding "agrarianism," an antiurban ideology based on "biological materialism" and "cooperative syndicalism," at times headed or participated in the government. The agrarians more often than not opposed the Communist parties and programs for they could not reconcile the Communist goals of a "dictatorship of the proletariat" and a propertyless peasantry with their vision of a peasant-ruled republic.

When the Communists took over, they had little to offer to a peasantry that, although eager for a better life, had a deep feeling of private property and a family-centered outlook and was not willing to participate in revolutionary experiments, least of all in their own expropriation and the building of a regimented urban-industrial society.

The Theoretical Framework

Communist agricultural policy cannot be fully understood without at least a brief reference to the place of agriculture and the peasant in Communist theory, to the "agrarian doctrine" of Marx and his followers.

It is no mystery that Communist doctrine, built around the negation of a capitalist industrial society and identifying itself with the industrial proletariat, reveals mistrust of, and even contempt for, the peasantry, and that it considers the peasantry unreceptive to the avowed Communist goals, particularly to the abolition of private property. History played an unfair trick on Marx and his disciples when rural, not industrial, Europe became the home of Communism; hence, the legacy of Marxist dogma today haunts the East European rulers, who, although aware of the deficiencies of the blueprint, are unable to redesign it. Total nationalization of the land, the conversion of peasants into agricultural workers, and the concomitant but no less important rooting out of peasant independence and outlook remain the official goals. It should thus be clear why an open or latent conflict between the Communists and the peasants is bound to persist as long as Marxist dogma colors Communist thinking and action.

Communist economic theory, in so far as it affects agriculture, must also be considered in this connection. One of the priority goals is the compulsive industrialization, with emphasis on heavy industry. While few would argue against the need for and benefits of industrialization, especially in overpopulated Eastern Europe, an indiscriminate drive in an area with an inadequate resource base, and at no matter what cost, is neither the only nor the best alternative. But the blueprint requires that agriculture be neglected, although urbanization places increasing claims on farm produce, that labor be recruited *en masse* from the agricultural sector, and that the peasant pay the heaviest price for industrial achievements without obtaining benefits comparable to his sacrifice.

A second dogma is the exigency of rigid planning and control of the entire economy. Applied to agriculture—which involves climate, weather, and soil, as well as personal initiative and care, and thus requires greater flexibility and more individual responsibility than industry—central and detailed direction often works against economic rationality.

Another tenet, which at first glance seems much more plausible, involves the principle of "economies of scale." Under most conditions, integrated and large farms are more efficient, because they lend themselves to modern technology, a factor much praised by Marx and his followers. But "gigantism" per se, without corresponding capital investments in agriculture, without discrimination on the basis of specific crops, climate, and soil, and without due consideration of concrete labor-capital relationships, is of dubious value. It is obvious that beyond a given optimum size, economies may turn into diseconomies, or

that large farms are to be preferred when labor is relatively scarce and capital abundant. But since the opposite conditions prevail in much of capital-deficient and overpopulated Eastern Europe, a course different from that advocated by "scientific Marxism" would appear logical, unless, as it seems, gigantism is motivated more by other than economic considerations.

All this points to the conclusion that dogmas and sociopolitical goals, even when contrary to the dictates of common sense and sound economics, mold the Communist attitude toward agriculture and the peasant. The "dictatorship of the proletariat" and the "socialist transformation of agriculture" form the ideological framework within which the peasant-agrarian society is molded to conform to an irrational concept.

The Road to Collectivization

Communist agricultural policy has passed through several stages, reflecting the conflict between theoretically dictated measures and empirical stumbling blocks, a conflict that results in oscillating tactical compromises. Yet despite such conflicts, Communist planning never abandons the goal of total collectivization with its broader concomitant aims. The Soviet example has been the over-all guide. Differences between the Soviet and the East European experiments—the fact that outright nationalization of all the land has not taken place in the satellites (even though the collectivization drive started sooner after the Communist accession to power than it did in the Soviet Union), or that the timing and intensity of collectivization policies in individual bloc countries vary, or that drastic deviations have occurred in Yugoslavia and Poland—are due not so much to a lack of enthusiasm by the Party leaderships as to prevailing international and domestic conditions that demanded different approaches.

The first phase extended from the end of

the war (1945) to the time of consolidation of Communist rule (1948–49). The local Communist parties, before the seizure of power and until genuine coalitions with non-Communist parties were no longer needed, proclaimed as their goal the distribution of the land to "those who work it" and rejected any allegation that they would disturb private ownership of land. In fact, the land reforms they, jointly with coalition parties, undertook immediately after the war were mostly in conformity with their protestations, and the nationalization of the "no man's land" in German-depopulated areas of Czechoslovakia and of new Poland could not be used as evidence of Communist bad faith. [The reforms affected about one-fourth of the total agricultural area of Eastern Europe, with Poland leading in the redistribution (43 per cent) and Bulgaria trailing (2 per cent), but in every instance the state kept about one-third of the expropriated land.] Still, the general arbitrariness, the excesses, the discrimination against the large landowners (a relative term meaning different things in latifundic Hungary and in dwarf-household Bulgaria), as well as the beginnings of collectivization here and there, were like warnings of a gathering storm. The end effect of this initial land reform was, in fact, a further breakup of farm land, a further increase in subsistence holdings (farms now averaged 12–25 acres per family throughout the region), and consequently a reduction in marketable surpluses. This, of course, ran counter to Communist economic theory and goals, but was found expedient in political terms, eroding as it did the strength of the medium and large farmer and neutralizing the peasantry.

It should be pointed out that this phase coincided with the nationalization of industry and the period of economic reconstruction, so that, when the end of the decade was approached, long-range planning could be undertaken within a regimented nonagricultural sector and attention could be devoted to regimenting the agricultural sector as well.

The about-face in Communist policy came almost unexpectedly and abruptly, although Bulgaria and Yugoslavia had started modest collectivization as early as 1945. As it became known later on, the decision to push ahead at the fastest pace possible was made at the June, 1948, meeting of the Cominform and implemented with great vigor in the early 1950's, until Stalin's death. The priority goals were: in the political field—to do away with the peasants' independence; in the economic —to subject agriculture to strict government planning and control, so as to extract forced savings from the peasant majority for industrial investment, to shift manpower to industry, and (as a professed long-term objective) to provide the basis for large-scale modern farming. That this objective played a subordinate role is evidenced by the fact that more efficient farming could have been encouraged by methods not affecting private ownership, especially since planned state investment in agriculture almost nowhere exceeded 10 per cent (and was actually much lower), and private investment could not be expected to be forthcoming in any appreciable degree.

In view of its motivation, the collectivization drive had to rely on force and drastic economic measures rather than on persuasion. Opponents were branded "kulaks" and treated accordingly. The exceedingly discriminatory economic measures used against them included higher compulsory delivery quotas, steeper tax rates, higher interest, and higher charges for the use of machinery, seeds, and fertilizers. As if conscious of the unpopularity of their policy, the Communists avoided using the term "collective" at all, preferring instead the traditional designation "cooperative," and enacted statutes extolling the "voluntary" and "democratic" character of the new institutions. In most countries, more than one and up to four types of "cooperative farms" were organized: the looser forms (types I and II), in which joint work did not affect property, and the advanced types (types III and IV), where collective property became the rule. It goes without saying that the regimes pressured toward the latter group, and the peasants, when given a choice, preferred the former.

The end of this hectic period saw collectivization embrace over 50 per cent of the agricultural land in Bulgaria, and 20 to 40 per cent in Czechoslovakia, Hungary, and Yugoslavia (excluding the looser cooperatives). The remaining countries were about 10 per cent collectivized, but if the state farms' area is added (which was most prominent in Hungary, Poland, East Germany, and Rumania), the joint "socialist sector" comprised from one-fifth (Poland) to two-thirds (Bulgaria) of the cultivable land, except in Albania, in which about 10 per cent was collectivized. The average collective farm ranged from 370 acres (East Germany) to 2,200 acres (Bulgaria) and included up to 200 former individual farms.

It is evident that the results of this first pull were neither total nor the same in each of the countries. This divergence was due to differences of individual Communist regimes — different degrees of subordination to Soviet leadership and different national characteristics resulting in different methods. But the underlying motives and trends were similar (with the exception of Yugoslavia, where a reappraisal was already indicated), and so were the results.

At the time of Stalin's death, an appraisal of this first round of collectivization revealed a serious setback in agriculture and near despair among the peasants. Aside from the inadequacy of available capital and skills for such a rapid and drastic transformation, the price and procurement system and the discrimination against the private sector destroyed personal incentive and cut into farm income and production. The compulsory delivery quotas set for all major crops and livestock based on acreage and type of ownership were irrationally large, and prices disproportionately low (at least one-half and down to one-fifth of the prices paid by the state for above-quota deliveries, not to mention free-market comparisons), and thus acted as a severe tax on farm income. On the other hand, prices of goods sold by the state were purposely set high (including "turnover" sales taxes and profit markups), thus further reducing the farmers' purchasing power. Furthermore, payments by private farmers to machine-tractor stations — the monopolists of farm machinery — were set three to four times higher than those required from collective farms. It is, therefore, not surprising that the rural areas were depressed and that, while industrial output doubled over the prewar level, agricultural production fell way below. (The average grain and potato crops in 1948–52 were at least 15 and as much as 25 per cent lower than in 1934–38.) What was surprising was that the abused and shrinking private sector (including individual plots of members of collectives) continued to contribute most of the agricultural output and about three-fourths of the marketable grain (except in Bulgaria), while the collectives, especially the state farms, had to be heavily subsidized. There was little doubt that the collectivization and agricultural policies in general would ultimately lead to a dead end.

Zbigniew K. Brzezinski

ECONOMIC ACHIEVEMENTS BY 1953

The nationalization policy, particularly in industry but also in handicrafts, by 1950 had resulted in the fairly general adoption of state ownership throughout the area, thereby breaking with the former pattern of diversification. As a result, at the beginning of the long-range socialist planning, all the People's Democracies could boast that the major means of production, save the agricultural sector, were in the hands of the proletariat. Socialist transformation was now to be accompanied according to the tried Stalinist experience, by a radical and rapid industrialization of the individual states, unhindered by private enterprise. This industrialization would result, together with collectivization, in a radical destruction of the old ways of life, bring to the cities hundreds of thousands of new laborers, produce extensive urban development, and shatter once and for all the remnants of former habits, traditions, and nonsocialist characteristics. The repetition of the Soviet experience of the thirties would be bound to create an environment essentially like the Soviet environment.

The plans, admittedly prepared with the assistance of Soviet economic advisers, emphasized the priority of the development of heavy industry, to which the major investments would be assigned. The funds were to be used to expand the existing industrial plants and also to launch several spectacular schemes which were to symbolize the new socialist era and stand as lasting monuments to the socialist order. Each People's Democracy boasted of some such project: the Nowa Huta Steel Works in Poland, the Gottwald Steel Plants in Czechoslovakia, the Stalin Works at Dunapentele in Hungary, and the Dimitrovo Steel Plant in Bulgaria.

Without evaluating the plans and their fulfillment, it is worth noting that within a few years of almost superhuman effort and tremendous social sacrifice, the various countries of East Europe could point to certain genuine achievements. Considerable strides were made in such sectors as steel production and coal extraction, and by 1953, total steel production was roughly equal to West Germany's and about twice as much as before the war. The area's hydroelectric capacity was more than doubled, and by 1953 Czechoslovakia, Poland, and Hungary roughly tripled their engineering production as compared to the prewar level. By 1952, Poland's annual industrial production reached 194.8 per cent of the 1949 level (by comparison, in agriculture the total was only 104.9 per cent), and in Czechoslovakia the comparable percentage was 198.9 per cent. The area, with all its deficiencies and problems, was emerging into the industrial age even though its economies were still largely unintegrated and developed on a semiautarkic pattern.

Internally, the *politically* significant consequence of this process of industrialization was the rapid increase in bringing the nonagricultural labor force into the organized, and hence more politically controllable, industrial process and urban life. According to the most exhaustive study available on the economics of East Europe, "between 1948 and 1953 there was a net increase of the nonagricultural labor force of about 400,000 in Bulgaria, 465,000 in Yugoslavia, close to 600,000 in Czechoslova-

Reprinted by permission of the publishers from Zbigniew K. Brzezinski, *The Soviet Bloc*, (Cambridge, Mass.: Harvard University Press), pp. 99–103. Copyright 1960 by the President and Fellows of Harvard College.

kia, 750,000 in Hungary, 825,000 in Rumania, and over 1.9 million in Poland." This amounted to an increase of about 33 per cent in the industrial labor force, telescoped into the remarkably short time of five years. During this period the rural population, while remaining generally stable in absolute numbers (with some small decreases), declined in terms of ratios between urban and rural populations as the new industries drained off the rural youth, having previously absorbed whatever surplus town labor had existed (in the form of the unemployed and the female labor force).

The new proletariat, housed in temporary barracks and workers' hotels, with no privacy, individuality, or family ties, was to help build the new tomorrrow, the socialist society. The conditions under which it labored have been best described by the poets and novelists. But to many of these workers, the new environment did at first offer an improvement over previous conditions, or at least an opportunity of breaking away from a life which many of them no longer thought meaningful or desirable. Many of them did not have a clear image of what tomorrow would bring, but many did have a vague feeling that today was no longer for them—a feeling which Communist agitation stimulated. The masses flocking to the cities and industrial work sites were hoping for something they did not clearly grasp; but by coming they were helping to weaken the existing social bonds, to undermine the social institutions of the past which the Communists felt had to fall. The effect of industrialization was to create a revolutionary social situation in which the only source of cohesion would be the party, the only source of direction the leadership's will.

Under these conditions, the Soviet methods of labor discipline and organization were rapidly adopted. The trade unions were usually subordinated with the absorption of the Social Democratic parties and with the nationalization of the last areas of private enterprise. One-man management assisted by party committees became the norm, and the factory became merely a unit within a hierarchically organized industrial pyramid, characterized by the strictest discipline and subordination. Laws of labor regulation, such as penalties for absenteeism and lateness, and a system of sanctions patterned on the Soviet model were adopted, together with specified norms, "socialist competitions," and premiums. Labor discipline was strictly enforced and labor recruitment subjected to state control. Announcing the introduction of strict state surveillance over employment, the Czech Minister of Labor stated:

By this new regulation the entire existing system, which was based on the voluntary movement of labor under state supervision, will be abandoned, and a new system applied which will directly control labor recruitment for the most important sectors of our industry in the same manner as our entire Socialist economy is directed.

The submerging of society in the state, a process characteristic of totalitarian development, was accordingly to be one of the major by-products of the internal transformation.

The application of these new concepts meant that the People's Democracies were becoming replicas of the Soviet system, though somewhat less advanced (in the Marxist historical sense). In effect, they duplicated the Stalinist pattern of "economic war communism," that is, a rigid system of limited priorities to be achieved at the cost of other, less essential, economic sectors, particularly agriculture, housing, and light industry. The previous diversity among East European states was giving way not only to common patterns but also to a fundamental affinity between their domestic patterns and those of the USSR.

At this stage one might again raise the question: which of these changes had been motivated by ideology and which by power considerations? Power alone cannot explain the emphasis put on rapid collectivization unless the peasant is considered by those in power to be an imminent political threat. But if he is, then the very act of such consideration is colored by ideological assumptions about the implications of private enterprise. Industrialization was badly needed by the area — and Communist power was admittedly strengthened by it, initially at least. But the nature of the industrial development, based on Soviet experience, again was affected by the image of the society desired and the forces said to oppose it. In this manner policy reflected the impact of a peculiar normative perspective on reality as well as the assumed existential imperatives of that reality for those in policy-making positions.

As far as relations among Communist powers were concerned, it followed from Marxist thinking that these necessary internal changes were also creating political and economic bonds between the Soviet and East European societies. The result would be a solid, spirited, and single-minded phalanx which would stand together under any circumstances. The parties, by becoming Stalinized, by purging themselves and destroying such sources of deviationism as the Social Democrats, would tend to be more oriented toward the USSR. Terror used against the population at large would destroy any sources of potential opposition to the regime and introduce such fear that compliance with the policies and purposes of the system would be assured. Collectivization would carry the class struggle into the countryside and weed out the normally conservative orientation of the peasants, driving them into collective institutions where they could be subjected to organized political and economic control. Economic transformation through nationalization and, more significantly, through industrialization would create the objective basis for socialism while ripping apart the social fabric to such an extent that the Communist Party — Stalinist and dependent on the Soviet Union — would be the only source of social cohesion, the only organization to which the youth, in particular, could turn for guidance. The revised theory as applied would create the material bases for an internally cohesive socialist bloc. It would serve as a solid foundation for Stalinism as an interstate system.

THE IDEOLOGICAL BACKGROUND

The extension of Soviet influence in Eastern Europe not only caused an upheaval in the world balance of power; it also called for a complete reappraisal of communist theory with regard to world revolution on Marxist lines. According to orthodox Marxism-Leninism, revolutions outside the U.S.S.R. resulting in the overthrow of the bourgeois state structure would be followed by a dictatorship of the proletariat. This was not the actual case in the countries of Eastern Europe. No political revolutions were forthcoming, and the somewhat hesitant process of political transformation that took place in the countries subject to Soviet influence did not allow for the early establishment of a dictatorship of the proletariat. How could the position be described in such an anomalous regime as existed in Czechoslovakia after the war?

The Soviet answer was provided in the title of the People's Democracy, a phrase first used by Tito in 1945 at the Congress of the Yugoslav Fatherland Front. The People's Democracy was neither a Soviet Republic (the very idea of this analogy would have been enough to arouse panic in Western statesmen after the war) nor a bourgeois state: it was a mongrel form lying somewhere between the two. It was not a clear-cut definition of a static phenomenon. Rather it was intended as a temporary guide to and description of the existing reality, for use by communists whose duty it was to understand the political structures they were working on and constantly changing by their own action. As an article of dogma it was in the Leninist tradition rather than in that of more rigid Marxism.

The concept altered as the Soviet grip tightened over Eastern Europe. In November 1946 Gomulka, the secretary of the Polish Workers' Party, asserted that "our democracy is also not similar to Soviet democracy, just as our social system is not similar to the Soviet system."

In 1947 the economist Eugene Varga got into trouble with the theorists for having laid too much stress in his book of 1946 on the bourgeois elements in the economic structure of the People's Democracies: he was not keeping up with the times. By December 1948, after the onset of the new hard line in Soviet foreign policy, Georg Dimitrov, the Premier of Bulgaria, was practically contradicting Gomulka's statement of 1946.

Georg Dimitrov

PEOPLE'S DEMOCRACY

The character of a people's democracy is determined by four major factors:

1) The people's democracy represents the power of the toiling people—of the overwhelming majority of the people, under the leadership of the working class.

That means, first, that the rule of the capitalists and landlords is overthrown and the rule of the toilers from the towns and villages, under the leadership of the working class, established, that the working class as the most progressive class in contemporary society is playing the principal role in state and public life. Second, that the state serves as a tool in the fight of the toilers against the exploiting elements, against all efforts and tendencies aimed at re-establishing the capitalist order and the bourgeois rule.

2) The people's democracy is a state in the transitional period, destined to ensure the development of the state on the path to socialism.

That means that although the rule of capitalists and landlords is overthrown and their property handed over to the people, the economic roots of capitalism are not yet extirpated; capitalist vestiges still persist

Georg Dimitrov, excerpt from political report from the Fifth Congress of the Bulgarian Communist Party, December 19, 1948.

and develop, trying to restore their rule. Therefore, the onward march towards socialism is possible only by waging a relentless class struggle against the capitalist elements for their liquidation.

Only by advancing directly on the route to fulfil socialism, can the people's democracy stabilize itself and its historic vocation. Should it cease to fight against the exploiter classes, and to eliminate the class elements, the latter would inevitably gain the upper hand, and would bring about its doom.

3) The people's democracy is built in collaboration and friendship with the Soviet Union.

Just as the liberation of our country from the fetters of imperialism and the establishment of a people's democracy were made possible by the aid and liberating mission of the USSR in the fight against Fascist Germany and its satellites, so the further development of our people's democracy presupposes the safeguarding and further promotion of close relations and sincere collaboration, mutual aid and friendship between our state and the Soviet state. Any tendency toward weakening this collaboration with the USSR is directed against the very existence of the people's democracy in our country.

4) The people's democracy belongs to the democratic anti-imperialist camp.

a) Only by participating in the unified democratic anti-imperialist camp, headed by the mighty Soviet state, can every people's democracy ensure its independence, sovereignty and safety against the aggression of the imperialist forces.

b) Under the conditions of the military collapse of the Fascist aggressor states, of the abrupt sharpening of the general capitalist crisis and of the immense strengthening of the power of the Soviet Union and the existing close collaboration with the USSR and the new democracies, our country and the other new democracies were enabled to realize the transition from capi-

talism to socialism, without the establishment of a Soviet order, through the regime of a people's democracy, on condition that it gets stabilized and develops, and by leaning on the USSR and the other new democracies.

c) Embodying the rule of the toilers under the leadership of the working class, the people's democracy, under the existing historic setup, as already proven by experience, can and must successfully perform its functions of proletarian dictatorship for the liquidation of the capitalist elements and the organization of a socialist economy. It can crush the resistance of the overthrown capitalists and landowners, quell their attempts to restore the rule of capital, and organize the building of industry on the basis of public ownership and planned economy. The regime of the people's democracy will succeed in overcoming the vacillations of the urban petty bourgeoisie and middle class peasantry, in neutralizing the capitalist elements in the village and in rallying the toilers around the working class for the onward march toward socialism.

The regime of the people's democracy will not change its character during the implementation of this policy which aims at eliminating the capitalist elements from the national economy. The key positions of the working class in all spheres of public life must continuously be stabilized and all village elements rallied who might become allies of the workers during the period of sharp struggles against the *kulaks* and their cronies. The people's democratic regime must be stabilized and improved in order to hamstring and liquidate the class enemies.

d) The new democracies, including Bulgaria, are already marching toward socialism, in ceaseless struggle against all domestic and especially foreign enemies. They are now creating the conditions necessary for the building of socialism, the economic and cultural basis for a future socialist society.

So far in this book we have only dealt with Eastern Europe, the major area of Soviet influence at the end of the Second World War. Although problems in this sphere kept Russia's hands busy, she also had a finger in the Asian pie as a reward for entering into the war against Japan in the closing stages of the war. In Europe the Soviets claimed the Baltic States, Bessarabia, and other territories as their own; in Asia the theme was repeated with the acquisition of southern Sakhalin, the Kurile Islands, and naval bases in Dairen and Port Arthur. The Eastern European pattern was also followed with regard to areas occupied by Soviet troops in the course of their campaigns against the Axis powers; in Asia they took over Manchuria and the northern part of the Korean peninsula.

After the failure of the Moscow Council of Foreign Ministers Conference in December 1945, the Soviets proceeded to set up a provisional puppet government in North Korea on lines similar to those employed in Eastern Europe. Headed by Kim Il Sung, a Moscow-trained communist, the "Provisional People's Committee of North Korea" carried out political and economic reforms of the type that were put through in Europe.

Manchuria was the biggest prize of Russia's Asian loot. Industrially it was more advanced than any other part of Asia except Japan, which had been, during its occupation of Manchuria, responsible for the progress made there. As in Eastern Europe, Russia carried out large-scale removals of equipment under the guise of reparations to strengthen her home base. In view of the fact that Manchuria would have to be returned to China, and a China soon to fall under communist rule, Stalin's policy appears to have been more shortsighted in Manchuria than in Eastern Europe. But Stalin was no more able than American observers to foresee the rapid deterioration of the Chinese Nationalist forces under Chiang Kai-shek from 1946–8; what he could see was the desperate state of Soviet industry.

In the period immediately after the war, the nationalist side of Stalin's thinking was certainly to the fore in the Asian arena. In September 1945 he declared that the Japanese defeat in Manchuria had been wished for by Russians of the older generation ever since the Russo-Japanese war of 1904–5. Three years later, in 1948, Stalin admitted to the Yugoslav communist Djilas that he had been wrong in recognizing the Kuomintang regime at the end of the war, thus temporarily abandoning the Chinese communists: "True, we too can make a mistake. Here, when the war with Japan ended, we invited the Chinese comrades to reach an agreement as to how a *modus vivendi* with Chiang Kai-shek might be found. They agreed with us in word, but in deed they did it their own way when they got home: they mustered their forces and struck. It has been shown that they were right, and not we."

Russia's chameleon-like attitude to the Chinese communists was shown in her treatment of Manchuria. Having completed half of the stripping operation in the area, the Soviet command offered Chiang Kai-shek joint Sino-Soviet management of the remaining industrial plant, but Chiang refused. Subsequently, in the process of withdrawing from Manchuria in the autumn of 1945 according to the terms of the Sino-Soviet pact arranged at Yalta, the Russians duly handed over the cities to the Kuomintang, but permitted the communists to occupy the rural zones and gave them large supplies of Japanese arms. In the course of the scramble to take over Manchuria before the communists, Chiang dangerously overextended his military communications—later in the civil war his most efficient troops were cornered in Manchuria and had to be supplied by air—and it may be that the Soviet Union had deliberately lured him into the trap.

Stalin's Chinese policy at this time and indeed up to the victory of the Chinese communists in 1949 remains obscure, probably because it was a hesitant, undetermined policy which hung on events. Cautious by nature, Stalin was also inclined to such a course by various other factors, two of which were personal. First, he appeared to dislike the Chinese as people and was apt to decry their capabilities. Secondly, once before, in 1926–7, he had advocated a policy of wait-and-see in the struggle between the Chinese communists and their opponents and had brushed aside Trotsky's call for aid to the communist side. Here again, as in so many other fields the aging dictator was perhaps leaning heavily on past experience in his dealings with China after 1945.

If he had openly supported the Chinese communists in 1945, Stalin would have run counter to his policy of initial restraint, a policy demonstrated by Soviet noninterference in Greece and by Soviet pressure on Yugoslavia to prevent her antagonizing the West too much over the question of Trieste. There was no point in carving up the wartime alliance of the Big Three while it was still offering surprising advantages to Russia, of which one of the most significant included her postwar concessions in Asia. A more deepseated reason was probably Stalin's mistrust of independently inspired communist revolutions, which was brought home to him by his experience with Yugoslavia in 1947–8. China with her vast potential in manpower could present a far more serious problem than Yugoslavia unless she was carefully assigned to her proper place in the communist hierarchy of nations.

The upshot of Stalin's policy or lack of one was that the Kuomintang forces lost the Chinese civil war mainly because of their own weakness and corruption, and not because the Soviet Union offered substantial aid to the communists.

Howard L. Boorman

THE MOSCOW-PEKING AXIS

After the Chinese Communists had carried out their epoch-making Long March from Kiangsi to the remote hills of northwest China, reliable information about their relations with the Russians became exceedingly elusive. Mao's followers displayed a careful orthodoxy in their theoretical statements and a respectful deference toward Moscow, and they executed a thoroughgoing program aimed at building up a tightly disciplined Communist party along strict Leninist lines. Yet, in retrospect, one cannot point to a large body of concrete data bearing upon the political or personal contacts of the Chinese Communist leaders with Stalin and the contemporary top leadership of the Soviet Union.

Even later, following the Japanese surrender in 1945 and the emergence of Mao Tse-tung and his followers from the caves of Yenan, the Communist march to total power in China left behind few clues as to the precise nature of Russian support or influence. In fact, in this respect the years between 1945 and 1949 are particularly obscure, even for the specialized student of relations between the Soviet and Chinese Communist Parties.

There had been collaboration in Manchuria between the Russian units which appeared there after the war against Japan had been won in the Pacific and the Chinese Communist forces which speedily made their way overland to that critical arena of conflict. Yet the extensive Russian removal of important industrial equipment from an area which was so soon, as it turned out, to come under complete Communist domination raises the question as to the degree of confidence with which the Russians viewed their Chinese counterparts in the immediate postwar period. A few years later, in the discussion groups organized in China to implant the new revolutionary creed, there was no question more difficult for a Chinese Communist political commissar to answer satisfactorily than the query: If the Russians are really such good fellows and such superior disciples of Marx and Lenin, why did they behave like a mob of hoodlums in Manchuria in 1945–46?

During the years following the Japanese surrender, when the Chinese Communists were fighting their way to power, their own political line with respect to the Soviet Union was both consistent and correct. Their radio station in northern Shensi paid dutiful homage to Moscow, and Liu Shao-ch'i's essay, *On Internationalism and Nationalism,* published in November 1948, supported the Soviet stand in the Tito apostasy of that year. It is debatable whether the Chinese Communists had organized their diplomatic assumptions into a coherent whole as early as the end of 1948, at a time when they were still preoccupied with the military aspects of the civil war then being fought in China. In any case, it seems clear that the senior leaders of the Chinese party viewed their orientation toward Moscow as both necessary and, in terms of their own interests, highly desirable. In July 1949, even before the establishment of the new National Government in Peking, Mao Tse-tung formally outlined the Chinese Communist position with respect to Sino-Soviet relations. His "lean-to-one-side" speech announced forthrightly that the new regime would base its policies on

From Howard L. Boorman, *Moscow-Peking Axis* (New York, 1957), pp. 2–13. Reprinted by permission of the Council on Foreign Relations, Inc.

close cooperation with the Soviet Union, not with the non-Communist "imperialist" world.

Until 1949, while the Chinese Communists were fighting for victory, the Soviet attitude toward the National Government of China was ambiguous. At the official level, it was scrupulously proper. The Russians continued to maintain formal diplomatic relations with the National Government, the sworn enemy of the Communists in China. At the operational level, the Soviet attitude was cynical and enigmatic. As late as 1949, the Soviet ambassador in China continued to negotiate with the National Government over important economic and transportation concessions in Sinkiang, apparently with a view to obtaining for Russia a special position in the province during the very months when the Chinese Communist armies were driving rapidly into the northwest.

The scanty evidence regarding conversations and agreements between the Russians and the Chinese Communists during 1947–49 is both incomplete and contradictory. It is relatively simple to sketch the broad outlines of the design, but difficult to fill in the fine detail. Possibly official Soviet representatives in China were not always *au courant* of developments in the Communist-controlled areas of the country in which they were stationed. And it is probable that Stalin, much farther removed from the rapidly changing circumstances in the hinterland of China, was not adequately prepared for the new political situation which was then being created by the startling military advance of the Chinese Communist armies as they drove southward and westward from Manchuria.

Certainly the balance in the Sino-Soviet Communist Party relationship was now drastically altered from what it had been a generation before, in the 1920's, when the Chinese Communist Party was young, inexperienced, and firmly under Moscow's direction. By 1949, Chinese Communism had grown into a vigorous and self-confident force which, if not yet fully mature, was clearly enjoying the brash assurance of late adolescence. It possessed a tightly knit political organization, then numbering over 3 million members, and a battle-toughened army of over 1.5 million men. During the two decades when it had been growing to this stature, the Communist Party of China had probably been less under direct Soviet control than Communist parties elsewhere. Its revolutionary armies were native to the soil and had not required active support from the Soviet Red Army to plan their campaigns or win their battles. By 1949, the Chinese Communist leaders possessed a background of practical political and administrative experience in their own country far more extensive than that which the leaders of the Bolshevik revolution in Russia had possessed in 1917 or even in 1921.

Stalin and the New Ally in Peking: 1949–1953

The Central People's Government of the People's Republic of China was formally established on October 1, 1949. The Soviet Union at once accorded it recognition, and the large Russian embassy on Legation Street, closed since the Chinese Communist occupation of Peking, reopened for business. Early in October, N. V. Roshchin—who had served as Soviet ambassador to the National Government of China as recently as May 1949, when he departed for Moscow—arrived in China again as the first foreign diplomat accredited to the new Communist regime there. Mao Tse-tung, in turn, dispatched the first Chinese Communist ambassador to Moscow.

The establishment of formal diplomatic relations and the exchange of official representatives, while noteworthy, were nevertheless routine. Neither these developments nor the tidy political slogans which poured unceasingly from Peking could provide adequate answers to the basic security and ideological problems involved in the new phase of contacts between the Russians and the Chinese Communists. It was left to Mao Tse-tung himself to travel to the Soviet Union to discuss these issues personally with Stalin. Mao's mission to Moscow underscored the fact that, for a prominent Communist, he was still in a decidedly irregular position. Ruler of the most populous Communist nation, he had never visited Russia, spoke no Russian, and had had relatively little contact with the Russians. His journey to negotiate with Stalin at the end of 1949, when the Soviet dictator was already seventy, was Mao's first venture outside his native China, and, to date, his only pilgrimage to the Mecca of world Communism.

It was doubtless an extraordinarily difficult period of negotiation for the two Communist leaders in Moscow, for both were tough political realists, not vague theorists. It is probable that Stalin, increasingly rigid in his later years, viewed Mao Tse-tung as an Asian and an inferior. Mao, for his part, knew very well that Stalin's failure, two decades earlier, to understand the realities of the Chinese political situation had led Moscow in 1927 to issue unrealistic directives to the Chinese Communists and had resulted in staggering Communist losses at the hands of the Kuomintang. Whether Stalin and Mao reviewed the past or discussed the theory and practice of Communist revolution in Asia is uncertain. All the effusive propaganda about Sino-Soviet friendship could not, however, conceal the probability that the negotiations must have been devoted, essentially, to hardheaded practical bargaining. Mao Tse-tung stayed in Moscow for nine weeks—from December 16, 1949, until February 17, 1950—at what was one of the most important Communist conferences of the postwar period. On February 14, 1950, a joint communiqué announced the conclusion of three new Sino-Soviet agreements, signed in the Kremlin by the late A. Y. Vyshinsky,

then the Soviet Minister of Foreign Affairs, and Chou En-lai, the Chinese Communist Foreign Minister.

The first was the Sino-Soviet Treaty of Friendship, Alliance, and Mutual Assistance, the foundation stone of the new alliance between the two major Communist powers. This treaty is valid until 1980 and may be further extended by mutual consent. Its focus is Asia; its nucleus is a military alliance ostensibly directed against defeated Japan. In it, Moscow and Peking agree to take all necessary measures to prevent the resumption of aggression on the part of Japan "or any other state that may collaborate with Japan directly or indirectly"—a clear reference, in this context, to the United States. If either Communist China or the Soviet Union is attacked by Japan "or any state allied with it" and thus becomes involved in a war, the other party will immediately render military and other assistance by all means at its disposal.

The second agreement covered the respective rights of the Russians and the Chinese Communists in Manchuria, the major border area in which both have significant strategic interests. It stipulated:

That the principal railroad network in Manchuria, the Chinese Changchun railway, would continue to be operated under joint Sino-Soviet administration (as had been provided earlier in the agreement signed between Moscow and the National Government of China in August 1945).

That the important naval base, Port Arthur, would also continue to be "jointly used," with Russian troops garrisoned there (as they had been since 1945), and would be employed to support joint military operations in the event of war with Japan or any country allied with Japan. Both of these arrangements—that concerning the Chinese Changchun railway and that concerning Port Arthur—were to be terminated upon the conclusion of a peace treaty with Japan or at the end of 1952, whichever came earlier.

That the administration of Dairen, the principal port at the southern end of the Chinese Changchun railway, was confirmed as belonging entirely to the Chinese. Since 1945, it had been under Soviet control.

The third agreement dealt with Russian financial assistance to Communist China. The Russians granted a credit which, at the official rate, amounted to U.S. $300 million, at an interest rate of one per cent per year. This credit arrangement covered the five-year period from 1950 through 1954, with one-fifth, or U.S. $60 million, to be made available annually. Communist China was to use this loan to pay for deliveries of industrial and railway supplies from the Soviet Union: equipment for electric power stations, metallurgical and engineering plants, mining equipment, railway and other transport equipment, rails, and "other materials for the restoration and development of the national economy." China was to repay the credit in ten equal annual installments, the first at the end of 1954 and the last at the end of 1963.

At the same time, the Soviet and Chinese Communist governments exchanged notes covering two other matters. The treaty and other agreements concluded on August 14, 1945, between the Soviet Union and the National Government of China were now declared null and void, and the independent status of the Mongolian People's Republic (Outer Mongolia) was guaranteed by both governments.

The developing alliance between the Soviet Union and Communist China was extended by other agreements signed in the spring of 1950. These provided for the establishment of a network of Sino-Soviet joint-stock companies to operate in the borderland areas of China:

Two companies to undertake the exploitation of non-ferrous and rare minerals, and petroleum in Sinkiang (Chinese Turkestan), the vast province in the far northwest of China adjacent to Russian Central Asia.

A civil aviation company to operate flights between Peking and the Soviet Union via Manchuria, Outer Mongolia, and Sinkiang,

A company to build and repair ships at Dairen, the commercial port adjacent to Port Arthur in southern Manchuria.

And, in the spring of 1950, the two Communist allies completed initial negotiations on trading arrangements under which the Soviet Union was to supply industrial equipment while Communist China would, in return, export raw materials.

The forging of the Moscow-Peking axis was thus well begun before the outbreak of the Korean war in mid-1950 and the ensuing Chinese Communist intervention, in October. From 1950 through 1952, the government in Peking was in the difficult position of having to push through its initial programs of political unification and economic rehabilitation at home, while at the same time deeply involved in a costly and risky military engagement in Korea. Viewed from one standpoint, the Korean war was useful to the Communists in China, for it permitted them to consolidate domestic controls and mobilize human and material resources more rapidly than would otherwise have been politically feasible. In the midst of a war, internal opposition, or even criticism, could be dealt with as treason committed in favor of the "imperialists." By mid-1952, however, there were indications that the rulers in Peking were more anxious to push forward with their internal development programs than to continue what were for them increasingly pointless military operations which were also placing a severe strain upon scarce resources.

Caution suggests that the interpretation of the diplomatic history of the Korean war be left to the future, since the present evidence is as overabundant as it is incomplete. Sino-Soviet relations during the Korean conflict are, in many respects, still a riddle. At times, Russian and Chinese moves seemed perfectly timed to present a common Communist front. Yet there were instances in the United Nations negotiations where, it would appear, the Russians failed to take complete advantage of tactical opportunities favorable to them and made only inconclusive gestures toward advancing Chinese interests. Certain it was, in any event, that Communist China felt by mid-1952 that the point of diminishing returns had been reached in Korea.

Further high-level political discussions between the Russians and the Chinese were now required. The most pressing problem was the joint consideration of issues outstanding under the agreements of February 1950 on the Chinese Changchun railway and Port Arthur. Thus, in the early autumn of 1952, a delegation headed by Chou En-lai flew to Moscow for new negotiations with the Soviet leaders. In mid-September, an official communiqué outlined the areas of agreement. The Soviet government was to transfer to China, with full title and without compensation, all Russian rights in the joint management of the Chinese Changchun railway and all property belonging to it. A second exchange of notes declared that the Chinese government "suggests and asks the Soviet government to agree to postpone the withdrawal of Soviet troops from the jointly-used Chinese naval base of Port Arthur" until peace treaties had been concluded between the Communist governments and Japan. This exchange of notes, incorporating Peking's "request" and Moscow's "agreement," was retroactively made a component part of the Sino-Soviet Treaty of 1950.

Implementation of these revised arrangements proceeded on schedule. The transfer of the Manchurian rail network from joint Sino-Soviet to full Chinese control was carried out at a formal ceremony in Harbin at the end of 1952. This was a significant event in the Communist bloc, as it marked one of the first instances in Stalin's post-1945 career when the Russians had voluntarily relinquished valuable economic

rights once they had been acquired. While giving up its control over the principal railway in Manchuria, Moscow tightened and prolonged its hold on the important Far Eastern naval base of Port Arthur. In view of the generally unsettled situation in the Far East and the continued military stalemate in Korea, it is possible that Communist China, possessing only a tiny naval force of its own, may have felt in the autumn of 1952 that the continued garrisoning of Soviet forces there was actually desirable from the standpoint of its national security. The terminology of the notes exchanged was nevertheless of interest in indicating the deliberate care apparently taken to demonstrate that the extended stay of Russian forces in Port Arthur was at China's request and by China's grace. The net result, in any event, was that the Soviet Union continued to maintain its own military and naval establishment at a major base within Chinese territory.

The negotiations of August and September 1952 also touched upon the issue of Outer Mongolia. The three governments —"with a view to strengthening their mutual economic and cultural ties"—worked out a tripartite Sino-Soviet-Mongol agreement on the construction of a new strategic rail link through the Mongolian People's Republic, to connect the rail systems of the Soviet Union and Communist China. This agreement, concluded in 1952, was not announced publicly by the Communists until two years later, in October 1954.

It seems likely that Chou En-lai's negotiations in Moscow must also have dealt with the Korean war, which was dragging into its third year with no clear indication of an armistice, and with no slackening of Communist military commitment in Korea. There was, however, no public mention of this subject, nor of Sino-Soviet economic relations, although it was clear that the issue of long-term Russian assistance was of pressing concern to the Chinese Communists as they prepared to move into their first Five-Year Plan of "large-scale economic construction," scheduled to begin in 1953. Indeed, after Chou En-lai and some of his delegation had returned to Peking late in September 1952, other experts and advisers who had accompanied him to Moscow stayed behind, apparently to continue detailed economic negotiations which lasted well into the following year.

An event of major significance in the Communist world at this time was the Nineteenth Congress of the Communist Party of the Soviet Union, held in October 1952. The first since 1939, this Congress was an important general gathering of Communist parties, with many sending their most senior leaders to Moscow for the occasion. The Communist Party of China was represented by Liu Shao-ch'i, who offered the official greetings of the Chinese party to the Congress at the session of October 8.

That Mao Tse-tung should have selected Liu Shao-ch'i to speak for the Chinese Communist Party at the Soviet party Congress was not surprising, for Liu had clearly established his pre-eminence as deputy to Mao in the realm of party affairs in China. This was Liu's first trip to Moscow since the distant days when he had studied there as a neophyte of the Comintern from 1920 to 1922, and it would be interesting to speculate on his personal impressions and reactions to the changes which had taken place in the Soviet capital. On his 1952 trip Liu remained in Moscow for slightly over three months. Yet his return to Peking in mid-January 1953 was accompanied only by the briefest of official announcements which told nothing except that he had been met at the airfield by virtually the entire membership of the Political Bureau of the Chinese Communist Party. Nor did Peking make any subsequent statements regarding his trip, the subject of his negotiations, if any, with the Russians, or the degree of success of his mission. That this visit, the most extended stay in Moscow of any key member of the Chinese Communist Political Bureau since 1950, was devoid of significance is doubtful. There would seem little reason—aside from medical consultation—for a senior Communist with the manifold responsibilities which Liu had in Peking to linger in the Soviet Union for over fourteen weeks except for the purpose of conducting serious discussions. The fact that his extended sojourn in Moscow took place during the final months of Stalin's life offers grounds for speculation. But the visit was, and remains, an enigma.

Many aspects of the relations between Moscow and Peking during the Stalin period are still obscure. It is not clear, for example, how far Stalin may have attempted to go in penetrating the internal control apparatus of the Chinese Communist dictatorship. It is, however, reasonably clear that he was reluctant to cast the People's Republic of China in what might be construed to be a co-starring role on the international Communist stage.

But if the director was aging and obdurate, Communist China—the youthful aspirant from the East—was both resilient and realistic, confident that its very energy would ensure general recognition in the end. Whatever Mao Tse-tung's private estimates may have been during these years, he apparently felt it important during the final weeks of Stalin's life to lay public emphasis upon the essential solidarity of the Sino-Soviet bloc in checking any "aggressive moves of imperialism" in the Far East; upon the lack of strain in Moscow-Peking relations; and upon the continuing Russian support for Peking in the pursuit of the basic—still unattained—national goals of China.

Howard L. Boorman

SOVIET POLICY IN OUTER MONGOLIA

After the communist victory in China and the withdrawal of Soviet troops from Manchuria, North Korea was the only newly won area of Soviet influence in Asia that was molded on East European lines and given satellite status. However we have not yet dealt with Outer Mongolia, a Soviet satellite in fact if not in name since 1924.

In the twentieth century the status of Outer Mongolia, which has been discussed sporadically in the United Nations, has been very ambiguous in the eyes of the non-Communist world. The Mongolian People's Republic has apparently claimed to be an independent state ever since it was formally established in 1924. For over two decades, however, the Soviet Union was the only state which maintained diplomatic relations with it or recognized it as an independent political entity.

Outer Mongolia was for many years a persisting political and diplomatic issue between the governments of China and Russia. Aside from a short-lived tripartite agreement concluded between Tsarist Russia, China, and Mongolia in 1915, the problem was in diplomatic limbo until the Sino-Soviet Treaty of August 14, 1945, and the subsequent plebiscite, the results of which, to nobody's surprise, were reported as overwhelmingly in favor of "independence." In January 1946, the National Government of China recognized the Mongolian People's Republic as an independent state, but this formal gesture on China's part was not followed by the establishment of diplomatic relations.

Immediately after the establishment of the Central People's Government in Peking, Marshal Choibalsan, then Premier and Foreign Minister of the Mongolian People's Republic, notified Peking, on October 6, 1949, of the decision of his government to establish diplomatic relations with the People's Republic of China and to exchange diplomatic representatives. Chou En-lai, the Foreign Minister in Peking, at once agreed.

The question of Sino-Mongol relations within the Communist bloc had to await a settlement of far more important questions. In February 1950, at the time of the conclusion of the new Sino-Soviet Alliance, the status of Outer Mongolia was formally dealt with in an exchange of notes between Chou En-lai and Vyshinsky. The two governments agreed that the treaty concluded in August 1945 was now null and void, and that "the independent status of the Mongolian People's Republic is fully guaranteed as a result of the plebiscite of 1945 and the establishment with it of diplomatic relations by the People's Republic of China." It is interesting to note that the first step in the new pattern of Sino-Soviet cooperation, a step which affected Outer Mongolia, was arranged directly by the Russians and the Chinese Communists without Mongol participation. This was the agreement, signed in Moscow on March 27, 1950, which provided for the establishment of a Sino-Soviet Civil Aviation Company, one of whose lines was to fly from Peking to Irkutsk by way of Kalgan and Ulan Bator, capital of the Mongolian People's Republic.

It was not until after the outbreak of the

From Howard L. Boorman, *Moscow-Peking Axis* (New York, 1957), pp. 166–173. Reprinted by permission of the Council on Foreign Relations, Inc.

Korean war in June 1950 that Peking and Ulan Bator proceeded to exchange diplomatic representatives. On July 3, 1950, Bayaryn Jargalsaihan, the first Mongol ambassador accredited to a Chinese government in the twentieth century, called on Mao Tse-tung. And one week later Chi Ya-t'ai, a Mongol by origin, presented his credentials as the first official Chinese representative to Ulan Bator since 1921.

Since 1950 the pattern of Sino-Mongol-Soviet relations has developed gradually, almost imperceptibly. Many problems are still unanswered; many issues are still in doubt; many basic questions of attitude and orientation are still unclear. But one thing is certain: Outer Mongolia, like all areas in Eastern Asia, cannot be isolated, much less insulated, from the broad implications of the fact of total Communist control on the mainland of China and from the political and strategic implications of Communist China's growing power. . . .

In broader terms, it does not appear likely that the issue of Outer Mongolia is of sufficient political importance to cause basic difficulties within the Sino-Soviet alliance in the near future. It is doubtful that the Chinese Communist leaders are capable of challenging Russian primacy at this time. It is still true, as it has been for many years, that the senior Mongol Communist leaders in Ulan Bator are oriented toward Russia, not China. Their military alignment is delineated in the Soviet-Mongol Treaty of Friendship and Mutual Assistance of February 1946, and Ulan Bator has no comparable treaty with Peking. One *tughrik*, the unit of currency in Outer Mongolia, is still equivalent to one ruble, and the recently completed rail line is Russian-style broad gauge across Outer Mongolia to the Chinese border.

Possibly, therefore, it is more realistic to view the Mongolian People's Republic, not as a major area of immediate political contention between Communist China and the Soviet Union, but rather as an increasingly important geographic area across which the two Communist giants are strengthening their strategic and economic links. Neither Moscow nor Peking has any interest in stirring up potentially disruptive issues of Mongol nationalism or pan-Mongolism, and it appears that the leaders in both capitals are capable of resolving the larger issues involved in their policies toward Mongolia within the general framework of the Sino-Soviet coalition.

Without opportunity for independent investigation in Outer Mongolia itself, it would be presumptuous to attempt to estimate the degree of pro- or anti-Russian or pro- or anti-Chinese sentiment which now prevails among the Mongols there. But the feelings and ambitions of the non-Communist Mongols, no less than the strategic interests of the Soviet Union and Communist China, are still to some extent involved in the politics of the area. The observations of one student of contemporary Mongolia may be pertinent in defining that elusive factor, the Mongol national tradition.

In any case it is remarkable that though faced with powerful neighbors, the individual Mongol has tried to retain one quality which is omitted from so-called Marxist interpretations of events — his ardor for independence, which is as much part of his nature as it is that of the eagle.

It befits the Mongol's pride in his past, for it is his country's earlier history and not his immediate ancestors (as with the Chinese) on which his heart is set. It falls in with his sturdy, but easy-going nomadic life; with the vast spaces of his land, difficult to control from the center, and with the mobility of his constant companion and other self — the Mongol pony. The Mongol can pitch his tent, i.e., his home, just in front of the imposing new buildings of the capital or move it out of reach of stony walls and officials. (In any case, that is what he would like to do, whatever restrictions may exist as to the moving into or moving out of Ulan Bator.) No wonder therefore that he has always shown a strong aversion to the building of railways in and across his country.

Still more must the many manifestations of Soviet-inspired planning in an economy of scarcity run counter to their individualistic habits. Their breeding and rearing of sheep and other cattle was in fact highly inefficient in the past, but with the coming into being of the Mongolian People's Republic they have been deprived of the right to sell the cattle at the place and in the manner they liked. We realize that they are now protected from the sharp business practices of the Chinese merchants. But even supposing such do not obtain at all in any form under the new conditions, there will always remain some human beings endowed with enough naiveté — and the travellers are legion who have testified as to this enthralling characteristic of the Mongols — who prefer being cheated as free men of the plains to being shielded as controlled men of "collectives," "artels," etc.

SOUTH EAST ASIA

Turbulent South East Asia seemed to present an ideal opportunity for Soviet intervention in muddy colonial waters at the end of the Second World War. In the event, great chances for communist expansion in the area between 1945 and 1948 were hopelessly lost. Why was this so? Stalin was more concerned with internal affairs and with the delicate situation in Eastern Europe, which was easier to supervise due to the presence of the Red Army. Eastern Europe offered a much more convenient field for the imposition of Soviet communism as developed by Stalin. The area had sizable industries and possibilities of economic expansion together with a growing proletariat susceptible to communist propaganda. In Asia Stalin was confronted by lethargic peasant economies to which the Soviet export model would have great difficulty in adapting itself without considerable modification: Stalin had neither the right character nor the right age for indulging in experimentation.

Furthermore, it was events in Europe that first set the communist and capitalist powers against one another, and although this antagonism was eventually to have great repercussions in China and in the Far East, in these areas it was not initially of the kind that urged Stalin to speed up the communization process in Eastern Europe. The mere proximity of Soviet and British armies in Europe, where Bonn, the capital city of West Germany was only a little over 120 miles from Soviet-controlled Thuringia, increased the neurosis that led to the cold war. The postwar struggle between the two political systems came into focus much more slowly in Asia. During the war period the United States had often been critical of British imperialism, and for their part the British, and not the Russians, were the first to lead the campaign against the American assumption of sole authority in Japan. At Yalta Roosevelt and Stalin had apparently come to an amicable agreement over the future of China: only at the end of 1945 did Russia and the United States clash over the situation in that country.

Soviet political thought on the introduction of communism in Asia remained extremely scholastic in nature. Theoretical wrangles over the various stages of Marxist development in Asian countries were bereft of any relevance to actual conditions in the area. The existence of the many multi-racial societies in South East Asia was ignored, and no new solution was put forward with regard to the economic problems connected with under-development. By preserving his dichotomic view of the world, Stalin lumped together the capitalist nations and their ex-colonies in the same camp and thus failed to grasp the opportunity of wooing over the infant governments in Asia at the time when colonial passions were most heated.

Once again the economist viewed the Asian scene with more foresight than his political masters; he reasoned that the great accumulation of sterling credits by a free country like India demonstrated that political and economic independence could be achieved gradually in ex-colonial territories: but for Stalin India still remained a lackey of imperialism.

The result of Moscow's inability, lack of interest, and rigidity was that communism remained a virtually irrelevant factor in South East Asia in the vital years 1944 – 48. Independence was achieved in India and Pakistan in August 1947 and in Burma in February 1948. The dissolution of the Comintern in 1943 was not followed by an indication from Moscow as to whether the line of the United Front should be continued or not, and its only direct successor with ties in Asia, the World Federation of Trade Unions, established in February 1945, gave no substantial aid to Asian communists. A trickle of confused guidance came from the communist parties of Europe, which was all there was to go on except for scattered Soviet press and radio statements. The dithering attitude of national communist parties in Asia was in sharp contrast to that of the nationalist leaders, who were quite sure that independence was their aim and rose to power on their convictions.

Communist lack of initiative was evident in all areas except Vietnam. In Indonesia the communist party found itself taking part in a coalition supporting the moderate Sjahrir government against the more strongly anti-Dutch nationalists. Burma also presented a pretty picture of communist disarray. Three political groups considered themselves Marxists; one of them put forward a variant of the heretical policy advocated by the American Earl Browder, to the effect that there was no need to attack the imperialist power, since it had joined in the revolutionary movement of its own accord.

The Malayan communist party got off to a better start by organizing the most efficient resistance movement to Japanese occupation in all Asia. It was kept together by fierce Chinese nationalism and was virtually an extension of the Chinese communist party. After the Japanese surrender, however, the party dissipated its efforts in attempting to dominate the labor movement in Malaya instead of continuing with the guerrilla struggle which might have carried it on to victory in 1945.

Indochina provided the only bright communist hope in the immediate postwar years. The brilliant communist leader Ho Chi Minh proclaimed the "Democratic People's Republic of Vietnam" in September 1945. In May 1946 he signed an agreement with the French for the inclusion of an independent Vietnam within the French Union, but the incompatibility of his regime and French rule resulted in the outbreak of open war in December 1946. Ho Chi Minh was the only resolute communist leader thrown up by the Asian nationalist movement. He owed nothing to support from Moscow, indeed he came to victory on the strength of his independence from the Kremlin line, which originally played down his achievements at first because they were embarrassing to the French communists, who occupied a more central position in Soviet foreign policy. Ho Chi Minh embarked on open resistance about one year before Russia finally made her intentions in Asia clearer with the proclamation of a renewed "hard" line.

Stalin's decision to accelerate the creeping advance of communist influence in Europe through the creation of the Cominform in September 1947 and his subsequent power thrusts in Czechoslovakia, Berlin, and Yugoslavia had their counterparts in Asia, where his concept of slow infiltration had met with much less success than in Eastern Europe. The onset of open civil war and the repeated victories of the Communist forces in China after the early months of 1947 gave him encouragement. But whereas the continued momentum of the Chinese communist effort over many years bore fruit with the establishment of the People's Republic of China in 1949, Russia's late start in Asia on a militant basis paid far lower dividends.

Although the chief mouthpiece of the new line, the Youth Conference held in Calcutta in February 1948, had been arranged in Prague as early as August 1947, a month before the formation of the Cominform, it came more than two years late to have much impact. This was illustrated by the sending of two Burmese delegations to the conference. The smaller one was communist-inspired and dedicated to the overthrow of the newly independent Burmese government which, however, was represented by the larger delegation. Nationalist groups had already won the ascendancy in the majority of Asian countries and for the most part remained impervious to armed communist uprisings after 1948.

Moscow changed its strategy, but hopelessly outmoded theory still prevailed. In the course of one of the main addresses to the conference, Palme Dutt of the British communist party referred to the "veiled imperialism under the form of slave-controlled 'independence'" by which India and other ex-colonial territories were still supposed to be bound to their mother countries.

Only after 1952 did the Soviet leaders realize the true strength of noncommunist nationalist governments in Asia and turn to their third postwar policy: wooing them with gifts instead of ignoring or openly attacking them. But even this more realistic line was to achieve only mediocre success by 1961. The golden opportunities existing in the period immediately after 1945 had gone, perhaps forever.

Direction of Asian uprisings from Moscow was at first as indecisive as the previous policy. In his report to the first Cominform meeting Zhdanov had little to say on the subject of Asia, and up till the end of 1948 the communist party of India, the most important in Asia after the Chinese party, was unsure as to whether its new "left" strategy met with Moscow's approval. Coordination of the communist movements in the area was finally handed over to the Permanent Liaison Bureau of the World Federation of Trade Unions, established at the conference of Trade Unions of Asia and Australasia held in Peking in November 1949. The Chinese, not the Russian, member of the Bureau apparently directed its activities. After the communist victory in China, Chinese influence over communist movements in South East Asia increased substantially mainly among Chinese minorities in the area.

Insurrections broke out in Burma, Malaya, and Indonesia within six months of the Calcutta conference. None of them was successful, although those in Burma and Malaya caused trouble. Only in Indochina did Ho Chi Minh move on from strength to strength. In January 1950 the Peking regime accorded communist Vietnam diplomatic recognition, and Moscow followed suit shortly afterwards.

THE KOREAN WAR

China's direct participation in the Korean war, which represented the climax of Soviet efforts in Asia to enforce the new hard line after 1948, added to her stature within the communist world. Korea had been divided into two areas at the end of the Second World War: the North Korean government was recognized by the Russians in October 1948, and the Southern Korean Republic by the United States in January 1949. Both powers withdrew their troops from the peninsula, but in June 1950 the North Korean army, trained and equipped by the U.S.S.R., attacked South Korea by advancing over the thirty-eighth parallel.

It is highly probable that the U.S.S.R. encouraged this intervention. The Korean war appeared as the natural climax to aggressive Soviet action in Asia. Although Stalin thought initially that the North Koreans would win without any Western intervention, the war turned out to be advantageous for the Soviet Union from the strategic point of view since it tied down large Western forces in a remote area of the world.

Politically it confirmed the fresh bonds between communist China and the Soviet Union. If it was won over, the Korean peninsula would prove a valuable asset to a land-locked power that had previously engaged in long struggles with Britain for the control of the Turkish Straits, and with Japan for Korea itself. Finally, the peninsula pointed like a dagger at southern Japan. Success in Korea might easily lead to the rise of communism in Japan. Left to her own devices,

Japan would probably reemerge as a major power in the Far East, thus discouraging Chinese aggression in the area and also offering China trading opportunities that could pull her away from economic dependence on the U.S.S.R.

The Soviet-inspired thrust into South Korea and the ninety-day occupation which followed provide a unique picture of a coup arranged in Moscow which eventually failed; in Eastern Europe Soviet military occupation had always been succeeded by political communization, thanks to the lack of hostile military forces.

Through the summer of 1950 Seoul, the capital of South Korea, was subjected to propaganda techniques familiar in Eastern European capitals.

J. W. Riley, Jr. and W. Schramm

THE REDS TAKE A CITY

Seizure of Radio Seoul was the first recorded action of the occupation forces in respect to the communications system. They began at once to broadcast messages to the populace: Your government has fled, the People's Republic is now in control. Go back to your work. Everyone will be forgiven if he goes back to work.

It seems strange that Radio Seoul, which had an output of 35 kilowatts and covered all Korea, should be so immediately available to them. When it became clear that the city could no longer be held, it would seem that good military policy would have dictated its destruction or immobilization by the South Koreans. Possibly the Rhee government, which broadcast a fighting message shortly before its precipitous flight, wanted to keep the station on the air to cover its departure; perhaps it was due to the presence of fifth-column activity within the station; or it may have been simply that no adequate demolition plan existed.

The North Koreans brought with them men from their own radio system for the top personnel jobs of Radio Seoul (the chief engineer had been trained in Moscow). Every effort, however, was made to keep the station's lower personnel, particularly the technicians, in their jobs. The engineers, the writers, the announcers, were assured that they had nothing to fear if they would co-operate. Thus, the occupation government controlled the program content but the work of putting it on the air was carried on by the usual South Korean personnel.

All seven newspapers in Seoul were suspended by the occupation authorities. In their place, they reinstated the *People's Daily News* and the *Liberation Daily News*, two papers previously suspended by the R.O.K. government because of their Communistic lines. It appears they reinstated also the South Korean Communist editors of the earlier publications. The papers were nationalized. They were printed in Seoul's largest newspaper offices which had been confiscated for the purpose. All news services except TASS were also forbidden. In

J. W. Riley, Jr., and W. Schramm, *The Reds Take a City* (New Brunswick, 1951), pp. 103–107. Reprinted by permission of Rutgers University Press.

addition to TASS, most of the news that was to be printed came from the many releases and articles sent to the newspaper offices by the Public Information Office. Here, too, we see the common pattern in operation: continue to use the same technical personnel (printers, circulation men, etc.), but put the control of the policy line and content into the hands of the Party and the government (Communist editors, TASS, the Public Information Office).

For several weeks these newspapers were distributed gratis, apparently in the ratio of one paper to every six or eight homes. Each family which received a copy was asked to read the paper, then hand it to a neighbor. Then, after several weeks a charge was made for the papers, although apparently some free circulation did continue. After the occupation had ended, it was impossible to obtain accurate information on circulation trends and patterns.

Control of the motion pictures shown in Seoul theatres was maintained through the Cultural Bureau of the Home Ministry. United States and British films were excluded. It was estimated that three out of every five films shown were of Russian origin. A few films from China or other "non-capitalist" countries were also shown. Pictures were chosen for their ideological and propagandistic content, and there appears to have been a considerable repetition of films shown.

During the first few weeks of occupation, admission to the theatres was free, which contributed greatly to the popularity of the occupation government and kept attendance high. Then, so it is said, one night during the performance the theatre doors were locked and all able-bodied men of military age in the audience were seized and conscripted into the army. As a result attendance thereafter fell to a small percentage of its former size. This story is encountered so often there seems little reason to doubt it.

The same news and many of the same articles would appear in both newspapers, and the newspapers would often be read over the radio. The same political articles would be sent by the Public Information Office to both papers and radio, and news for all the media was filtered through TASS. Reports all agree that there was a great sameness of content in all mass communications during the occupation period regardless of media. The movies, with their strong ideological content, repeated the same line, with many of the same illustrations, that was given in the newspapers and on the radio.

There is also general agreement that in the newspapers, radio, movies, there was a high percentage of formalized political content — political speeches and discussions, letters and messages to and from leading Communists, explanation of doctrinary points. This obviously was at the cost of entertainment on the radio and of social news in the papers. "Radio Seoul," said one resident, "was just talk, talk, talk." "There was no charm in press and radio," said another. "The radio was just mechanical propaganda," said a writer. "Of course the Communists didn't have a privately owned press," a publisher remarked wryly, "they only had to consider what went in, not how nor what the people thought of it."

The Communists, of course, depended on their monopoly to remove their need of competing for an audience. They did not have to worry if their newspapers and radio programs were a little on the dull and preachy side. They conceived the press and radio, and especially the former, as a kind of textbook, and used them as such. At the culture hours, the newspaper was read to the meeting. "We had to pass on to others the exact content of the speeches given by leaders without adding a single word of our own," explained one Seoul resident.

Never forgetting their ultimate purpose, the Communists made several important changes in media form and content. To reach the larger audience which was more familiar with Korean phonetic characters than with the more commonly printed Chinese ideographs, use of the Korean characters was emphasized. There is also testimony that they rearranged the contents of the papers to make them easier for unlearned readers to use. On Radio Seoul they frequently reserved spots for laborers and farmers to be interviewed and to speak their political thoughts.

Such changes as these, of course, were made as a gesture to their audience. Changes were also made in the interest of building up the Party. They used the front page of the newspaper for speeches by Russian Communist leaders or for messages to and from Kim Il Sung. On the radio, they programmed a generous amount of military music, and a great many political talks. These talks were "sometimes one and a half hours," one respondent said, and were "often read mechanically, without pause, from the newspaper." They carried an uncommon amount of abuse for the United States and the United Nations, but only favorable news when it concerned the Communists.

During the ninety days of occupation, it appears the Communists did not accomplish too much through the radio and other mass media. There are indications that, if there had been time to develop their program further, public reaction might have been more responsive. Another factor operated against immediate Communist success. Their audience was one which had been accustomed to a relatively free press and it was not wholly isolated from an entertaining radio. Many complained that the news was the same in all media. Some said they became surfeited with the mutual admiration of the top Communists. One person interviewed, however, said, "The information we got through the press and radio was just like the contents of a textbook on Communism." Perhaps he had come nearer the Communists' purpose than he realized.

THE END OF THE KOREAN WAR

Russian and Chinese hopes in Korea were dashed by the swift intervention of American and eventually United Nations troops under General MacArthur. No Soviet veto was cast against this action, because the Soviet delegate had quitted the Security Council in January 1950 in protest at the rejection of communist China as a member of the United Nations, and he had not returned. After initial hesitations, the United Nations forces repulsed the North Koreans and in October 1950 advanced over the thirty-eighth parallel, approaching the Soviet and Chinese borders. This move provoked an attack by Chinese "volunteers" who in their turn threw back MacArthur's troops. Truce negotiations began in July 1951 and went on for two years until after Stalin's death. Efforts on the part of the Japanese communists to disrupt political life in Japan at this time met with little success. In September 1951 the United States signed a peace treaty with Japan but was not followed by the Soviet Union, communist China, or other Asian powers.

The effective resistance which the Soviet Union encountered in Berlin and Korea was eventually to persuade her leaders that they had run into a blind alley with the policy of the hard line enforced after the founding of the Cominform in 1947. But the lethargic manner in which the Korean war was allowed to drag out showed that no new positive policy lay ready at hand, and it was not until after the death of Stalin that a marked change came about in Soviet foreign policy.

III. Stresses and Strains in the Communist Bloc, 1953-1956

THE NEW COURSE

In the period covered by this chapter Soviet relations with the rest of the communist world departed widely from Stalinist traditions. At the Twentieth Congress held in 1956 Molotov was to say, "We not infrequently still remain prisoners of habits and patterns formed in the past. . . . We not infrequently still suffer from an underestimation of the new possibilities opened before us in the postwar period."

What were the "new possibilities" in the year of Stalin's death? In the first place the Soviet Union could now further its interests abroad from a home base that was immeasurably more secure economically and politically than it had been in 1945. Time appeared to be on the communist side in the bipolar struggle for the world which had arisen since the reaffirmation of the cold war. Malenkov's announcement to the Supreme Soviet in August 1953, that Russia as well as the United States possessed the hydrogen bomb, reinforced this view.

The communist homeland, which had survived alone until after 1945, was now surrounded by a protective zone of states with similar governments, none of which could as yet remotely contest Russia for the leadership of the communist bloc. Also, the carefully built-up group of states in Eastern Europe had been unexpectedly joined in 1949 by communist China. In March 1953 the only cloud of any dimension on the Soviet horizon was Yugoslavia. Soviet-Yugoslav relations were an omen of much future dissension within the Sino-Soviet bloc.

The course of future history may show that by the time of Stalin's death the world communist movement had reached an all-time peak in terms of solidarity, if not of geographical expansion.

No longer hindered by the whims of an aging dictator whose weakness lay in a rigid theory-bound view of Soviet foreign policy, the new leaders slowly adapted themselves to the realities of the world situation. The doctrine of peaceful coexistence announced at the Twentieth Party Congress in 1956 was merely the intellectual crystallization of the pragmatic moves made after Stalin's death. These moves were based on the hypothesis that the cold war in Europe had reached a stalemate; for the time being there seemed to be little chance of Soviet advances farther west. Further consolidation in Eastern Europe was therefore the chief aim, and this included a settlement of the German and Austrian questions which would be favorable to Russia.

Subsequently more attention could be paid to Asia and other parts of the world where there were opportunities for communist subversion.

In Eastern Europe the aim of consolidation was not realized during this period, and it became an even wilder dream after the Polish and Hungarian uprisings of 1956. The Soviet Union's own policy prevented its implementation as much as did recalcitrance on the part of the countries under Soviet influence. At the time of Stalin's death men like Rákosi in Hungary, Bierut in Poland and Ulbricht in East Germany were willing to submit to consolidating trends in Soviet policy, as they had been in the past. But being loyal Stalinists they were ill-equipped to understand and imitate the subtle gyrations of the new "soft" line in Soviet policy carried out by a somewhat undecided collective leadership. Furthermore they did not agree with the wing of the collective leadership headed by Malenkov, which increased attention to consumer goods production and slowed the pace of heavy industrial growth; this was anathema for East European Stalinists.

There were, it is true, influential communists near the top of the East European parties who wholeheartedly agreed with Malenkov's New Course. But their views on other subjects veered even further away from the Stalinist line and did not coincide with those of any member of the Soviet collective leadership. They were eager to acquire some measure of independence from Moscow in matters of economic planning and the conduct of their foreign relations.

Thus within the Soviet-controlled countries of Eastern Europe the collective leadership had to choose between two unpalatable alternatives — on the one hand, the subservient Stalinist bosses in power, who knew only too well how to align themselves with Moscow and carry out a policy of consolidation, but who looked askance at the new elements of Soviet domestic and foreign policy; on the other hand, slightly less prominent leaders, who could be relied upon to implement the new line, but who were likely to resist a policy of consolidation. Indeed their views contained more than a whiff of Titoism.

The years between the death of Stalin and the final settlement of the problems raised by the Hungarian revolution in 1956 witnessed the evolution of a makeshift compromise between the Stalinist and Titoist extremes. The Soviet attempt to impose the frequently conflicting policies of consolidation *and* relaxation met with numerous setbacks and opened up wide rifts in the governments of some of the East European countries. The uncertain course of Russian policy, caused by the changing fortunes of the members of the rapidly disintegrating Soviet collective leadership, only served to enhance the general instability. Until the emergence of Khrushchev as Stalin's successor in the summer of 1957, Soviet foreign policy in Eastern Europe presented a bewildering picture, both with regard to its implementation by the Russians and its reception in the countries concerned.

The immediate reaction to Stalin's death both in government circles and among the masses in Eastern Europe was almost the opposite of that in Russia. At first there was no change in Stalinist policies at the top, but considerable ferment occurred at lower levels. As might be expected, Czechoslovakia and Bulgaria, both heavily committed to Stalinism, continued to apply the old hard line. In June 1953 the Czech government enforced a severe currency reform in an effort to make the labor force work harder; as late as September 1954 trials reminiscent of the later Stalinist period were staged in Bulgaria. There was also no immediate change of policy in Poland, where it was announced that Gomulka, who had been removed from power in the purges of 1949, was about to be tried.

On the other hand the summer of 1953 was marked by the first wave of serious popular outbreaks in Eastern Europe (the second wave, far more significant in its implications, was kept back until the summer and autumn of 1956). In June a strike occurred at the former Skoda works in Pilsen, Czechoslovakia, and in the same month a general strike and disturbances on a much larger scale took place in Eastern Germany. The local police was unable to quell the disorder in Eastern Germany and Soviet troops intervened.

After the initial upheavals in Eastern Europe the Soviet Union attempted to impose a system which appeared to come closest to Malenkov's domestic line of economic relaxation, while conserving Stalin's political ideas. Following on Malenkov's announcement of the New Course on August 8, 1953, planning commissions in Eastern Europe adapted their programs to the Soviet model; a brake was put on the development of heavy industry and greater attention was paid to the output and exchange of consumer goods.

In the spring of 1954 the Council for Mutual Economic Aid was revived: it had been formed by Stalin in January 1949 to weld together Soviet-controlled economies in Europe but had remained a dead letter. It was now admitted, at least tacitly, that Stalin's effort to mold each East European country on Soviet lines had resulted in the uneconomic duplication of heavy industrial plants within national boundaries, thus making for over-investment in primary production and economic separatism. At the same time the transfer of scarce labor, materials, and foreign exchange from half-finished investment projects to consumer industries was considered ruinous by economists in Eastern Europe, where heavy industry was far less advanced than in the Soviet Union.

The pattern of East European agriculture in the years 1953–56 revealed the same muddled outline. Toward the end of 1953 substantial concessions were made to the peasants in Poland, Czechoslovakia, and Hungary. In some cases they were even allowed to revert to private farming after having been members of collectives. By 1954 a partial reaction to this policy set in.

Inevitably, economic relaxation brought in its wake hopes for some measure of political détente. The spark that set off the strike of the Czech workers at Pilsen was the currency reform which slashed their wages, but the memory of the short period of American occupation at the end of the war and the deeper remembrance of the more liberal past spurred them on to protest against the political regime as well. Symbolic gestures were made by East European governments in response to this and other outcries. In 1954 elections were held in some countries and National Fronts were revived temporarily in an effort to woo sectors of public opinion which appeared to be deviating from the party line. A more permanent liberal trend was imported from the Soviet Union: the execution of Beria and the considerable diminution of the powers of the secret police had direct repercussions in Eastern Europe, where to a great extent Soviet domination of the police was abandoned. The national police systems released their grip on the parties and the population.

In the period under review Hungary may be taken as an interesting, though untypical illustration of the impact of Soviet influence on the Eastern European countries. More than any other country in the area, Hungary reflected the vacillations in the Soviet attitude, and showed how economic changes led in turn to political innovations.

The wildly fluctuating reactions to Russian events and pressure, which were to culminate in armed revolt in 1956, were partly due to the internal situation in Hungary and partly to Soviet changes of mind. At the time of Stalin's death the Hungarian population was engaged in an industrial program which was more arduous than that existing in any other country of Eastern Europe and which had been hastily imposed on a backward economy. The political purges in Hungary had also been exceptionally harsh.

At one blow this legacy from the Stalinist era was removed in June 1953 by the replacement of the Premier, Mathias Rákosi, by Imre Nagy. Rákosi had been personally responsible for the policies applied prior to 1953, whereas Nagy was known to be a supporter of Malenkov's New Course. In fact the change in the government was arranged by the Soviet collective leadership at a meeting with Rákosi and Nagy in Moscow in May and June of 1953. The Soviet leaders apparently decided to apply their concept of a balance of power to the Hungarian political scene. Nagy was given the equivalent of Malenkov's post as chairman of the Council of Ministers, while Rákosi was maintained as First Secretary of the party, equivalent of the post that was to fall to Khrushchev in September of the same year.

Rákosi's views were, however, much more Stalinist than Khrushchev's, and Nagy's new economic program immediately led to demands for greater political freedom, which did not happen in the Soviet Union. The strain imposed on Hungary by a "collective leadership" made up of leaders with diametrically opposed views eventually proved too great. The collective leaderships broke up in both Russia and Hungary, with consequences that were far more violent in the latter country.

After his appointment, Nagy made various price reductions and wage increases, slowed down heavy industrial production, and abolished some compulsory agricultural deliveries to the state. Peasants were allowed to leave the collective farms in large numbers. The contrast with the pre-1953 period was very great. Political changes took place in the wake of economic reform. A serious effort was made to resuscitate the Independent People's Front which was now joined by "Titoists" newly released from prison.

In Hungary the political spring that had been wound by Moscow-inspired communists over the years since the end of the war was suddenly uncoiling and running down the Stalinist state machine. The mere fact that Hungary was now acting differently toward other East European countries showed that the rigid conformity to Russian practice of the period from 1948 to 1953 was rapidly becoming a thing of the past.

In the following passages Nagy explains and defends the working of the New Course in Hungary.

Imre Nagy

THE NEW COURSE IN HUNGARY

The Third Congress of the Hungarian Workers' Party confirmed the thesis that the June 1953 resolution of the Central Committee had opened a new course in the building of socialism in Hungary. Summarizing the resolutions in five points, the essential character, and specific traits of the New Course are defined and described on pages 31 to 33 of the congressional report of the Central Committee. However, the definition of the gist and specific traits of the New Course lacks a good theoretical foundation and is not complete or satisfactory.

A correct definition of the concept, essence, and character of the New Course is of great importance because the unclear definition of the essence of the New Course is responsible for certain views, according to which the New Course is tantamount to an anti-Marxist, rightist deviation. Such views and the charge of anti-Marxism-Leninism will reveal that the classics of scientific socialism alternately used the expressions of "course" (*étape*) and "period," meaning the same thing. The principle and concept of a "New Course" is,

therefore, not in contradiction with the theory of Marxism-Leninism. Stalin divided the New Economic Policy (NEP) into two "courses" or "periods," emphasizing that strategic tasks did not change in the former or in the latter course.

For an exact Marxist-Leninist theoretical definition of the New Course, needed to avoid misinterpretations or to refute them, and for amending the incomplete and inadequate statements concerning the New Course voiced at the Third Congress of the Hungarian Workers' Party, it must be established that the New Course initiated by the June 1953 resolution of the Central Committee did not set new strategic tasks for the Party. The former strategic task— laying the economic foundations of socialism and building socialism in Hungary— had been left untouched. Therefore, the policy of the New Course had been directed toward the solution of the old strategic task by changing and improving the former bad tactics. The New Course gives expression to this tactical change. Arguments on the terminology and charges of anti-

---

I. Nagy, *On Communism*, (New York, 1957), pp. 80–86, 128–135, 154–156. Reprinted by permission of Frederick A. Praeger, Inc.

Marxism are only forms in the fight against the important economic and political measures stipulated by the June resolution.

The main strategic task, the Party's strategy, is based on historic "turns" and embraces whole periods. Therefore during the period of transition from capitalism to socialism the strategy and its main goal remain unchanged. At the same time, however, there are definite changes within the given periods, which are best expressed by the word "course." Within the unchanged principal strategic direction, these changes are expressed in new tactics. Thus, in the *étapes* of development, *within* the strategy, there can be and definitely will be changes. Such a change, in Hungary, was the New Course, the new tactic.

One of the main characteristics of the transitional period is the struggle between capitalist and socialist elements. Within the transitional period, the economic and political goals of the New Course were determined by these same basic tasks. The economic policy of the New Course is, therefore, the proper application of the teachings of Marxism-Leninism to the specific Hungarian conditions, on the basis of specific traits in the transitional period and the objective needs of building socialism in the field of socialist transformation and development of the people's economy. . . .

It was a serious shortcoming of the New Course that in many important fields it brought about only half-solutions. The economic policy of the New Course showed serious shortcomings because of the resistance of the Party and state organs, especially in the field of economy, and also because objective economic laws were not always correctly applied as a result of not having been scientifically analyzed, and because specific Hungarian conditions were not clearly defined. The main error was not that we established the New Course in Hungary for building socialism, but rather the fact that we did not follow this course consist-

ently and fully. This, on the other hand, makes us draw the logical conclusion that the New Course must not be liquidated but rather should be fully realized, eliminating its shortcomings and paying great attention to those specific tasks that are necessitated by specific conditions in Hungary. . . .

Economic and political developments in the summer of 1953 necessitated the initiation of the New Course:

A. In the economic field we were faced with a completely hopeless situation. Main target figures in the economic plan were greatly exaggerated and impossible to meet. We had enforced the fulfillment of heavy industrial plans to a much too great extent. The rate and proportions of developing heavy industry were much higher than in countries that had more favorable conditions, and we had exceeded all the other People's Democracies in developing our heavy industry. Industry began to show a steady shortage of materials. The quality of products was deteriorating rapidly. Export difficulties became everyday phenomena, and foreign debts were rising steeply. Development of agricultural production had come to a standstill, and there was a danger of it going downhill altogether. The area of uncultivated land increased. The standard of living was deteriorating, and a further decrease became a certainty. The economic basis for the worker-peasant alliance had been shaken. Increasing dissatisfaction could be observed in the ranks of the workers' class. The keeping and consolidation of political power as the principal task facing the Party showed up in its full extent.

B. Politically, we had skipped several stages of development through which the Soviet Union had passed.

C. Faced with these specific conditions of our development, the Party should have done everything in its power to discuss the motives of its day-by-day policy with the membership, to teach the members how to form independent political opinions, to develop in the Party the practice of criticism coming from below, to realize the principle of collective leadership in all Party organs, and to apply consistently the Leninist principles of democratic centralism. Instead, the method of convincing by arguments was replaced by giving instructions. Criticisms and objections on the basis of principles or justified concern were branded more often than not as the voice of the enemy or at least as a petty bourgeois lack of judgment.

Economic difficulties piling up under such circumstances had to lead to the deterioration of the living standard, and consequently to a blow to confidence, to increasing mistrust, to the exaggeration of difficulties, and the belittling of achievements.

All this actually happened in the spring of 1953 and made it necessary that a turn be taken with the introduction of the New Course.

The government program for carrying out the June resolution was received with tremendous enthusiasm. The same enthusiastic reception was given by the Party members and the working people to resolutions on the restoration of socialist legality, the enforcement of the principle of collective leadership, the extension of democratism,

the greater assertion of criticism and self-criticism against dogmatism and schematism; on the struggle to be fought in the ideological and cultural fields; on a national cooperation resting on a wider basis; on the People's Front and the greater power given to local councils. All these resolutions were correct and necessary. Their correctness was proved by the unfolding political activity of the masses, by the flourishing of Party life, by the consolidation of the link between the Party and the masses, by the sudden invigoration of criticism and self-criticism, by the consolidation of the worker-peasant alliance, and by the greater trust of the nonproletarian masses in the state of the workers' class.

The freeing of the spirit of self-criticism and criticism brought about the inevitable consequence that the Party membership and the working masses themselves began to criticize the leadership. To a Communist, this should not have been a surprise: our Party has continuously emphasized that it was not afraid of frank criticism or self-criticism and was not worried that the enemy would try to take advantage of this. It was a mistake, however, that the Party did not give appropriate guidance to the extensive work of enlightenment and thus left the field open to counterpropaganda.

Nagy defends himself against the accusation that he opposed industrialization in general: it is interesting to note that in order to do this, he quotes Stalin's views on the subject in the 1920's; destalinization had not yet touched even the most revisionist East European country, and was only being vaguely hinted at inside Russia itself.

It can be ascertained from my own work done during the past twenty months in the field of socialist industrialization, that neither I nor the government of the Hungarian People's Republic under my leadership, nor its economic policy, have ever given up the idea of continuing socialist industrialization. On the contrary, it has been regarded from the very beginning as the principal means for building socialism. The June policy pointed out that within industry individual branches of the people's economy have to be regrouped, and that in the course of socialist industrialization consideration must be given to the fact that we are not building socialism alone, as the Soviet Union had to do it at one time for a long period; further that, with respect to industrialization, we must take into account our existing possibilities, the load that the country can support, and the international division of labor.

Nagy expresses himself with similar pungency on the heated problem of agricultural collectivization. He agreed to it in the long run, but opposed the notion, put forward by Gerö, one of Rákosi's close associates, that collectivization should be forced through as fast as possible, which in Nagy's view would lead "to the stifling of the rural productive forces and to a decrease in agricultural production."

We must also deal with Ernö Gerö's extreme "left-wing" agrarian views, before they bring about even greater chaos in the ranks of the Party and grievously damage our people's economy. The economic policies represented and directed by Ernö Gerö once did bring us to the brink of catastrophe in the summer of 1953, and according to the conclusions of the Central Committee's session of June 1953 were irresponsibly reckless policies. Then his anti-Party and anti-people views were revealed by unlimited forced industrialization, resulting in an overexpanded heavy industry that lacked the necessary conditions for development. Now, as he declared in his June 12, 1955, *Szabad Nep* article, "On the Way Up," he wants to put into operation the same conception in our agrarian development. In those days, as we know, Ernö Gerö excused the forced speed-up of industrialization in the raised Five-Year Plan by saying, among other things, that without this the socialist reorganization of agriculture could not be realized; on the other hand, he excused the forced speed-up of farm collectivization by saying that without it socialist industrialization could not be realized. He linked both aims to the prospect of a significant rise in living standards. In the course of the Five-Year Plan he didn't take into account the fact that for long years to come excessive industrialization would deprive our producers and consumers of the resources of the people's economy, while, on the other hand, the increase in the number of workers and the increased need to import raw materials require a significant increase in food production, even in the event of only a minimal increase in living standards. It became evident that agricultural production could

not be increased simultaneously with forced collectivization. The speeding of the socialist reorganization of agriculture presupposes a great increase in agriculture's productive forces, which would devolve primarily on heavy industry and the building industries. Inasmuch as heavy industry, under the First Five-Year Plan, primarily produced for itself—as a result of the improper trend of forced industrialization—the quantitative increase of industrial goods produced for agriculture lagged far behind the needs, in fact fell off in many areas. Yet, concurrently, the accelerated collectivization of agriculture demanded significant food reserves to insure proper supply of the working class and city dwellers in general; but we have not had such reserves since 1951, precisely because of the grave financial sacrifices demanded by forced industrialization.

One of the most important lessons of the First Five-Year Plan was that the resources of our people's economy cannot assure the simultaneous realization of two goals so huge as forced socialist industrialization and the forced collectivization of agriculture.

It seems Gerö either forgot this or, worse still, in the face of all experience, now is repeating the past mistakes that severely damaged our people's economy.

Gerö now goes so far that, after the increased forced industrial development of the Five-Year Plan—which without the June resolution and the subsequent New Course would have imperiled the existence of the People's Democracy—he proceeds to announce his plan for intensified collectivization. In the years 1949 through 1952 it was proved that the raising of agricultural production and living standards is an empty phrase when coupled with extreme industrialization and the emergency development of heavy industry. Party and state documents as well as statistical data show that agricultural production, and with it the living standards of the workers, have greatly declined. Now Ernö Gerö, simultaneously with a crash program for heavy industry, would have the Party and state plan not only to increase agricultural production significantly, but also to realize the plan for intensified collectivization. In the course of the First Five-Year Plan the country could not bear the double load of extreme industrialization and the increase of agricultural production; so at this point we can still less realize the triple programme of extreme industrialization, forced collectivization, and the increase of agricultural production without a drastic decline in the living standards of the workers.

THE RAPPROCHEMENT WITH YUGOSLAVIA, MAY 1955

It gradually became apparent to the more liberal Soviet leaders that a place could even be found for outlawed Yugoslavia within the looser system of communist states as it was now evolving. Yugoslavia's reentry into the communist bloc would be a big step toward consolidation in Eastern Europe. The slow rapprochement with Yugoslavia that took place from 1953 to 1955 was conducted entirely from the Soviet side, to the surprise and for the instruction of the rest of the communist bloc.

The Soviet approach was insistent. As early as April 29, 1953, the Yugoslav chargé d'affaires in Moscow was sounded out on the subject of reestablishing normal diplomatic ties. By the end of the year, no doubt with Russian encouragement, Bulgaria, Hungary, and Albania had entered into negotiations with Yugoslavia with the intent of reducing tension. Once again economic changes preceded political openings; a barter agreement between Russia and Yugoslavia was concluded in September 1954, and in May 1955 an announcement that a delegation of Soviet leaders was going to Belgrade with the aim of achieving "a further improvement of relations" heralded the decisive Russian move. It proved to be a twentieth century Canossa.

The Soviet delegation included Khrushchev, Bulganin, and Mikoyan, but Molotov was ostentatiously omitted. After making an abject apology in public for the way in which Yugoslavia had been treated since 1948, the Soviet Union proceeded to negotiate for an agreement. Russia's aim was to reestablish full party relations, but Tito not unnaturally wavered because in their apology the Soviet leaders frequently rejected the Cominform resolution of November 1949 accusing the Yugoslavs of many crimes, but little mention was made of the 1948 declaration, which had dealt explicitly with ideological errors. The joint statement issued at the end of the Soviet visit merely stressed the inter-state, as opposed to the inter-party, relations between the two countries, which were now to be renewed. Economic and cultural exchanges figured most prominently in the agreement, although lip service was paid to the desirability of ideological rapprochement.

This major diplomatic move on the part of the Soviet Union could not help but have far-reaching consequences, especially in the context of the other measures of relaxation that had been taken by Russia since the death of Stalin. Until May 1955 Eastern Europe could presume that her *economic* grievances would be heard to some extent; in May it became clear that even outright *political* opposition to the Soviet Union was not always followed by annihilation. Khrushchev's revelations on Stalin at the Twentieth Congress were the final stimulus responsible for the second and much larger wave of uprisings in Eastern Europe in 1956.

Amongst the Soviet leaders only Molotov appeared to foresee the dangers inherent in Soviet foreign policy. At a Presidium meeting in March 1955 he opposed the plan for a rapprochement with Yugoslavia and did not join the Soviet delegation to Belgrade two months later. At a plenary meeting of the Soviet Central Committee in July he was criticized for his opinion. He also wished to maintain the *status quo* as it existed at the time of Stalin's death with regard to a number of other foreign policy issues. For instance he did not agree to the proposed signing of peace treaties with Austria and Japan, nor to Khrushchev's and Bulganin's goodwill visits to Asia in this period. His obstinacy must have caused considerable embarrassment at first to Malenkov and Khrushchev, who both wanted changes in Soviet policy, although they did not agree on their extent. Stalin had delegated so little authority to his lieutenants that on his death no single Soviet statesman had an overall view of the political problems involved in running the country's affairs. The only man who had long experience of foreign policy was Molotov, who was thus in a position to influence and possibly to thwart his colleagues' intentions in this field.

Seweryn Bialer

SOVIET CONTENTION OVER YUGOSLAVIA

The political struggle between Khrushchev and Molotov over the Yugoslav problem is described below by Seweryn Bialer, a member of the Central Committee of the Polish Communist Party who had access to the minutes of the Soviet meetings at which the quarrels took place.

In the spring of last year, the Politburo held a meeting at which Molotov was criticized as Minister of Foreign Affairs for his attitude towards the Yugoslav problem and several other international problems. Molotov was accused of having hampered the reestablishing of Soviet-Yugoslav relations by all means.

Khrushchev and Molotov Battle Over Tito

Before the Khrushchev and Bulganin departure for Belgrade, the Politburo held another meeting at which Molotov opposed the visit. Molotov was for reestablishing international relations with Yugoslavia but, for ideological reasons, resisted reestablishment of Party relations with the Yugoslav Communist Party. What he had in mind was not only Khrushchev and Bulganin's visit to Belgrade but also the character of their visit.

These facts were given by Khrushchev in his opening speech to the secret part of the July Plenum. As a result of Politburo discussions, Khrushchev continued, Molotov still had not changed his attitude. The disagreement found its expression in the adoption of two Politburo resolutions. In one, the majority of the Politburo recognizes the necessity of the Belgrade visit and the necessity of attempting to reconstitute inter-Party relations with Yugoslavia. In the second resolution, Molotov's attitude

was described, appraised by Khrushchev and the rest of the Politburo, and a decision was taken to put it up for discussion at the earliest Plenum of the Central Committee of the CPSU.

At the July Plenum, Khrushchev once again charged Molotov with having prevented the reestablishment of international relations with Yugoslavia, and denounced his attitude on this issue as both erroneous and against the Party line.

Molotov Battles . . .

The stenographic record showed that Molotov addressed the meeting after Khrushchev's speech and explained his viewpoint. However, in the discussion which followed and lasted for several days, the Plenum of the CC declared itself against Molotov's position. In addition to Khrushchev, Bulganin, Mikoyan, Kaganovich, Susslov, and Shepilov criticized Molotov severely. The discussion was accompanied by a series of personal skirmishes, abusive remarks flowed freely, and time and again speeches were interrupted. This was particularly true of Molotov's speech.

I shall give an example. When Molotov was explaining his viewpoint that Party problems should not be discussed with Tito because Tito was anti-Soviet and his views far removed from Communism and rather close to those of anti-Communists,

From Seweryn Bialer, *Hearings before the Subcommittee of the Committee on Judiciary, U.S. Senate 84th Congress, Second Session on the Scope of Soviet Activity in the United States,* pp. 1562–63.

Khrushchev interrupted him, shouting: *"But in 1939 you could talk to Ribbentrop!"* Incidentally, it occurred to me while I was reading the minutes that the comparison to Ribbentrop was not very flattering for Tito.

. . . and Capitulates

As a result of the violent discussion, Molotov made a short declaration toward the end of the secret meeting, occupying not more than one page of the shorthand minutes, in which in an extremely formal manner, he listed Khrushchev's charges and admitted that they were well founded. He also said that he yielded to the Central Committee's view of the Yugoslav problem. His declaration was so formal that I had no doubt when I read it that it was only Molotov's attempt to save what still could be saved. It was an attempt to take away from Khrushchev all the arguments which could be used for Molotov's dismissal.

Allegedly "Impersonal" Encounter

The shorthand minutes showed that the discussion was full of Khrushchev's personal remarks about Molotov. Khrushchev therefore devoted a great deal of space in his closing speech to assurances that there was no question of a personal misunderstanding between him and Molotov. Personally, he said he had nothing against Molotov; his sole concern was Party matters. These assurances were so numerous that I understood them to mean their opposite. Besides, even in his closing comments, Khrushchev could not resist making a personal remark leveled at Molotov. He said, and I remember that passage extremely well, "Vyacheslav Mikhailovitch, all this is your wife's fault. It would be much better for you if you didn't listen to her. She pushes you and makes you ambitious. She is your evil spirit."

Such was the general outline of the showdown with Molotov at the secret session of the Plenum last July.

Nikita Khrushchev

SPEECH AT BELGRADE AIRPORT, MAY 6, 1955

Dear Comrade Tito, members of the government and leaders of the Yugoslav Communist League, dear comrades and citizens: . . .

The Soviet delegation has come to your country to determine, together with the Yugoslav government delegation, the roads for further development and consolidation of friendship and cooperation between our peoples, to consider our joint task in the struggle of our countries for prosperity, for reduction of tension, for strengthening peace in general and the security of peoples.

The peoples of our countries are linked by ties of long brotherly friendship and joint struggle against the enemy. This friendship and militant collaboration were particularly strengthened during the time of difficult trials in the struggle against the Fascist invaders during the Second World War. During these difficult years all the

Nikita Khrushchev, Speech on arrival at Belgrade Airport, May 26, 1955.

Soviet people followed with great feeling the heroic struggle of their Yugoslav brothers, headed by the Communists, and hailed with all their hearts the courageous feats in battle of the National Liberation Army of Yugoslavia under the leadership of Marshal Tito.

Our peoples will always remember that Yugoslav and Soviet soldiers joining forces in the battle for Belgrade, hit the enemy hard and liberated this ancient Slav city from the Hitlerite invaders. The peoples of the Soviet Union ardently welcomed the creation of the Federal People's Republic of Yugoslavia.

As we know, the best relations developed during those years between the peoples of the Soviet Union and Yugoslavia, between our states and our Parties. However, later these good relations were destroyed.

We sincerely regret what happened and resolutely reject the things that occurred, one after the other, during that period. On our part, we ascribe without hesitation the aggravations to the provocative role that Beria, Abakumov and others—recently exposed enemies of the people—played in the relations between Yugoslavia and the USSR.

We studied assiduously the materials on which the serious accusations and offenses directed at that time against the leaders of Yugoslavia had been based. The facts show that these materials were fabricated by enemies of the people, detestable agents of imperialism who by deceptive methods pushed their way into the ranks of our Party.

We are profoundly convinced that this period of the deterioration of our relations has been left behind us. For our part we are ready to do everything necessary to eliminate all obstacles standing in the way of complete normalization of relations between our states, of the consolidation of friendly relations between our peoples. . . .

The desire of Yugoslavia to maintain relations with all states both in the West and in the East has met with complete understanding on our part. We consider that the strengthening of friendship and ties between our countries will contribute to consolidation of peace in general.

Zbigniew Brzezinski

THE FORMATION OF THE WARSAW TREATY ORGANIZATION

In the same month that the Soviets went on pilgrimage to Belgrade, they cast out another line in their general attempt over this period to draw a slightly less rigidly totalitarian Soviet system. The idea of a defense pact uniting Eastern Europe against the capitalist powers ranged against them in the NATO alliance was received with customary submissiveness and some enthusiasm as well in Russia's communist satellites. An account of the structure and function of the Warsaw Treaty Organization up to 1960 is given below.

The Warsaw Treaty Organization is both a political and a military organization. Established formally on May 14, 1955, under the Treaty of Friendship, Cooperation, and Mutual Assistance, it is composed of eight of the twelve Communist States, with China "associated" but not a member, and North Korea, North Vietnam, and Mongolia remaining outside of the pact. It is thus primarily a European organization, serving externally as a counter to NATO, internally as the formal device for the perpetuation of close ties between the Soviet Union and its European satellites. In fact, to this day it constitutes the single most important formal commitment binding the European Communist states to the USSR, officially limiting their scope for independent action by precluding their participation in other alliance systems (Art. 7).

The founding meeting of the WTO provided for a Political Consultative Committee which was empowered to establish supplementary multilateral organs. The Committee exercised this power in its January 1956 Prague meeting by setting up a regular secretariat, with representatives from member states, and a standing commission for foreign policy co-ordination. The meeting also decided that the Committee was to meet not less than twice yearly. However, when Khrushchev ad-dressed the next consecutive meeting, he had to concede that "more than two years have passed since the Political Consultative Committee last met in Prague in 1956." Since the Committee did not convene again until February 1960, it appears that the 1956 decision has lapsed. Two hypothetical explanations may account for this: the resistance of the Poles to such meetings, or (what is more likely, since the Poles could hardly prevent them) the unwillingness of the Soviet Union to push the development of the WTO too far lest it become a genuine consultative organ.

At the present time, meetings of the Political Consultative Committee serve primarily as forums for the articulation of a common stand on important international issues and, in effect, for implicitly delegating the USSR to be the spokesman of the bloc in dealing with the West. The May 1958 session was primarily devoted to an analysis of the international situation, with special emphasis on the program which the Soviet leaders would submit at a summit meeting with the Western Powers. Particular stress was put on troop reductions within the bloc as proof of the bloc's stability and peaceful intentions. The 1960 meeting in effect served to endorse the position which the Soviet leadership was to adopt at the expected May 1960 summit

From Z. Brzezinski, "The Organization of the Communist Camp", *World Politics*, (January 1961), pp 176–178. Reprinted by permission of *World Politics*.

meeting, with the only discordant note coming from the Chinese observer, who attended the meetings in keeping with China's status as "associated" with the WTO.

Judging from the three sessions—the second and third lasting merely one day—it appears that the Political Consultative Committee does not serve as an active policy-making agency, comparable to some of the multilateral meetings of party chiefs. The political importance of the WTO is that (1) it provides a formal framework binding the various states together, (2) supplies the juridical basis for limiting the exercise of their sovereignty, and (3) serves as a useful forum for the articulation of unanimity, expressing ritualistically the bloc's support of Soviet foreign policy initiatives. It is significant that one of the charges most often cited against Imre Nagy was that he violated the unity of the bloc through his unilateral decision to leave the Warsaw Pact.

The essentially static, restrictive function of the WTO is evident also in its military aspects. The original agreement provided for a Unified Command of the armed forces of the signatories, and, indeed, the signing of the treaty was followed immediately by a communiqué announcing that a joint command had been set up. Soviet Marshal I. S. Konev was appointed commander-in-chief, another Soviet officer became joint chief of staff, and the command headquarters was to be situated in Moscow. Defense Ministers of the participating states have attended ostentatiously the three sessions of the Political Consultative Committee and Marshal Konev (recently replaced by Marshal Grechko) delivered reports to these sessions on the military situation. Probably some strategic "division of labor" has also been made. However, to the extent that it can be determined, this exhausts the military aspects of the WTO. The international military command has not been set up. The various states have not delegated their ranking officers to serve in it, nor have liaison officers been appointed. In this case, the Soviet Union's fear of arousing new anti-Soviet sentiments was combined with its desire not to share Soviet military secrets with its allies. Since the uprisings of 1956, the stationing of Soviet troops in East Europe has been regularized by bilateral agreements which used the Warsaw Treaty as their point of reference, but they could have easily been concluded independently of such a treaty.

CULTURE IN POSTWAR EASTERN EUROPE

Let us stand aside from the flow of politics in Eastern Europe for a while, and instead examine the effect of Soviet influence on cultural life in the area in the years 1945–1955. The Soviet example was constantly referred to in this period. In Eastern Europe education, the arts, religion, all had to take their cue from the Soviet model. Up till 1956 the Soviets managed to impose their system with increasing thoroughness; the slight "thaw" in the economic sphere which has been noted above was not at first accompanied by much relaxation in cultural life. Only after the Soviet Twentieth Party Congress in the spring of 1956 did the East European intelligentsia begin to throw off its chains.

Hugh Seton-Watson

CREATING A NEW INTELLIGENTSIA

The care of the intelligentsia consists of the professional class—the doctors, lawyers, engineers, and teachers. But as at present interpreted in Eastern Europe it extends also to a part of the bureaucracy and of the industrial managers and business experts. If the national economic plans are to be fulfilled, every man and woman possessing special skill or knowledge is urgently needed. But the pre-war intelligentsia was brought up in a spirit unsympathetic or hostile to communism. It was infected with the prejudices of bourgeois education. It had not mastered "Marxist-Leninist methodology," and was in fact unlikely ever to master it.

Consequently the treatment of the intelligentsia by the new regimes is a mixture of cajolery and persecution. They have continued to employ a large number of the former doctors, teachers, engineers, bureaucrats, and even army and police officers. Some experts, especially technicians and writers, are offered extremely generous salaries and material conditions. They have to work very hard, but they enjoy a good standard of living as long as they keep their job. They have, however, no real security. At any moment the communist leaders may have a bout of panic suspicion, or need a scapegoat for their own faults, or simply wish to make a few examples _pour encourager les autres_. Then without warning the unhappy manager, official or journalist is torn from his life of luxury and cast into prison, to appear in due course in court as an agent of Western imperialism, spying for the capitalists or defaming his country's good name, or deliberately sabotaging

production. The new regimes' attitude to the intelligentsia is in fact the same as that of the Soviet regime in the 'twenties. It inevitably induces unwillingness to take responsibility, and determination to please every whim of the new masters rather than perform the work the way that knowledge and experience would show.

The communists of course regard this as an unsatisfactory transitory stage. Their aim is to produce as quickly as possible a new intelligentsia, trained in Marxist-Leninist principles. This new intelligentsia will include not only the professions which in the West might be termed intellectual, but also the whole higher administrative personnel—the leading bureaucrats, the factory managers, the trade union bosses, and the cadres of the Communist Party itself. This new intelligentsia will not have a lower social standing than the workers and peasants; it will form the new ruling class, as is the case in the U.S.S.R. Of course even at present those administrators and experts who are docile Communist Party members enjoy greater social prestige than any other group. But for the most part they do not call themselves either intellectuals or bureaucrats, but "workers," though many have long abandoned the factory-bench for the life of professional party organiser, and some were never at the bench all their lives.

The new intelligentsia is to be created by the new system of education. The positive side of the new system is that poorer children get a better opportunity of mounting the educational ladder. Between the world wars, it is true, great progress was made in

From Hugh Seton-Watson, _The East European Revolution_ (New York, 1951), pp. 282–286. Reprinted by permission of Frederick A. Praeger, Inc. and Methuen & Co., Ltd.

education throughout Eastern Europe. Primary education was greatly developed, and where it was not effective the obstacles lay as much in the difficulty of communications and the prejudices of the parents as in the policy of the governments. Secondary and higher education were also greatly improved in comparison with the Russian or Ottoman empires, or the Hungarian half of the Habsburg empire. But they were still quite inadequate. What had been a luxury for the aristocracy and the wealthy bourgeoisie became accessible to children of medium peasants and small state officials; but for children of poor peasants or factory workers exceptional ability and good fortune were necessary to secure a higher education. The present regimes have set out to favour children of workers and to a lesser extent of poor peasants. In Hungary even before the war a movement was started to create "people's colleges" for poor peasants' children. The pioneer was a certain Györffy, whose name was given to the first college. The movement was led by the left-wing group of intellectuals and peasants connected with the National Peasant Party. But in 1948 the movement was rebuked by the communists for paying too much attention to peasants and too little to workers. The colleges were brought under closer control by the communists, and the social composition of the pupils received was changed to the advantage of workers. Nevertheless, though less favoured than workers, poor peasants have a better chance to get their children educated throughout Eastern Europe than they had before the war.

Besides helping children of the poor, the new regimes also discriminate against the children of the formerly wealthy. It is made increasingly difficult for ex-bourgeois children to attend universities. This represents a loss, for such children have the advantage, which should not be underestimated, of growing up in a more cultured background. It should be by no means im-

possible for the regimes to win over many of these children at school and university; they prefer, however, to treat them as enemies, irremediably corrupted by the reactionary prejudices of their parents.

The main concern of the educational reformers has been to create a uniform type of school. It is considered more important to standardise teaching than to enable the abler pupils to rise quickly. This was the purpose of the Act passed in April 1948 in Czechoslovakia and of a series of laws passed in Hungary in the same year. Hungary's Catholic schools were nationalised in June 1948. The Rumanian educational reform was introduced in April 1948. During the summer foreign religious and other schools were closed in both Rumania and Bulgaria. The ban eliminated such fine institutions as the American College of Sofia and French foundations in Rumania. In Czechoslovakia, the Slovak religious schools had been taken over by the state during the rule of the "independent" Slovak government of the Catholic Mgr Tiso; the new regime kept its control, though of course applying it in a very different spirit, especially after February 1948. In the Czech lands obstacles began to be placed in the way of Catholic schools from 1948 onwards. The same process was slower in Poland.

The purpose of the new education is technical proficiency and Marxist-Leninist indoctrination, rather than preparation of the pupils to think for themselves. The emphasis on scientific and technical knowledge is to a large extent justified. Before the war all Eastern Europe suffered from a surfeit of law graduates expecting as of right employment in the civil service. On the other hand there were too few doctors, and far too few industrial and agricultural engineers. But the need to remedy these defects does not justify the regimentation of thought which is becoming universal in the education system of the whole region.

Different countries are of course at different stages. Yugoslavia was the pioneer in Marxist-Leninist indoctrination until the Tito-Cominform breach. Since then, the doctrine has been interpreted so as to allow for emphasis on the variety of Marxist development possible in individual countries, and especially in Yugoslavia. A careful watch is kept for Cominformism, which is of course as much a heresy in Titoist eyes as Titoism in Cominformist. But there is no evidence that the exclusion of non-Marxist ideas is any less severe than before the breach. In Albania indoctrination is made easier by the very slight previous growth of non-Marxist democracy. Between Islamic traditionalism and Marxism-Leninism the intermediate stages are almost absent. Hoxha and his friends are therefore faced with a task of modernisation not unlike that of the Soviet Bolsheviks among the Tadjiks or Turkmens. The Marxist schools are the first modern schools for most Albanians. In Bulgaria already in 1946 entry to the university depended on presentation of a certificate from the branch of the communist-led Fatherland Front in the student's home area that he or she was politically reliable. Indoctrination is intense from the primary school upwards. In Rumania, schools and university faculties have "educational councillors" and "spiritual guides," appointed by the Minister of Education, whose task is to indoctrinate not only pupils but also their parents. Committees of students and school-children are encouraged to spy on their comrades and report them. In Poland a subject called "Polish contemporary history" is taught in the schools. It is a euphemism for Marxist propaganda. In Czechoslovakia things have moved more slowly. But at the ninth congress of the Czechoslovak Communist Party, in May 1949, the Minister of Information, Vaclav Kopecky, declared that the government intended to "conduct the entire state education, both in and out of school, in the spirit of our ideology, in the spirit of our scientific truths, of Marxist-Leninist theory."

There is of course no doubt that before the war not only the important works of Marx, but also the whole field of the social sciences, were neglected throughout Eastern Europe. Czechoslovakia was the only country where they were at all adequately considered. But the forced growth of Marxism-Leninism under the new regimes is more than a corrective to the reactionary romanticism of the past. Marxism-Leninism means in practice the parrot-like repetition of the slogans of the Agitprop department of the Central Committee of the All-Union Communist Party in Moscow. As the number of educated Marxists, really familiar with the writings of Marx, Engels and Lenin, is extremely small, slavish repetition of phrases learned by heart is the only safeguard for teachers who know that they will be severely punished if they deviate from orthodoxy which most of them do not yet understand. Lectures on French literature, Plato's philosophy or hydrostatics have to be spiced with quotations from Marx, Lenin, Stalin, or—in Yugoslavia—Tito and Kardelj. Little collections of quotations on all subjects by these great men are made available for the benefit of teachers.

The minds of adults are cared for hardly less thoroughly than those of children. Press, radio and publications are of course controlled by the Communist Parties. But perhaps more grave is the fact that censorship extends not only to ideas expressed today but to those expressed in the past. Public libraries are purged by stages. Publishing is nationalised, with very few exceptions. This means that the Communist Party can decide what books shall be reprinted. As the war left a severe book shortage throughout Eastern Europe, common text-books and classics from before the war are hard to obtain.

Books in private possession are bound to dwindle. Perhaps the main reason for this is the shortage of housing space. As residential building has a low priority in all the national economic plans, and all also provide for an enormous increase in the number of industrial workers — and so of the urban population — pressure on living space will steadily increase. Already regulations are being introduced to force ex-bourgeois families to give up some of their rooms — the only asset remaining to them — and in some cases to leave the capitals or principal cities. Inevitably within a few years housing conditions in East European cities will resemble those which have long prevailed in Soviet cities. Forced to move into one room with their families, owners of books will have to jettison them. As the new privileged are unlikely to wish to buy them, they will find their way to the dustbin. Before long sources of non-Marxist-Leninist knowledge will have disappeared.

This system is based on force, and could not be made to work without force. It is bitterly resented by many people, and there is no independent evidence to suggest that it is welcomed by any but the small minority of convinced communists and the rather larger number of cynical careerists. There is certainly no evidence for the view, widely held by apologists for communism in Western Europe, that "only a few intellectual malcontents" care about intellectual freedom, that the workers and peasants care only for their daily bread and a job. Neither in Eastern nor in Western Europe do workers or peasants care only for material comfort. There are no doubt individual workers and peasants, like individual bureaucrats, capitalists or members of any other social group, who care only for these things. But no Western apologist for communism, nor any outside observer of any political complexion, has the right to decide whether the workers and peasants of Eastern Europe are capable of "appreciating freedom of thought."

Wiktor Weintraub

SOVIET CULTURAL IMPERIALISM IN POLAND

When the Russian-sponsored government took over the administration of Poland in 1945, the situation on the "cultural front" was desperate. During the years of German occupation, all Polish schools, cultural institutions, publishing houses, were closed, and their property often destroyed. Cadres were severely depleted by death and emigration. In order to give some idea of the enormity of this cultural disaster, it is enough to point out that during the war 85 per cent of all books in Polish public libraries were destroyed.

This situation created difficult administrative tasks for the Communist regime, but in one respect it was very favorable for the regime. After almost six years of enforced inactivity everyone was eager to resume his duties, and after having suffered the terrible devastations of war, all institutions depended on government money. Nevertheless, the regime began very cautiously. The understanding on the part of the regime that the previous Russian rule in Poland left behind a deeply seated distrust must have been one of the reasons for this caution. At first no strict orthodoxy was imposed. Communists were put in key administrative posts, of course, and in every sphere of activity people who declared

From Wiktor Weintraub, "Soviet Cultural Imperialism in Poland" in *Soviet Imperialism*, ed. W. Gurian (Notre Dame, 1953), pp. 94 – 101. Reprinted by permission of University of Notre Dame Press.

themselves to be Communists were in privileged positions. But in order to enjoy the favors of the regime or, at least, to be left unmolested, it was sufficient to be what was then called "progressive." At the beginning the term was interpreted fairly broadly, except for one point: in order to be acknowledged as "progressive" one had to be pro-Russian. From the very beginning the censorship was extremely sensitive to everything concerning Russia, not only Soviet Russia but Russia of the past as well. Thus, for example, it was possible for the famous Polish economist, Adam Krzyzanowski, to present a paper overtly criticizing Marxist doctrine at the Polish Academy in Cracow, and get a résumé published in the *Bulletins* of the Academy. It is true that Professor Krzyzanowski was later deprived of his chair and violently criticised by the Communist press. But the fact remains that it was possible for the Academy to accept such a paper and to publish it in its *Bulletins*. I do not know, however, of any Polish scholarly contribution with an anti-Russian tinge published after 1945. The same refers to literary production.

At first, the government tried to attract everyone active in the cultural field, irrespective of his political past. It was far more successful among writers than among scholars. From the very beginning, a fairly large number of writers and artists in general, although certainly not all of them, started to collaborate with the regime and to take orders from administrative officials. Thus, it was relatively easy for the administration to bring all the artistic activities of the country under its control. As the instruments of this control, professional unions of writers, painters, musicians, actors, etc., were chosen. Their role is similar to that played by corresponding unions in the USSR; that is to say, their aim is not the protection of professional interests but the supervision and guidance of the professional activity of their members. The Soviet

example is often referred to as a model to be followed.

At first, every artist willing to collaborate was accepted with open arms and declared "progressive." There was little fuss about his pre-war activity and almost none concerning his social origins. Enabling them to receive high fees, the administration managed to create for its favored artists conditions of life which, seen against the general low standards of living, can be characterized as luxurious.

Very soon, administration control began to tighten. The most visible and sudden change came in 1948 after Tito's defection. Artists' accomplishments started to be measured by the yardstick of that queer doctrine of wish-fulfilment, "socialist realism," and much of it was rejected as "petty bourgeois," "cosmopolite," "decadent." The process affected some of the most devoutly pro-régime writers. Even the leading Communist poet, Broniewski, was not exempt. One should admit, however, that in his case a certain exception to the customary procedure was made; he was granted the privilege of self-flagellation. He declared that, since he noticed the workers did not like some of his poems—finding them too fanciful, too personal—he had decided not to publish them again. Today the government's grip on literature and the arts is very firm. Very soon, one of the most abject features of the Soviet literary life, articles in which writers repent their past "errors" and declare their total submission, started to appear in Polish periodicals.

With regard to scholars, the government had a far harder nut to crack. Originally, very few scholars went over to the Communist camp. Most of them fought a desperate rearguard action. From the very beginning they had to comply with a strict rule enforced by the censorship. Nothing that tended to be in the least bit anti-Russian could appear in print. This restriction seriously hampered research in modern Polish history. Thus, while there was a spate of important new books on medieval Polish history, very few original contributions in modern Polish history could appear. We know, for instance, that the leading Polish authority in the field of modern history, the late professor Konopczyński, wrote seven books during the last twelve years, only two of which could be published. But apart from this restriction, scholars tried hard to maintain their prewar level of production, their prewar orientation, and their ties with the West. They fought against terrible odds, against the crushing administrative machine of a totalitarian régime. Because of their perseverance, solidarity, and caution, they were able to continue the tradition of independent Polish scholarship until 1952.

Hugh Seton–Watson

THE CHURCHES IN EASTERN EUROPE

Communist control of the schools was bound to lead to conflict with the Christian churches. No church can consent to the forcible indoctrination of children with Marxist-Leninist atheism. It must put up a fight.

Eastern Europe is divided between the Roman Catholic and Orthodox churches, with several small but influential Protestant communities as minorities. Poland, Czechoslovakia, Hungary, and the northern provinces of Yugoslavia (Slovenia, Croatia and the Voivodina) are mainly Catholic. The Orthodox church is dominant in Rumania, southern Yugoslavia (Bosnia, Montenegro, Serbia, Macedonia) and Bulgaria. In Transylvania there was an important minority belonging to the Uniate (or "Greek Catholic") Church.

The Protestants fall into three main groups. Calvinists amount to about a quarter of the population of Hungary, and are also numerous among the Hungarian minority in Transylvania. Czech Protestants include various groups which trace their spiritual descent from the medieval reformer John Hus. The third branch are the Lutherans, who form about 20 per cent of the population in Slovakia, have a following in Hungary, and predominate among the "Saxons" of southern Transylvania, the older of the two German communities in Rumania.

Finally Islam predominates in Albania, and there are important Moslem minorities in Bosnia, Sandjak, Macedonia and eastern Bulgaria, extending more sparsely along the Black Sea coast of Rumania.

The attitude of East European communists to the churches, like that of the Soviet government, is largely determined by their international connections. The Catholic church, owing allegiance to a supreme international authority residing outside the Soviet zone, is considered a dangerous enemy. The dependence of the Vatican on the American imperialists is a favourite theme of communist propaganda within and without the Soviet zone. The Protestant churches have much looser but important connections with the Protestants of the Anglo-Saxon countries, Scandinavia and Germany. They are therefore regarded with suspicion. Moslems are to some extent

From Hugh Seton-Watson, *The Pattern of Communist Revolution* (London, 1953), pp. 287–295. Published in the United States as *From Lenin to Khrushchev*. Reprinted by permission of Methuen & Co., Ltd., and Frederick A. Praeger, Inc.

suspect of sympathy with Turkey, the base tool of the Western imperialists. The Orthodox church has connections with Greece and with the Orthodox communities of Lebanon, Palestine and Egypt. Hitherto Moscow appears to have believed that these connections could be used to further Soviet policy rather than be turned against it. Therefore, though the Orthodox church too is an ideological enemy, it has enjoyed a privileged position in Eastern Europe. . . .

The most serious church conflicts have concerned the Roman Catholic church. The first arose in Yugoslavia. A part of the Catholic clergy in Slovenia and Croatia gave a more positive support to the German or Italian invaders of Yugoslavia and to the Croatian fascists of Pavelić than merely religious duties required. Bishop Sarić of Sarajevo is perhaps the outstanding "collaborator." There were also individual cases where Catholic priests encouraged the massacres of Serbs and Jews. The resentment of many Yugoslav patriots at this behaviour, and the traditional dislike of the Orthodox for Catholicism, were exploited by Tito's government to make a direct attack on the church. Not only those who had helped the enemy suffered. The most striking case was Archbishop Stepinac of Zagreb, head of the Catholic church in Croatia. Performance of his religious duties had obliged him to have official dealings with Pavelić and with the occupation authorities. But there was little evidence that he had been in frequent conflict with them; no evidence that he had protected persons who were in danger. But he was an avowed opponent of communism, and it is for that sin that he received a sixteen-year prison sentence. On December 5, 1951 the Yugoslav government, probably in order to make a good impression on Catholic opinion in the United States, released Stepinac. His status remained unsettled. The Vatican still considers him Archbishop, while the Belgrade government denies this.

The head of the Hungarian Catholic church, Cardinal Joseph Mindszenty, was openly and loudly hostile to the government from the first days of the new regime. A brave and obstinate man, a narrow Hungarian nationalist, and a conservative with little understanding for social issues, Mindszenty was an almost medieval figure, a prelate from the heroic times of the Turkish invasions. He antagonised not only the communists but the large number of Hungarian democrats who at first believed that collaboration with communists was possible, and in any case wished as strongly as the communists themselves to transform the semi-feudal and chauvinist Hungary which the cardinal seemed to defend. But as the fraud and force used by the communists became ever clearer, Mindszenty seemed to be vindicated. He had from the first insisted that communists could not be trusted, and that no terms offered by them should be accepted because they would not be kept. He had criticised the land reform, not because he felt that peasants should not own land, but because it removed the revenue from which the Catholic church maintained its schools, which were some 60 per cent of all schools in Hungary. The government at first supported the Catholic schools from its funds, but Mindszenty did not trust its intentions. And in June 1948 the government nationalised schools, against the votes in parliament of the followers of the Catholic Baránkovics. The Catholic youth organization had already been dissolved, and the Catholic press reduced to one much-censored weekly. The government declared that though schools were nationalised, religious instruction would continue. But Mindszenty trusted the government less than ever. The Communist Party had its means of bringing pressure on working-class and peasant parents, and if necessary on the children themselves, to "request" the suspension of religious teaching at a later stage. So Mindszenty stubbornly opposed the government, and ordered teaching priests to

143

give up their jobs. About 2,500 teachers thus left. By the autumn the government claimed that two-thirds of the vacant places were filled. The cardinal continued his denunciations of the government. He became the symbol of all opposition, political as well as religious.

On December 27, 1948 he was arrested on a charge of conspiracy. The evidence at his trial showed that he had denounced the government in conversation with the American Minister, that he thought a third world war probable and that he hoped for the overthrow of the regime. The prosecution also maintained that during a visit to the United States he had conversed with the ex-Archduke Otto, Pretender to the throne of the Habsburgs. The sum total of evidence showed that he was a fanatical enemy of the government: this he had never denied, and he had good reason for it. If he believed another war was coming, so unfortunately did millions in Hungary, including many communists. No solid evidence showed that he had taken steps to overthrow the government or to start a war. But the government achieved an undoubted success by bringing him into court and making him confess that his previous attitude had been mistaken. Whether this was achieved by threats, torture or simply exploitation of his moral doubts on the best way to protect his flock, is not and cannot be known. The leading figure in the Hungarian church after Mindszenty's removal was Archbishop Groesz of Kalocsa, who did his best to protect Catholics by some compromise with the authorities. In August 1950 an agreement was signed by which the Catholic bishops promised that the clergy would not engage in political opposition (the three issues of the Five-Year Plan, collectivisation of agriculture and the Moscow-sponsored "peace campaign" were specifically mentioned), while the Government promised to ensure freedom of religious belief and activity, to restore a few schools to the church and to sup-

port it financially at a diminishing rate for the next eighteen years. But government attacks on the church soon revived. In June 1951 Archbishop Groesz in his turn was tried for treason, and he too confessed to his crimes. In July the bishops took the formal oath of allegiance to the Hungarian People's Republic. But the struggle for freedom of conscience continued.

In Poland the church for a time enjoyed more freedom than in neighbouring countries. Mgr Wyszynski, who became Primate of the Polish Church on the death of Cardinal Hlond in 1948, had a reputation for conciliation and diplomacy. But this did not prevent the Communists from denouncing the church as a centre of political reaction. In August 1949 a new law was passed which, while purporting to guarantee freedom to all religious beliefs, gives the authorities power to impose heavy penalties on priests showing dislike for the regime. In April 1950 an agreement was signed between government and episcopate on the same basis as the Hungarian agreement described above. By the autumn it had broken down. The government accused the church of breaking it, the church leaders replied that the violation had come from the government side, with arrests of priests and interference with the schools that remained under church control.

A feature of Communist attacks on Polish Catholicism has been the allegation that the Vatican favours Germany at the expense of Poland. A papal letter to the German bishops in 1948, which expressed sympathy for the plight of German refugees from territory annexed by Poland, was given much publicity and a tendencious interpretation. Since the war the Sees in these territories had remained vacant. The Polish church was pressed by the government to fill them, but could not do so without Vatican authority. In January 1951 the government declared that the Sees would be administered by five capitular vicars elected by the chapters. In practice the "election" meant nomination by the Communist Party. The purpose of this action was to mobilise Polish nationalism against the church in general and the Vatican in particular. . . .

The papal decision of July 1949 to excommunicate communists inevitably sharpened the conflict. The East European governments threatened with prison priests who should refuse the sacraments to communists, and in certain cases the threat was carried out. It now became clearer than ever that the aim of the regimes was to sever the links between the national churches and the Vatican. It is of course intolerable to the Soviet bosses that any organisation should exist in Eastern Europe which has connections with the West. The Catholic church, hierarchically subordinate to Rome, is far the most important such organisation that still remains. The link with Rome must be broken, and the churches deprived of the moral protection which that link still represents. Then the last stage and real objective of the communists, the destruction of the churches, and the suppression of religion, can be seriously begun. Defenders of the East European regimes have tried to win sympathy in Protestant north-western Europe by denouncing the reactionary record and international intrigues of the Vatican. The new regimes, they argue, are only doing what Henry VIII did. Their policy is also compared to that of Clemenceau and Briand forty years ago. These arguments are false. It is true that the Catholic church has been associated with political and social reaction, and that Mindszenty is a man of the extreme right. But the Catholic church is not being attacked because it has tolerated social injustice in the past, or because the Vatican has good relations with North or South America or Franco's Spain. It is being attacked because the new regimes are determined to exclude religious influence from national life. The "popular democracies" are not trying, like Henry VIII, to make national churches, or like the French radicals, to make religion a matter of individual conscience. Their aim is to destroy all religion, and to replace it by the totalitarian doctrine of Marxism-Leninism, to be inculcated into every child from the cradle upwards. This no church can accept without struggle.

SINO-SOVIET RELATIONS, 1953–1956

The period 1953–56 witnessed the fast growth of Chinese political power, although it was obscured to some extent by China's continued economic dependence on the Soviet Union and the almost unchanged nature of the Sino-Soviet relationship during these years. China's enhanced position in the communist bloc began to have its effect soon after the Soviet Twentieth Party Congress. The trade agreement between the two countries arranged in March 1953 did not differ from earlier pacts; Soviet aid was again directed mainly to Manchuria and Northern China, areas that had been Stalin's chief interest. In the theoretical sphere, Chinese communist experience provided Russia with a valuable link through which the other underdeveloped countries of Asia could be influenced politically. Although China's version of Marxism-Leninism as applied to her domestic problems was unorthodox by Soviet standards, it did not as yet affect Soviet ideological primacy within the communist bloc.

Chinese prestige grew with the cold war in Asia and with the cultivation of the new "soft" line. The Korean war, in which China played a leading role, was portrayed as a great communist victory and proved to the Chinese, as the Japanese had proved to the rest of Asia during the Second World War, that North American and European armies were not necessarily invincible. During the transition to peaceful coexistence communist China acted for the first time as a great international power in the settlement of the Indochinese problem, which could not be solved without her help. The Chinese leaders took advantage of the occasion to display themselves with pomp at Geneva in 1954. By 1955 Chou En-lai was scoring quieter, though no less impressive, gains for Chinese influence by attempting to minimize the difference of outlook between his country and the uncommitted nations at Bandung.

The celebration of the fifth anniversary of the communist Chinese regime in October 1954 was marked by the visit of a Soviet delegation headed by Khrushchev. Neither Malenkov nor Molotov took part in this goodwill tour, which resulted in Soviet concessions to China that implied some readjustment in the balance of power between the two states. The last Soviet forces in China left Port Arthur in 1955. The joint-stock Sino-Soviet companies formed in the Stalinist era and characteristic of its dominating ethos were liquidated by January of the same year. Also in 1955 Chinese influence made inroads into Outer Mongolia by means of greater economic aid and technical assistance. Sinkiang, another crucially located area near Soviet Asia, received increasing numbers of Chinese, who ran the communist machine there.

During this period China made substantial grants to North Korea and North Vietnam and also provided assistance for Outer Mongolia. These measures were extraordinary at a time when China was still obtaining vast loans from the Soviet Union, but they were indicative of her attitude. For reasons of prestige China wished to maintain her hold over the first two areas, which owed as much to her as to Russia in the recent past. The Chinese communist leaders and the Chinese population as a whole were in the early stages of shedding a national inferiority complex brought on by past humiliations. Recent Chinese victories had received scant recognition from Stalinist Russia and none at all from the noncommunist world. The Chinese Nationalist Government still lay like a thorn in her side on the island of Formosa. An overwhelming majority of nations still refused to give diplomatic recognition to the communist régime.

Nikita Khrushchev

THE DIFFERENT ROADS TO SOCIALISM

In connection with the radical changes in the world arena, new prospects are also opening up in regard to the transition of countries and nations to socialism.

As far back as on the eve of the great October socialist revolution, V. I. Lenin wrote:

All nations will arrive at socialism — this is inevitable — but not all will do so in exactly the same way. Each will contribute something of its own in one form or another form of democracy, one or another variety of the dictatorship of the proletariat, one or another rate at which socialist transformations will be effected in the various aspects of social life. There is nothing more primitive from the viewpoint of theory or more ridiculous from that of practice than to paint this aspect of the future in a monotonous grey "in the name of historical materialism."

Historical experience has fully confirmed this brilliant precept of Lenin's. Now, alongside the Soviet form of reorganizing society on socialist foundations, we have the form of people's democracy.

This form sprang up in Poland, Bulgaria, Czechoslovakia, Albania, and the other European people's democracies and is being employed in conformity with the specific historical social and economic conditions and peculiarities of each of these countries. It has been thoroughly tried and tested for years and has fully proved its worth.

Much that is unique in socialist construction is being contributed by the Chinese People's Republic, possessing an economy which was exceedingly backward and bore semi-feudal and semi-colonial character till the triumph of the revolution. Having won over the decisive commanding positions, the people's democratic state is

pursuing a policy of peaceful reorganization of private industry and trade and their gradual transformation into components of the socialist economy in the course of the socialist revolution.

Leadership of the great cause of socialist reconstruction by the Communist Party of China and the Communist and Workers' Parties of the other people's democracies in keeping with the peculiarities and specific features of each country is creative Marxism in action. In the Federal People's Republic of Yugoslavia, where power belongs to the working people and society is founded on public ownership of the means of production, unique specific forms of economic management and organization of the state apparatus are arising in the process of socialist construction.

It is quite probable that the forms of transition to socialism will become more and more varied; moreover, achieving these forms need not be associated with civil war under all circumstances. Our enemies like to depict us Leninists as advocates of violence always and everywhere. True, we recognize the need for the revolutionary transformation of capitalist society into socialist society. It is this that distinguishes the revolutionary Marxists from the reformists, the opportunists. There is no doubt that in a number of capitalist countries violent overthrow of the dictatorship of the bourgeoisie and the sharp aggravation of class struggle connected with this are inevitable. But the forms of social revolution vary. And it is not true that we regard violence and civil war as the only way to remake society.

Khrushchev, *Central Committee Report to the Twentieth Party Congress.*

Howard L. Boorman

MAO AND STALIN'S HEIRS

The death of Stalin in March 1953 introduced a distinct note of uncertainty into the relations between the two major powers of the Communist bloc. The outward propaganda manifestations, however, continued to be characterized by stress upon political and ideological unity, and the general atmosphere of amity was punctuated by persisting protestations that the Sino-Soviet bloc was impregnable, unbreakable, and invincible. No other non-Chinese figure in modern times has, through his death, occasioned the overwhelming, unspontaneous Chinese attention which Stalin called forth. There was an official mourning meeting in Peking, with over a half a million people present, and a required five-minute period of silence throughout the country. Peking automatically produced a special essay, signed by Mao Tse-tung and dedicated to Stalin, entitled *The Greatest Friendship.* It was noteworthy that Mao himself did not hasten to Moscow, an omission which some observers interpreted as an assertion, both to the Russians and to the world at large, of the heroic personal stature of the leader of the only successful major Communist revolution in Asia. However, like many of his less prominent compatriots, both Communist and non-Communist, Mao Tse-tung has a strong aversion to air travel, and, in view of the necessity for prompt action, his decision not to fly to the Soviet capital may have been a routine one.

From the outset, it appeared that the post-Stalin leadership in Moscow, perhaps in some degree concerned during its first days in power over the possible actions of Mao Tse-tung, had concluded that the most realistic attitude was to leave no doubt of his continuing status as the principal Soviet ally in Asia. The new Russian regime made a definite attempt to treat the Chinese with cautious politeness and signs of public respect. At Stalin's funeral, Chou En-lai, who headed the official Chinese Communist delegation, was given precedence over all other non-Russian Communist leaders and was placed on a virtually equal footing with the top-ranking members of the Soviet party and government. He walked abreast of Khrushchev, Beria, Malenkov, Voroshilov, Kaganovich, Bulganin, and Molotov behind Stalin's bier — a most unusual honor for the Russians to accord to a foreign Communist at a Soviet function. In the funeral speeches, the Russian leaders made a clear distinction between "the great Chinese people" and the "countries of people's democracy," the phrase used in referring to the satellite states in Eastern Europe. Both by their statements and by their treatment of Chou En-lai, the new Russian rulers indicated that they regarded the Sino-Soviet coalition as the key to their Far Eastern policy. . . .

During the second half of 1954, Chinese prestige in the Communist world continued to climb. At the Geneva Conference in the summer, Foreign Minister Chou En-lai went far in establishing Peking's point that the settlement of Asian problems would inevitably involve Western negotiations with Communist China. And in the autumn of 1954, a large Russian delegation, headed by Khrushchev and Bulganin, paid an official visit to Peking. The results of the new conversations between the Russians and the Chinese Communist leaders, as

From Howard L. Boorman, *Moscow-Peking Axis* (New York, 1957), pp. 13–27. Reprinted by permission of the Council on Foreign Affairs, Inc.

announced in mid-October 1954, represented a further advance for the Chinese and a further reinforcement of the Moscow-Peking axis. Had there previously been doubt on the question, it now appeared even more unlikely than before that either Moscow or Peking would, in the near future, embark upon fundamentally incompatible international policies. In the political and military spheres, as in the economic, there would be continuing close coordination.

The new agreements between the Communist powers, as worked out in Peking, were the subject of two joint government declarations and a number of official communiqués.

The first declaration dealt with Sino-Soviet relations and Communist foreign policy. It affirmed that the two governments were "in full agreement" with respect to both Sino-Soviet cooperation and "all

questions concerning the international situation." Recalling the 1950 Treaty of Friendship, Alliance, and Mutual Assistance, scheduled to bind the two nations until 1980, the declaration confirmed the determination of the two governments to consult on all questions touching the "common interests" of the Soviet Union and the People's Republic of China, with a view to achieving "unity in action directed to safeguarding the security of the two states and maintaining peace in the Far East and throughout the world."

The declaration also announced that there would be general coordination of policy and approach between Moscow and Peking on Asian problems. It endorsed the "five principles" on which Nehru and Chou En-lai had previously agreed, and set forth Communist attitudes toward Indochina, Taiwan, Korea, and Southeast Asia.

THE CONSEQUENCES OF ANTI-STALINISM

The entire communist camp was to change radically in nature as a result of two pronouncements made at the Twentieth Congress.

The first concerned the Soviet admittance of different roads to socialism; from that time on the Soviet prototype was apparently not to be applied indiscriminately to other communist states. The new line sprang from the desire of Stalin's more reasonable successors to normalize contacts with Eastern Europe. The practical effects of this policy have already been seen in their initial stages in the New Course as applied to Hungary; during the same period (1953–1956) Czechoslovakia for instance still adhered to Stalinist economic policy, thus diverging considerably from her communist neighbor. An even more surprising departure from past insistence on complete compliance with Moscow was provided by the Soviet-Yugoslav rapprochement of 1955. The Twentieth Congress translated these expedient moves into ideological terms.

The second major pronouncement at the Congress which affected the communist camp in particular dealt with Stalin's reputation. Khrushchev's denunciation of Stalin at the Congress had direct repercussions on the immediate future of foreign policy. His fulminating account of his late master's errors was almost entirely confined to the sphere of domestic policy, though amongst other points brief mention was made of Stalin's "shameful role" in the Yugoslav quarrel of

1948 and his neglect of India after her emancipation. Khrushchev's speech contained no references to Stalin's method of dealing with the People's Democracies which implied that the Soviet leaders themselves would subsequently decide for Eastern Europe the extent to which the Stalinist heritage could be dismantled.

However the matter was not settled so easily as that. By releasing violent criticism of Stalin at this particular juncture in East European affairs, the Soviet leaders committed what was perhaps their biggest blunder in foreign policy since Stalin's lack of foresight in neglecting to prepare for the Nazi attack of 1941. They overlooked the fact that it was ludicrous to attempt to pin all the blame for the evils in the Soviet system on one man and that in denigrating Stalin they were also criticizing the whole regime. Exactly this point was made soon after the Congress by no less a person than Togliatti, the head of the Italian Communist Party. He was backed up by Tito and Gomulka. Apart from this, the revelation of Stalin's mistakes sounded the death knell for his puppets who in most cases still held the power in Eastern Europe. They had risen to the top on the crest of Stalin's infallibility; now the ground was suddenly cut from beneath them.

The undermining of the Soviet Union as the exemplary image of a socialist state and the loss of prestige of Stalinist leaders in the People's Democracies both of them fortuitous byproducts of Khrushchev's secret speech on Stalin opened wide the gates of revolution in Eastern Europe. The right climate for leanings towards independence had already been fostered by the economic and political détente of 1953–1955 and the readmission of Yugoslavia to the Communist fold. Soviet foreign policy blithely pursued an unswerving course for a months after the Congress despite shocked reaction of East European delegates Khrushchev's speech. In April 1956 the Cominform (that erstwhile symbol international communist conformity) was finally dissolved, and in June joint declaration of the CPSU and the League of Yugoslav Communists affirm

> . . . that the roads and conditions of Socialist development in different countries, that the wealth of the forms of socialist development contributes to their strengthening, and . . . that any tendency one's own views in determining the roads and forms of Social ment are alien to both sides. . . .

Six days after Tito left Moscow riots broke out in Poznan, Poland announced in mid October 1954, represented a further advance for the Chinese and a further reinforcement of the Moscow-Peking axis. Had there previously been doubt on the question, it now appeared even more unlikely than before that either Moscow or Peking would, in the near future, embark upon fundamentally incompatible international policies. In the political and military spheres, as in the economic, there would be continuing close coordination.

The new agreements between the Communist powers, as worked out in Peking, were the subject of two joint government declarations and a number of official communiqués.

The first declaration dealt with Sino-Soviet relations and Communist foreign policy. It affirmed that the two governments were "in full agreement" with respect to both Sino-Soviet cooperation and "all

questions concer
uation." Recalling international situation." Recalling international sit-
Friendship, Alliance 1950 Treaty of
ance, scheduled to Mutual Assist-
until 1980, the declare two nations
determination of the tconfirmed the
consult on all questions to vernments to
mon interests" of the Soviet the "com-
People's Republic of China, ion and the
achieving "unity in action di a view to
guarding the security of the two d to safe-
maintaining peace in the Far es and
throughout the world.' st and

The declaration also announced that there would be general coordination of policy and approach between Moscow and Peking on Asian problems. It endorsed the "five principles" on which Nehru and Chou En-lai had previously agreed, and set forth Communist attitudes toward Indochina, Taiwan, Korea, and Southeast Asia.

THE CONSEQUENCES OF ANTI-STALINISM

The entire communist camp was to change radically in nature as a result of two pronouncements made at the Twentieth Congress.

The first concerned the Soviet admittance of different roads to socialism; from that time on the Soviet prototype was apparently not to be applied indiscriminately to other communist states. The new line sprang from the desire of Stalin's more reasonable successors to normalize contacts with Eastern Europe. The practical effects of this policy have already been seen in their initial stages in the New Course as applied to Hungary; during the same period (1953–1956) Czechoslovakia for instance still adhered to Stalinist economic policy, thus diverging considerably from her communist neighbor. An even more surprising departure from past insistence on complete compliance with Moscow was provided by the Soviet-Yugoslav rapprochement of 1955. The Twentieth Congress translated these expedient moves into ideological terms.

The second major pronouncement at the Congress which affected the communist camp in particular dealt with Stalin's reputation. Khrushchev's denunciation of Stalin at the Congress had direct repercussions on the immediate future of foreign policy. His fulminating account of his late master's errors was almost entirely confined to the sphere of domestic policy, though amongst other points brief mention was made of Stalin's "shameful role" in the Yugoslav qua

The death of Stalin in March 1953 introduced a distinct note of uncertainty into the relations between the two major powers of the Communist bloc. The outward propaganda manifestations, however, continued to be characterized by stress upon political and ideological unity, and the general atmosphere of amity was punctuated by persisting protestations that the Sino-Soviet bloc was impregnable, unbreakable, and invincible. No other non-Chinese figure in modern times has, through his death, occasioned the overwhelming, unspontaneous Chinese attention which Stalin called forth. There was an official mourning meeting in Peking, with over a half a million people present, and a required five-minute period of silence throughout the country. Peking automatically produced a special essay, signed by Mao Tse-tung and dedicated to Stalin, entitled *The Greatest Friendship*. It was noteworthy that Mao himself did not hasten to Moscow, an omission which some observers interpreted as an assertion, both to the Russians and to the world at large, of the heroic personal stature of the leader of the only successful major Communist revolution in Asia. However, like many of his less prominent compatriots, both Communist and non-Communist, Mao Tse-tung has a strong aversion to air travel, and, in view of the necessity for prompt action, his decision not to fly to the Soviet capital may have been a routine one.

From the outset, it appeared that the post-Stalin leadership in Moscow, perhaps in some degree concerned during its first days in power over the possible actions of Mao Tse-tung, had concluded that the most realistic attitude was to leave no doubt of his continuing status as the principal Soviet ally in Asia. The new Russian regime made a definite attempt to treat the Chinese with cautious politeness and signs of public respect. At Stalin's funeral, Chou En-lai, who headed the official Chinese Communist delegation, was given precedence over all other non-Russian Communist leaders and was placed on a virtually equal footing with the top-ranking members of the Soviet party and government. He walked abreast of Khrushchev, Beria, Malenkov, Voroshilov, Kaganovich, Bulganin, and Molotov behind Stalin's bier—a most unusual honor for the Russians to accord to a foreign Communist at a Soviet function. In the funeral speeches, the Russian leaders made a clear distinction between "the great Chinese people" and the "countries of people's democracy," the phrase used in referring to the satellite states in Eastern Europe. Both by their statements and by their treatment of Chou En-lai, the new Russian rulers indicated that they regarded the Sino-Soviet coalition as the key to their Far Eastern policy. . . .

During the second half of 1954, Chinese prestige in the Communist world continued to climb. At the Geneva Conference in the summer, Foreign Minister Chou En-lai went far in establishing Peking's point that the settlement of Asian problems would inevitably involve Western negotiations with Communist China. And in the autumn of 1954, a large Russian delegation, headed by Khrushchev and Bulganin, paid an official visit to Peking. The results of the new conversations between the Russians and the Chinese Communist leaders, as

Edward L. Boorman, *Moscow-Peking Axis* (New York, 1957), pp. 13–27. Reprinted by permission of the Council on Foreign Affairs,

Nikita Khrushchev

THE DIFFERENT ROADS TO SOCIALISM

In connection with the radical changes in the world arena, new prospects are also opening up in regard to the transition of countries and nations to socialism.

As far back as on the eve of the great October socialist revolution, V. I. Lenin wrote:

All nations will arrive at socialism—this is inevitable—but not all will do so in exactly the same way. Each will contribute something of its own in one form or another form of democracy, one or another variety of the dictatorship of the proletariat, one or another rate at which socialist transformations will be effected in the various aspects of social life. There is nothing more primitive from the viewpoint of theory or more ridiculous from that of practice than to paint this aspect of the future in a monotonous grey "in the name of historical materialism."

Historical experience has fully confirmed this brilliant precept of Lenin's. Now, alongside the Soviet form of reorganizing society on socialist foundations, we have the form of people's democracy.

This form sprang up in Poland, Bulgaria, Czechoslovakia, Albania, and the other European people's democracies and is being employed in conformity with the specific historical social and economic conditions and peculiarities of each of these countries. It has been thoroughly tried and tested for years and has fully proved its worth.

Much that is unique in socialist construction is being contributed by the Chinese People's Republic, possessing an economy which was exceedingly backward and bore a semi-feudal and semi-colonial character until the triumph of the revolution. Having taken over the decisive commanding positions, the people's democratic state is pursuing a policy of peaceful reorganization of private industry and trade and their gradual transformation into components of the socialist economy in the course of the socialist revolution.

Leadership of the great cause of socialist reconstruction by the Communist Party of China and the Communist and Workers' Parties of the other people's democracies in keeping with the peculiarities and specific features of each country is creative Marxism in action. In the Federal People's Republic of Yugoslavia, where power belongs to the working people and society is founded on public ownership of the means of production, unique specific forms of economic management and organization of the state apparatus are arising in the process of socialist construction.

It is quite probable that the forms of transition to socialism will become more and more varied; moreover, achieving these forms need not be associated with civil war under all circumstances. Our enemies like to depict us Leninists as advocates of violence always and everywhere. True, we recognize the need for the revolutionary transformation of capitalist society into socialist society. It is this that distinguishes the revolutionary Marxists from the reformists, the opportunists. There is no doubt that in a number of capitalist countries violent overthrow of the dictatorship of the bourgeoisie and the sharp aggravation of class struggle connected with this are inevitable. But the forms of social revolution vary. And it is not true that we regard violence and civil war as the only way to remake society.

Nikita Khrushchev, *Central Committee Report to the Twentieth Party Congress.*

1948 and his neglect of India after her emancipation. Khrushchev's speech contained no references to Stalin's method of dealing with the People's Democracies, which implied that the Soviet leaders themselves would subsequently decide for Eastern Europe the extent to which the Stalinist heritage could be dismantled.

However the matter was not settled so easily as that. By releasing violent criticism of Stalin at this particular juncture in East European affairs, the Soviet leaders committed what was perhaps their biggest blunder in foreign policy since Stalin's lack of foresight in neglecting to prepare for the Nazi attack of 1941. They overlooked the fact that it was ludicrous to attempt to pin all the blame for the evils in the Soviet system on one man and that in denigrating Stalin they were also criticizing the whole regime. Exactly this point was made soon after the Congress by no less a person than Togliatti, the head of the Italian Communist Party. He was backed up by Tito and Gomulka. Apart from this, the revelation of Stalin's mistakes sounded the death knell for his puppets who in most cases still held the power in Eastern Europe. They had risen to the top on the crest of Stalin's infallibility; now the ground was suddenly cut from beneath them.

The undermining of the Soviet Union as the exemplary image of a socialist state and the loss of prestige of Stalinist leaders in the People's Democracies both of them fortuitous byproducts of Khrushchev's secret speech on Stalin opened wide the gates of revolution in Eastern Europe. The right climate for leanings towards independence had already been fostered by the economic and political détente of 1953–1955 and the readmission of Yugoslavia to the Communist fold. Soviet foreign policy blithely pursued an unswerving course for a few months after the Congress despite shocked reaction of East European delegates to Khrushchev's speech. In April 1956 the Cominform (that erstwhile symbol of international communist conformity) was finally dissolved, and in June a joint declaration of the CPSU and the League of Yugoslav Communists affirmed

> . . . that the roads and conditions of Socialist development are different in different countries, that the wealth of the forms of socialist development contributes to their strengthening, and . . . that any tendency to impose one's own views in determining the roads and forms of Socialist development are alien to both sides. . . .

Six days after Tito left Moscow riots broke out in Poznan, Poland.

D. Shepilov

DISCUSSION OF KHRUSHCHEV'S STATEMENT

This extract from a speech by D. Shepilov at the Congress is interesting in the light of the Sino-Soviet rift after 1956. At the Congress China is praised by the Russians for taking a lead in the new ideological trend by striking out on the road to socialism with a good measure of independence. In later years she was to be accused of having taken too independent a line.

. . . Our homeland was the first country in the world to break with capitalism and embark on the path to socialism. Centuries and millenniums will pass, but grateful mankind will always pay homage to and honour the working class of Russia, the heroic Party of Communists and immortal Lenin, those who raised the sacred banner of man's struggle for liberation and, by securing the victory of the great October revolution, opened up a new era in world history—the era of Communism.

Nearly four decades have passed since that epoch-making event. The world situation has changed radically. The mighty camp of Communist countries of democracy and socialism where the ideas of Communism represent the views of many hundreds of millions of people, has come into being. The victorious struggle of peoples of colonial and dependent countries against the imperialist yoke is spreading. In the countries where capitalism still prevails millions of people are deeply drawn to socialism. Are not the workers who follow the Labour Party and the trade unions in Britain really supporters of socialism? We need not even mention the militant and glorious working class in France and Italy, which has given so many proofs of its devotion to socialist ideals.

In these circumstances only formalists and Marxist dogmatists can think that such deep upheavals as the transition from one social system to another can be carried out according to a single pattern, according to a stereotyped plan, let us say the same way in Denmark as in Brazil and the same way in Sweden as in Malaya. This is a distortion of the *essence* of Marxism, of its creative spirit. History fully confirms the great Lenin's foresight in saying that the "development of revolution in various countries proceeds in different forms, at different rates (and can not proceed otherwise)." Everything depends on the specific conditions within each country.

The creative efforts of the masses, of the Communist and Workers' Parties gave rise to much that was new and specific during the very profound social transformations in each of the Europ nople's demcracies. The progress of th in China has been even the revolutionary establish ple's rule, the Chinese Comm creatively applying Marxism-L came to the conclusion that in the c tions of China "it is not only possible t replace private ownership by socialist, collective ownership, but it is also possible to replace capitalist ownership by socialist ownership, through the medium of peaceful methods, i.e., methods of persuasion and education," Comrade Mao Tse-tung points out. Having isolated and rendered harmless the comprador bourgeoisie, which was the rabid enemy of the people,

D. Shepilov, Discussion of Khrushchev's Report to the Central Committee at the Twentieth Party Congress.

the Chinese state is step by step transforming exploitative ownership into socialist ownership in its various forms.

From the point of view of pedant Marxists such an approach to the question of transforming exploitative ownership into socialist ownership almost amounts to flouting the principles of Marxism-Leninism. But in reality this is creative Marxism-Leninism in action, a masterly application of Marxist dialectics to the specific conditions of China, boldly and wisely carried out by the heroic Communist Party of China.

Seweryn Bialer

POLISH GRIEVANCES BEFORE THE TWENTIETH CONGRESS

As we shall see in the next part of this section, the first serious resistance to continued Soviet domination of Eastern Europe after the Twentieth Congress occurred in Poland. It is therefore of some interest to note some of Poland's grievances that were felt in the period before the Congress, but which the events of the Congress served to whip up to boiling point. In the following passage, Seweryn Bialer, the Polish Communist defector whom we have already met, comments on the nature of Soviet-Polish relations on the basis of the record of a Soviet Central Committee meeting held in July 1955.

The Soviet Ambassador to Poland Is Not a Diplomat But a Proconsul

The stenograph record of the secret part of the Plenum of the CC of the CPSU also contained many matters which pertained to Poland and Polish-Soviet relations. The question of the real role of the Soviet ambassadors to Poland, particularly Popov and Lebiediev, confirmed a state of affairs I had suspected for a long time. The Soviet ambassador in Poland was more a proconsul interfering in the internal affairs of the country than the diplomatic representative of a friendly nation. He does not take into account either the feelings of the people, or the Party leaders' ambitions. There is, of course, nothing new in this. What is new is that it was described in this manner at a Central Committee meeting in Moscow with Khrushchev and Kaganovich there.

How was it that the question of the behavior of the Soviet Ambassadors to Poland was discussed at the secret meeting of the July Plenum? It so happened that Molotov's activity as Minister of Foreign Affairs had already been examined, and in order to substantiate their criticism of him, Khrushchev, Kaganovich, and others cited facts which either directly or indirectly discredited him. Among other things, the activities of the Soviet ambassadors to Poland emerged. Long before I read the shorthand minutes of the July Plenum, I heard rumors and sometimes even full details which threw light on the real role of the Soviet ambassadors to Poland. Besides, I was in personal contact with other Soviet inspec-

From Seweryn Bialer, *Hearings before the Subcommittee of the Committee on Judiciary, U. S. Senate, 84th Congress, Second Session on the Scope of Soviet Activity in the United States,* pp. 1563–1567.

tors in Poland. Thus, I often met Professor Alexandrov, ideological tutor of some of the Polish training schools, Comrade Nietchkina, guardian of the Polish philosophers, Professor Kuzminov, who occasionally came from Moscow to inspect the Polish economists and their work, Comrade Pankratova, member of the Central Committee in Moscow and patron of Polish historians, and many others. On the basis of these contacts and seeing their condescending attitude toward Poles, I could easily imagine how the Soviet ambassador, whose rank was much higher, behaved. But it is quite a different thing to imagine things and to find a confirmation of one's suspicions in Khrushchev's or Kaganovich's speeches, and the stenographic minutes of the July Plenum secret mission confirmed them amply.

Kaganovich Admits that Popov Liked to Give Orders

At the Plenum Kaganovitch criticized Molotov's activities as Foreign Minister and, among other things, appraised the Soviet ambassador's work in Poland. Kaganovitch maintained that Popov's behavior was simply inexcusable. What was this inexcusable behavior? According to the report, *Popov thought* he was fully entitled to issue orders to the Comrades in the leadership of the Polish Party. He grossly interfered in Polish internal affairs. Kaganovitch said that Popov was intriguing among the Polish Party leaders and inciting them one against the other. Moreover, Popov spoke disparagingly, in the presence of Polish comrades, of the Polish Party leadership. Such behavior on the part of a Soviet Ambassador to Poland, Kaganovich said, was inadmissible.

While I read the above criticism of the Soviet Ambassador's behavior by Kaganovich, I involuntarily asked myself the following questions: First, Popov became ambassador to Poland in June 1953 and remained at his post until March 1954. He was, therefore, Ambassador after Stalin's death, after Beria's purge, and when Khrushchev was made First Party Secretary, and came to Warsaw on several occasions. It is hard to believe that the Soviet leadership was unaware of Popov's behavior, yet in spite of this his activities in Warsaw were tolerated.

Second, I wondered how meek the PZPR[1] Politburo was if it had tolerated Popov's actions for so long. This same Popov was not even a member of the Central Committee of the CPSU. They even tolerated him when they were no longer obliged to listen to Stalin's orders.

But the criticism of the Soviet ambassadors to Poland made at the July Plenum was not limited to Popov only. In his closing speech at the secret session of the Plenum, Khrushchev violently attacked another Soviet ambassador to Poland, Lebiediev. . . .

Mikoyan on the "Brotherly Soviet Aid"

One of the most interesting problems discussed at the secret session of the July Plenum in Moscow was the problem of economic relations between the Soviet Union and the People's Democracies. Mikoyan devoted a good deal of space to that problem in his speech. I read those passages with a good deal of interest because I had written a series of articles on those relations for Party and economic publications. One of my articles, published in Trybuna Ludu, was reprinted in the Cominform paper, *For a Lasting Peace, for a People's Democracy*. Why do I speak of that now? Because I had closely followed the Party line in my articles, yet when I read Mikoyan's speech I saw that everything I had written in those articles *was simply a lie*. Of course I

---

[1] Polska Zjedoczona Partia Robotnicza

knew many facts which proved that the Soviet Union was taking advantage of many privileges in the economic relations with Poland, but only after reading Mikoyan's speech did I realize that economic discrimination was applied to all of the captive countries. Mikoyan denounced these discriminatory measures and plainly implied that it was not exceptional but the general rule. What was this general economic discrimination with regard to the captive countries? I shall mention some of the examples I found in the stenographic record of the secret session of the July Plenum.

Joint-Stock Companies for Exploitation, Not for Help

The problem Mikoyan discussed particularly extensively was that of the so-called mixed companies' activities. Mixed companies were commercial or industrial enterprises set up by the Soviets in almost all the captive countries. In such a company there are two partners: the Soviet Union and the People's Democracy in which the company operates. According to the statutes of these companies, there is complete equality between the two partners.

In all the variety of forms of so-called Soviet brotherly help extended to the People's Democracies, the mixed companies always set up as an example of the Soviet Union's sacrifices for its younger brothers. The Romanian Premier Gheorghiu-Dej once said that mixed companies were the most efficacious and profitable form of Soviet brotherly aid offered to the countries building socialism. The mixed companies were given an ideological training as an example of proletarian internationalism. This was the official Party and ideological line. However, at the secret session of the July Plenum, Mikoyan said that the mixed companies were the most conspicuous form of Russian interference in the domestic economic affairs of the People's Democracies. They were, in Mikoyan's opinion, a sign of Soviet nationalism, a form of exploitation of the People's Democracies which is why they had to be dissolved.

Chinese Communists Slap Moscow's Face

But the mixed companies were dissolved not only because they were inconsistent with the principle of proletarian internationalism. And Mikoyan himself admitted it. Here is a passage of the shorthand minutes which I remember particularly well: "Did we need those mixed companies?" Mikoyan asked. "Were we very happy when our Comrade Mao Tse-tung put our nose out of joint by refusing to allow similar companies to be established in China? Shouldn't we draw a lesson from past mistakes and dissolve those companies?"

Mikoyan then explained in detail how the Soviet nose had been put out of joint by Mao Tse-tung. This even took place *after Stalin's death* when the Soviet Union proposed founding such mixed companies to China, for the production of tropical fruits in China which would then export a certain quantity of them to Russia. Mao Tse-tung did not agree to the offer and proposed instead that China export tropical fruits on a normal commercial basis. Thus, Mao gave a very eloquent appraisal of the mixed companies' activities from the point of view of Chinese interests.

In my opinion, these experiences explain why it was decided to wind up the mixed companies. However, while Mao was putting the Soviet nose out of joint about mixed companies in China, mixed companies in the European People's Democracies continued to be a symbol of Soviet brotherly aid. In December 1954 I was in Moscow and heard a certain Meinshikov read his paper on Mixed Companies, Symbol of Soviet Brotherly Aid Offered to the People's Democracies, to a Conference of Social

Sciences at the Soviet Central Party Committee. As we know, most of the mixed companies have been dissolved, but some of them still exist. Secondly, what struck me particularly when I read the minutes of the secret session was that the dissolution of the companies was not in the least explained by the arguments given by Mikoyan to the secret session of the July Plenum.

On the contrary, in the communiqué announcing their dissolution, I read that they had played a very important role in the development of the People's Democracies, that they had been a symbol of the brotherly Soviet aid offered to these countries, that they had been dissolved merely because their task had been completed. The Soviet dictators of the mixed companies received the highest decorations from the countries in which they had operated. That is why I was amazed at the fantastic hypocrisy of the Soviet Party leaders, and their unwillingness to tell the truth, when I saw the minutes of Mikoyan's speech. In practice, I saw one of the aspects of the alleged open sincerity of the political life in the new post-Stalin era.

Soviet Experts Are Arrogant and Overpaid

In another passage of the record of the secret session, Mikoyan also gave a fair assessment of the behavior of the Soviet experts and delegates in the People's Democracies. The work of our experts abroad, Mikoyan said, necessitates a good deal of tact and modesty. In no case can we hurt the feelings of the local population. But in practice, Mikoyan said, our experts have constantly violated this rule. They have been patronizing and arrogant. They thought that everybody could learn from them, and that they had nothing to learn. In this way they often did a disservice to the cause of friendship between the Soviet Union and the People's Democracies. Mi-

koyan also admitted that the excessively high salaries of Soviet specialists were a source of discontent among local workers and employees.

Mikoyan devoted a great deal of space to Soviet-Yugoslav economic relations. He admitted that the breaking of the trade agreement with Yugoslavia in 1949 was a violation of international law, and there were many other instances, on a larger and smaller scale, of breaking trade agreements. Indeed, they were imperialistic moves, Mikoyan said.

Principles Are Principles: But Business Is Business

When I read this exceptionally frank statement of Mikoyan's I remember several cases of unilateral breaking of trade agreements with Poland by the Soviet Union. I know, for example, that in the past few years, the Soviets broke the agreement on supplying wheat and cotton for Poland, and besides, the Soviet Union never paid any indemnity. Poland, on the other hand, was forced hastily to look for new sources of grain and cotton supplies on the Western markets.

From the minutes of the secret session, it emerged clearly that Mikoyan had violently condemned all discriminatory practices concerning the People's Democracies. Last January I could ascertain how sincere this condemnation of past mistakes was. I was told that Mikoyan had delivered an address at the Conference of Mutual Economic Aid which had been held last December in Budapest. There, the Polish delegation proposed, quite justifiably after all, that the export of Polish coal and farm products to the Soviet Union and the other People's Democracies should be decreased. The Polish delegation also called attention to the necessity of increasing exports of machines because this was the only way to improve Poland's difficult economic situation.

In a long speech, Mikoyan said, among other things, that Poland's traditional exports were coal and farm produce and that she should continue to export them. I wonder how Mikoyan would have described this sort of economic aid last July?

POLITICAL UNREST IN POLAND

On June 28, 1956, riots broke out amongst workers in the industrial city of Poznan, Poland. As in Czechoslovakia and East Germany in 1953, economic grievances soon gave place to political outcries against Soviet domination. The Russians, still in a liberal mood, made concessions. Many Stalinists were expelled from the Central Committee of the Polish United Workers' Party. But on October 15 the Polish Politburo decided to have Gomulka elected as First Secretary; this was the man who had been imprisoned for some years for opposing Stalin. In taking a unilateral decision of this nature and refusing to go to Moscow for consultations, the Poles were openly defying the Soviets. The Soviet Presidium ordered Russian troops in Poland to move nearer to the towns and arranged for Rokossovsky, their faithful supporter, to stage a coup if negotiations between Russia and Poland broke down. At this moment of crisis, the fragmented Soviet leadership rallied together temporarily. Khrushchev, Molotov, Kaganovich, and Mikoyan went to Warsaw to mediate with the Poles, who had their way by proceeding to elect Gomulka. The bloodless October revolution in Poland triumphed, unlike the almost simultaneous uprising in Hungary. Gomulka's program was more radical than Moscow would have liked, but at least it flowed naturally from earlier thaws in a domestic policy that left unscathed the two principles on which Soviet-Yugoslav relations had foundered in 1948—continued membership of the Soviet bloc and agreement on the role of the party.

Bulletin on the Poznan Incidents

For some time imperialist agents and the reactionary underground have been trying to use the economic difficulties and shortcomings at several Poznan enterprises to incite outbursts against the people's rule. It is no accident that the enemy selected Poznan, where an International Fair is in progress, as the place of provocation. They intended to cast a shadow on the good name of People's Poland and to impede development of peaceful international co-operation.

On June 28, enemy agents succeeded in provoking street disorders. Matters went so far that several public buildings were attacked, with casualties resulting.

Relying on the politically conscious part of the working class, the authorities gained control of the situation and restored order to the city.

Representatives of the Government and of the Polish United Workers Party, led by

Trybuna Ludu, June 29, 1956.

Jozef Cyrankiewicz, Chairman of the Council of Ministers, came to the scene of the events.

The organizers of the destruction, a broad and carefully prepared provocative-diversionary action, will be punished to the full extent of the law.

In view of the Poznan events, all workers and patriotic forces of the people must be particularly vigilant against all antistate attempts and demonstrations inspired by the enemies of People's Poland.

The Poznan provocation was organized by the enemies of our fatherland at a time when the Party and Government are greatly concerned with eliminating shortcomings in the life of the workers and making our country more democratic. Every patriot and every honest person in Poland must realize this.

The Government and the Central Committee of the Polish United Workers Party are convinced that every attempt to provoke disorders and to act against the people's rule will be duly rebuffed by all the workers and citizens to whom the welfare of the country is dear.

The Soviet Reaction to the Poznan Riots

The hostile provocation failed. The politically conscious section of the Poznan working class helped the authorities to gain control of the situation and to reestablish order in the city. The Polish Press Agency reports that by 7.00 a.m. on June 29 the majority of the workers from the striking enterprises returned to their jobs. Streetcar and bus services have been resumed in the city. The workers express their indignation over the infamous activities of the diversionists who tried to organize a demonstration against the people's rule. Preliminary investigation of the case of the arrested saboteurs and bandits reveals their ties with the reactionary underground.

On June 29 Jozef Cyrankiewicz, Chairman of the Council of Ministers of the republic, who is in Poznan, delivered a radio address to the Poznan workers. He stated that bloodshed in Poznan lies on the imperialist centers and the hostile reactionary underground, the direct organizers of the events. However, Jozef Cyrankiewicz stressed that the Poznan events will not impede or weaken the efforts of the Party and Government toward a further democratization of our life, toward a better fulfillment of our tasks, toward development of the economy and national culture, toward a further rapid improvement in the workers' living conditions.

The Polish working class and all the workers of the country express decisive indignation over the insolent imperialist attack in Poznan. Mass meetings and open Party gatherings are taking place in enterprises of Warsaw, Lodz, Lublin, Silesia, the Baltic coast area, and other regions of the country at which the workers are holding up to shame the organizers and inspirers of the provocation against the people.

Such a mass meeting took place at the Warsaw Dimitrov Plant. Worker Hauser stated: "Imperialist provocateurs tried to cast a shadow on our achievements. They wanted to destroy the peaceful life of the Polish people. Our people paid too dearly for the victories achieved under a people's democratic system. We demand severe punishment for the organizers of the provocation." The participants of the meeting adopted a resolution expressing profound indignation over the imperialist agents' provocation.

The workers of the Warsaw Automobile Plant state in a resolution adopted at a meeting: "We will not permit a split in the unity of the working class and its Party in the struggle for further democratizaton of our lives."

The collective of the Kedzierzyn Nitrate

Fertilizer Combine adopted a resolution which states: "We will not permit the forces which detest whatever is our weal and our hope to try to destroy all the fruits of the constant labor of our workers and engineers, dedicated to the prosperity of our people's motherland."

Communiqué on the Reinstatement of Wladyslaw Gomulka as a Member of the Polish United Workers Party, August 4, 1956.

The Seventh Plenum of the PUWP[1] Central Committee resolved to annul the resolution of the Third Plenum of the PUWP Central Committee of November, 1949, in the part concerning the unfounded and wrongful accusations of tolerance with regard to enemy agents formulated against comrades Wladyslaw Gomulka, Marian Spychalski, and Zenon Kliszko.

After the Seventh Plenum, representatives of the Politburo of the PUWP Central Committee had a talk with Comrade Wladyslaw Gomulka during which, among other things, the fundamental problems of the Seventh Plenum of the PUWP Central Committee were discussed.

The Politburo, having heard a report on the course of this talk, decided to restore to Comrade Wladyslaw Gomulka his rights as a Party member.

Gomulka's Account of the New Polish Policy to a Citizens' Rally in Warsaw, October 24, 1956

Comrades! Citizens! Working People of the Capital! I greet you in the name of the Central Committee of the Polish United Workers Party which at its last plenary session turned over the helm of the Party to a new leadership.

A great deal of evil, injustice, and many painful disappointments have accumulated

in the life of Poland during the past years. The ideas of socialism, imbued with the spirit of the freedom of man and respect for the rights of a citizen, have been greatly distorted in practice. The words were not borne out by reality. The heavy toil of the working class and of the entire nation did not yield the expected fruits.

I deeply believe that these years belong to an irrevocable past.

The Eighth Plenum of the Central Committee of our Party executed a historic turn. It created a new period in our work, a new period in the history of socialist construction in Poland, in the history of the nation.

The leadership of the Party has told the working class and the entire nation the whole truth, the unvarnished truth, leaving nothing unsaid about our economic and political situation, about difficulties which will have to be overcome in order to march forward and to achieve a lasting improvement in the life of the workers in Poland.

The leadership of the Party does not want and will not give empty promises to the nation. We turn with full confidence to our class, the working class, to the intelligentsia, to the peasants.

We are telling them: We have powerful forces of production built by the effort of the working people during the past years, but these are not fully utilized. We have considerable resources in our national economy, in thousands of factories and mines, in industry and agriculture, which are still being squandered, to no small degree, due to wastefulness and poor management.

We have numerous ranks of the working class, of working men who love their profession, who mastered new techniques, whose labor productivity, however, is still low; we have real opportunities of increasing agricultural production, production of food, and raw materials for industry, but

---

[1] Polish United Workers Party

Trybuna Ludu, August 5, 1956; Trybuna Ludu, October 25, 1956.

they are still tied up by the errors of agricultural policy of the past years.

Workers and employees of all sectors of national economy! Help the Party and the Government in the great work of improving the socialist economy of People's Poland! . . .

Our last meeting with the delegation of the CPSU allowed the Soviet comrades to orient themselves better in the political situation in Poland.

Recently, we received assurances from the First Secretary of the Central Committee of the CPSU, Comrade Khrushchev, to the effect that he does not see any obstacles to the development of our mutual Party and state relations on the basis of the principles outlined by the Eighth Plenum of the Central Committee of our Party. [*Prolonged ovation*]

All concrete matters pertaining to our internal affairs will be solved in accordance with the estimate of the Party and the Government. The question whether we need Soviet specialists and military advisers, and for how long we need their aid, will depend on our decision alone. [*Prolonged ovation*]

At the same time, we received assurance from Comrade Khrushchev that within two days Soviet troops in Polish territory will return to their locations, in which they are stationed on the basis of international treaties, within the framework of the Warsaw Pact. [*Ovation*]

This is closely connected with the presence of the Soviet troops in the German Democratic Republic. As long as there exist bases of the [North] Atlantic Pact in Western Germany, as long as the new Wehrmacht is rearming there is fomenting chauvinism and revisionism aimed against our frontiers, the presence of the Soviet Army in Germany will correspond to our highest state interest. It also is in accord with the interest of the toiling masses of the GDR, against whom the arming and the threats of the militaristic and revanchist circles of Western Germany are also directed.

In these circumstances, we should reject, with even greater decisiveness, all attempts at anti-Soviet agitation undertaken by the reactionary and anti-popular forces, and all maneuvers of the international reaction which desire to weaken the alliance between our fraternal nations.

Comrades! The Eighth Plenum of the Central Committee of our Party has received a warm welcome from the working class and the widest masses of the people. At thousands of meetings throughout the entire country, workers, the intelligentsia, students, soldiers, and all the toiling people had expressed their approval and support, and their trust in the new leadership.

Nothing is more important for us, for the Party, for its leadership, than this trust and support. There is nothing more important for the nation, for the realization of its desires and aspirations, than unity between the Party and the people, a unity stronger than ever before.

In the name of the Central Committee, I am expressing warmest thanks to the workers of many industrial enterprises who, in a noble upsurge, expressed their readiness to work overtime, and even to float a state loan, although there is no need for it at the present moment, and for voluntary deductions from their earnings in order to help the people's authority and the new leadership of the Party. I thank the students of the Polish universities who demonstrated in these days so much enthusiasm for and trust in the Party. I thank the soldiers and officers of the Polish Army who demonstrated their loyalty to the Party and to the Government and their support for the results of the Eighth Plenum.

The nation can completely trust its army and the command of the army [*ovation*], which, in our country, as everywhere in the world, is completely and entirely subordinated to the government of ·its country.

[*Applause*]

Comrades! The tremendous wave of the political activity of the masses brought about by the Eighth Plenum here and there has encountered forces hostile to socialism, opposed to the Polish-Soviet alliance, inimical to the people's authority, forces which would like to distort, hinder, and retard socialist democratization.

Comrades! Let us not allow reactionary troublemakers and various hooligans to obstruct our way. Let them keep away from the pure current of the struggle of socialist and patriotic forces of the nation! Drive away the provocateurs and reactionary loud mouths! The state authority will not tolerate for a moment any action directed against the Polish state interests and against our state system.

Comrades! Time is pressing. The Party must embark on the solution of daily, difficult problems of our economy and state life. How can you help the Party and the Government today? Above all, every one of you should stand at your work-bench, at your post, and demonstrate your loyalty and devotion to our cause by intensified work or study.

Today we turn to the working people of Warsaw and of the entire country with an appeal: enough meetings and demonstrations! Time has come to embark on daily work—full of faith and consciousness that the Party united with the working class and with the nation will lead Poland on the new road to socialism.

Long live the unbreakable bond of the Party with the working class and with the entire toiling people!

Long live socialism!

Long live People's Poland! [*Ovation*]

THE HUNGARIAN REVOLUTION

In October 1956 the Polish experience was repeated in Hungary, though we shall see that the Hungarian uprising was far more violent and widespread, and ended differently. The Hungarian nation gave expression to the most pronounced rejection of the Stalinist past in Eastern Europe. The Stalinist Rákosi had to resign as First Secretary in June 1956, under the impact of Khrushchev's secret speech on Stalin, but even the policies of his successor, Ernö Gerö, were not sufficiently liberal for a people who had tasted more freedom under Nagy in the very recent past. On October 23 revolution broke out in Budapest. Nagy was reinstated as Premier with the consent of Mikoyan, who was in Budapest with Suslov to control the revolution. For a period of six days the Hungarians enjoyed the luxury of a government that tried to be independent from Moscow. The reaction to Rákosi's "hard" line was extreme. The Hungarians wished to end the political monopoly of the communist party and withdraw from the Warsaw Pact, thus putting themselves even further out of the Soviet grasp than the Yugoslavs had been from 1948 to 1955. This the Soviets would not allow. By crushing the revolt on November 4 with Soviet tanks and troops against the will of a nation, they put a halt to the retreat from Stalinism that was as abrupt as its initiation at the Twentieth Congress, and far more damaging to Soviet prestige.

Thus at the very moment when Russia was trying to disperse some of the negative elements in her heritage, she had to reaffirm them in order to preserve the existence of the communist bloc in any form. One is reminded again of the French Republicans: "they believed themselves to be cosmopolitans, they were that only in their speeches . . . the Revolution degenerated into an armed propaganda, [*in the Russian case the period 1945–1953*] then into conquest. . . ." [Hungary, 1956]

Paul Kecskemeti

THE UNEXPECTED REVOLUTION

The Elite

For months before the revolt, the intra-Party opposition had been demanding the rehabilitation of Nagy and the reorganization of the government under his leadership; otherwise, the opponents of the Old Guard warned, there would be an explosion. The opposition, however, had no thought of forcing the hand of those in power. To all Party men, however critical of the regime, a change in leadership not decided upon by the appropriate Party authorities was unthinkable. Events, however, outran the sluggish tempo of intra-Party developments. The explosion came, but the old leadership was still in place, and no preparations had been made for reshuffling the top positions in the Party.

Nagy himself was out of town when the students began preparing their mass demonstration. It was the wine harvest season, and he had gone to a small country place he owned in the wine district of western Hungary. There, on the evening of October 22, Nagy was guest of honor at a wine harvest festival, while the Budapest students were holding meetings and formulating revolutionary demands, including the one that called for a new government under his leadership. Nagy learned about this from the radio on the 23rd, and decided to return to Budapest. Nothing, however, was further from his thoughts than taking advantage of this irregular popular movement in his favor in order to crush his old Party antagonists and impose himself as leader. According to Meray, who himself was an active member of the intra-Party opposition and conversant with Nagy's political attitudes at that time, some of the students' demands, notably those directed against Soviet domination, were far too radical for Nagy to swallow. Moreover, Nagy would not have considered taking any political initiative outside Party channels.

The only Party people imaginative and undisciplined enough to take direct action to bring about a last-minute change of government were the journalists of the Party newspaper *Szabad Nép*. After an impromptu meeting at the newspaper's offices, they sent a delegation to the Central Committee, urging the leadership to bow to the will of the people. Gerö, who received the delegation, waved the suggestion aside.

Reprinted from *The Unexpected Revolution* by Paul Kecskemeti, pp. 106–116, with the permission of the publishers, Stanford University Press. © 1961 by the RAND Corporation.

During the afternoon of the 23rd, when the city was already in an uproar, Nagy stayed at home. With great difficulty, some of his supporters, including the novelist Tamás Aczél, persuaded him to go to the parliament building, in front of which a huge crowd was clamoring to hear him. Nagy, having no instructions from the Party authorities, at first refused to talk to the crowd. When, finally, he appeared on the balcony and spoke a few words, it was a near disaster. He began with the word "Comrades" and was roundly booed. In his short address, he stressed the need to proceed within the framework of "constitutional order and discipline." The crowd then began to disperse; many went to the radio building, where fighting broke out soon afterward.

During the night, the Central Committee finally decided to appoint Nagy Premier. Installed in power, however, Nagy did not, at first, act like a revolutionary leader. His primary endeavor upon taking office was to restore order and disarm the insurgents. His appeals to the fighters to lay down their arms were fruitless (understandably enough, since Soviet tanks were in action in the capital), and his initial popularity declined rapidly.

The Communist intellectuals, who had been the most radical and outspoken critics of the regime before the revolution, were thoroughly frightened by its outbreak and did everything in their power to steer events into a peaceful course. Gyula Háy, for example, spoke as follows in a broadcast to young Hungarians on October 25:

There must be a change-over to peaceful methods without the slightest delay, the armed struggle must stop immediately. Even peaceful demonstrations are not suitable at this time, because they can be misconstrued. There must now begin an implacable, uncompromising, democratic clash of thoughts and ideas in which the spokesmen of the new, the young in age and spirit, will gain a brilliant, universally resounding victory.

According to Háy, Gerö's removal from power guaranteed that all legitimate revolutionary aspirations would be satisfied under the new government.

The Communist writers' efforts to call a halt to violent action indicated no change in their fundamental attitudes. They did not give up their convictions, either then or later. Their determination "never again to tell lies" held good, after the crushing of the revolution, under the Kádár regime. Háy, Déry, and other leading Communist critics of the pre-revolutionary regime who stayed in Hungary never recanted; they went to prison rather than submit. Their behavior showed a remarkable consistency before, during, and after the revolution; they wanted to reform the regime, to rid it of its aberrations, but they had no idea of discarding Marxist socialism as the basis of political order and starting out along entirely new lines.

Nagy, too, was consistent; he thought he could save the situation in 1956 by reviving the New Course of 1953. Only gradually did he perceive that the dynamism of the revolution had rendered that stage hopelessly obsolete. When he did recognize this fact, he prepared himself to make a revolutionary break with the past. The formation of a government of national union, announced on October 27, represented the beginning of such a break; it was followed by more radical steps in the same direction, culminating in the attempted withdrawal from the Soviet bloc. Nagy, however, did not choose this radical course spontaneously; he was forced into it by the uncontrollable, overwhelming upsurge of the masses' revolutionary *élan*.

The Social Background of the Combatants

The proportion of active fighters in the revolution varied from one social group to another. A survey conducted by the Audience Analysis Section of Radio Free Europe, Munich, gives the following breakdown of the proportion of active fighters within the various social categories: professionals, 14 per cent; white-collar, 2 per cent; industrial workers, 13 per cent; farmers and farmhands, 6 per cent; and others (including students), 20 per cent.

This breakdown shows the highest incidence of active fighting in the last group, the youngest in age, who were not yet classifiable in any occupational category other than that of students. The urban occupational groups, except clerical workers, follow next. The peasantry shows a much lower percentage, and the office workers the lowest of all. (Of the total white-collar group, 82 per cent are shown as having been "inactive"; that is, as not even having participated in non-fighting activities.)

The peasantry had its own pattern of revolutionary activity. This class seems to have been in sympathy with the most aggressive revolutionary groups, the active fighters; it did not want a "reformed" Communism but was seeking something radically different. The peasants showed their sympathy by supplying the fighters with food. Their own activity, however, was concentrated largely upon dismantling the kolkhozes, their constant objective throughout the Communist era. Their behavior, somewhat like that of "elite" rebels, showed continuity rather than an abrupt change from submission to rebellion.

Some continuity also could be observed in the behavior of the intelligentsia; the members of this category reveled in proclaiming publicly what they had long been saying *sotto voce* in private. They devoted much energy to creating a democratic political machinery. There was a proliferation of newspapers and political parties reflecting every shade of opinion. Interview material reveals that many of the fighters (students, in particular) felt this activity to be both excessive and premature; it deflected energies from the main task. The intelligentsia, however, were extremely active in every field of revolutionary endeavor,

literary and organizational work as well as armed combat; the Radio Free Europe survey shows that the proportion of the "inactive" in this class was only 6 per cent, as compared to 61 to 82 per cent in the other classes.

The extremely low participation quota among office workers is striking; it suggests that this category remained demoralized even after the outbreak of revolution. The group as a whole was apparently unable to develop an organizational framework of its own, or to attach itself to the various councils in which the industrial workers, the intelligentsia, and the students ranged themselves.

Extreme combativeness manifested itself in the Hungarian Revolution primarily among three categories of people: street crowds who assembled in spontaneous fashion, the youngest age group, and industrial workers. Each group had its own characteristic style of revolutionary behavior.

The Street Crowds

In the crowds, tension built up gradually during the afternoon and evening of October 23. What attracted them to begin with was the sight of marching students; this was something entirely new and exhilarating. But at first the street crowds were mere onlookers, curious to see what would happen. As time went by, however, the people's mood gradually changed. When the crowds grew denser and showed no inclination to disperse, it dawned upon those in them that a historic moment was at hand. We find in the interviews such statements as: "We simply felt that it was impossible to leave without having done something decisive"; and "Something big was bound to happen." The crowds now sought outlets for this accumulated tension. The statue of Stalin offered itself as a target. Vast numbers converged upon the parliament building, clamoring for Imre Nagy, whom the street had designated premier, and upon the radio building, where they took up the students' demand that their manifesto be put on the air. When the police attacked, nobody thought of dispersing. The provocation drove the crowd to frenzy, and the possession of arms, obtained from sympathizers among the military, gave it a feeling of unlimited power. The crowd's ruling impulse was to destroy the symbols of Communist and Soviet domination and to get even with the terror and publicity apparatus of the regime. The offices of the Party newspaper (by then under the control of Communist dissidents) were wrecked; bonfires were built of Communist literature; the hated red star emblem was torn down everywhere. Above all, the crowd stormed the strongholds of the political police and overpowered the units manning them. There were many lynchings.

This phase of the revolution exhibited many of the well-known features of mob violence: rage, a passionate desire for revenge, cruelty. Yet one of the classic symptoms of mass action, the breakdown of cultural restraints and inhibitions, was lacking. Mass aggression was extremely selective, pinpointed upon the political police. There was no looting, no storming of shops, no general breakdown of discipline. The crowds did not even start an indiscriminate persecution of Communists. Even in small towns, where Party members were highly conspicuous, "decent" Communists were left unharmed. On the whole, destructive impulses were vented only upon the political police and the inanimate symbols of Communist rule.

The Young People

The revolution entered a new, fateful stage after the entry of Soviet occupation troops in the early morning of October 24. During this stage, the revolutionary struggle consisted mainly of street battles with Soviet tanks, and in these the youngest age group played the most conspicuous part.

To a very considerable extent, the street battles were fought by the young: students, apprentices, and schoolchildren. A good many older people participated too, but it seems certain that the struggle would not have been sustained as long as it was if it had not been for the death-defying, desperate determination of the very young.

According to the above-mentioned survey of Radio Free Europe, 11 per cent of the population up to 20 years of age, and 19 per cent of those aged between 21 and 29, were active fighters in the revolution. Among those between 30 and 49 years old, however, only 5 per cent fought actively, and of those aged 50 years or more, 1 per cent. The fall-off after 29 years of age is significant. How can this be explained? Whereas it is not surprising that people aged 50 and over showed little inclination to participate in street battles, men in their 30's are not too old to fight. On the other hand, those aged 32 or more in 1956 were old enough to have seen military service in World War II. They had had experience with Soviet tanks and could estimate the odds against successful resistance. This, presumably, was the reason why they showed less inclination to fight than those who had not been in the war. A Hungarian war veteran whom I interviewed was very positive on this point. He said that ex-soldiers considered military resistance to the Russians hopeless; only boys too young to have seen service were ignorant enough to fight. This extreme formulation certainly overstates the case, but the general point seems valid.

The very young among the active fighters did not, in fact, base their action upon any sort of realistic weighing of odds. There was in their combativeness an element of psychic compulsion, as though they were caught in a somnambulistic trance. It did not matter whether they lived or died. Only one thing counted: getting weapons and using them as much and as long as possible.

How did such a pattern of behavior develop among children? Lack of suitable data makes it impossible to answer this question conclusively. On general grounds, however, it seems that decisive weight must be given to peer-group solidarity and imitation. When some children got weapons and went out to fight, this apparently started a teen-age epidemic: the others felt they could not remain behind. Not every child fought, of course; presumably, *all* parents did what they could to restrain their own children, and many succeeded. However, the Radio Free Europe figure of 11 per cent for active fighters in the age group up to 20 by no means gives the true measure of the scope of the teen-age epidemic in Budapest. For one thing, the sample is nationwide, but most of the active fighting took place in Budapest; for another, the age span includes the many children not yet in the teen-group who were immune to the epidemic or could be controlled by their parents.

Whereas children mostly fought in small gangs, the combat activity of more mature young men, particularly students, showed a more organized pattern. The students had organizations of their own to begin with. Within these, various teams were formed for specific purposes (the printing and distribution of leaflets; liaison with the workers, the army, and the government; active fighting; and logistic support). Interviews with students indicate that they considered themselves the nerve center of the revolution. They found that they could easily establish contact with any group —workers and peasants as well as government officials, professionals, and army officers. They used this easy access to all strata in order to co-ordinate revolutionary policies and activities.

The Industrial Workers

It was the industrial workers whose revolutionary activity lasted longest and was the best organized. They were active in street battles in Budapest and elsewhere; but their weightiest contribution to the rev-

olutionary struggle was the organization of workers' councils and, its principal outcome, the revolutionary general strike.

The first workers' council was set up at the Incandescent Lamp Factory in Budapest on October 24. From there, the movement spread rapidly; within three days a network of councils covered the entire country. The councils' activity was concentrated on national politics. For example, on October 26, one of the most articulate of the councils, that of the industrial region of Borsod County, north of Budapest, broadcast a manifesto of twenty-one points, which a delegation took to Budapest and submitted to Premier Nagy.

The Borsod program contained a number of demands reflecting the social welfare aims of organized labor (better wages, workers' control of plants, decentralization of industry, and so on), but the significant thing about it was that it put the greatest emphasis not on social but on national grievances. It urged revision of the trade treaties with the Soviet Union, the exploitation of the Hungarian uranium deposits for the country's benefit, and, above all, the withdrawal of Soviet occupation troops by January 1, 1957, at the latest. To give effect to these demands, the Borsod workers proclaimed a general strike, to last until the occupation was lifted. In the sequel, the activity of all workers' councils was concentrated upon this basic point. Work stopped in all plants. The workers knew that the strike would bring great hardships, but they did not care; if existing conditions could not be altered radically, they felt, life was not worth living anyway. When the revolution seemed to be victorious, the councils made preparations to end the strike. But after the second Soviet intervention, they decided to keep it up, and the condition for resuming work remained the same: the withdrawal of the Soviet troops. The workers simply disregarded the verdict of military action, refusing to believe that their collective effort could be frustrated by it.

To my knowledge, this was the first time in history that the syndicalist myth of the revolutionary general strike, as set forth by Georges Sorel, actually became the basis of sustained political action by the entire industrial population of a country. It is safe to say that the Hungarian workers who organized the councils and conceived the idea of a general strike against the Russian occupation had never heard of Sorel and his theory of the "myth," but they acted in accordance with it. There was only this difference: Sorel thought that the proletariat would rise to sweep away a rotten, degenerate bourgeois order, but to his unwitting Hungarian disciples the antithesis between "bourgeoisie" and "proletariat" was of no immediate interest. The significant antithesis was between "Soviet" and "Hungarian," and the social and political order to be swept away was not a bourgeois but a Communist one, set up by the disciples of Lenin whom Sorel had greatly admired. The idea of workers' councils seems to have been inspired by the example of Yugoslavia, where a new type of "industrial self-government," based upon the creation of plant councils, had been introduced in 1950. A council movement inspired by the same example arose in the autumn of 1956 in Poland, where the councils mobilized the industrial masses and created popular pressure strong enough to compel a relaxation of the dictatorship and some easing of Soviet control. In Poland, however, the councils never became supreme, because the Party apparatus was not smashed, but merely revamped under Gomulka's leadership. By contrast, the Hungarian councils were able to steer a radical revolutionary course. They insisted upon the total elimination of all Party influences from economic management as well as from national politics. The end of Soviet occupation was the underlying aim of all this, and the council movement became primarily a national liberation movement.

The workers' revolutionary behavior showed a sharp break in continuity. Outwardly quiet until the outbreak of street fighting in Budapest, the Hungarian industrial population instantly mobilized itself in a determined bid to wrest political power from the Party. This explosive transition from total discipline to total rebellion was characteristic of the "mass pattern" of the Hungarian Revolution, in contrast with the smooth, continuous nature of the "elite pattern." Not that the revolutionary behavior of the mass represented a completely new departure; the Hungarian Revolution consciously imitated historical models. The memories of 1848 – 49 (Kossuth's and Petöfi's revolution) were ever-present. In addition, the industrial workers in revolting against the Party were inspired by the Social Democratic traditions of the organized labor movement of Hungary. These traditions, suppressed under the Communist regime, suddenly came to the fore when the workers regained their freedom of action.

RADIO AND PRESS STATEMENTS DURING THE HUNGARIAN REVOLUTION

Radio Address by Ernö Gerö, First Secretary of the Hungarian Workers Party, October 23, 1956

Dear Comrades! Dear friends! Working people of Hungary! The Central Committee of the Hungarian Workers Party adopted important resolutions in July of this year. The membership of our Party, our working class, our working peasantry and intellectuals, our people received these resolutions with approval and satisfaction.

The essence of the July resolutions was the fact that we further develop socialist democracy on the basis of Party unity based on solid foundations in our Party, in state life, in the field of production, and in our entire society. By rectifying numerous mistakes of the past and relying on our achievements we build socialism in our country, and according to our capacity and possibilities, gradually raise the standard of living of our working class and nation.

Following the July resolutions the initiative of the working masses began to develop widely throughout the country. During the brief period that has elapsed since the resolutions were passed, numerous measures have been taken to implement them.

It goes without saying, however, that the resolutions could not be fully implemented during the short spell of a few months. At the same time mistakes, too, have occurred in the course of their implementation. The July resolutions, furthermore, could merely indicate the direction and place the main tasks in the forefront, without providing a solution for all the problems which confront our country and people. Many of these problems require further thorough examination to find solutions that best correspond to the real situation of our country, to our national characteristics, and to the interests of our working class and people.

The leadership of our Party is firmly resolved to direct—in the spirit of the July resolutions—the continued building of socialism, relying ever more widely on our working class; on our cooperative, and all working, peasantry; on our intelligentsia; and on the millions of our people. It is our resolute and unalterable intention to develop, widen, and deepen democracy in our country, to increase the participation of the workers in running the factories, state farms, and various economic bodies and institutions.

We, of course, want a socialist democracy and not a bourgeois democracy. Our Party and, in our opinion, our working class and people are jealously guarding the achievements of our People's Democracy and will not allow anybody to harm them. We will defend these achievements under any circumstances from whatever quarter they may be threatened.

The main endeavor of the enemies of our people today is to try to undermine the power of the working class, loosen the worker-peasant alliance, undermine the leading role of the working class in our country, and shake our people's faith in their party—the Hungarian Workers Party; to try to loosen the close friendly ties between our country, the Hungarian People's Republic, and the other countries building socialism, in particular between Hungary and the socialist Soviet Union. They endeavor to loosen the relations which link our Party to the glorious Communist Party of the Soviet Union, the Party of Lenin, the Party of the 20th Congress.

They heap slanders on the Soviet Union. They assert that we are trading with the Soviet Union on an unequal footing, that our relations with the Soviet Union allegedly are not of equality, and that our independence must allegedly be defended not against the imperialist but against the Soviet Union. All this is impudent untruth, hostile propaganda which does not contain a grain of truth. The truth is that the Soviet Union not only liberated our country from the yoke of Horthy fascism and German imperialism but even then when our country lay prostrate at the end of the war, she also stood by us and concluded agreements with us on the basis of full equality, and ever since she has been and is pursuing this policy.

Announcement of the Hungarian Government's Appeal for Soviet Military Assistance, October 24, 1956

Attention! Attention! The dastardly armed attacks of counter-revolutionary gangs during the night have created an extremely serious situation. The bandits have penetrated into factories and public buildings and have murdered many* civilians, members of the national defense forces, and fighters of the state security organs.

The Government organs have not reckoned with the bloody dastardly attacks and therefore applied for help, in accordance with the terms of the Warsaw Treaty, to the Soviet formations stationed in Hungary. The Soviet formations, in compliance with the Government's request, are taking part in the restoration of order.

The Government is appealing to inhabitants of the capital to keep calm; to condemn the bloody havoc wreaked by the counterrevolutionary gangs and support everywhere the Hungarian and Soviet troops seeking to maintain order. The liquidation of the counterrevolutionary gangs is the most sacred cause of every honest Hungarian worker, of the people and Fatherland. At this moment we are concentrating all our strength on that task.

A Plea for Order and a Promise of Hope: Proclamation by Imre Nagy to the Hungarian Nation, October 24, 1956

People of Budapest, I announce that all those, who in the interest of avoiding further bloodshed, stop fighting before 1400 [2 p.m.] today and lay down their arms will be exempted from summary jurisdiction.

At the same time I state that with all means at our disposal we will realize as soon as possible, on the basis of the June 1953 Government program as I expounded it at that time in Parliament, the systematic democratization of our country in every field of Party, state, political, and economic life. Heed our appeal, cease fighting, and secure the restoration of calm and order in the interest of the future of our people and country. Return to peaceful and creative work.

Hungarians, comrades, my friends! I speak to you in moments pregnant with responsibility. As you know, on the basis of the confidence placed in me by the Central Committee of the Hungarian Workers Party and the Presidential Council, I have taken over the leadership of the Government as Chairman of the Council of Ministers. Every possibility exists for the Government to realize our political program by relying on the Hungarian people, under the leadership of the Communist Party.

The essence of this program, as you know, is the far-reaching democratization of Hungarian public life, the realization of a Hungarian road corresponding to our own national characteristics in the building of socialism, and the realization of our lofty national aims, the radical improvement of the workers' living conditions.

In order, however, that we should be able, together with you, to make a start with this work, the first necessity is the creation of order, discipline, and calm. Hostile elements joining the ranks of peacefully demonstrating Hungarian youth have misled many well-meaning workers and turned against the People's Democracy, against the power of the people. The paramount task now facing everyone is the urgent consolidation of the situation.

Afterwards we will be able to agree on every question, since the Government and the majority of the Hungarian people want the same thing. By referring to our joint and great responsibility toward national existence I appeal to you, to every man, woman, youth, worker, and peasant, and intellectual to stand fast and remain calm, resist the provocateurs, and help restore order and assist our forces to maintain order. By common effort we must prevent bloodshed and we must not let our sacred national program be soiled by blood.

The Hungarian Government is preparing for peaceful and creative work. The Government is determined not to allow itself to be diverted from the road of democratization and of the realization of the program corresponding to the interest of the Hungarian people as discussed with the broad strata of the people. We want a policy not of revenge but of reconciliation. For this reason the Government has decided that all those who voluntarily and immediately lay down arms and cease fighting, as in the case of the groups which have already surrendered, will not be brought before summary jurisdiction.

Workers, defend the factories and machines. This is our own treasure. He who destroys or loots causes damage to the whole nation. Order, calm, discipline — this is now the slogan. This comes before everything else.

Friends, Hungarians! I will soon expound in detail the Government's program, which will be debated in the National Assembly when it meets soon. Our future is at stake. The great road of progress of our national existence lies ahead of us. Line up behind the Government. Secure peace, the continuation of peaceful and creative work.

Make it possible for every worker in our country to work undisturbed for his own and his family's future. Line up behind the Party! Line up behind the Government! Trust, that learning from the mistakes of the past, we will find the correct road for the prosperity of our country.

The Interpretation of the Hungarian Revolt by the Principal Newspaper of Budapest, "Szabad Nép," October 29, 1956

The latest issue of *Pravda* carries a dispatch from its own correspondent about the events in Hungary entitled "Collapse of the Antipopular Adventure in Hungary." This is an error. What happened in Budapest was neither antipopular nor an adventure. What is more it did not collapse. For five days bombs exploded and machine guns were active, spreading death. For five days this city, torn by fate, shed blood and suffered. But through hundreds of deaths, the ideals of true patriotism and democracy were burning in the fires.

The slogans of socialist democracy were the loudest to be heard and not those of the reaction and counterrevolution. The revolutionary people of Buda and Pest want a people's freedom without tyranny, terror, and fear. They want more bread and national independence. Is this then an antipopular adventure?

What collapsed could indeed be called antipopular. It was the reign of the Rakosi-Gerö clique.

The *Pravda* article further states that manifestations of the people of Pest and the revolt were instigated by the subversive work of the British and American imperialists. We can safely say that all 1.5 million inhabitants of Budapest are deeply hurt and insulted by this assertion. In body or in spirit, a large portion of the population of Budapest was present at the demonstrations on Tuesday [October 23]. They sympathized or agreed with the basic patriotic and democratic aims of the great popular uprising.

The bloody, tragic, but at the same time ennobling fight, lasting five days, was not instigated by some sort of subversive work. It was caused, alas, by our own faults and crimes. The greatest of our faults and crimes was our failure to protect the sacred flame which our ancestors had bequeathed to us—our national independence. What does the Hungarian nation want, asked the youth in March 1848? The independence of the nation, was the answer given by Petofi and his friends in the first of his twelve points.

Let us at last talk frankly. This is the first answer today too. This is the first demand of the nation. Hungary shall be a free and independent country and will live on this basis in peace and friendship with its neighbor the USSR. This is what we have fought for and this is what we want. This is what writers and journalists—fighting with their pen—want. This is what engineer and workers, peasants and demonstrating students, and the Premier of the country want.

A heavy stone rolled off our hearts when the new Government and new leaders of the Party espoused this demand. From behind the dark clouds the sun is rising, red in color because it is bathed in blood, but it is the sun of liberty and peace.

While we are at it, we must make another comment about the deplorable *Pravda* article. It is true that evil fratricide raged for days. Now, we believe that at last it is over. It will be necessary to punish those who, clinging to their power and fearful for their lives, instigated the fight. Punished must be those who ordered fire on the unprotected [demonstrators] in front of the Parliament. Punished also must be those criminal elements who, freed from prison, jumped on the wave of the revolution.

Yes, it will be necessary to punish, but this is quite different from what the *Pravda* article calls "liquidation." No one could,

and now no one wants to liquidate the fight of the Hungarian people. Even if at a high price, this fight has nevertheless borne fruit: the victory of the ideals of freedom. And with this and only this will it bring at last the silence of arms on a soil bathed in blood; beautiful peace, new beautiful bloodless struggles, and the beginning of our constructive work.

Proclamation by Imre Nagy on the Restoration of a Multi-Party System and a Coalition Government, October 30, 1956.

Working people of Hungary! Workers, peasants, intellectuals! As a result of the revolution, which is unfolding with tremendous strength, and the mighty movement of democratic forces, our Fatherland has reached a crossroads. The national Government, acting in complete agreement with the Presidium of the Hungarian Workers Party, has arrived at a decision, vital for the nation's life, of which I want to inform Hungary's working people.

In the interest of the further democratization of the country's life, the Cabinet abolishes the one-party system and places the country's Government on the basis of democratic cooperation between the coalition parties, reborn in 1945. In accordance with this it sets up an inner Cabinet within the national Government. The members of this Cabinet are Imre Nagy, Zoltan Tildy, Bela Kovacs, Ferenc Erdei, Janos Kadar, Geza Losonczy, and a person to be nominated by the Social Democrat Party. The Government will submit a proposal to the Presidential Council of the People's Republic to elect Janos Kadar and Geza Losonczy as Ministers of State.

The national Government appeals to the headquarters of Soviet forces immediately to begin the withdrawal of Soviet troops from the territory of Budapest. At the same time, the national Government informs the people of the country that it will begin negotiations without delay with the Government of the USSR about the withdrawal of Soviet troops from Hungary.

I announce, on behalf of the national Government, that it recognizes the democratic organs of local autonomy which have been brought into existence by the revolution, that it relies on them and asks for their support.

Hungarian brethren, patriots! Loyal citizens of the Fatherland! Safeguard the achievements of the revolution, safeguard order by every means and restore calm. No blood should be shed in our country by fratricide. Prevent any kind of disturbance and safeguard life and property by every means at your disposal.

My Hungarian brethren, workers, peasants! Stand beside the national Government in the hour of this fateful decision. Long live free, democratic, and independent Hungary!

Interview with Imre Nagy, October 31, 1956

QUESTION: Do you believe that in your negotiations with the Russians on the withdrawal of Soviet forces from Hungary you will be successful only if this takes place within the framework of all Warsaw Pact nations, or do you believe that Hungary can be a separate case?

NAGY: Yes, I believe so, yes. I do not know exactly what is provided by the Warsaw Pact, but independently, I think, we will be able speedily, I think, to solve this question.

Q: What about the Warsaw Pact now? Are you in it or not?

NAGY: At present, we are in it.

Q: Do you wish to leave the Warsaw Pact, if the Hungarian people desire this?

A: Today we have begun negotiations on this matter and other questions connected with this problem.

Q: Would it be of any help to you if the American, British, French, and the other allies in West Germany would simultaneously offer to withdraw their forces from West Germany in case the Russians are willing to withdraw from Poland, Hungary, Rumania, and the other People's Democracies, and particularly from East Germany? Do you think that such negotiations could take place?

A: I cannot speak for the Polish and Rumanian . . .

Q: But in your opinion?

A: When this comes up for discussion we will have to take a stand. We will have to give our opinion on this matter then.

Q: It will now be necessary to reconstruct Hungary economically. Will you apply to the Western Powers for aid in the reconstruction of Hungary?

A: It seems to me that we will have to count on all economic forces to help us emerge from this situation.

Q: Will you continue to recognize the German Democratic Republic?

A: I think so, yes.

Q: Also in the future?

A: It appears to me that this is not up for discussion right now. In our foreign policy we do not want to lean only in one direction, but wish to maintain good and friendly relations.

Q: Also with the German Federal Republic?

A: Well, presently we have no relations. It seems to me that this question, too, is premature. We will have to decide later on.

Q: What will be your future relations with the Soviet Union?

A: Very good, I think. Good diplomatic and friendly relations.

Q: According to the agreement you have now concluded, are the Soviet forces now withdrawing to their original bases in Hungary?

A: At present the forces in Budapest, it seems, have already withdrawn, and have returned to their bases.

Q: In Hungary?

A: Yes, in Hungary. I do not know exactly from where they came.

Q: There are also some Soviet forces which came across the border from other states. Are they also withdrawing to where they came from?

A: I think so, yes. I do not know from where they came, but they will return from where they came.

Q: You said just a few minutes ago that you were put under pressure to bring in the Soviet troops, that it was not you who invited the Soviet troops to move into Budapest. Who invited them?

A: It was not me—that I can say. At that time I was not Premier; I was not a member of the Central Committee of the Party.

Q: How then did the opinion appear that you invited the troops?

A: I do not know. At that time I was not a member of the leadership. It may have been this way: At first it was said it was the Government; and then later on, after 2 or 3 days, I was made Premier, and the masses are unable to differentiate. Two days ago or now, it is all the same to them.

Q: But did you not approve of the invitation to the Soviet troops afterward?

A: No.

Q: Did you say it was necessary for the reestablishment of peace and order, or did you not?

A: No, no, no. I did not say such a thing, and I must say that their appearance has caused much damage.

Q: What will now be the first measures of the Government?

A: It is too difficult to give a government program right here.

Q: But perhaps you can tell us the next step?

A: We have very grave economic problems. The most important problem is to restore order here and to reestablish economic life. Today I talked with the workers delegation from Csepel. They will be able to give you some information.

Statement by Premier Imre Nagy Announcing an Attack by Soviet Forces on the Hungarian Government, November 4, 1956

This is Imre Nagy, speaking. In the early hours of this morning, the Soviet troops launched an attack against our capital city with the obvious intention of overthrowing the lawful, democratic, Hungarian Government. Our troops are fighting. The Government is in its place. I inform the people of the country and world public opinion of this.

Appeal by Imre Nagy to the Hungarian Representatives on the Mixed Hungarian-Soviet Commission, November 4, 1956

Imre Nagy, Premier of the National Government, appeals to Pal Maleter, Defense Minister; Istvan Kovacs, Chief of the General Staff; and the other members of the military mission who went to the Soviet Army Headquarters at 10 p.m. last night and have not yet returned to return immediately and to take charge of their respective offices.

Formation of the Hungarian Revolutionary Worker-Peasant Government; Radio Appeal by Ferenc Munnich, November 4, 1956

Open letter to the Hungarian working nation!

Compatriots, our worker and peasant brethren!

The undersigned, Antal Apro, Janos Kadar, Istvan Kossa, and Ferenc Munnich, Ministers, former members of the Imre Nagy Government, announced that on November 1, 1956 [?], severing all our relations with that Government, we left the Government and initiated the formation of the Hungarian Revolutionary Worker-Peasant Government.

We were prompted to take this responsible act by the realization that the Government of Imre Nagy had come under the pressure of the reaction and become impotent. Within that government we had no opportunity whatever for action, in the face of the ever growing strength of the counterrevolutionary threat menacing our People's Republic, our worker-peasant power, and our socialist achievements with extinction.

Esteemed champions of the working class movement with several decades of service have been murdered—Imre Mezo, the secretary of the greater Budapest executive committee of the Party; Comrade [?] the seasoned fighter of the labor movement in Csepel; Sandor Sziklai, the director of the museum of war history. In addition, other generally esteemed sons of the workers and peasantry have been exterminated en masse.

We could not longer stand by idly as members of the Government, incapable of action, while under the cover of democracy counterrevolutionary terrorists and bandits were bestially murdering our worker and peasant brethren, keeping our peaceful citizens in terror, dragging our country into anarchy, and putting our entire nation under the yoke of counterrevolution for a long time to come.

Hungarian workers, compatriots, worker-brethren, comrades! We have decided that we will fight with all our strength against the threatening danger of fascism and reaction and their murderous gangs. We appeal to every loyal son of our People's Republic, every follower of socialism—in the first place the Communists—workers, miners, and the best sons of the peasantry and the intellectuals to support every measure of the Hungarian Revolutionary Worker-Peasant Government and its entire struggle for the liberation of the people.

Budapest, November 4, 1956
Antol Apro, Janos Kadar,
Istvan Kossa, and
Dr. Ferenc Munnich

Program and Composition of the Revolutionary Worker-Peasant Government Announced by Janos Kadar, November 4, 1956

Appeal to the Hungarian people!

The Hungarian Revolutionary Worker-Peasant Government has been formed. The mass movement which started on October 23 in our country had the noble aims of remedying anti-Party and antidemocratic crimes committed by Rakosi and his associates and defending national independence and sovereignty. Through the weakness of the Imre Nagy Government and through the increased influence of counterrevolutionary elements who edged their way into the movement, socialist achievements, our people's state, our worker-peasant power, and the existence of our country have become endangered. . . .

Our nation is passing through difficult days. The power of the workers and peasants and the sacred cause of socialism are in danger. So are all the achievements of the past twelve years which the Hungarian working nation, and above all you Hungarian workers, have created by your own hands and by your heroic and self-sacrificing work.

With growing impudence the counterrevolutionaries are ruthlessly persecuting the followers of democracy. Arrow Cross members and other beasts are murdering the honest patriots, our best comrades. We know that many questions are still awaiting solution in our country and that we have to cope with many difficulties. The life of the workers is still far from what it should be in a country building socialism. Simultaneously, with the progress attained during the past twelve years, the clique of Rakosi and Gerö has committed many grave mistakes and gravely violated legality.

All this has rightly made workers dissatisfied. The reactionaries are seeking their own selfish ends. They raised their hands against our people's democratic regime, which means that they want to return the factories and enterprises to the capitalists, the land to the big estate owners.

The gendarmes and prison wardens of Horthy and the representatives of the hated and cursed oppressive system have already set out to sit on the neck of the people. If they had won, they would not have brought freedom, well-being, and democracy, but slavery, misery, unemployment, and ruthless fresh oppression. Making use of the mistakes committed during the building of our people's democratic system, the reactionary elements have misled many honest workers and particularly the major part of the youth, who joined the movement with honest and patriotic intentions.

These honest patriots wanted the further democratization of our economic and social life and thus the securing of the consolidation of the foundations of socialism in our country. They raised their voice for the strengthening and flourishing of Hungary so that she would become a free and sovereign state which maintains friendly relations with the other socialist countries. For this reason it is wrong and criminal to accuse them for having taken part in this movement.

At the same time one must not lose sight of the fact that, by utilizing the weakness of Imre Nagy's Government, counterrevolutionary forces are indulging in excesses, murdering and looting in the country, and it is to be feared that they will gain the upper hand. We see with deep sadness and a heavy heart into what a terrible situation our beloved Fatherland has been driven by those counterrevolutionary elements, and often even well-meaning progressive people, who willy-nilly abused the slogans of freedom and democracy and thus opened the way to reaction.

Hungarians, brethren, patriots, soldiers, citizens!

We must put an end to the excesses of the counterrevolutionary elements. The hour of action has struck. We will defend the power of the workers and peasants and the achievements of the people's democracy. We will create order, security, and calm in our country. The interest of the people and the country is that they should have a strong government, a government capable of leading the country out of its grave situation. It is for this reason that we formed the Hungarian Revolutionary Worker-Peasant Government. . . .

IV. *Toward a New Concept of the Soviet Bloc, 1956-1960*

SOVIET EFFORTS FOR RECONCILIATION WITH EASTERN EUROPE, 1956–1958

The Soviet act in Hungary shed new light on the concept of different roads to socialism, which admittedly had not been outlined in any detail at the Twentieth Congress. By November 1956 it was at least clear that the Yugoslav agreement of 1955 with the Soviet Union was not intended as a model for the rest of Eastern Europe, which would be obliged to restrict its divergences from the Soviet prototype to certain limits. The definition of these limits formed the subject of the often painful dialogues that occupied Russia and her allies until the Moscow Declaration of the ruling communist parties in November 1957.

Before entering into the details of these discussions, we may stand back from our review of Soviet policy in Eastern Europe at this point and observe that the autumn of 1956 marked a watershed in intra-bloc relations. Since that time the People's Democracies could no longer be considered as an undoubted asset to the Soviet Union. Politically some of them proved their unreliability in 1956, and the wounds that opened up then were never completely healed afterwards. From the economic angle the more generous trade and credit terms that Russia gave to her allies after the Hungarian and Polish revolts in order to pacify them represented a definite drain on her resources which was no longer compensated for by war reparations and Soviet-controlled joint stock companies, two amongst several forms of earlier Russian economic domination. In military terms also, Soviet confidence in the reliability of East European troops waned after the events of 1956. Besides, the launching of an accurate ICBM in the summer of 1957 heralded the close of an era when it was vital for Russia to retain Eastern Europe as a protective zone.

Nevertheless, the sudden release of the People's Democracies on their own terms would have struck a major blow at Soviet prestige and as an act of policy would have contradicted the ideological dream of world communism and Russian national expansionist trends since Stalin's time. In the autumn of 1956 the situation was very precarious. If the opposition to Russia in Poland, Hungary, and Yugoslavia had triumphed and joined hands across national borders, Russia's geographical link to the more faithful Czechoslovakia and East Germany would have been restricted to the narrow eastern tip of Slovakia. With

Western aid Germany could have attempted to reunite her two halves, and Austria might have retreated from neutrality in view of her new position in Europe vis-a-vis the two power bloc. But in view of their inability to unite, partly because of their deliberate isolation from each other by Russia, partly through their own national proclivities which had kept Eastern Europe weak against Russia, Austria and Turkey across the centuries, the Soviet bloc remained intact.

Russia had to tread very warily after the Hungarian revolution. In the first months following on the crisis it was a case of temporarily patching up the dike against revisionism until communist interstate relations could be reestablished on some new and firmer basis. In an important speech of November 6, 1956, the Soviet ideologist Suslov made it clear that national roads of communism were still permissible, but were subject to certain well-defined Marxist laws which had been rigorously applied in the past to the Soviet Union; therefore, some elements of the Russian experience had acquired universal meaning and were pertinent to the present situation in Eastern Europe.

At this crucial moment in Soviet relations with the communist bloc, China stepped into the arena. In an article of December 29, 1956, the newspaper *Jen Min Jih Pao* virtually reiterated Suslov's line of the previous month, making it doubly clear that while some local deviations from orthodox central policy might persist, they would not be allowed to override the general unity of the bloc under Soviet guidance. In one respect the article was more precise than Suslov had been. Yugoslavia was directly chided for attacking other communist parties and causing a split in the socialist movement. From this moment it became increasingly obvious that Yugoslavia could scarcely be included in the revised Soviet system, even in the rather more liberal version that was about to evolve.

Just as grievances in Eastern Europe had thrived on economic grudges before turning to political ills, so now the Soviets applied economic palliatives before concentrating on political problems. Soviet credits were handed out to critical sectors in Poland, Hungary, and East Germany. With an eye to the more distant future, Russia pumped new life into the Council for Mutual Economic Aid. In the summer of 1957 draft development plans for all of Eastern Europe were set in motion, covering from ten to fifteen years. Gradually the People's Democracies were allowed to play a greater role in the organization and even to dispute some of the Soviet proposals. At the same time, however, Russia soon began to make good use of the council's multilateral conferences as a means of forcing majority decisions on recalcitrant members like Poland, who would not submit to pressure from a purely political body, such as the revived version of the Cominform now suggested by the Soviets.

The idea of a new International was naturally repugnant to the Poles, and above all to the Yugoslavs, who had been the direct target of the Cominform. When the Soviets sounded out foreign communist parties on the matter toward the end of 1956 and through 1957, it became apparent that the Chinese and the

Italians were also reluctant to agree to the notion. Backing down somewhat, the Soviets proposed that a leading periodical for the communist parties should be established (apart from its distinctive anti-Yugoslav aim, the Cominform had consisted of little more than an editorial machine in Belgrade). The Poles, the Italians, and especially the Yugoslavs, still resisted, but in September 1958 the first issue of the *World Marxist Review* finally appeared, significantly in faithful Prague, under a Soviet editor.

After the bitter experience of the recent past, the Soviets found it impossible to resurrect a new communist international organization of a permanent nature, with all that it implied in the sense of Soviet domination. The Italian idea of a continuous series of bilateral or multilateral meetings of communist parties was finally adopted. Throughout the latter part of 1956 and most of 1957 Russia held bilateral meetings with the leaders of all the East European countries, at which she gradually formed her impression of the way in which the wind would blow at a multilateral meeting.

By the summer of 1957 the decisive nature of Khrushchev's final victory over the anti-party group inside Russia allowed him to take a more decisive line in Soviet foreign policy. The hesitations and blunders of the years after Stalin's death were due, as we have seen, as much to the rifts in the Soviet leadership as to growing recalcitrance on the part of the People's Democracies. After July 1957 Khrushchev was soon able to carry out his foreign policy compromise that lay between Molotov's old fashioned Stalinism and the unbridled revisionism that had affected some parts of Eastern Europe. Gone were the days when Molotov could try to thwart the executive through his control of administration. In July 1957 Khrushchev said of his new foreign minister "Gromyko only says what we tell him to . . . if he doesn't we'll fire him and get someone who does."

Although the Polish and Yugoslav communist parties held a bilateral meeting of their own at Belgrade in September 1957 where they expressed agreement with each other's views, a wedge had already been driven between them as early as January 1957, when Gomulka promised the Chinese foreign minister Chou En-lai, mediating for Moscow in Warsaw, not to exacerbate Polish differences with the Russians. Tito never flinched from holding up Yugoslav practical and ideological deviations from the Soviet line as examples for export to other East European countries, even if it meant the dissolution of the communist camp. His purpose veered closer to the Hungarian heresy of October 1956 than to Gomulka's milder indiscretions.

By the autumn of 1957 Khrushchev could afford to gamble on the hope that at a multilateral meeting of the world communist parties, Yugoslavia could be safely isolated and Poland bludgeoned by a compelling majority to reenter the Soviet fold. The launching of the first earth satellite on October 4, 1957 gave a fillip to Russian prestige, just before the convention in November of the leaders of sixty-four communist parties in Moscow to celebrate the fortieth anniversary of the Russian Revolution.

Yugoslavia remained stubborn. Tito sent Kardelj and Rankovic to Moscow instead of coming in person, and the Yugoslav delegation refused to sign the important declaration of the twelve ruling communist parties confirming Russian leadership. Poland thus found herself isolated, especially after Mao Tse-tung's open recognition of Soviet supremacy at the meeting. She bowed to the strong and signed the Moscow Declaration. However, the final document reflected some of her opinions in that the draft theses of the Soviet communist party was modified in the final version. The Soviet Union was more often referred to as merely the first state in the bloc and not as the leader; comments in the theses on the "pernicious ideas" of "national communism" were replaced by less harsh admonishments of revisionism and dogmatism.

Khrushchev's final dealings with Yugoslavia and Poland after the signing of the Moscow Declaration reflected the new spirit. They were characterized by unusual flexibility combined with a calm view of the ultimate aim springing from Khrushchev's knowledge that he was no longer likely to be thwarted by opposition in the Presidium. Khrushchev also continued to rely on the support of friendly foreign communist leaders, as Russia had had to do in 1956–57, although it was not quite such a vital makeweight as before.

With the Moscow Declaration behind her, Russia had little trouble in neutralizing the effect of the Yugoslav threat in 1958. When Tito expressed a negative approach to both the Warsaw Pact and Western capitalism in a new draft program for Yugoslav communism and Rankovic openly attacked the Soviet leaders at the Yugoslav Congress in April 1958, Khrushchev at last aligned himself clearly with the Chinese attitude toward Tito by stating at Sofia on June 3rd that the Soviet Communist Party had never withdrawn its approval of the condemnation of Yugoslavia by the Cominform in 1948. On June 17th, after accusing Tito of having taken an active part in the Hungarian rebellion, the Soviets executed Nagy. In the same period Russia postponed two loans promised to Yugoslavia. Relations between the two countries sank to the low level that had characterized the interval between Stalin's death and the reconciliation of 1955.

Poland had neither the strength nor the inclination to resist bloc pressure by 1958. She made a last stand at the Yugoslav Congress in April by refusing to walk out after Rankovic's criticism of the U.S.S.R., but the execution of Nagy forced her into either creating an open rift with Russia by still supporting Nagy's image or else acquiescing. Her historic urge to self-immolation was no longer powerful enough to make her cling to Tito's principles, which in any case differed in some ways from her own. On June 28th Gomulka criticized Tito and Nagy in a speech which cemented Poland to the Soviet bloc once again.

After five years of trial and error since Stalin's death the Soviet Union had partially succeeded in achieving its aim of consolidation and relaxation in Eastern Europe. The cost was high, the final result not entirely satisfactory from the Russian point of view. Yugoslavia's continued neutralism was a reminder of bitter disputes throughout Eastern Europe that had taxed Soviet diplomacy to the utmost.

M. Suslov

SOVIET RECOGNITION OF DIFFERENT ROADS TO SOCIALISM

These general features and laws in no way preclude possible and indeed inevitable variations in the forms and means of the conquest of political power by the working class, the rate at which the basic means of production are socialised and other social transformations carried out and in the forms of socialist democracy in each of the countries taking the path of socialism, determined by the concrete conditions of their development. Each country contributes its share to the theory and practice of socialism, thus confirming the creative character of Marxism-Leninism. During the past years the People's Democracies have accumulated a wealth of experience in socialist construction. This experience must be attentively studied and exchanged by the socialist countries on the principle of equality and proletarian international-ism. . . .

It would be wrong to imagine that the radical reconstruction of social relations affected during the past ten years in the People's Democracies could take place without difficulties, painlessly and without mistakes.

After the Twentieth Congress of the C.P.S.U. the fraternal Communist and Workers' parties in the People's Democracies began to change and improve methods of Party and administrative work, paying due regard to the peculiarities of their countries and resolutely correcting the mistakes committed in the past.

Unfortunately things in Hungary developed in a different way. The former Hungarian leadership, which made a number of grave mistakes, failed to appreciate the demands of the moment and acted all too late, with the result that mass discontent set in. Reactionary, antisocialist elements, on the instigation of international reaction, immediately seized on this in order to launch an attack on the people's democratic system. By means of false slogans they succeeded for a while in leading astray fairly large masses of people and especially the youth. There was a moment when the counter-revolutionary forces created an extremely dangerous situation for socialism in Hungary. The Nagy Government, which had been formed in this situation, surrendered position after position to the reactionary forces and, having paved the way for counter-revolution, actually disintegrated. Counter-revolutionary gangs unleashed terror, brutally murdered prominent public figures, hanged and shot Communists. There was an intensive flow across the western frontier into Hungary of arms and big groups of officers and soldiers who had served in Hitler's and in Horthy's fascist armies. The country was reduced to a state of complete chaos and lawlessness. It was directly threatened with restoration of the capitalist and landlord system and the re-emergence of fascism.

The victory of reaction and fascism in Hungary would have signified not only the loss to the Hungarian working people of all the gains won by them in the struggle against the landlords and capitialists, it would have signified also a threat to the other socialist countries by bringing imperialist bases closer to their frontiers.

At this fateful moment in the life of the Hungarian people the socialist forces in the country adopted the only correct decision—to form a Revolutionary Worker-Peasant Government capable of barring the way to reaction and fascism [Prolonged applause]

By now the socialist forces of People's

M. Suslov, Speech delivered at a celebration meeting of the Moscow Soviet, November 6, 1956 (extracts).

Hungary have smashed the forces of reaction and counter-revolution, have prevented the counter-revolution from trampling upon the gains of socialism. . . . [Prolonged applause]

The Declaration issued by the Soviet Government on October 30th, in which it reaffirmed the line of the Twentieth Congress of the Party concerning strict observance of the Leninist principles of equality in relations between the socialist countries, is of enormous importance for the development and further strengthening of friendship and co-operation between the Soviet Union and the other socialist countries. [Applause]

In the future, too, the U.S.S.R. will seek agreement with those circles in the Western countries who favour a solution of controversial issues not by means of the bankrupt "positions of strength" policy, but on the basis of a sober analysis of the interests of other countries. The Soviet Union is determined to improve its relations with the Great Power in the West—the United States of America. We are aware, of course, that certain elements in the United States are still speculating on international difficulties, and accentuating Soviet-American differences. However, a policy of this kind is harmful to the United States and the sooner it is ended the more universal peace and security of all peoples, including the American people, will gain.

The Soviet Government is expending no little effort to improve relations with Britain and France. We hope that the peace-loving forces in these countries will not let the aggressive elements disrupt the friendly contacts between our people.

Comrades, never before has the banner of the Great October Revolution waved so high over the world as at the present time. Never before have such powerful forces of communism, democracy and peace rallied around the sacred socialist banner. Many difficulties have still to be overcome on the road to the final triumph of the cause of the working class and working people of all countries, but the basic line of contemporary world development has been defined once and for all. Now that socialism has triumphed in such great countries as the U.S.S.R. and China, now that there is a socialist world system, that the people of the great India, Indonesia and many other countries of the East have won independence and that additional millions of people in the countries of Europe and Asia, Africa and Latin America are fighting for liberation, the final outcome of the world-wide struggle is no longer in doubt. Today the words of our leader and teacher—the immortal Lenin—that the final victory of socialism is fully and unconditionally assure, ring with renewed force. . . .

Zbigniew Brzezinski

WESTERN COMMENT ON THE CRISIS IN THE SOVIET BLOC

In 1953 the Soviet bloc was characterized by ideological unity and dictatorial centralization of power. Today, Soviet supremacy in Eastern Europe is at stake. And whatever happens between the Elbe and the Bug rivers, between the Baltic and the

Zbigniew Brzezinski, "Ideology and Power: Crisis in the Soviet Bloc," *Problems of Communism*, No. 1957, pp. 12–17.

Adriatic seas, is likely to have grave consequences not only for the USSR as a world power but also for internal Soviet life. The intricate relationship between ideology and power, built up over many years by Stalin, has been dissipated by his successors.

Stalin's death deprived the Soviet System and its peripheral satellites not only of strong leadership but also — and in the long run more important — of the elements of fear and unity of purpose, all component parts of the Stalinist system. It was this system which gave the bloc a coherent frame of reference, and local leadership could in sense anticipate Moscow reactions by basing itself on the fundamental tenets of Stalinism. The result was fawning imitation of Soviet patterns of development and the application of Stalinist methods to local circumstances. Stalin's death did not provoke an immediate abandonment of Stalinism but led rather to a stage of experimentation in the USSR, and consequently also in the peripheries. New solutions to domestic and external problems had to be tested. The death of the dictator left a certain gap, and as a result the succession leadership badly needed some common basis as a point of reference for its decision making. Under these circumstances ideology became more important than it had been for some time.

Disintegration of Ideology and Power

Efforts to cope with existing problems were further complicated by a struggle for power in the top ranks of the Moscow leadership. A crucial by-product of that struggle, important not only for the USSR but above all else for later developments in Eastern Europe, was the weakening of the police apparatus. Since the satellite police networks in the past had been directly tied to the Moscow MVD, the decline of police power caused considerable dislocation and, as is now apparent, also demoralization in the local police establishments. A significant instrument of control was thus lessened and the factor of fear lost its potency.

One of the crucial international issues which faced the succession leadership was the problem of Soviet-satellite relations. This necessarily involved the Yugoslav question. Feeling apparently that Stalin's reaction to Tito was largely a product of the late dictator's pathological hatreds and phobias (see Khrushchev's secret speech), and that domestically Tito was a good Stalinist (a fact certainly true in 1948), some Soviet leaders were inclined to think that the Soviet bloc would be strengthened by a rapprochement with Tito and that international communism would thereby gain increased prestige. It appears further that among the Soviet leaders only Molotov fully understood the disruptive implications of Titoism and warned early in 1955 against this policy, suggesting that while Tito may have been in fact a real Stalinist in the past, a policy of apologia would have unsettling consequences elsewhere in the Soviet bloc. Khrushchev's and Mikoyan's arguments, however, carried the day and the famous B-K [Bulganin and Khrushchev] trip to Belgrade followed in the summer of 1955.

The Soviet leadership, it seems, assumed that Tito was basically still the same dictator he had been in 1948, and that by meeting his demands for local authority a pattern would be established for similarly firm Communist regimes elsewhere. That their assumption was not too far-fetched is suggested by the paradoxical fact that it was not Tito but rather Stalin and Molotov who first appreciated the implications of "Titoism" as a competitive system of "socialism." Tito's position developed slowly. At first it was merely a cry of outrage of a local Stalinist leader against the Stalinist system which could not tolerate little Stalins. Gradually, through internal reforms, policy statements and new clashes with Stalin, a more coherent Titoist line began to emerge. By 1955, however, it was still not a coherent ideology ready for export to supplant Stalinism as the frame of reference for the Soviet bloc.

The Soviet leaders, quite understandably, wanted to reach the broadest ideological cooperation with Tito, believing that this would strengthen their ties with the satellites. This aim was in keeping with their assessments. But Tito, gradually emerging with a theoretical framework of his own, succeeded in June 1955 in holding out for a limited state agreement. He thereby preserved his own ideological independence while still not attempting to export his own position. Stalinism as the frame of reference was still the official if somewhat tarnished doctrine of the Soviet bloc. It was only after Khrushchev's attack on Stalin at the Twentieth CPSU Congress (the motives for which are outside the scope of this paper) and the Kremlin's concomitant lip service to the concept of "separate paths to socialism," that Stalinism was finally shattered and Titoism emerged as a full fledged theory, read to fill the resulting vacuum.

The June 1956 joint declaration of the CPSU and the League of Yugoslav Communist meant to Tito the acceptance of the principle . . . that the roads of conditions of socialist development are different in different countries, that the wealth of the forms of socialist development contributes to their strengthening and . . . that any tendency to impose one's own views in determining the roads and forms of socialist development is alien to both sides. . . .

Curiously, it now appears that even then Khrushchev and others (with the known exception of Molotov) still did not quite realize that their signatures meant in fact giving their blessing to Titoism as the new theoretical statement of the norms for Soviet-satellite relations. Tito was no longer a local Communist dictator, imitations of whom could be set up elsewhere and controlled by Moscow, thereby strengthening the unity of the Soviet bloc. Tito was now

attempting to project his concepts into an overall principle of a multifold pattern of Communist development in Communist states, even in the USSR. The June 1956 declaration opened the way for him, and in 1956 Tito was ideologically and politically prepared to step forward.

This ideological upheaval was paralleled in 1956 by the increasingly apparent disintegration of Soviet control in Poland and Hungary. Years of forced industrialization on the Soviet model had produced widespread poverty in the satellites, serving as a catalyst for mass disillusionment. This, coupled with Stalinist police terror, had alienated the intellectuals; by 1955 they gradually began to speak out in criticism of the existing state of affairs. In both Poland and Hungary it was the intellectuals who spearheaded the growing ferment, and in both countries Communist writers were among those in the first ranks of disaffected critics. In Poland Wazyk with his "Poem for Adults" and Kott with his attacks on socialist realism matched people like Hay and Dery in Hungary. The neutralization and subsequent demoralization of the police apparatus made administrative repression difficult, while the broad support that these people enjoyed among the masses made less violent measures ineffective.

The impact of the intellectuals on the Polish and Hungarian populations (particularly the youth) was enhanced by the fact that they enjoyed an almost complete monopoly of the press, to which they had previously gained access as apologists for the regimes. Furthermore, in both countries the intellectuals traditionally had played a significant political role, formulating and proclaiming national ideals at such times when these countries lacked statesmen or military leaders and were under foreign domination.

The growing protests of the intellectuals over recent months not only influenced the masses but also produced gradual demoralization among the local ruling cadres of the party. An important reason for this was the disproportionately large size of the Communist (Workers) parties in both Poland and Hungary as compared to the more tightly knit party apparatus of the USSR or Yugoslavia. It came as no surprise that under these circumstances the Communist hard core found itself outnumbered even within the party itself.

Stalinist efforts of counterattack in Poland were made difficult not only by the weakness of the ruling group once the police power disappeared but also by the fortuitous circumstances of Bierut's death. This removed from the scene an able organizer and an established ruler. His successors were forced to manipulate rather than to act brutally, while at the same time they were probably unwilling to reveal their internal weakness by calling on Moscow for help. In Hungary, Rákosi's belated moves against the writers in the summer of 1956 were rendered harmless by the outside pressure of Tito, whom the Soviet leadership was willing to accommodate (and also by the Rajk scandal). The June 1956 Tito-Khrushchev declaration, furthermore, gave this ferment a certain ideological content which the Stalinist faction lacked. The latter responded, as in Poland, without firm ideological formulations and was finally reduced to slogans such as "the press and the race are responsible for the present evils," a crude appeal to anti-intellectualism and anti-semitism.

The Soviet Reaction and Policy Alternatives

Soviet recognition of the gravity of the situation appears to have been belated. In the fall of 1956 a secret circular letter was sent out to the various satellite capitals, allegedly warning against the pitfalls of the Yugoslav experience. The time when a mere Moscow letter could turn the clock back had clearly passed, however. The subsequent rushed flight of the Soviet leaders to Warsaw in October suggests that they had underestimated the gravity of the situa-

tion, and that their local stooges possibly had misled them for the sake of their own local interests.

The recent events in Poland and Hungary need no reciting. What might be pointed out again, however, is that Soviet action in Poland and Hungary was one of accommodation to the unfolding situation, with some pattern of hesitation and uncertainty in the Hungarian case. Moscow's reaction in the latter case need not be viewed as inconsistent with its line towards Poland since the revolution in Hungary went so much farther. But what is surprising is the somewhat confused nature of the reaction, ranging from halfhearted intervention, to withdrawal, to brutal repression. Partially, this can be explained in logistical terms. But a further reason is suggested by Tito's Pula speech in mid-November and an article in the Italian Communist organ L'Unita of November 25th. It appears from these presumably well informed sources that the Soviet leadership is itself uncertain and split on what further policies to adopt in Eastern Europe. Having belatedly appreciated both the disintegrative consequences of the ideological vacuum created by the destruction of established doctrine, and the weakness of the local regimes once the political terror decreased, the leadership now has to reassess the entire situation.

The alternatives open to it are basically twofold:

The first is to use force on a large scale to reestablish firm Soviet control in Eastern Europe and to cow any future Gomulkaists. The difficulty with this proposition, apart from the increased danger of war, is that such a policy is probably impossible unless accompanied by a reversion to Stalinism in the USSR itself. The latter would involve considerable resort to force, as the "non-Stalinist" faction (using the term loosely) probably enjoys more widespread support than the "hard policy" group. For this reason the liquidation of the "non-Stalinist" would become necessary if the alternative policy were to prevail. The unanswerable question at this stage is whether the capacity for the reintroduction of fullfledged terror still exists in Moscow. Other possible consequences also would have to be weighed—namely, the weakening effect on world communism, an increase of tensions between Moscow and Peiping, and continuing loss of support in Asia once the policy of brutality were adopted on a larger scale.

Moscow's second alternative is to tolerate and manipulate the present trends in Eastern Europe, using force only when they become excessive, hoping eventually to contain them, and counting at the same time on the continued development of revolutionary trends in other parts of the world. The use of violence in Hungary can still be compatible with this policy. Eventually, it may be hoped in Moscow, Gomulka will fall victim to internal difficulties and the situation will adjust itself. If not, there is always time to adopt the first alternative.

Whichever solution is finally adopted, the monolithic unity of the Soviet bloc has ceased to exist. What in the spring of 1956 Togliatti called "polycentrism" is rapidly becoming, despite Moscow's intentions, a political fact in Eastern Europe. And this fact will not be easy to change. Return to a policy of Stalinism, even if practicable, probably would mean large-scale bloodshed, war, and the further splintering of world communism, including the alienation of China, even though in Eastern Europe it could temporarily lead to a reassertion of Soviet control. But the adoption of the second solution, which the Soviet leadership—barring some unforeseen explosion—apparently has decided to pursue for the time being, also results in the continued splintering of ideological unity and power in the Soviet bloc. Furthermore, the longer the present policy is pursued, with the consequent weakening of Stalinist positions of strength at home and abroad, the

more difficult it will be to abandon the present policy in favor of the first alternative.

Community of Hostile Communisms

Several concepts of socialism, of the methods of achieving it, and of the relations between socialist states already are in competition with each other in Eastern Europe. The Soviet concept, gradually emerging after the destruction of Stalinism and the disappointing experience with Tito, has been most clearly in the Suslov speech of November, 6th, and in the Pravda reply of November 23rd to Tito's speech at Pula a few days earlier. The Soviet position is much clearer on what the leadership wishes to avoid than on what it wishes to establish (thereby testifying again to a certain disunity). The Soviet leaders deny strongly that Stalinism must be combatted through major reforms in the system itself; they also continue to emphasize the preeminent role of Soviet experience although conceding the relevance of local circumstances. The emphasis is still on one-party dictatorship and control from above. They also justify the Soviet military intervention in Hungary as a necessity in view of the "reactionary counterrevolution" which Nagy was not able to control. In this they are supported by the political leadership of East Germany, Rumania, Czechoslovakia, Bulgaria, Albania (there Nagy has been called a "counterrevolutionary bandit"), and also that of Thorez in France. In fact, it is likely that the satellite leaders are putting pressure on Moscow to hold the line against further concessions.

The intermediary position is held by Tito, who, while advocating the complete independence of "socialist states" and the development of socialism along local lines, and denying that there is any need to follow the Soviet example, at the same time insists on the primary role of the Communist Party and will brook no internal opposition. Tito's position, in its outline, is supported by Togliatti who specifically stated (*L'Unità*, November 29th) "I feel that the formula of a 'a guiding party' is obsolete." While the Stalinist features which characterized Tito's Yugoslavia up to about 1950 far more than elsewhere in East Europe have been modified significantly, nonetheless the scope of internal freedom is more limited than in Poland. On the Hungarian issue Tito has gone on record as recognizing with regret the necessity of the second Soviet intervention. Tito's stand in some respects corresponds, it would appear, to the Chinese position. The Chinese Communists recently condemned "big power chauvinism" and have given tacit support to the Poles, but their internal system has not undergone any major changes and is still largely Stalinist. Chou's forthcoming visit to the USSR and Eastern Europe probably will attempt to maintain "the achievements of destalinization" but also will strive to restrain any further moves either by Moscow or Tito or the Poles which could widen the existing breach. This was probably the purpose of the Chinese Communists' pre-New Year statement warning against excessive attacks on Stalinism.

The extreme position is held by Gomulka. While insisting on the same external privileges that Tito gained, internally his concessions have gone much further. The press is relatively free and outspoken, the jamming of foreign broadcasts has ended, books by Polish emiges are being published, Polish sailors can now work on foreign ships, trade unions are being democratized, compulsion in agriculture is being abandoned, large-scale rehabilitation of political victims has been undertaken, the Church has regained its authority in internal matters, the Communist youth organization, patterned on the Komsomol, has broken up, etc. All of this, of course, is at least partially the result of his difficult internal situation since, unlike Tito, Gomulka has to depend for his support on the masses and not on a militant party backed by the police. Nonetheless, even ideologically Gomulka has veered far from the Soviet position in defining socialism as meaning essentially the elimination of exploitation of man by man. This ideal, according to Gomulka, can be achieved in all sorts of ways by all sorts of people, including even Catholics: "Impoverished is the thought that socialism can be built only by people with materialist viewpoints." The Moscow agreement of November 19th between Gomulka and Khrushchev, however, did not go far in giving the Poles ideological equality and the right to mutual criticism as did the analogous agreement with Tito. This suggests again that Moscow is attempting to contain Gomulka, hoping for his internal collapse but shrinking from the use of force for the time being. Yet even in Moscow the Poles refrained from endorsing either of the two Soviet interventions in Hungary, while their press has openly espoused the Hungarian cause.

Today we are witnessing in Eastern Europe a dialogue among Communist parties such as has never been heard before. States which recognize each other as "socialist" are at the same time accusing one another, often in intemperate terms, of a variety of ideological offenses. The Poles and Yugoslavs have gone far in suggesting that the Soviet system is itself responsible for Stalin's excesses. The East Germans have defended Stalinism, have denied Polish claims that a "second revolution" has occurred in Poland, and have stated that Polish outbursts against Stalinism place their authors "in the company of counterrevolution." The Poles have countered by stating that East German Stalinists are afraid of socialism. French Communist leaders have backed the East Germans and have attacked Gomulka. The Czechs have criticized the Yugoslavs. The Soviets have held up the Czechs and the East Germans as an example for other Communist parties to emulate and have condemned Polish statements that relations between Communist parties ought to be based on the principle of "coexistence" (e.g. see Pravda, December 23, 1956, pp. 3–4). The Yugoslavs have clashed publicly with the USSR (the Nagy abduction being a major irritation symptomatic of general strain); while their relations with Albania have degenerated to the level of mutual namecalling. In his Pula speech Tito referred to Enver Hoxha in contemptuous terms; in reply *Zerii Popullit,* the organ of the Albanian party, published a long attack on Tito, referring to him throughout as "Josip Broz-Tito" without the usual prefix "comrade." Putting Tito's Marxism to doubt, the paper alluded to Tito's statements as "anti-Soviet lies" suggesting that they were made for the benefit of the "imperialists." The paper also quoted with approval Suslov's statement that "all the countries which have entered the road of socialist development are generally using the main principles drafted during our revolution and applied in life during the development of the Soviet Union." The Yugoslavs also have clashed with the French and have suggested that the logic of the French defense of Stalin should lead the French CP to a full rehabilitation of Beria.

This dialogue is significant and it is likely to get even louder. In the past all such discussion was synchronized in Moscow and its tone set by an authoritative outburst from the centre. Some interpreters have been inclined to interpret the present exchanges as being similarly directed by Moscow. However, their uneven pattern and the marked variations in their tone and content suggest that local Stalinist leaders are attempting to force Moscow's hand and push it in a direction more in keeping with their own local vested interests. This again is significant if compared to the monolithic pattern of the past. The defense of Stalinism is no longer primarily in Soviet hands.

Implications for the Future.

Future developments depend in great measure on what happens in Poland. The Hungarian's tragic struggle, so moving in its courage that it already has earned a lasting place in history, has resulted in a great political defeat for the USSR. It has finally buried the dream of Khrushchevism: that of manipulated and Moscow-controlled national Communist regimes. It was for the sake of this policy that Moscow embarked on the rash Tito rapprochement. The recourse to force in Hungary, brutal yet without the consistency of the Stalinist pattern, suggests that even in the USSR itself destalinization continues to grapple with forces of Stalinism. The outcome is uncertain and cannot be specifically predicted, either in terms of further Hungarian development or of the broader Soviet picture.

As for Poland, Gomulka has many difficulties ahead of him, including not only a ruined economy but above all else his own precarious position: he must steer in the direction of communism without Moscow support and without a well-organized party, amidst seas of anti-Russian hatred. If he can maintain control, however, it seems safe to judge that the existing ferment in Poland will in time have increasing effect on the internal life of his Communist neighbours, including the USSR itself. Hints of scattered ferment in the Soviet Union itself already have come to the outside world; there have been some indications of minor student unrest and even reports of a workers' sit down strike. The Hungarian revolt must have had a devastating effect even on the very orthodox. For here, in a sense, was a classic Marxist revolution: capitalism (of a state type) had so accentuated the material exploitation of the proletarist which it had created through rapid industrialization, that the workers, supported by the population, rose in spontaneous rebellion. New difficulties must certainly arise in a situation where some Communist states ruled by an iron hand must coexist side by side with other, more relaxed Communist regimes (assuming the latter can succeed in maintaining themselves). If Poland remains officially in Soviet good graces and retains the status of a "socialist state," then inevitably Soviet intellectuals, students, and workers will begin to wonder whether the Polish type of socialism is not preferable to their own. Their questions will be difficult to answer. It will be impossible to dismiss workers' councils or even limited intellectual freedom as examples of "bourgeois sham-democracy." However, it would be idle to expect a repetition of the Hungarian or Polish experiences in the USSR itself. There the regime has not been imposed from the outside, has far greater capacity for survival, and doubtless enjoys a greater measure of popular support or at least acceptance.

As for Moscow's satellite policy, the worst to be feared is a Kremlin decision that its own interests will best be served by a military suppression of Poland, carried out with impunity along the pattern of suppression pursued in Hungary. Under certain circumstances, Soviet leaders might conclude that disillusionment abroad, even in China, is a lesser price to pay than instability at home. But such a calculation would be logical for the Kremlin only if it had advance certitude of a free hand. In the absence of such conditions, the problems of ideology and power in Eastern Europe are likely to continue plaguing the Soviet leadership for a long time to come—and ever closer to home.

E. Goodman

THE CONCEPT OF A COMMONWEALTH OF SOCIALIST STATES

The Moscow Declaration of November 1957 referred to the Soviet orbit variously as "the socialist camp" "the world socialist system" and "the commonwealth of socialist states." Some observers have concluded that the commonwealth idea, connoting a loose grouping of sovereign, independent socialist states, effectively negates the goal of a single supranational Soviet world state. It would seem to be a gross misreading of the evidence, however, to identify the "commonwealth of socialist states" with the idea clustered about "commonwealth" as it is, for example, in the British Commonwealth of Nations. "The world camp of socialism," a Soviet spokesman has explained, "is a monolithic commonwealth of free and sovereign states with common interests and purposes, in which there is not and cannot be antagonism."

The commonwealth idea, in Soviet usage, is of Stalinist origin. Far from negating the world state idea, the term "commonwealth" had been used to describe the future organization of mankind, which, in the same Stalinist tract, was alternately characterized as "a single World Socialist Republic." Similarly, the present basically confederal pattern for East Central Europe

From E. Goodman, *The Soviet Design for a World State*, (New York, 1960), pp. 351–355. Reprinted by permission of Columbia University Press.

goes back to Stalin's proposal of 1920, when it was clearly understood that this transitional form of interstate relations in no way contradicted the idea of a world state.

In the post-Stalinist period the "commonwealth" term first came into prominence with the Soviet Declaration of October 30, 1956, issued at the height of the Hungarian revolt. As has already been noted, the Declaration, claiming that "the great commonwealth of socialist nations" was founded upon "the principles of complete equality, of respect for territorial integrity, state independence and sovereignty and of noninterference in one another's affairs," was followed almost immediately by the brutal and massive Soviet armed intervention in Hungary. Soviet theorists then upheld these acts as examples of fraternal Soviet aid and respect for the independence of sovereignty of Hungary. It must be recalled that national independence and national sovereignty, according to Soviet theory, are attained in their most perfect form when a nation achieves statehood as a Union Republic in an expanding USSR.

"The participants in the great commonwealth of socialist nations," the Soviet ideologue Koronvin asserted in 1958, see that "the consolidation and unity of the socialist countries is a sure guarantee of their national independence and sovereignty." This is manifested, for example, in "the selfless support and help typical of economic relations between the countries of the socialist commonwealth," based on the "socialist division of labor" and "the long term joint coordination of plans for economic development.

All this is an illustration of the masterly prophecy made by Lenin when he spoke of a "tendency towards the creation of a single world economy, regulated" in accordance with a general plan "by the proletariat of all nations" and which "should certainly be further developed and fully consummated under socialism."

The further development and full consummation of the existing socialist "commonwealth" is still explicitly found in Lenin's vision of 1920, as codified in the Theses of the Second Comintern Congress. The lives of all nations, Lenin had specified, would come to be regulated by a single common world economic plan operating within the framework of a Soviet world state.

Another of Lenin's theoretical prescriptions of 1920 has obviously served to guide Khrushchev's seeming improvisations. Though Khrushchev has not succeeded in his gambit to win over Tito, it is enlightening to recall the initial Soviet explanation of its entente with Yugoslavia of June 1955, as an indication of how Khrushchev hoped to deal with national differences within the various Communist-controlled states. In an official clarification of its recently signed accord with Tito, Moscow granted that, "given unity in the most important and basic matter of guaranteeing the victory of socialism, different forms and methods of deciding the concrete problems of socialist contruction can be applied in different countries, depending upon historic and national peculiarities." Subsequently, it seems to have been impossible to achieve unity in those matters which Khrushchev deemed "important and basic," but this formula has supposedly found its application within the socialist "commonwealth," where, it is claimed, a basic unity of views exists.

Khrushchev's formula would appear to be little more than a paraphrase of Lenin's admonition of 1920 that "national and state differences exist among peoples and countries, and these differences will continue to exist for a very long time, even after the dictatorship of the proletariat has been established on a world scale. What was required of the working class movement in all countries, therefore, was "not the elimination of variety, not the abolition of national differences (that is a foolish dream at the present moment), but such an application of the fundamental principles of communism . . . as will correctly modify these principles in certain particulars, correctly adapt and apply them to national and national state differences." Although the post-Stalinist Soviet leadership was forced to moderate Stalin's senseless demand for a rigid, mechanical imitation of the Soviet Russian pattern in its every aspect, Khrushchev could conveniently hark back to Lenin's pragmatic, flexible approach that would sanction the play of national variations within the general framework of the "valid" Russian pattern.

Khrushchev was also unquestionably aware of Lenin's fundamental purpose in taking account of national peculiarities. By so doing he hoped to neutralize and minimize national resentments and antagonisms so that, as Lenin added in the next breath, Moscow could "create a really centralized, leading center, capable of directing international tactics of the revolutionary proletariat in its struggle for a World Soviet Republic." Lenin's ultimate image of a world society was totally centralist, and he wanted the tightest possible integration of all nations into a Soviet world state. While he condemned the imposition of a centrally devised plan upon all nations as "a foolish dream at the present moment," it was precisely this dream that lay at the end of his intended historical journey.

From Lenin's point of view, Stalin could not be censured for the direction in which he was moving by imposing an increasingly uniform pattern on all nations under his control, but only for the miscalculation of time required for such national refashionings to take hold. Within the Soviet Union it took several decades of terror, mass purges, deportations, and even repression of open armed rebellion to install the Soviet system of controls in the rimlands surrounding Great Russia. The constant struggle against "nationalist deviations" in the Ukraine; prolonged guerrilla warfare with the Basmachi in Soviet Central Asia; armed uprisings in the Transcaucasus, such as the Azerbaijani riots of May 1920; the Armenian rebellion of February 1921, that drove the Soviet administration out of the capital of Erivan, and the August 1924 national uprising in Georgia that temporarily paralyzed Soviet rule, an uprising whose reverberations were apparently still being heard in the Tiflis riots of March 1956; all these are but samplings of the encounters that Moscow had with non-Russian nations long before the Polish and Hungarian rebellions of 1956. Viewed in this perspective, the rebellion of the East European satellites is hardly novel. Stalin's innovation was his attempt to compress the process of assimilating the People's Democracies into the Soviet body politic in a briefer span than had been required for the non-Russian nations of the former Russian Empire, where the imprint of political independence was more remote and less well established than in the newly acquired East European satellites.

It is little wonder that the relaxation of Stalinist pressures following his death set loose rebellious elements that lay beneath the veneer of imposed conformity. Stalin's embarrassing failure to master the forces of Yugoslav communism, compounded by the Polish and Hungarian explosions, made the Kremlin painfully aware that it needed time to digest recalcitrant nations successfully. The "many roads" theory, it would seem, was devised as a calculated play for time, to entice, cajole, and finally to attempt to coerce deviants back onto the single, ever-narrowing path marked out by Moscow. Although Khrushchev has only met with partial success in this program, can it be doubted that his ultimate "solution," like Stalin's, is the total subservience of the peripheral nations to the Russian center? If there must be an uncomfortable, unavoidable, even prolonged interim before achieving this acceptable "solution," it must still be considered an interim.

One of the requirements for charting a steady course in the desired direction is the absence of serious dissension among the top policy makers in the Kremlin. When the power struggle among Stalin's heirs was aggravated by the vacillation and confusion of the destalinization process, the satellite leaders were emboldened to weaken Moscow's channels of control. As might be expected, the resolution of factional differences in the Kremlin, such as resulted from the purges and demotions of Khrushchev's major rivals (Malenkov, Molotov, Kaganovich in June 1957, Zhukov in October 1957, and Bulganin beginning in March 1958), have helped remove the restraints and indecision that had momentarily stayed the hand of the strong centralized authority over the outlying satrapies.

In the future, Khrushchev predicted in 1959, the importances attached to state borders in Central and Eastern Europe will progressively diminish, after the pattern already in evidence among the Republics of the USSR. He cited the controversies over the borders of a divided Germany and over the territorial lines between Poland and the Soviet Union, Yugoslavia and Hungary, Rumania and Hungary, and Rumania and the Soviet Union as examples of the legacy of capitalism which is doomed to extinction. Then going beyond the further integration of European states, he announced flatly: "With the victory of communism on a worldwide scale, borders among states will disappear."

A. Zauberman

ECONOMIC INTEGRATION OF THE BLOC: PROBLEMS AND PROSPECTS

After long and ineffectual reliance upon intra-bloc trade as the primary mechanism for integrating their individual economies, the Soviet Union and its East European orbit partners have at last accepted the logic of their own internal form of centrally-controlled and planned economy and are seeking to achieve bloc-wide economic integration through extra-long-term supra-national planning. This important new phase of orbit economic development, although foreshadowed as early as 1955, began to take definite shape only much more recently and, as yet, still remains in its infant stage. Nevertheless, it is perhaps not too early to try to place it in historical perspective and to examine, if only in tentative

fashion, some of the problems it is likely to encounter.

Efforts at economic coordination of the Soviet sphere of control in Eastern Europe date all the way back to its establishment at the close of World War II. During the postwar phase of Stalinist rule, the East European economies were subjected to direct Soviet intervention on a broad scale, ranging from the imposition of delivery quotas—either as "war reparations" or under some other heading—to the stationing of Soviet "advisers" at key points in the satellite economic structures and the establishment of Soviet-operated industrial enclaves in East Germany. The overall effect of these measures was to put in operation

A. Zauberman, "Economic Integration: Problems and Prospects," *Problems of Communism*, No. 4. (1959), pp. 23–29.

an extremely crude sort of integrating machinery. Needless to say, it operated in a manner that was harmful to the East European economies, but it served the purpose of Moscow's "get-rich-quick" policies of the time.

Post-Stalin Policy

Even before the Stalinist epoch came to an end, changing conditions made it apparent that this one-sided, exploitative type of integrating mechanism had outlived its usefulness, and steps towards dismantling it began. Later political developments in the Soviet Union and elsewhere in the orbit served to speed up the dismantling process. Today, the only area in which a remnant of the old outmoded system continues to operate—and even here in much attenuated form—is the extraction and processing of nuclear fuel.

In the meantime, the early 1950's saw the crystallization of a new Soviet policy stressing maximum development of the economic potential of the East European bloc. Such an objective necessarily entails the most efficient possible utilization of available resources, and this in turn demands that individual commodities be produced where their respective production costs are comparatively lowest. In other words, to be fully effective, the Soviet policy of maximizing the economic potential of the whole bloc logically required the formation of an integrated bloc economy in which production would be organized strictly on the basis of comparative advantage.

In fact, thoroughgoing integration on these lines has proven extremely difficult to attain for various reasons, not least of which has been the persistent postwar tendency of the individual economies within the bloc to pursue autarkic policies and hence to become self-sufficient entities. Although Khrushchev now insists that he repeatedly cautioned the orbit countries—Hungary in particular—not to overindulge in such poli-

cies, their strong predilection for autarky has stemmed, in large part, from the very economic strategy which Moscow prescribed for the orbit to follow. One of the basic principles of this strategy, of course, is the priority development of capital goods industry—a rule derived from Marxist-Leninist theory and therefore sacrosanct. (It is interesting to note that the view of a Polish economist challenging the universality of this principle was sharply condemned as "heretical" by the Moscow guardians of economic orthodoxy as recently as mid-1958.)

The very fact that all members of the bloc were required the same strategy inevitably resulted in the multiplication of identic economic structures and narrowed the possibility of dovetailing them. It also produced some striking economic follies. To cite an extreme example, Hungary tried to develop a steel industry in the face of the fact that the foreign-exchange cost of imported raw materials per ton of steel produced in Hungarian mills exceeded, by itself, the cost of a ton of finished steel purchased from abroad.

Another factor which spurred the bloc countries to strive after self-sufficiency was the unreliability of supply sources within the orbit. In fact, experience has shown that the same impulsion operates at every echelon of a Soviet-type economy, from the individual enterprise on up. The desire to be as independent as possible from uncertain and unpredictable outside suppliers is a well-known and readily understandable element in the psychological make-up of the Soviet firm manager. It is entirely natural that this trait should have projected itself upward into the psychology of orbit economic planners at the top national level.

Trade as an Integrator

Besides the tendency towards autarky, there was a further impediment to effective economic integration, namely the bloc's primary reliance upon the intra-bloc trade network as the integrating mechanism. Trade can, indeed, be a powerful engine of coordination and unification. It can effectively integrate a market economy within national frontiers, and where effective international markets operate, it can perform the same function on the international scale. Competitive markets automatically reveal the cheapest sources of supply and tend to channelize productive resources accordingly. Hence in order to integrate a group of national market economies in accord with the rule of comparative advantage, all that is necessary — in principle — is to assure the effective operation of a competitive international market by eliminating trade barriers such as customs tariffs and all types of quota restrictions. In practice, however, as the recent experience of such international agencies as the Organisation for European Economic Cooperation (OEEC), the European Coal and Steel Community (ECSC), and the European Economic Community (EEC) has shown, the dovetailing even of market economies, under contemporary conditions, requires supplementing the trade mechanism with a good deal of further coordination of various economic elements through some sort of intergovernmental planning.

In a family of centrally-planned economies of the Soviet type, on the other hand, there is incomparably less scope for achieving overall integration along lines of maximum productive efficiency through the operation of trade alone. Their domestic prices are divorced from external markets and consequently provide scant guidance as to which among them is the least expensive producer of any given commodity. Each member's whole pattern of production is consciously insulated against the pressure of market forces; it is governed, as are all areas of domestic life, by the national economic plan. Thus, it is demonstrable in logic that, just as the orbit countries rely upon their respective plans to regulate and

integrate their economies on the national plane, so must they turn to supranational planning as the appropriate method of integration for the whole group, as an entity.

Why, then, did the Soviet Union and its orbit partners persist in relying chiefly on mutual commerce for this purpose — clearly the wrong instrument in an environment of planned economies? The internationally know economist Dr. Gunnar Myrdal, in an illuminating study, has rightly stressed the paradox presented by this restriction of the tools of integration basically to trade when the states concerned wield unlimited powers over all the means of production in their economies. By way of explanation a Soviet official who plays a prominent role in the current phase of economic integration efforts of the bloc, came forward recently with the argument that the concentration of intra-bloc trade was dictated by international political and economic conditions in the late 1940's, specifically by the "economic boycott of the socialist camp countries." It may be conceded that once Stalin had slammed the door against further cooperation with the West, the substitution of intra-bloc trade channels for those severed with the West naturally must have been a matter of immediate concern. But this still would not explain why the system instituted to cope with this emergency subsequently was retained as a mechanism of bloc economic integration. Perhaps Dr. Myrdal is near the truth when he surmises that the explanation has something to do with the doctrinal survival of Stalin's concept of "socialism in one country" at a time when it already had become anachronistic.

Brakes on Intra-Bloc Trade

A further point deserves mention. One partner in a group of countries is handicapped in its search for trade opportunities if it cannot use currency earned from exports to another member of the group in order to purchase goods from any third member. Hence, a group of market economies seeking to assure better integration tends to develop "multilaterality" of trade through the adoption of some kind of arrangements making the currencies of the member countries mutually "transferable" so that a member acquiring a credit balance vis-à-vis another need not worry about being able to make the best use of it elsewhere. This was the purpose, for example, of the West European payments union which was set up within the framework of the OEEC.

By contrast, trade within the Soviet-East European orbit has consistently tended towards "bilaterality": that is, individual pairs of countries conclude separate trade agreements which, as a rule, are long-term and provide for strictly-balanced exchanges of goods. In fact, any other system would hardly be workable inasmuch as what a bloc member can sell to another is fixed by its national economic plan, which obviously would be thrown out of kilter if the system permitted an unscheduled demand for goods to be made by a third country. It is thus apparent that little room exists for transferability, or convertibility, of currencies in trade arrangements among countries with centrally-planned economies. Still, there have been constant complaints from bloc members that the lack of currency convertibility under the bilateral system restricts their opportunities and hinders trade growth. In response to these grumblings, an attempt has been made since 1957 to provide machinery for the current settlement of intra-bloc trade balances by having the Soviet State Bank act as a clearing house. As was to be expected, however, this makeshift arrangement has not been successful, and its failure is now being frankly admitted by Soviet spokesmen.

True, the volume of intra-bloc exchanges of commodities has swelled appreciably over the years (roughly two and one-half times during the 1950's) and they now account for 60 per cent of the total foreign trade of bloc members — 70 per cent if trade with non-European Communist countries is included in the intra-bloc figure. In 1957, for example, intra-bloc trade channels supplied four-fifths of the members' total imports of machinery and capital equipment; 75 to 100 per cent of their imports of fuel, iron ore and pig-iron, fertilizers, grains, and timber; and half of their cotton imports. Nevertheless, there has been a growing awareness that the intra-bloc trade mechanism does not, of itself, forge the bloc economies into a coherently integrated whole based on a rational division of labor, and that the lack of such integration not only causes enormous waste but also hampers the economic growth of the entire bloc. It was only when the Communist leaders finally realized the urgency of this problem that serious efforts began to be made to integrate the bloc economies by methods more compatible with their basic character.

Birth of a New Approach

The Council of Mutual Economic Aid established by Stalin in 1949 as a counterpoise to the OEEC and West European economic consolidation under the Marshall plan, has furnished the framework for these efforts. Despite its ten-year existence, the CMEA actually has had only three or four of active life; its function for several years seems to have been confined largely to lending titular sponsorship to bilateral trade agreements concluded between its members, but since the mid-1950's, its institutional framework has been rapidly expanded and life has been infused into what was formerly little more than one of Stalin's dummies. Starting with the sixth session at Budapest in 1955, successive CMEA meetings have delineated broad boundaries of economic specialization within the bloc, and individual committees dealing with practically every area and facet of economic activity have sought to develop the habit of intra-bloc cooperation on the technological plane.

All this represents progress but nonetheless within rather narrow limits. In the area of specialization there have been frequent reports that the CMEA has allotted the leading role in hard-coal mining and zinc and sulphur production to Poland; in brown coal mining and processing, to East Germany; in oil and natural gas production, to the USSR and Rumania; in bauxite extraction and aluminum products to Hungary. Within the particular field of engineering industry, Poland and East Germany are directed to concentrate, *inter alia,* on shipbuilding; Czechoslovakia chiefly on heavy machinery, East Germany on precision instruments, and the Soviet Union, *i.a.,* on steel mill equipment. Most of these "allocations," however, merely reflect the pattern of specialization resulting from natural endowment or from historically developed special skills. It is only when one goes beyond the allotment of general fields of specialization to the assignment of the thousands of different items making up the product-ranges of such diversified industries as engineering and chemicals that the real job of coordination begins.

The CMEA has, it is true, already ventured into this complex area by compiling detailed catalogues of specialization. According to a recent Soviet report, the May 1956 CMEA session at Berlin, for example, indicated lines of specialization for several hundred different products of the machine-making industry. Still, this has not prevented Czechoslovakia, a small country with a limited home market, from continuing to produce 80 per cent of all items covered by the international nomenclature of engineering. Moreover, intra-bloc trade movements have not given evidence of greater specialization, whereas real progress in this area would naturally tend to reflect itself in stepped-up exchanges of products within the bloc. This has not been evident in industry; it also entails reallocation of fuel supplies and shifts in manpower, and may further require augmentation of ship-building and steel-making capacities by the addition of new yards, coke ovens, furnaces, and rolling mills. Such an involved process of adjustment necessarily takes time, since years must elapse before a newly programmed mine, steel mill, or shipyard actually enters operation. Moreover, extra capital is required to build and equip them, posing the question of whether to seek foreign credits or attempt to "squeeze" it out of the domestic economy through enforced savings, with inevitable repercussions upon the popular welfare. Schematic as this hypothetical example may be, it suffices to show how bloc action to adjust and correlate production projects for a single item may necessitate a whole gamut of additional decisions on a bloc-wide scale, including in particular those affecting the distribution of national income and the balance of payments of individual bloc members.

New Principles of Integration

It is precisely on the points just outlined that responsible Soviet economists now appear to have recognized the defects and shortcomings of the abortive 1955 experiment in intra-bloc coordination. Their keener perception of the root causes of failure has led to the formulation of new principles according to which, in addition to being multilateral, coordinated economic planning for the bloc (1) should be detailed and comprehensive in scope, and (2) should be carried out on the basis of a much longer plan-period, perhaps as long as 15 years. These new concepts were considered important enough to be given formal endorsement at the "summit" conference of bloc leaders held at Moscow in May 1958, and a month later the 8th CMEA session at Warsaw took the first steps toward their implementation. As a result of these developments, the bloc has moved appreciably nearer to a system of supra-national, extra long-term planning as the logical method of economic integration.

Logical as the system may be, however, its implementation confronts intra-bloc economic planners with at least as many new problems and dilemmas as it solved. An examination of the various difficulties involved has fortunately been facilitated by the fact that, after years of secrecy, some information is at last being published with regard to how the CMEA goes about its business. Thus, it has recently been revealed that the fundamental method relied upon by the CMEA in implementing economic coordination is one based on the concept of "material balance of output and use of individual products, for the world socialist system as a whole and, first of all, for the member countries of the CMEA."

Intrinsically the method contains nothing new, for it merely projects into intra-bloc planning a concept which has long been basic to the methodology of Soviet (and hence the other orbit countries') national economic planning. Reduced to simple terms, the method as applied nationally involves the planning, regulation, and adjustment of all factors governing output (supply) on the one hand (labor, materials and equipment input, etc.) and of product-use (consumption) on the other, so as to bring these elements into equilibrium and thus establish a "balance" in each individual sector of the economy. The balances for different but interrelated sectors must necessarily be dovetailed together, e.g., the balance for the iron and steel industry must be dovetailed with that for energy sources, from which it gets its coking-coal and electric power; with the balance for ore mining, on which it depends for raw materials; and doubly with the balance for engineering industry, which not only supplies capital equipment to the steel industry but inversely obtains from it its supplies of steel. All the numer-

ous balances are, of course, closely related to the key balance of labor supply and use. Hence, it is obvious that the task of working out the individual balances and of interlocking them into a coherent, dynamic whole is already formidable enough on the national scale. It stands to reason that, on a vastly enlarged international scale and with a prolonged plan-period, the problems and pitfalls facing the planners will multiply more than proportionately. In fact, by the time they extend their coordinating efforts to cover half a generation of economic activities spread over an area from the Elbe to the Pacific, it can safely be predicted that the difficulties will assume nightmare dimensions.

Major Economic Problems

While shunning technical intricacies, the writer would like at this point to make specific though very cursory mention of a few of the major hurdles which confront the orbit planners. First of all, their fundamental task is to determine which bloc country has the best conditions for developing a certain line of production — or, in other words, in which country investment in a given branch of productive activity will be most fruitful. In a Soviet type economy, however, the planner experiences enormous difficulties in trying to compare potential yields from alternative uses of capital — one of the snags being that, according to Marxian ideology, only labor, and not capital as such, can have value-creating property. The difficulties are great enough within the bounds of a single economy but are so much the greater on an international scale, as for example when trying to figure out whether it would be more economical to sink another coal mine in Poland or to invest instead in a new Rumanian oil well in order to obtain a given increment to the energy balance.

A closely-related problem is that of pricing. In order to choose the most efficient producer among several countries, it is necessary to know and compare their production costs. However, costs can be compared internationally only if the prices on which they are based are internationally comparable. The point is that, in the orbit economies, they are not. As has already been pointed out, prices in each bloc country are completely divorced from the outside world. And even though ingenious yardsticks have been devised to help the national planners obtain some idea whether a given commodity had best be imported or produced at home (and perhaps exported), the simpler formulas are too crude to be of much use, and the more refined too unwieldy for practical application. Here again, if the problem is a difficult one for the national planner, it is vastly more difficult on the international, i.e., intra-bloc, scale.

One more vital problem has to do with the emergent realization that effective integration of the bloc economies implies a high degree of intra-bloc mobility of capital, labor, and managerial and technical skills. The question of capital mobility is largely one of Soviet capacity and willingness to help finance economic development in the rest of the orbit. This recalls to mind the excellent article by Victor Winston which appeared in these pages some time ago, and which (for the first time to the present writer's knowledge) broached the question of whether the dependent orbit countries have become an economic liability to the USSR. As one who broadly subscribes to Winston's affirmative answer, the present writer would however like to offer one qualification. Although, as far as one can judge, the period of ruthless Soviet milking of the orbit economies does appear to be a thing of the past, the criterion of whether or not they now are a "liability" to the USSR is the drain on Soviet resources for financing their growth. Actually, there is little prospect of any substantial flow of

Soviet capital to the East European dependent area because the USSR itself is a capital-hungry nation and will remain so in the foreseeable future; its present query for Western credits should dispel any fallacious ideas that have gained currency on this score. Moreover, should the Soviet Union commit itself further to helping China finance her industrialization program, reversing the present trend in the Sino-Soviet balance of payments, Soviet resources which could be spared for developing the East European orbit economies would be very sharply reduced. It is highly significant in this connection that the only extra long-term national economic plan that has so far been published in detail by a bloc country — the Polish plan, extending to 1975 — assumes self-sufficiency in capital, despite the fact that the severe pressure of population on Polish resources makes an influx of capital indispensable if there is to be substantial economic growth.

The absence of mobility in respect of the manpower factor has a different background. The dependent bloc economies include some with a surplus of manpower and a measure of more or less disguised unemployment, as well as others where progress is severely hampered by a chronic and acute manpower deficit — notably East Germany and Czechoslovakia. Yet, with one or two quite marginal exceptions (such as the small scale and mainly seasonal migration of Bulgarian workers to the Soviet Union), there have been no indications of any intra-bloc move to equalize these imbalances of labor supply through increased mobility. Here, of course, the obstacles are political and psychological, rather than economic.

Political Stumbling Blocks

Indeed, while the whole focus of the present article has deliberately been economic, it must not be forgotten that the movement toward bloc economic integration has far-reaching political implications, just as some of the problems it faces are political in nature. Economic integration means greater economic strength, and greater economic strength means increased external political strength for the bloc as a whole. But this is not all. As a long-range policy, economic integration also may commend itself to Soviet policy makers as a means of strengthening intra-bloc ties and thereby consolidating Soviet political hegemony over Eastern Europe—the more so because they may see in it the way that is comparatively least provocative and hence least likely to evoke resistance and trouble.

It would appear, however, that these implications have also not escaped the leaders of the dependent orbit countries, and that their political sensitivities constitute one of the stumbling blocks in the way of bloc economic integration. This is indirectly evidenced by the fact that Soviet leaders and economists have been prone to insist that the CMEA is not a supra-national body and does not affect national sovereignties. A. N. Kosygin, head of the Soviet State Planning Commission, for example, has gone on record with an emphatic statement that there is no single master plan in the CMEA. Again, the same sort of assurance was the leitmotif of the congratulatory address delivered by the permanent secretary of CMEA, Fadeyev, at the tenth anniversary session of the organization held at Tirana in May 1959.

In contrast to its meetings of the preceding few years, the Tirana session seems to have discreetly side-stepped the thorny central problem of overall planning for integration—possibly because it was considered hardly fitting to air fundamental issues and difficulties on such a gala occasion. Most of the session's attention was devoted to bottlenecks in certain sectors (coking coal and non-ferrous metals) and projects, already long discussed but as yet not matured, for interconnecting power grids across national boundaries. In short, technical problems rather than basic economic issues dominated the discussion.

As pointed out above, moreover, the basic economic issues are inextricably linked with political ones. Despite Soviet assurances that the CMEA is not a supra-national organ seeking to impose a single plan such an authoritative Soviet economist as Professor O. Bogomolov has, in effect, qualified these assurances with a highly significant "not as yet." The qualification seems to reflect tacit recognition that the process of integration will be fully consummated only if and when the orbit economies are directed as a single unit in accordance with a single plan drawn up and implemented from a single center of authority. This would practically make the forging of an organic political entity a necessary precondition for full-fledged economic integration—and such a development can hardly be contemplated as a real possibility in the post 1956 political climate of Central and Eastern Europe.

In any event, it is abundantly clear that the bloc of centrally-planned economies, though hardly past the threshold of its new, more "logical" approach to economic integration is already discovering obstacles to which, as the same Professor Bogomolov admits, no satisfactory solutions have yet been found. In the writer's view, the experience of the CMEA lends strong support to the proposition—theoretically evolved by the well-known American economist Professor Jacob Viner—that it is far more difficult to integrate centrally planned socialist economies than market economies, without the suppression of national identities.

Herein lies the fundamental dilemma of the Soviet planners in Eastern Europe.

CZECHOSLOVAKIA'S VIEW OF HER ECONOMIC ROLE IN THE SOVIET BLOC

Solving the Main Economic Task

The task of tipping the scales in world production in favor of the socialist system, as against the capitalist system, is being solved by all socialist countries on the basis of the socialist international division of labor, co-ordinated long-term planning, specialization and co-operation in production, and extensive scientific and technical exchanges. Each socialist country is doing its bit for the common victory in economic competition with the capitalist world.

Among the countries which have taken the path of socialism, no small part is played by Czechoslovakia. Czechoslovakia is contributing substantially to the economic progress of the entire socialist camp. A country with a highly developed industry before the war, the new Czechoslovakia has made great progress, particularly in machine-building. By 1958 its industrial output had more than trebled compared with pre-war, with machine-building registering a fivefold increase. Today, industry accounts for over four-fifths of the gross output of the country.

Czechoslovakia is successfully competing with the leading capitalist countries in the economic field. It has outstripped many of them in per capita output for a number of items. For example, it has surpassed France, Italy, and Japan in per capita generation of electric power; Japan, Italy, Austria, Canada, and Sweden for pig iron output; France, Austria, and Sweden for steel output; France, Canada, Japan, Sweden, and Italy for coal extraction.

A nation's way of life, however, is determined not only by output, but also by the level of consumption. Per capita consumption of a number of foodstuffs in Czechoslovakia is also higher than in many capitalist countries: meat consumption, for instance, is higher than in Austria, Holland, Norway, and Italy; consumption of milk and sugar is higher than in Belgium, West Germany, France, and Italy. Footwear purchased in Czechoslovakia amounts to 3.8 pairs per head of the population—the highest for all European countries. It should be pointed out that this sharp rise in consumption has taken place during the years of socialist construction. For example, compared with 1936 per capita consumption of sugar has risen from 23.2 to 34.9 kgs; fats from 14.1 to 17.5 kgs; meat from 34 to 54 kgs; eggs from 138 to 170; and fruit from 42.9 to 61.5 kgs.

In the period from 1953 there were seven successive price reductions in Czechoslovakia, resulting in a gain for the population of some 18 billion crowns a year and in a 25 per cent rise in the purchasing power of the crown.

In the third quarter of 1959, compared with June 1953, the general index of expenditure of a working class family on food, rent, clothing and other essentials dropped to 79.7 points, that of a peasant family to 76.2 points.

Simultaneously with this, wages and incomes rose. Real wages of factory, office and other workers went up approximately 38 per cent, compared with 1937, with the wages of factory workers increasing at a faster rate. The income level of the peasant family has in recent years drawn closer to that of the working class family. These facts testify to a steady rise in real wages; unem-

World Marxist Review, No. 2 (1960) pp. 11–15

ployment has been abolished, and the annual intake of workers in the national economy is at a rate of about 1,000,000 a year.

Under socialism the well-being of the people is determined, in addition to wages, by the constantly developing social services. Take, for example, the generous children's allowances, old-age pensions and the big state allocations for social and cultural services. The sum paid in allowances for three children adds up to about a third of the average wage and increases proportionately with the number of children, plus a simultaneous substantial tax reduction. Pensions are granted not only to factory, office and other workers but also to country people, including individual peasants. Public welfare (pensions, scholarships, health insurance) amounts to one-fifth of the income of the working man. In nearly all capitalist countries the cost of living is rising. According to bourgeois statistics, which hardly give the full picture, expenditure on rent, medical treatment and education in the United States, Britain, France, and West Germany adds up to about 20 per cent of the family income. In Czechoslovakia rent averages 2 to 3 per cent of the family expenditure, while health services, medicine, and education are free.

Czechoslovakia's high standard of living makes nonsense of the contention of capitalist apologists that industrial development in the socialist countries takes place at the expense of the well-being of the people. . . .

Czechoslovakia in the Socialist Commonwealth

In keeping with the decisions of the Moscow conference of the Communist and Workers' parties of the member countries of the Council for Mutual Economic Aid, and the recommendations made at the IXth session (1958) of the Council in Bucharest, bilateral talks on economic co-operation were held between Czechoslovakia, on the one hand, and Albania, Bulgaria, Hungary, the German Democratic Republic, Poland, Rumania, and the Soviet Union, on the other.

Practical questions of co-operation were discussed in the commissions and at sessions of the Council. This stage of coordinating plans envisages further co-operation in trade and in carrying out important economic measures.

Long-term agreements signed by Czechoslovakia for 1958–60, especially the agreements for 1961–65, provide for a considerable growth of trade with the Council's members; in 1965 this trade will be double the 1957 volume. These agreements act as stabilizers for the economy and determine its prospects on the basis of the growing socialist international division of labor.

This is particularly true of machine-building—the key branch—which will turn out machinery for the chemical, power, iron and steel, food and light industries and equipment for building materials enterprises; as well as metal cutting lathes, forging and pressing equipment, electric and diesel locomotives, automobiles, tractors, diesel-engines and computers.

Foreign trade plays an important part in the economy of the country. Czechoslovakia ranks first in the socialist camp for volume of foreign trade per head of the population; twenty-five per cent of the national income derives from this trade. At the same time our economy depends largely on imports of iron ore, non-ferrous metals, rubber, cotton, wool, hides and foodstuffs (mainly grain and meat).

Since imports of staple raw materials and foodstuffs and exports of machinery and equipment are vital for the country, Czechoslovakia, naturally, is interested in an all-round extension of trade with the socialist countries. At the moment this trade is over 70 per cent (the figure for the Soviet Union being 33 per cent) of her total foreign trade.

. . . Co-operation between the socialist countries, based on planned development, furthers the economic advance of these countries and paves the way to specialization and coordination of production in accordance with the natural resources, economic potential and the traditions of each country. It ensures a more useful and more advantageous allocation and development of the productive forces of the socialist camp as a whole and a more rational utilization of the natural resources of each country in the interests of the socialist world. This immeasurably increases the economic potential of the socialist countries, strengthens the international positions of socialism and ensures rising standards of living for hundred of millions.

The economic co-operation between the socialist countries has entered a new phase, when the advantages of the socialist world system will make themselves felt in even greater measure, advantages which accelerate the progress of all members of the socialist camp. The division of labor between the socialist countries reinforces the friendship which unites them in the struggle for the common goal—the building of socialism and communism, preservation of peace, and victory in economic competition with the capitalist world.

THE NEW LOOK IN THE COMMUNIST CAMP

After the Soviet Twenty-first Congress in 1959, it was no longer the revisionist countries in Eastern Europe which embarrassed the Russians, but rather those members of the bloc that were neo-Stalinist by inclination.

Why was this so? In the first place, it should not be forgotten that Khrushchev's original aim in delivering the secret speech had been to steer Russia and the communist bloc into a new political phase, leaving behind the legacy bequeathed by Stalin's rule. Soviet suppression in Eastern Europe later in 1956, although reminiscent of Stalinist policy, was not deliberately prepared by Khrushchev, but was carried out in order to cut short a revolt that had been inadequately foreseen inside Russia. It represented an unpremeditated flashback to the past that merely held up the planned advance to a more liberal future. When calm was restored in 1959, it was seen that the neo-Stalinist countries were now the ones which were out of line with Soviet policy. On the neo-Stalinist wing, the solidarity of views shared by East Germany, Czechoslovakia, and to some extent Bulgaria became more apparent. In June 1960 the Soviet leaders found it necessary to criticize "dogmatism" through the medium of the press. Scarcely veiled accusations were leveled at Ulbricht, the Secretary of the East German Communist Party.

Taken on their own, the dissenting views of these countries were not sufficiently influential to cause the U.S.S.R. much trouble, but the real danger to Khrushchev lay in the fact that their opinions on ideology and foreign policy appeared to veer closer to Chinese rather than to Soviet attitudes at a time when the Sino-Soviet conflict was blowing hotter. As we shall see when we come to consider relations between Russia and China in this period, the latter did not discard Stalinist tenets, but flaunted them like a red rag in Russia's face and rallied to the side of other communist states that held similar political views. In the case of East Germany and Czechoslovakia, the ties were economic as well as political, as China relied to a great extent on supplies from them for crucial portions of her industrial program.

The firm attitude of Czechoslovakia and East Germany had helped to anchor the bloc firmly to Russia again after the uprising of 1956, but their continued adherence to a "hard" policy after 1957–58 was embarrassing to the U.S.S.R. The Russians feared that these two countries might eventually imitate Stalinist Albania, which towards the end of this period allied herself directly with China against Russia.

Albania's position was in some ways similar to China's. She too suffered from economic and social backwardness in relation to the rest of the communist world and to Russia in particular. Both Albania and China had taken on communist governments without direct Soviet military aid, and neither of them could tolerate the existence of a neutral Yugoslavia—China mainly for ideological reasons, Albania chiefly on account of her traditional hatred of an overbearing neighbor. Together they struggled to win over other countries in the bloc to their point of view at inter-party meetings held in Bucharest in June 1960 and in Moscow in November of the same year.

The Stalinist countries in the communist camp worried the Soviet Union in yet another way. Just when Khrushchev was making an all-out attempt to woo the less-developed countries into joining the new socialist commonwealth which was painted in glowing terms for the outside world, China and her communist sympathizers took pains to make it quite clear that their attitude towards nationalist governments in the uncommitted areas of the world did not differ one jot from the line Stalin had taken between 1945 and 1953, which had had such disastrous effects. Once again it looked as though Russia was hamstrung between the swinging pendulum of left and right opinion within the communist camp.

By the time of the Soviet Twenty-second Congress in 1961, the East European communist bloc, which had reached the height of its unity at Stalin's death, had become a much more loosely knit group of partly self-willed countries. The totalitarian empire was fast dissolving into a socialist commonwealth.

We have noted the developments that led to this change; it might be useful to give a brief sketch of the revised institutional framework still binding the camp to Russia at the end of the period covered by this book.

By 1961 Soviet relations with the East European People's Democracies as a whole were marked by more reliance on formal institutions like the Warsaw Treaty Organization and the Council for Mutual Economic Aid, and less on the unofficial ties through party channels that had bound the bloc to the Soviet Union in Stalin's lifetime. New life was pumped into these two bodies, which in earlier years had been mere propaganda fronts. Ties with Moscow were put on a more normal inter-state basis.

Zbigniew Brzezinski

THE REVISED ORGANIZATION OF THE COMMUNIST BLOC

Insofar as the organization of the Communist camp is concerned, recent years have seen concrete efforts in the direction of (1) the regularization of relations among its members; and (2) the intensification of such relations. Many of the earlier sources of tension were due to the essentially informal and indirect system of Stalinist controls, to the blurred lines between central authority and domestic autonomy, to the air-tight compartmentalization of the camp's members, each surrounded by an iron curtain and beholden only to Moscow. The regularization of these relations, and their concomitant intensification, have been designed to reduce the number of tension points, and to liquidate the earlier ambiguities in the division of power between the center and its dependencies and/or allies. While foreign affairs, military affairs, and ideology still remain primarily in the Soviet domain (excepting the special case of China), a limited measure of autonomy in regard to the tempo and specific character of domestic social and economic policies is gradually developing insofar as the other Communist states are concerned. Although the Soviet Union yielded to this development with hesitation and often painfully, the regularization of relations and their simultaneous intensification were both necessities dictated by this concession and responses to the new situation. Most of the organizational aspects of the promotion of unity became important only in the last few years.

The great emphasis on the organizational aspects of the camp has certain implications for its greater character. For one thing, since its unity now involves much more conscious effort on the part of the various ruling elites than was the case earlier, one can note something which could not have occurred in Stalin's day—namely the appearance, albeit still very timid, of constellations or "in-groups" within the camp. On a number of important issues, it would appear that the East German and Czechoslovak leaderships share similar approaches, and quite often they seem to enjoy Bulgarian support. Furthermore, on occasions they have displayed more sympathy for some of the Chinese attitudes, both on ideology and on foreign policy. For the time being, the Poles, the Rumanians, and the Hungarians have been closer to the Soviets with respect to international affairs even though the Czechs and the East Germans are relied upon by Moscow to promote the internal line of bloc unity.

Finally, the regularization and intensification of relations within the camp, and the abandonment of the relatively informal Stalinist pattern, have revealed a striking differentiation in the formal institutional structure of the camp insofar as the Asian group of Communist states is involved. They are not in the formal alliance system nor in CMEA, and their contacts with the other parties appear to be less intense. Furthermore, since much of the Soviet hope for the future political and ideological unity of the camp is based on the present drive for closer economic interdependence, an autarkic Chinese development means that in the years to come Chinese unity with the rest of the camp will rest almost entirely on

From Zbigniew Brzezinski, "The Organization of the Communist Camp," *World Politics* (January 1961), pp. 206–209, 183–189. Reprinted by permission of *World Politics*.

the ideological-political plane. While this is not tantamount to disunity, it does reflect a somewhat less homogeneous reality than the Communist leaders would have the world believe.

This leads to two further points. The history of the camp can now be evenly divided into the Stalinist and the Post-Stalinist period, each lasting about seven years. From a historical standpoint, these are very short phases indeed. What is striking, however, is the difference between them. In the first place, the camp no longer seems as monolithic and as invulnerable to change as during Stalin's lifetime. Because of that, the alternative to it seems less likely to be violent upheavals. Today, in some ways the camp is better equipped to absorb the strains which occur in any multinational organization, and particularly in one dominated by a single national group. By suppressing such tensions through terror, accompanied also by economic exploitation, Stalin created the preconditions for a revolutionary situation. This no longer appears to be the case. On the other hand, because of the greater elasticity which now absorbs the strains and prevents an explosion erupting from stored up frustration, the danger of a gradual erosion of the camp's ideological unity seems greater than ever before. Even the small measure of diversity which now exists, even the formal steps taken to regularize and improve relations, can gradually become impediments to the maintenance of the Leninist-Stalinist type of internal organizational discipline, so necessary to the unity of a camp founded on a doctrinaire ideology. This is particularly the case since the camp is still undergoing evolutionary change requiring a continuous adjustment of the ideology to varying and often conflicting national circumstances. Furthermore, to the degree that the Soviet leadership finds it necessary to mobilize the support of other Communist regimes in opposition to some Chinese

stands, the relationship of political power between Moscow and the other capitals becomes increasingly less asymmetrical.

Secondly, it seems fair to note that the camp in its first phase was in effect a national empire, centrally directed and run largely to the advantage of the dominant Soviet party. In some ways, if one for a minute overlooks the ideological elements, it was much like the Roman or French or English empire in their earlier day. Precisely because of that, it did not require elaborate machinery. The present development within the camp is increasingly transforming it into an international Communist empire, dominated by various Communist elites, bound together, to be sure, by Soviet power but also by common interests and aspirations. While united in their efforts and in their vested interest in keeping their ideologically oriented empire together and their populations suppressed, they increasingly find it necessary to express their unity through various organizational devices. The need for such organizational devices is felt to be particularly great because in the current Communist thinking "socialist" and subsequently even Communist countries will continue to exist as separate entities until a world-wide Communist society emerges. During this transitional, but probably lengthy period, unity between the ruling parties is to be cemented through continuing efforts to develop even closer political and economic ties among the countries ruled by them. To the extent that such ties do establish normative principles (if only in theory), particularly the principle of equality and independence, they will gradually consolidate the transition from a national to an international empire. By preserving state forms but emptying them gradually of their content, the ultimate hope is to surmount the traditional forces of nationalism and to create in effect an interlocking supersociety. While many obstacles still remain and others may arise, particularly with the further development of China, the West would do well not to underestimate the importance of the organizational development of the Communist camp.

* * *

Institutional Aspects of the Communist Bloc

This multilateral framework is buttressed by a web of bilateral agreements. Of these, the most important are the friendship and mutual aid agreements. They are usually directed against a specific outside threat — either Germany or Japan, and their possible allies — and they contain pledges of mutual support. In that sense, an effort is made to relate the alliance to a concrete danger, activating deeply felt anti-German or anti-Japanese popular feelings existing within some of the Communist-ruled states. However, it would be specious to argue that a treaty of friendship and mutual assistance between, let us say, Rumania and the Soviet Union represents a meaningful partnership. Rather, the treaty is essentially a cloak for a relationship of political subservience, with the juridical fiction of equality serving both to mask this relationship and to perpetuate it. Quite another matter is the Soviet-Chinese treaty of alliance. Here, the two contracting partners have in effect formalized a relationship of alliance and have expressed it in terms which impose meaningful obligations on both sides.

The Soviet Union has entered into friendship and mutual aid treaties with all but three of the Communist states — East Germany, North Vietnam, and North Korea, all divided nations. It seems likely that the Soviet Union does not wish to create a juridical situation which could simply impede the unification of these nations under Communist auspices, and premature ties might possibly constitute such an impediment. Furthermore, in the past at least, the Soviet Union may have considered the possibility that ties of alliance could in-

volve the Soviet Union in local conflicts which might easily erupt (or be provoked) between the opposing sides of the divided nations. However, it is likely that in the foreseeable future the Soviet Union will conclude treaties with these states so as to eliminate an anomalous distinction increasingly less necessary with the apparent consolidation of the outer limits of the camp. East German membership in the WTO and attendance of its sessions by North Vietnamese and North Korean observers would seem to augur this. At this stage, the East European states, while bound to one another by treaties of mutual aid and friendship, do not have such treaties with any of the Asian states; rather, the expedient of the vaguer friendship and co-operation treaty has been used. Symptomatic of certain political affinities noted in part II, China has concluded such friendship and co-operation agreements only with East Germany (December 25, 1955) and Czechoslovakia (March 27, 1957).

All of the mutual aid treaties were concluded by 1950 — i.e., in Stalin's lifetime. It is noteworthy that the treaties did not provide a juridical basis for the stationing of Soviet troops on the territory of the members of the camp. A provision for Soviet bases abroad was contained in the multilateral WTO, and even that agreement was very general in its wording. In a way, therefore, the most substantive bilateral political agreements concluded among the Communist states were those which for the first time formalized and rendered explicit the basis for the presence of Soviet troops on the soil of the other Communist-ruled states.

The model for such agreements was the Polish-Soviet treaty of December 17, 1956 (ratified by both parties in February 1957), concerning the status of Soviet troops "temporarily" stationed in Poland. This treaty reflected the new situation created by the changes that took place in Poland in October 1956 and was designed to meet long-standing Polish grievances. The political foundation for it was laid by the agreement reached by the Soviet and Polish government and party leaders in a conference held in Moscow in mid-November, and expressed by the joint declaration of November 18, alleviating many past Soviet abuses and explicitly defining the principles which govern the status of Soviet troops in Poland. The declaration imposed severe restrictions on many unilateral Soviet activities, explicitly prohibited the use of Soviet troops for political purposes in Poland, enjoined the Soviet command to co-ordinate their disposal, transportation, and numbers with the wishes of the Polish government, and made their personnel and dependents subject to Polish law. These provisions were reaffirmed in the formal treaty and a mixed Polish-Soviet commission was established to settle any disputes that may arise.

The Soviet-Polish treaty, while perpetuating Soviet military presence in Poland, marked a definite step forward for Poland and the negotiation of this treaty did involve a measure of bargaining and definite Soviet concessions. Even the subsequent consolidation of Soviet influence within the bloc, which necessarily gave the Soviet Union new opportunities for exerting pressures (any formal limitations notwithstanding), did not undo this arrangement. Furthermore, the concessions won by Poland could not be denied to the other, more loyal Communist states. As a result, a mere three weeks after the signing of the Polish-Soviet treaty, a Soviet-East German declaration (of January 7, 1957) announced that a formal agreement regularizing the presence of Soviet troops on German soil would soon be concluded. Such an arrangement had been prefigured by the Soviet-East German treaty of September 20, 1955, defining the relations between the two countries, and granting East Germany "full freedom" as a sovereign state. However, it seems clear that it was the change

in Soviet-Polish relations which prompted the execution of this commitment, and on March 12, 1957, a formal agreement was signed between the USSR and the GDR (East Germany), regularizing the presence of Soviet troops in East Germany. Similar agreements were concluded shortly thereafter with Hungary (the March 28, 1957, joint Soviet-Hungarian political declaration laid the basis for it, and the formal agreement was signed on May 27, 1957), and with Rumania on April 15, 1957. The Rumanian and Hungarian agreements were similar to the one concluded with Poland, except that they did not cede control to these states over the entry and exit of Soviet forces. The agreement with East Germany was even more restricted, in that it did not involve the restrictions cited in the Polish case, although asserting East German "sovereignty." The greater concessions made to the Poles reflected the relatively involuntary character of the Soviet adjustments.

Insofar as Poland and Hungary are concerned, the joint Polish-Soviet and Hungarian-Soviet governmental and party declarations of November 18, 1956, and March 28, 1957, respectively, represent the most important bilateral agreements concluded within the bloc. The first of these made it possible for the Polish Communist leadership to remain within the bloc while pursuing policies of relative domestic autonomy, some of which were at the time obviously displeasing to the Soviets. Nonetheless, the granting of compensation for past Soviet economic exploitation, the withdrawal of Soviet overseers from Poland, and acceptance of the Soviets of the Gomulka regime, and the restrictions imposed on the Soviet troops in Poland all were substantive measures designed to normalize and improve Polish-Soviet Communist relations. In the case of Hungary, the March 28 declaration was also designed to improve Soviet-Hungarian relations and involved economic concessions and promises of aid. However, unlike the Polish case, the declaration was much more a unilateral effort on the part of the Soviet government to improve the domestic position of a satellite regime recently imposed on the population by the force of Soviet arms, than an agreement between two states. Nonetheless, it did involve a step forward for the Hungarians as well, expecially when compared with the earlier period. Generally speaking, the agreements subsequent to October-November 1956 can be seen as reflecting a recognition on the part of the Soviet leaders of the need to regularise the semi-colonial pattern of relations prevailing between the Soviet Union and most of the other Communist states. An expression of this recognition was the declaration issued by the Soviet Union (and prompted directly by the Hungarian revolution) on October 30, 1956, promising to liquidate the most obnoxious aspects of the Stalinist pattern of Soviet-satellite relations.

Bilateral trade treaties also serve to unify the camp and are meant to create a common and enduring interest in its preservation. Since about 1957 these treaties have been designed to express in more detail and in binding manner the recommendations of CMEA. Given overall state control of the economy such treaties govern the totality of trade among its members, and since most of the foreign trade of the Communist states takes place within the camp (see Table 6, part II), these agreements have an important bearing on the future livelihood and development of the signatories. In recent years, there has been a veritable flood of statistics on the volume, composition, direction, etc., of trade between and among the Communist states, and there have been many valuable discussions of the degree of discrimination practiced by the Soviet Union against its weaker neighbors. There can be no doubt that such relations in the past did favor the Soviet Union and there is some evidence that they continue to do so. However, since 1956, the Soviet Union has become more actively engaged in issuing credit to the bloc states, and this has offset some of the still prevailing discrimination and, at the same time, has constituted an important bond. There is no need to cover the same ground here. Insofar as the trade agreements are concerned, it should be noted that they are usually concluded for relatively long-term periods, varying from two to seven years. In the early stages of the bloc, annual trade agreements were favored, since long-term planning co-ordination had not yet been effected.

The long-term agreements include a protocol valid for one year, providing a much more detailed breakdown of items to be traded. The protocol is usually renegotiated for subsequent single years and sometimes a price adjustment is made. In some cases, the agreements also outline a longer-range "perspective," sketching out the anticipated volume of trade over a longer period than the actual agreement; on occasions the agreements envisage co-ordination of capital investment and co-operation in production, as well as credits. This enables the contracting parties to plan several years ahead and to remain reasonably confident both of their supply and of their external markets. This is particularly important to states, like Poland, which are just developing certain branches of their industry—for instance, ship-building—and which would find it difficult to compete on the world market against the more advanced industrial states. However, at the same time the dependence of the more industrially developed Communist states (Czechoslovakia and East Germany) on Soviet supplies of raw materials, and of the less developed states (e.g., China) on Soviet machinery, is even further intensified by such long-term commitments. A corollary of these trade agreements is an extensive exchange of scientific knowledge and scientific cadres, and numerous bilateral arrangements between the various national institutes and academies as well as the bilateral commissions for scientific-technical collaboration established not only between the Soviet Union and the other Communist states, but among the People's Democracies as well.

The final link in the formal web of ties that deserves brief mention is provided by the cultural agreements concluded between the Communist states. Since art, culture and science are subject to state control under the Communist system, all cultural contacts between the various members of the camp must be regulated through official and formal channels. During Stalin's lifetime, however, such contacts were very much limited and only began to develop with the gradual lifting of the internal iron curtains by which the old dictator had isolated each Communist state. Thus, although European Communist states concluded cultural collaboration treaties with one another and also with China quite early in the history of the bloc (1947–1948, except for China and East Germany, which concluded such treaties in 1951 and 1952, respectively), cultural contacts remained essentially dormant until the middle 1950's.

The Soviet Union displayed ostentatious contempt for such arrangements, and refrained (with only one exception) from concluding such cultural collaboration agreements until the mid-1950's. This abstinence, however, did not prevent the Soviet Union from concluding a whole series of limited agreements with the members of the bloc, providing for the training of their citizens in Soviet institutions of higher learnings, for "co-operation" in radio programs and subsequently also in television, and finally for collaboration between their respective Academies of Science. It was only in the wake of the attack on Stalin and within the context of very hurried efforts to improve and normalize Soviet relations that the Soviet Union concluded cultural collaboration agreements with all the Communist states. These agreements provided for expanded contacts in education, art, music, literature, the theater, films, press, radio, television, sports, and even tourism. In effect, they were meant to establish a broad social basis for contacts with "the first country of socialism," hitherto sealed off hermetically. In all but four cases, the agreements were to run for five years; in the case of Mongolia, half-absorbed by the USSR, and of Soviet-controlled Korea and what was still Rákosi's Hungary, they covered ten years; and in the case of Vietnam, only three. In an effort to remove obvious discrimination, in the course of 1956–1957 the Soviet Union set up friendship societies with China, Bulgaria, etc., to match analogous friendship societies with the Soviet Union which had existed in the other states since the late 1940's. During 1957–1958 friendship societies also were established among all the Communist states.

The fact that these formal institutional aspects have in the majority of cases been developed or given substance in the post-Stalin phase of the camp's history is not without meaning. It would seem to suggest that these various devices, in spite of their original propagandistic purposes, have become more important to the Communist, and particularly the Soviet, leaders as instruments for the preservation and expression of their camp's unity. Indeed, as if to underscore this development, the old word "camp" (*lager* in Russian) now has a new equivalent: *sodruzhestvo,* or, roughly, "commonwealth." This in itself suggests a degree of maturation within the bloc, its growth from a relatively simple, informal combination of personal dictatorship and "big nation" imperialism, to a more complex pattern which preserves the privileged position of the dominant state but expresses this relationship through a more formal institutionalized set of arrangements.

By the end of 1957 communist China had embarked on a new stage in her relations with the Soviet Union. Both in terms of ideological and power status, she effected a rapid climb in the years 1956–1957 vis-à-vis the most important country of the socialist camp.

Khrushchev's attack on Stalin at the Twentieth Congress crippled the reputation of the camp's erstwhile ideological leader, and it was not until the Twenty-first Congress in 1959 that an attempt was made to elevate Khrushchev to the role of a major theoretician. In the interval the only possible claimant on the basis of long experience and originality of thought was Mao Tse-tung. The Twentieth Congress enhanced Mao's standing by officially adopting his "soft" line at that time towards the underdeveloped countries of Asia, although Lenin and not Mao was referred to as the authority for the change in policy.

In terms of sheer power, China was still a long way behind the Soviet Union even in 1959, but gratifying progress in domestic programs, which was accompanied by less violence and social upheaval than had been the case in Soviet history at a comparative stage, was now linked with growing diplomatic prestige abroad, at least within the communist orbit; China scored a success as the mediator in the Soviet discussions with Eastern Europe in 1956–1957. In January 1957, at a crucial stage both in bloc and domestic politics, Khrushchev toned down his anti-Stalinist inclinations and temporarily adopted the less critical Chinese image of the dead leader.

By weighting the scales more heavily against revisionism than against Stalinist dogmatism in the final reappraisal of international communist relations expressed in the Moscow Declaration of November 1957, Khrushchev prevented a possible cleavage in the bloc between Soviet- and Chinese-orientated satellites. Early in 1958 China adopted a much "harder" political line so that if Khrushchev in November 1957 had championed the claims of revisionist Poland and Hungary, Stalinist Czechoslovakia, Bulgaria, and Albania might conceivably have forsaken Soviet for Chinese leadership in the following year. In the event Russia maintained her leadership, although by 1960 Albania had transferred her allegiance to China.

Like Russia, China reverted to a "harder" line after an experiment in relaxation. Mao's attempt to appease the Chinese intelligentsia by means of the "Hundred Flowers" campaign begun in February 1957 unleashed criticism of the government that was hushed by a return to orthodoxy; this was not a diluted version of the original, as was the case in Russia. The result was a growing discrepancy between Soviet and Chinese domestic and foreign policies. At home the Chinese pursued radical aims like wages based on equal pay and the commune system, both of which had been abandoned in Russia during the years after the Revolution. On the strength of what they considered to be short cuts to communism, the Chinese were now reluctant to agree with the Soviet thesis that the U.S.S.R. would enter the stage of communism before any other country in the bloc, including China.

Some of the Sino-Soviet differences on domestic affairs came up for discussion at the Twenty-first Congress, but questions of foreign policy required an earlier solution. In 1958 China abandoned the seductive approach she had employed towards the uncommitted nations at Bandung in 1955, for although she had played a big part in opening up the path for Soviet influence in Asia, she had reaped scant benefit for herself since. Russia too was becoming more impatient with regard to neutralist countries, but not to the same extent. With an eye on Formosa, still occupied by hostile Chinese Nationalist forces, China now insisted that local wars could not be avoided, whereas the Soviets believed they could. In the summer of 1958 it seemed as though the Chinese had managed to persuade Khrushchev, on a visit to Peking, to give in slightly to their point of view. After Khrushchev's departure the Chinese campaign against Formosa was sharpened with the full backing of the Soviet press. Russia also withdrew her request for a summit meeting among the major powers.

Chinese influence in Soviet affairs increased at a startling rate after 1958. This was partly due to the continuing rise of Chinese power and prestige, but was more noticeable also on account of the growing disparity of Soviet and Chinese views on foreign and domestic policy.

Strong bonds held the Soviet Union and communist China together in a largely hostile world, but differences in stages of economic and political development threatened to sever them by 1960, since these differences set up incompatible views on national policies and ideology. China's lower level of economic wealth, her fresher revolutionary zeal, and her anti-white imperialism all served to estrange her from her communist partner. The rift had grown steadily since 1956, when China had a relatively "soft" policy, but widened faster after 1956 with her reversion to a "hard" policy at home and abroad.

Indications of the Sino-Soviet quarrel appeared first on the ideological plane. Although the practical consequences of the split could be enormous, the divergence of views remained for the most part in the minds of the protagonists and was but scantily translated into actual power politics by the time of the Twenty-second Congress in 1961. The ideological battle was all the more fierce in that is was conducted on several fronts. From 1958 to 1960 the struggle centered on the question of the Chinese communes and the related subject of Soviet and Chinese proximity to communism. After 1960 interest was to switch to an appraisal of communist world strategy.

In August 1958 the Chinese resolution on the formation of communes announced triumphantly that "the attainment of Communism in China is no longer a remote future event." After some initial prevarication, Khrushchev decisively opposed the Chinese move in July 1959 in the course of a speech in Poland. He said that China had a poor understanding of how to build communism and drew attention to the failure of the commune idea in the Soviet Union during the period of War Communism.

The decisive Soviet stand on this topic was motivated by three considerations. In the first place, if Mao's commune idea was allowed to go uncriticized, it would seem as though Chinese communist ideology was taking over the initiative from the Soviet version and that China was likely to enter communism before the U.S.S.R. Second, this initiative could be put to material advantage by offering the commune system to the less-developed areas of the world as being more suited to peasant societies than the Soviet system. Third, as a result of the first two possibilities, the Soviet Union might lose its position as the political and economic prototype for the communist bloc.

Sino-Soviet differences over communist world strategy came to a head in 1960 at the Bucharest conference of the twelve communist governments in June and the Moscow meeting of November. They arose from China's reluctance to abandon the Leninist view of the inevitability of war between capitalism and communism that had been discarded by the Russians at the Twentieth Congress in 1956. Thus China viewed peaceful coexistence as a mistaken policy. Mao could still express nothing but hatred for communism in the West, whereas Khrushchev claimed that there were "progressive" as well as reactionary circles in capitalist countries. On the strength of his opinion, Mao held that local wars at least were inevitable and should be encouraged by the communist bloc if it was a case of supporting new countries against neo-colonialists. Furthermore he mistrusted the "national bourgeois" governments in developing areas and maintained that communist parties would have a better chance of coming to power through force than by acquiescing to such governments.

The Bucharest conference culminated in a very short communiqué which thinly covered up Sino-Soviet disagreement. At the Moscow meeting of eighty-one communist parties, the largest of its kind ever held, the Russians managed to hold out against the Chinese, who apparently only received full support from Albania. The Declaration issued at the end of the conference reaffirmed that communism could still win without resorting to war; its cautious tone reflected the Soviet view that the time had not yet come for a decisive showdown with capitalism. Nevertheless, every effort was made to accommodate the Chinese short of reverting to a policy of war, and Soviet policy after December 1960 hardened considerably with regard to the German problem and the situation in the Indo-Chinese peninsula.

These last two shifts of Soviet policy were among the few practical results of Sino-Soviet disagreement on points of theory. Relations between the two protagonists cooled to the extent that the Soviets refused to deliver atomic bombs to China and to set up a joint Sino-Soviet naval command in the Pacific. Russia also withdrew many of her technical experts from China. However the full implications of the Chinese line in foreign policy had yet to be felt in the sphere of international relations. They became increasingly apparent after 1961 only and therefore lie beyond the scope of this book.

Donald Zagoria

THE SINO-SOVIET DISPUTE

Conflict over the Inevitability of War

At the 20th and 21st Soviet Party Congresses Khrushchev had introduced important innovations in Leninist theory on the inevitability of war. At the 20th Congress he said that the present correlation of forces in the world indicated there was "no fatalistic inevitability of wars," and although the danger of war existed, the opportunity and conditions had been established for *"ensuring not merely a prolonged but a lasting peace."* At the 21st Congress Khrushchev stated his thesis more sharply when he said that the new balance of forces in the world would engender a "real possibility of excluding world war from the life of society even before the complete triumph of socialism," and that *"any* attempt at aggression" would be stopped short—thus implying that local wars could be avoided as well.

Soviet military and political leaders had for some time before the spring of 1960 been contending that local wars—given the nature of the opposed alliance systems and the nature of nuclear weapons—were bound to escalate. While such statements were and are undoubtedly meant to deter the West from local wars, they probably also reflect a genuine Soviet estimate that the West will not use force to thwart Moscow's aims provided the Communist powers do not initiate aggression and provided local Communists do not attempt to seize power by force themselves but use "front men" like Castro. Kuusinen fortified this impression in his anniversary reply to the Chinese, when he said that the "rapid stream" of historic progress was now flowing in a direction which would finally make "any war" impossible.

Perhaps the frankest statement of Soviet views on the question of local wars came in an article by A. Sovetov in *International Affairs* on the Lenin anniversary. Because the article was analytical rather than propagandistic in nature, it was probably intended as a reply to Chinese assertions on the subject rather than as a warning to the West. The section on war, for example, began not by warning the West against a local war strategy but by stating that the West *was* deterred from local as well as from global war. The balance of forces "exercises a restraining effect on the imperialistic powers as regards so-called local wars." Sovetov then went on to maintain that since 1941 the frequency of local wars had declined by about one-third as compared with past centuries. Moreover, he said, clearly in response to an alternative argument, not one of the local wars since 1945 "has brought a direct gain to the imperialist forces." Although there had been five local wars from 1945 to 1955, only one—the Algerian war—had occurred since 1955. In this quantitative decline of local wars, the "decisive" factor was the might of the socialist system.

The Soviet argument, then, was that local wars were becoming less and less likely because of the might of the Bloc, and that even where local wars had occurred the Bloc had succeeded in preventing the West from improving its position.

Of great interest was Sovetov's statement that the USSR would do all in its power to ensure that revolutions in various countries did not lead to civil wars in which the Bloc

Reprinted from *The Sino-Soviet Conflict, 1956–1961* by Donald Zagoria, pp. 310–316, 325–326, 365–369, by permission of Princeton University Press Copyright © by Princeton University Press.

might be forced into supporting one side while the West supported the other: "In the atmosphere of rapid social development, characteristic of the present era, peaceful coexistence, while not retarding social changes in countries where these changes are ripe, *must at the same time ensure a situation in which internal processes in particular countries do not lead to military clashes of the two antipodal systems.* The situation is shaping favorably to such a course of events." [italics supplied] If revolutionary gains must be made without risk of expanding violence, how was this to be done? In its next paragraph, the article contended: "This situation opens up new, unprecedented horizons before diplomacy. As methods of violence and *diktat* are relegated to the background, methods of negotiation assume even greater importance." In other words, the USSR hoped to make revolutionary gains via negotiations and without the risk of war.

Soviet views on the non-inevitability of war seemed to be the result of several converging elements in their strategic thinking as of the spring of 1960. First, the Russians had exhibited both in doctrine and in action a belief that the likely costs of general war in the nuclear era are prohibitive. Second, they appeared to believe they could attain their objectives in the middle run without the risk of general *or* local war. Third, Moscow's conservative thinking on war seemed intimately related to the instability of the so-called balance of terror. So long as neither side has an invulnerable nuclear retaliatory force, each must live with the ever-present danger that a deteriorating international situation may at some point encourage the other side to strike first, in order to reap the great advantage of surprise.

The first *Red Flag* article under the imprimatur of Yu Chao-li appeared on April 1 and was almost entirely devoted to refuting Soviet positions on war. Its central thesis was twofold. First, it agreed with the Soviet view that the West was deterred from general war, and it went on to imply that the Russians were acting too timidly under the circumstances. Second, it held that while a two-camp war was unlikely, local wars were inevitable. It contended that the Bloc should support those local revolutionary wars which were "just" and strongly oppose those imperialist-launched local wars which were "unjust."

Some Westerners mistakenly believe the essence of the Chinese position is that general war is inevitable. The Chinese doctrinal articles, like those of the Russians, hold that central war is *possible*, but they do not consider it either likely or inevitable in the near future. This view is quite explicit in Mao's "smokescreen" line, which was revived in the fall of 1958 and which occupied a central place in the Yu Chao-li article. According to Mao, the imperialist cliques are only "using the rumor that war between the USSR and the United States may break out at any moment as a smokescreen to hide their schemes to control the world." The imperialists are said to be using the threat of a two-camp war in order to apply pressure on their own peoples and as an excuse to expand into the "intermediate zone" between the United States and the USSR.

The "real and direct contradictions" in the world since World War II, said Yu in April 1960, "are not contradictions between the Soviet Union and the United States. The Soviet Union and the United States can and are actually coexisting peacefully." In relation to practical policy decisions, therefore, Chinese public doctrine shows less concern than Soviet public doctrine over the danger of a two-camp war.

The second central element in the Chinese view, closely related to the first, is that while general war is unlikely, local wars are not only likely but inevitable. The "real and direct" contradictions in the world are those "between the reactionary cliques of an imperialist country and its own people, . . . between the imperialist countries and their colonies and semi-colonies, and . . . among the imperialist countries." Such contradictions, say the Chinese, will inevitably lead to civil wars in the capitalist countries, to wars between the capitalist countries and the colonial countries, and to wars among the imperialist countries.

Of these three kinds of inevitable local wars, Yu Chao-li seemed to believe that "colonial" wars were the most likely. "The spearhead of U.S. aggression at present," he said, "is directed primarily against the colonial and semi-colonial states and independent countries." One of the "special features" of international development since World War II has been the surging movement for national independence in colonial areas and the "continual suppression and use of force by imperialism to smother the movement." The imperialists cannot voluntarily give up their plundering of the colonies and semi-colonies, because the very survival of imperialism depends on its obtaining raw-material-producing centers and markets. This being the case, "national liberation wars will remain inevitable."

Yu identified three different kinds of wars that had broken out between imperialism and the colonial areas: (1) wars launched by imperialism to suppress actual colonies; (2) wars of aggression against countries which had achieved national independence, and (3) "national liberation wars" in the form of civil wars to oppose imperialism and "its running dogs." All three kinds, he said, "are still being carried out both separately and simultaneously." He seemed to consider both Western-initiated and Bloc-sponsored or Bloc-supported colonial wars as a continuing feature of the world.

The second type of local war which Yu seemed to hold likely was civil war in a capitalist country. Quoting Lenin, and tacitly discarding Khrushchev's thesis on the possibility of peaceful takeover of power, Yu said: "Civil wars are also wars. Whoever recognizes the class struggle cannot fail to recognize civil wars which in every class of society constitute the natural, and under certain conditions, inevitable continuation, development, and intensification of the class struggle. All the great revolutions prove this. To repudiate civil war, or to forget about it, would mean sinking into extreme opportunism and renouncing the socialist revolution."

Finally, Yu decided there could be no guarantee that World War III would not break out as a result of the irreconcilable contradictions between the capitalist countries: "Who can guarantee that West Germany and Japan will not tread their old path? Again, who can guarantee that West Germany will not launch a new war of aggression in the West and Japan will not launce a new war of aggression in Southeast Asia? Furthermore, who can guarantee that there will not be a recurrence of the Pearl Harbor incident, or that there will not be a new world war among the imperialist countries?"

Chinese views on the inevitability of local war were stated even more revealingly by Central Committee member Liu Chang Sheng on June 8 in his speech to the WFTU meeting in Peking. Liu specified four types of inevitable local wars: imperialist wars of suppression against the colonial countries, imperialist wars of suppression against the people in their own countries, national liberation wars in the colonies, and people's revolutionary wars in the capitalist countries. The first two were "unjust," said Liu, the second two "just." It was the duty of the Communist Bloc, he said, to uphold just wars and to oppose unjust wars. It was "entirely wrong" to believe that such local wars could be avoided, and it was also wrong to talk indiscriminately (as the Russians did) about opposing war in general without "making a specific analysis of its nature."

The Chinese do not believe, as the Russians evidently do, that the West is deterred from local as well as from general war. The Chinese therefore estimate that the Bloc will have to use force against the West whenever the West initiates local war. Moreover, they believe that local revolutionary wars — whether or not of the Bloc's own making — are inevitable and should be fully supported and exploited. While the Russians have not disavowed "just" wars or aid and support to those fighting "just" wars, their emphasis in the spring of 1960 was on the possibility of eliminating *all* wars, including by implication both the "just" and the "unjust." Their lack of material support for the Algerian rebels indicates they did not believe that their interests would be served as well by stirring up colonial wars as by pursuing their diplomatic objectives *vis-à-vis* the "imperialist" powers.

It is fairly certain the Russians were in 1959–1960 seeking a *détente* which they believed they could utilize to their advantage, and that they were aware they could not have a *détente* and support local wars at the same time. The Chinese, believing as they did that a *détente* would work against both world Communism and their own interests, were interested in stirring up local wars which gave promise of spreading Chinese influence.

The Chinese Communist attack on Soviet ideology and the revolutionary strategy reflected in that ideology virtually accused the Russians of betraying Marxism-Leninism. Such a charge was tantamount to calling into question Khrushchev's leadership of the Communist movement. The three principal targets of the Chinese fire were the very three basic ideological innovations which Khrushchev had personally presented to the 20th Party Congress. They rejected Khrushchev's views on the possibility and advisability of seeking a more or less long-range *détente* with the West and contended the coexistence could mean only

an armed truce. They argued that, although general war could be avoided by persistent and defiant revolutionary struggle and a policy of strength, local wars were inevitable so long as imperialism remained, and that it was the Bloc's duty to foster and support "just" wars. They minimized the possibility of peaceful accession to power in the non-Communist world and suggested that those who emphasized this possibility were traitors to the revolution.

* * *

The Bucharest Conference

The Russians evidently came to the Bucharest Conference in late June with the intention of forcing a Chinese retreat. The idea probably was to demonstrate to the Chinese that they were isolated in the Communist world and that the vast majority of the Communist leaders agreed with Soviet policies and, in any case, would support the Russians in a test of Soviet authority. The Russians evidently brought with them to the conference a lengthy letter which had originally been sent to Peking on June 12. From accounts of the letter that have appeared in print, it seems to have been a restatement of Soviet strategic views and a criticism of those Chinese views that had been in contention for several years.

The Bucharest Conference was also the scene of a bitter exchange between Khrushchev and the Chinese representative, P'eng Chen, a Politburo member close to Mao. In this exchange, Khrushchev is reported by Edward Crankshaw to have attacked Mao personally and to have compared him to Stalin in being oblivious of any interests but his own and in spinning theories detached from the realities of the modern world. Khrushchev reportedly added that the Chinese knew little about the realities of modern war. P'eng is said to have replied with a bitter attack on the Soviet Party and on Khrushchev personally. He charged that Khrushchev had confused the basic issues and said that the Chinese Party did not trust Khrushchev's analysis of the international situation. He further charged that Khrushchev had called the Bucharest meeting for the sole purpose of undermining Chinese prestige, a further indication that the Russians probably took the initiative against Peking at the conference. He replied to Khrushchev's allegation that the Chinese lacked sophistication about modern war by saying the Chinese had already shown in Korea and against the Japanese that they knew more about war than most people.

Khrushchev's public speech to the Bucharest Conference also implicitly attacked Mao for an inability to apply Marxist doctrine "creatively." On June 21, Khrushchev used these words: "On the basis of Marxism-Leninism, we must think for ourselves, profoundly study life, analyze the present situation, and draw conclusions which benefit the common cause of Communism. One must not only be able to read but must also correctly understand what one has read and apply it to specific conditions of the time in which we live, taking into consideration the situation and the *real balance of forces. A political leader* acting in this manner shows that he not only can read but also can creatively apply revolutionary teaching. If he does not do this, he resembles a man about whom people say: 'He looks into a book but sees nothing.'" [italics supplied]

Here Khrushchev was reiterating the Soviet view that Mao overestimated the change in the balance of forces in the Bloc's favor and did not sufficiently appreciate the complex problems of the contemporary international scene. The essence of the passage was that it was necessary to adapt Leninist revolutionary doctrine to new conditions. In a striking departure from normal practice, *Jen-min jih-pao* failed to publish the full text of Khrushchev's speech to the Bucharest Conference, and the excerpt quoted above was not included in the abbreviated version carried in the Chinese Party paper. The Bucharest meeting did not end in complete disorder, although there is no evidence that the Chinese retreated an inch. A very short and uninformative joint communiqué was signed by the Russians and Chinese, as well as by the other Communist parties in attendance, evidently for the sake of presenting at least a facade of unity. That it was only a facade was evident within a week of the conclusion of the meeting when *Pravda* and *Jen-min jih-pao* presented divergent views on the significance of the communiqué.

* * *

Sino-Soviet Relations after the Moscow Conference

The Moscow Declaration constituted, in boxing terms, a victory on points for the Soviet Party. It was *essentially* a Soviet document in the sense that the Soviet grand strategy—aiming at the world-wide triumph of Communism without war—remained intact. The Chinese succeeded in qualifying and hardening certain Soviet theses, in leaving several crucial ones open to varying interpretations, and, in general, moving the manifesto further to the Left than it would have been if drafted by the Russians alone. They did not succeed, however, in establishing any of their principal points: that peaceful coexistence was a mirage; that local wars were inevitable; that the Bloc must lend military support to "colonial" wars even at the risk of local war with the West; that the newly independent governments in Asia and Africa were unreliable and must be overturned soon; and that the possibilities for peaceful accession to power of any Communist Party were extremely rare.

The document was *essentially* Soviet because its overall tone and contents, however qualified, continued to adhere to the Soviet view that the Bloc had not yet reached a decisive strategic superiority over the West and must therefore move cautiously; that, in any case, time was on the side of the Communist movement; that the economic race with the West would in the end be decisive; that the newly independent countries could be gradually alienated from the West politically and economically by Soviet aid, trade, and example; that the value of violence should not be overestimated; and that the dangers and likely consequences of war were great.

For three years the Chinese had been urging a radical departure from the Bloc strategy laid down by the Soviet leaders. The Chinese views were explicitly based on the belief that the Bloc had achieved a decisive strategic superiority over the West. In any case, the Chinese argued, time was not necessarily on the side of Communism; the economic race with the West would not be decisive as Moscow thought; the role of violence in advancing Communist aims had been underestimated by the Russians; and the likely consequences of war were not as bad as Moscow believed.

The Moscow Conference ended one phase of Communist history and began another which will have a lasting impact on Soviet policy, Sino-Soviet relations, and the future evolution of relations within the Communist movement. With regard to Soviet policy, the single most important upshot of the conference was that the Chinese seemed to have succeeded in part in their intention to rob Soviet diplomacy of some of its flexibility and room for maneuver. The signs of this were numerous both in the proceedings of the conference and in the international behavior of the Russians after the conference concluded. First, there was the fact that for the first time in recent Communist history, a Soviet leader recognized Soviet "obligations" to the world Communist movement. During the Stalin era and most of the Khrushchev era, the only "obligations" had been those of the Communist movement throughout the world to defend and to obey the Soviet

center. By 1960 the Chinese and other parties had brought so much pressure to bear on the Russians that the latter not only recognized their reciprocal obligations to those other parties but also stated publicly that they would not evade their responsibilities. While Khrushchev successfully fought to retain some flexibility in deciding how to meet those "obligations," the very recognition of them has forced Soviet diplomacy to take risks that have heretofore been avoided. Even before the conference convened, Khrushchev had begun to take a tougher line on international policy as early as June 1960, at the very time when he was moving toward a showdown with the Chinese. No sooner had the summit meeting collapsed than he shot down an American plane, scuttled the ten-power disarmament talks at Geneva, accused all the Western powers of backing Belgian military intervention in the Congo, made ICBM threats to the U.S. with regard to Cuba, gave *de facto* recognition to the Algerian rebels, and took to banging his shoes on the desk at the UN. While not all of these tactics can be explained solely as reactions to Chinese pressure, none of them, particularly the recognition of the Algerian rebels, can be explained without taking that pressure into consideration.

After the Moscow Conference had concluded, Khrushchev moved even further towards a "hard" policy toward the West, undertaking a large-scale airlift to supply the Laotian Communist rebels and renewing his ultimatum on Berlin. In both these instances, while they did not yet signal adoption of the Chinese strategy, the Soviet leader nonetheless moved closer towards the risk of local wars with the West that the Chinese had persistently argued were inevitable and that he had argued could be avoided. Although both of these actions can in part be understood in terms of Khrushchev's own strategic conception, there is little doubt but that he assumed greater risks than he otherwise might. He was seeking to fend off Chinese accusations that he was reneging on his duties to support worldwide revolution and other Communist states in their struggle with the West. Khrushchev is well aware of the danger to the Soviet position of allowing China to appear as the only ardent champion of the Communist revolution: militant parties and anti-Western nationalist insurgents would be driven into the hands of Peking.

Another indication of decreasing Soviet flexibility was the implied Soviet promise in the Moscow Declaration to give greater weight to the views and interests of the Chinese Communists both before and during any future negotiations with the West, and also in the general conceptualization of Bloc strategy and tactics. If such a promise is observed in practice, it may not prevent East-West negotiation, but it will clearly make it more difficult.

With specific regard to Sino-Soviet relations, the significance of the Moscow Conference and its declaration was that the Russians and Chinese could not, even after two months of negotiation and with the help of seventy-nine other parties, resolve their differences. Neither the question of the locus of authority in the Communist world nor the complex issues of strategy and tactics were defined with precision. The declaration represented, not a real compromise of Soviet and Chinese views, but a collation of them. While the document, in its broad outlines, must be regarded as a Soviet "victory," its ambiguities and qualifications were so numerous that it could hardly serve as a guide for any of the Communist parties. Both Russia and China could and did derive different conclusions from it. The ostensible Soviet victory was thus bought at the very heavy price of an unworkable compromise which served clearly to demonstrate that the Russians were no longer able unilaterally to dictate law for the entire international Communist movement.

The hollowness of the Sino-Soviet "compromise" achieved at the Moscow Conference would be demonstrated before the next twelve months had run their course. At the 22nd Congress of the Soviet Communist Party in October 1961, Khrushchev seemed determined to exact the Chinese surrender that he was not able to get in 1960.

In the light of this later blatant attempt by Khrushchev to force a Chinese retreat, the question must be asked why he did not choose to do so a year earlier at the Moscow Conference? There are several possible explanations. First, it is possible that Khrushchev genuinely hoped his willingness to accede to some Chinese demands, particularly by hardening his line toward the West, would relieve some of the Chinese pressure. Second, there may have been in 1960 a division within the Soviet Presidium on how far to go in risking an open break with China. Although it seems dubious that there is an internal opposition to Khrushchev strong enough to oust him from the leadership, there is abundant evidence of policy disputes within the Soviet hierarchy and some indication that Khrushchev has not been able to get his own way or has been reversed on certain matters affecting Soviet agriculture and military policy. Third, there is the possibility, mentioned earlier, that the Russians expected all of the Communist parties to support them in a show of strength with Peking but found that many parties, particularly those in Asia, would not do so. In such a situation, Khrushchev would almost certainly have been reluctant to force a showdown that might result not only in a Sino-Soviet schism but in a break-up of the world Communist movement into two wings, one of which would be led by China.

Whatever the reasons for Khrushchev's caution in 1960, these reasons apparently were not so compelling a year later. At this time, Khrushchev must have seen a good opportunity. China was in the midst of economic crisis so severe that it was forced to turn to Canada and Australia for grain. There were increasing reports of perilously low food supplies on the mainland. The commune system had been all but abandoned and the Left-wing economic policies that Khrushchev had condemned now seemed to be in disgrace. Surely Khrushchev felt he could now restore a Soviet authority in the international Communist movement to a pre-eminent position. What better target, therefore, than the tiny Balkan Communist state, Albania, which had —with Chinese economic and political support—increasingly defied the Kremlin throughout 1960 and early 1961?

Stavro Skendi

ALBANIA AND THE SINO-SOVIET CONFLICT

The conflict between little Albania and the Soviet Union is today at the center of the Soviet-Chinese rift. This first became apparent at the Bucharest Congress of June 1960, when of all the heads of Communist Parties of Eastern Europe only Enver Hoxha was absent. However, the clash between the two countries had been proceeding undercover for a long time. To understand its roots, let us first turn to Albanian-Jugoslav relations.

. . . The Albanian Communist Party was founded and organized in November 1941 by the Jugoslav Communist Party. It was brought under the control of the latter during the war, and there it remained until the Tito-Cominform break in 1948. When the Albanian Communist Party was freed from the Jugoslav grip, it began attacking Tito and the Jugoslav leaders as "deviationists" and "traitors." This continued up to Khrushchev's visit to Belgrade in June 1955. The Soviet leader's efforts to reestablish friendly relations with Jugoslavia acutely disturbed the Albanian Communists. They feared that this might lead to a restoration of Jugoslav control in Albania, endanger-

ing not only their positions but perhaps also their lives. They moderated their attacks, but were cautious in expressing satisfaction at the reconciliation.

Then in February 1956 came Khrushchev's de-Stalinization speech. It was a great blow to the Albanian Communists, for it had been through Stalin's action that they had won independence from Jugoslavia and it was through Stalinist methods that they ruled the country. Soon they began to feel Khrushchev's pressure. In April–May 1956, according to Hoxha's later testimony, the Soviet leadership, through important persons like M. A. Suslov, principal theoretician of the Soviet Communist Party, and P. Pospelov, a member of its Central Committee, tried to persuade the Albanians to rehabilitate Koci Xoxe, Hoxha's powerful rival, who had in reality been a man of the Jugoslavs. To rehabilitate him would mean opening the door to Jugoslavia again and would involve the Albanian leaders in a degree of self-criticism which would jeopardize their positions. Tirana refused to rehabilitate Xoxe, and in May 1956 Hoxha accused him of having

S. Skendi, "Albania and the Sino-Soviet Conflict," *Foreign Affairs* (April 1962), pp. 471–478. Reprinted by permission of *Foreign Affairs*.

prepared "the political and physical extermination" of the leaders. "The accusation against Xoxe and his partisans," he concluded, "was well founded and the verdict of our Party and government totally just."

The Hungarian revolt of October 1956 brought bitter exchanges between Tito and Hoxha. Hoxha made no secret of the fact that he considered the Jugoslav leader responsible for Albania's domestic difficulties, as well as for those of the satellite countries. In an article in *Pravda* (November 8, 1956), he guardedly accused the Jugoslavs of being at the root of the Hungarian revolt. A few days later Tito, knowing well who at the Kremlin stood behind that article, attacked Hoxha personally in his now famous speech at Pula, describing him contemptuously as a person who "knows only how to say 'Marxism-Leninism' and not a word more." He struck at what he called "obdurate Stalinist elements" in various Communist Parties, and, in a pointed allusion to the Albanian regime, added that these elements believed that "people of the Stalinist cast would be found in the Soviet Union to assist them to maintain themselves on the back of the people."

To make matters worse for the Albanians, Khrushchev let them know what he replied to Tito on November 9, 1956. As reported by Hoxha only last fall, the Soviet leader agreed with Tito that "now no particular importance should be given to the question whether the Jugoslav Embassy in Budapest acted rightly or not in giving asylum to Imre Nagy and his companions." He also expressed gratification that Tito agreed with him that Janos Kadar was the most suitable person to be the First Secretary of the Hungarian Communist Party. This letter convinced the Albanian rulers that Khrushchev was on Tito's side.

At this juncture, collaboration was apparently established between the Tirana leadership and the Stalinists in the Kremlin, for on February 13, 1957, in the Plenum of the Central Committee of the Albanian Communist Party, Hoxha took up the defense of Stalin in the most laudatory terms—a unique instance in the Soviet bloc. Having admitted certain errors—the cult of personality and "violations of Soviet law"—he added: "In spite of all these mistakes, Stalin remains a great Marxist-Leninist. Stalin was never mistaken in such questions as the protection of the interests of the working class and of Marxist-Leninist theory, the fight against imperialism and other enemies of socialism. He was and remains an exemplary figure. Stalin's tragedy was that when he made these serious mistakes he thought that they were necessary for protection of the revolution." Hoxha's apologia was not directed against Tito alone; it was more an answer to Khrushchev.

The Albanian leader's speech in defense of Stalin not only involved his country in the struggle for power in the Kremlin but also injected an ideological content into the conflict with Khrushchev and Tito; and with time this was to be intensified.

It is not known whether the Albanians were the first to approach the Red Chinese, or vice versa. In any case, Jugoslav "revisionism" brought them into the open hand in hand. Since May 1958, the press of the two countries has never stopped denouncing Jugoslav revisionism, linking it often to the principle of peaceful coexistence. In the course of the strife, the ties between Tirana and Peking grew closer; the staff of the Chinese Embassy in Tirana was enlarged; frequent visits were exchanged; the Albanian press stopped reproducing articles of *Pravda* and replaced with those of *Jenmin Jih Pao*, the Communist Chinese organ.

The reason given for Hoxha's absence from the Bucharest Congress of 1960 was Khrushchev's decision to force the Parties of the Soviet bloc to accept his policy of peaceful coexistence. The Chinese were on hand, however, and held their own in opposition to the Soviet Premier. Since that

219

time, the Tirana-Moscow rift has become steadily wider. Hoxha did not attend the General Assembly of the United Nations in the fall of 1960, where Khrushchev was escorted by the First Secretaries of the Communist Parties of Eastern Europe. Like Khrushchev, they all virtually ostracized Premier Mehmet Shehu, head of the Albanian delegation; on the other hand, Khrushchev had two talks with Tito. The conflict culminated in the meeting of the 81 Communist Parties in November 1960 in Moscow, when Hoxha, according to reports, denounced Khrushchev as "a traitor to the Communist idea, a weakling and a revisionist," and the Soviet Leader retorted that Hoxha was going to pay for the offense. Thus the personal element in the antagonism was reinforced.

In the Communist world, conflicts have to take an ideological form even when the real motives may be the interests of individuals or groups or the power politics of countries. The February 1961 Congress of the Albanian Communist Party reflected this fact clearly.

Although he inclined toward the Chinese viewpoint, Hoxha made efforts in his address—a good example of Communist double-talk—to show that he abided by the Moscow Resolution of November 1960, which was a compromise solution. The Marxist-Leninists did not deny the possibility of the peaceful road to socialism, he said; they simply did not understand it at all as a negation of class struggle. He then attacked Jugoslav revisionism.

P. Pospelov, the director of the Marx-Engels Institute in Moscow, was the chief of the Soviet delegation. Taking the Moscow Resolution of November 1960 as a clear Marxist-Leninist program of action of the international Communist movement, he advocated the principle of peaceful coexistence among states with different social systems, stressing that life itself had demonstrated that this "Leninist principle" was the only just and reasonable principle in

international relations. He then came to the point: "Now the question is posed thus — either peaceful coexistence or the most destructive war. There is no other way." The war against revisionism, he said, remained an actual and important task of the Communist Party, but he called also for a tireless war on the other dangers—dogmatism and sectarianism.

Li Hsien-nien, a member of the Politburo of the Central Committee of China, who headed the Chinese delegation, praised Albania as the vanguard of the war against the enemies of socialism and a strong support for the preservation of Marxist-Leninist purity. He said that the Albanian Communist Party, basing itself on the principle of close connection between the universal truth of Marxism-Leninism and its own practice in the country, had applied and developed Marxism-Leninism in a creative manner. Red China, he continued, regarded the successes of the Albanian Party and people as her own. He then added: "As long as imperialism exists, there exists also the foundation for aggressive wars. The danger is not yet over, and imperialism, with the United States at the head, may give rise to a new world war. . . ." He acknowledged the superiority of the Soviet Communist Party, but he also declared that the Communist Parties of all countries are independent and equal, although responsible to the interests of the international proletariat. This unequivocal ideological support of the Albanian leadership on the part of Red China was accompanied by substantial material aid—a considerable quantity of wheat and a credit of 112.5 million new rubles—at a time when China itself was in great economic need.

What, then, compelled Khrushchev to make a frontal attack on the leaders of the Albanian Communist Party at the 22nd Congress in Moscow? Did he hope that an offensive would succeed where internal and external pressures had failed?

It appears that in 1960 the Soviet Party

was earnestly concerned about the situation in Albania. The Albanian leaders, tied more and more closely to China, were growing more and more aggressive. There have been reports that the Soviet Ambassador in Tirana, Ivanov, endeavored to create a pro-Soviet faction, or at least a pro-Soviet current in the Albanian Communist Party, which could exercise pressure on Hoxha and Shehu. The leaders of this movement were Koco Tashko, president of the Auditing Commission of the Party and a former envoy to U.S.S.R., and Liri Belishova, an old Communist and a member of the Central Committee of the Party. In September 1960 they were dismissed from their responsible positions and arrested. Their fate is not known; Belishova was mentioned as an enemy of the Party in Hoxha's speech of November 8, 1961, but Tashko's name has been completely ignored. The fact that the Congress of the Albanian Communist Party was twice postponed (it finally took place in February 1961) was almost certainly due to domestic troubles. If it is true that Rear Admiral Temo Sejko and his companions, executed in May 1961, were also involved in the moment—Tirana's accusation that he was conspiring with Greece, Jugoslavia and the American Sixth Fleet to overthrow the régime is unconvincing—the Soviet attempt must have utterly failed. In any event, in January 1961 a new Soviet Ambassador, J. V. Shikin, arrived at Tirana, welcomed only by the Chief of Protocol of the Foreign Ministry, and four months later the Soviet submarines left their base on the island of Sazan (Saseno), opposite Vlorë.

Then came pressure from outside. The Soviet Union stopped abruptly all material and technical help to Albania and withdrew its experts and advisers. The satellites followed suit. Albania was ignored in the press of the Soviet bloc, and Khrushchev, in an interview, pointedly refrained from mentioning Albania as an ally, despite its continued membership in the Warsaw Pact.

Obviously, in attacking the Albanian leadership, Khrushchev had more in mind than the expulsion of Albania from the Communist bloc. He wanted also to strike at its ally China and other potential dissidents. But how could he expect China to recant? Although it was in economic straits and needed Soviet assistance, China was also a great power and could not allow itself to be humiliated. Chou En-lai, quickly and firmly, contested Khrushchev's right to make a one-sided public denunciation of a member of the Communist bloc. He also insisted on the observance of the principle of consultation and complete equality among members, thus questioning Moscow's leadership of the international Communist movement.

The Albanians, too, were swift to pass to the counter-offensive. Explaining why they had not been invited to the 22nd Congress in Moscow, Hoxha declared that the Albanian Party's words "would bring into the open the truth about Albanian-Soviet relations, would unmask his [Khrushchev's] anti-Marxist viewpoints and actions, would reject all his slanders and entirely unfounded accusations." It is possible that the Soviet Premier's personal hatred of Hoxha and Shehu was a factor in his miscalculation.

It is puzzling to see insignificant little Albania challenging the mighty Soviet Union. What is the secret of its strength? Is the régime capable of continued resistance?

The territory of Albania has been coveted by its neighbors for so long that the Albanian People have grown suspicious of all of them. The present régime has often exploited this popular feeling in order to strengthen its position. For example, in the spring of 1960, when Sophocles Venizelos wrote in the Athens papers that Khrushchev was going to speak to Hoxha about improving conditions of the Greek minority in southern Albania, he gave Hoxha another reason for not attending the Bucharest Conference that year. Before World

War II this Greek minority amounted to approximately 35,000 and Greece has always used it as a reason to claim the southern part of Albania, which it calls Northern Epirus.

Albania's geographic isolation from the Soviet bloc, which in the past was a drawback, has now become an advantage. As none of the satellite countries borders on Albania, the U.S.S.R. is at a disadvantage in undertaking direct or indirect action against it. But Albania's greatest strength, of course, lies in her alliance with China, since the Soviet Union has to take into account China's reaction to any contemplated step.

On the other hand, the Tirana regime is confronted with serious dangers. Albania has never been a self-sufficient country, and for years was sustained by the economic aid of the Soviet Union and its satellites. True, China has come to its assistance but, so far, not on the scale to which it had become accustomed. There are unfinished projects which the Chinese cannot complete because of lack of specialized personnel. Unemployment is likely to ensue. Moreover, Albania's trade was almost entirely with the Soviet bloc; now it must look for new markets. Some may be found in Italy, with which a trade agreement for approximately $8,000,000 was signed December 6, 1961, about two months after Khrushchev's attack on the Albanian leadership.

For the moment there appears to be no fear of a direct attack by neighbors. Much as Tito detests the Albanian leaders, it is doubtful that he could be induced by Khrushchev to invade Albania, under any pretext—even a "war of liberation." However, Jugoslavia might find a more subtle way of overthrowing Hoxha's régime: by infiltrating Albanian bands formed in Jugoslavia. The Jugoslav autonomous region of Kosmet (Kosovo and Metohija), bordering on Albania, is preponderantly inhabited by Albanians. The Secretary of the Communist Party in that region has been for many years Dusan Mugosa, a Jugoslav who was one of the founders of the Albanian Communist Party and the military boss of the Albanian Communist guerrilla bands during the whole period of the war. He has been continuously gathering intelligence on the situation in Albania and has not lost touch with Albanian fugitives in Jugoslavia. As a collaborator he can call on General Panajot Plaku, a former Under-Secretary of Defense, who fled Albania in 1956.

Yet if the plan to infiltrate Albania were carried out, it might have serious consequences. Albania, if not yet expelled from the Warsaw Treaty, would certainly appeal to the other members to respect their obligations, thus putting the treaty to a test. What would Red China's reaction be? Would it send military support to Albania? Would it appeal to the world Communist movement?

To expect that a way out of the Albanian impasse might be found by an understanding between the Soviet Union and China for a "reformed leadership" (according to Khrushchev's wishes) is unrealistic. In fact, the main defect of the Moscow Resolution of 81 Communist Parties is that it is not so much a compromise as only the semblance of a compromise. A general Sino-Soviet compromise on Albania would presuppose a closeness of views between the two powers; but what we witness today is a deepening of the split.

John Bradbury

SINO-SOVIET COMPETITION IN NORTH KOREA

Victimised by its strategic location throughout history, North Korea appears once again to be the scene of competition for dominant influence between its powerful neighbours. As the recent statement by Chairman Kim Il-sung . . . suggests, the Communist régime in North Korea was apprehensive about the mounting crisis in Sino-Soviet relations in the summer and autumn of 1960. What it did not reveal is that the issues involved in the Sino-Soviet dispute had already exercised a profound effect on the domestic and foreign policies of this Asian satellite for a period of several years.

Broadly speaking, the Sino-Soviet rift has emerged as the result of two fundamental attacks launched by Communist China against the traditional position of Moscow as the undisputed leader and arbiter of doctrine within the Communist *bloc*. The first challenge, the appearance of Communist China's commune and "leap forward" programmes in the fall of 1958, provided a distinctive Chinese road to Socialism and Communism which diverged sharply from Soviet precedent and experience. The second challenge took the form of a vigorous attack against Khrushchev's "peaceful co-existence" strategy for leading the *bloc* and international Communism to a final global victory. Both challenges were accompanied by the implicit claim that Mao Tse-tung, as the foremost living Marxist-Leninist theoretician, was uniquely qualified to provide ideological and policy guidance to the world Communist movement. They were also accompanied by the only slightly less grandiose pretension that Communist China was uniquely qualified to lead "the countries of the East" and,

by extension, all the underdeveloped areas of the world to Socialism and Communism. As a backward Asian country and, what is more, a vital buffer area along China's north-eastern frontier, North Korea has constituted a prime target in Peking's drive to win acceptance of its more radical approach to the domestic construction of Communism and its more militant approach to international Communist strategy.

Domestic Construction of Communism

The appearance of Communist China's commune and "leap forward" programmes in the summer of 1958 introduced a new element of discord into Sino-Soviet-North Korean relations which persists to the present day. Conceived as the instrument for achieving rapid economic and social development leading to the early advent of the Communist society, the commune epitomised a distinctive Chinese road to Socialism and Communism with special applicability to the underdeveloped nations of Asia.

The main outlines of the Chinese ideological challenge were present in a July *Red Flag* article entitled "Under the Banner of Chairman Mao." It was here that Mao Tse-tung was credited with discovering in the commune and "leap forward" programmes a special road enabling China to accelerate Socialist construction and to realise Communism "in the not distant future." Moreover, he had done this in accordance with Lenin's injunction to "the Communists of Eastern countries" to "creatively develop" Marxist theory "in the light of special conditons unknown to the European countries . . . realising that the

From *China Quarterly*, No. 6 (1961), pp. 15–28. Reprinted by permission of *China Quarterly*.

peasants are the principal masses." The implication was strong that Mao had solved the special problems of Socialist and Communist construction which confronted all Asian countries.

Communist China's "special conditions," which have been summed up by Chairman Mao in the phrase "poor and blank," are usually identified as an impoverished agrarian economy, a shortage of arable land relative to population, and cultural backwardness resulting from past imperialist oppression. In the Chinese view, a programme calling for total mobilisation of all available resources was necessary in order to break through these barriers of industrialisation and modernisation. As the radical social organisation designed to implement this programme, the commune was expected to perform the following economic functions: centralisation of control over all means of production in the countryside as a first step toward "all-people ownership" (*i.e.*, state ownership); mobilisation of the peasants to implement a "mass line" of industrial development featuring the "native" production of iron and steel; extension of more effective controls over peasant consumption through the commune mess-hall and the "free supply" system of distribution (hailed as the beginning of the Communist system of distribution "according to need"); and intensive exploitation of human labour to a degree unknown in modern history. In addition, the commune was expected to perform various ideological functions which were to play an equally indispensable role in China's leap to modernisation. The very term "commune" connoted—intentionally so—an advanced status on the road to Communism. Pleading special conditions, the Chinese Communists undertook to substitute moral and psychological incentives—the early attainment of Communism—for material incentives as the major stimulus for production. The claim of priority in the march to Communism was stated

explicitly: "Tomorrow we shall build a paradise of happiness never before attempted in history—Communism."

Communist China's pretension to have discovered a special road for Asian countries leading to the early achievement of Socialism and Communism evoked an enthusiastic response in North Korea. Deviating from its traditional role as a docile Soviet satellite, the Pyongyang régime embraced a whole series of Chinese Communist policies and programmes in the summer and autumn of 1958, even to the point of flirting with the heretical commune organisation.

Imitation of the Chinese example began in June at a Korean Workers Party plenum. At that time it was decided to launch a mass movement for construction of small industrial installations combining "native and modern" technology—a movement which followed closely, both in time and content, Communist China's "mass line" of local industrialisation. Even the propaganda slogans were the same, including exhortations to rely on the "activism and creativeness" of the masses in a campaign of "all the people operating industry." The next and far more significant step was taken at a September central committee plenum which inaugurated North Korea's "flying horse" programme of economic development and the simultaneous amalgamation of some 13,000 collective farms into 3,800 political-economic units of township size. In a major policy speech of November 20, Kim Il-sung revealed the extent to which these programmes had been inspired by the Chinese Communist model.

First, Kim referred to his people as "poor and uncultured" (calling to mind Mao Tse-tung's characterisation of China as "poor and blank") and, as such, compelled to engage in a "bitter struggle" for a "leap forward" in economic development which would permit "catching up" with the more advanced Socialist countries of Europe. As a capsule statement of the rationale of Communist China's "great leap forward" programme, this could hardly be improved upon. Next, Kim advanced claims for North Korea's "flying horse" programme of economic development which bore a striking resemblance to the "leap forward" pretensions in Communist China. Pyongyang had already "solved" the food problem and "within two to three years"—the same time-period featured in Chinese propaganda—food was to become "extremely abundant." An accelerated programme of agricultural development based on mobilising the peasants and a similarly spectacular development of industry would lead to completion of the stage of Socialist construction and initiation of the "transition to Communism" within four to five years.

Even more suggestive of Chinese influence was the clear implication that North Korea was incorporating salient features of Communist China's commune programme into its own reorganisation of rural society. Kim placed heavy emphasis on moral, rather than material, incentives as the stimulus for production, holding forth as the reward for "bitter struggle" the realisation of Communism "in the not distant future." He disclosed that North Korea was contemplating establishing "comprehensive, Communist, all-people ownership" (*i.e.*, state ownership) in the countryside, another basic characteristic of China's commune. Even more striking, he revealed that Pyongyang was considering introducing the commune system of distribution featuring the "free supply" of commodities determined "according to need." Kim made this point in the form of a conversation with a peasant woman during a visit to an agricultural co-operative.

When I asked her how she would like it if all textile products, rice and everything else were supplied free of charge; if the peasants were placed under the same wage system as the workers; and we proceeded thus in the direction of practising the Communist principle of distribution along with the Socialist principle of

distribution at the same time; she replied that that sounded simply wonderful.

The very same co-operative visited by Kim had already established, by the end of October, most of the collective livelihood institutions of China's communes, including public mess-halls, nurseries, kindergartens and sewing teams.

Immediately after this remarkable speech, Kim Il-sung spent three weeks in an extended tour of Communist China. The recipient of signal honours and popular demonstrations throughout his visit, the North Korean leader responded with an enthusiastic endorsement of Communist China's unorthodox programmes which by now were, to a significant extent, those of his own country. Asserting that "the two countries of Korea and China . . . are advancing to Socialism and Communism with flying leaps," he made the following laudatory appraisal of China's communes.

We are very much interested in the communisation movement. . . . As a result of setting up public mess-halls, nurseries, etc., you have achieved collectivisation not only of production but also of livelihood; this means that . . . you have advanced a step towards Communism. . . . We will certainly pass on to our peasants the great results you have achieved from your commune movement. Also we will strive hereafter . . . to strengthen our mutual co-operation in building Socialism and Communism.

Kim's endorsement of the Chinese model was made even more explicit after returning to North Korea, when he hailed the Chinese programmes as "an example of the creative application of Marxism-Leninism to the realities of their country and *a particularly good example for Socialist revolution and construction in countries which were backward and under colonial oppression in the past.*" (Emphasis added.)

It is important to assess the significance of this development—the Chinese initiative and the North Korean response—as viewed from Moscow. Whereas the argument of "special conditions" had been advanced earlier to justify the deviation of "national roads" to Socialism (*e.g.*, Poland), it was now being advanced to justify a separate and distinct road (what is more, a short cut) to both Socialism and Communism for the entire continent of Asia or even, by extension, for all underdeveloped areas of the world. By implicitly denying the validity of the Soviet model for the special problems of economic and social development in Asia, the Chinese were in effect staking a claim for hegemony over Asian Communism, and the North Koreans, by acknowledging a Chinese prototype for the underdeveloped areas, appeared to have recognised this claim.

The Soviet reaction revealed a thorough appreciation of the fundamental nature of Peking's challenge. In rapid succession, the Russian leadership attacked China's premature attempt to introduce distribution "according to need" as "unworkable" and as "discrediting Communism"; the Chinese undertaking, through the commune, to move rapidly to "all-people ownership" as a violation of "economic laws"; and the Chinese pretension to be in the vanguard in the march to Communism as a vulgar manifestation of "equalitarian Communism." By announcing Russia's own accelerated programme of Communist construction featuring a highly developed "material and technical base" and by stressing that rapid progress of the "economically backward countries" was dependent on Soviet aid, it was made quite clear that the Soviet Union intended to determine the pace and order of *bloc* progress to Communism and that Khrushchev, not Mao Tse-tung, would solve the "problems of Marxist-Leninist theory connected with the transition from socialism to Communism."

Soviet denial of the Chinese claim to have discovered a special road for Asian Communism was sharp and unmistakable. The strategy was first to stress the "general laws" of Marxism-Leninism which have universal application and then to assert the validity of the Soviet model, as the embodiment of these laws, for both Europe and Asia. In a November 6 speech in Peiping commemorating the October Revolution, Soviet Ambassador Yudin emphasised that both "Europe and Asia," in accordance with Lenin's prediction, "must sooner or later" follow the "correct" Soviet road. The Draft Theses of Khrushchev's Report to the 21st Party Congress was even more explicit.

V. I. Lenin foresaw that the Soviet Union would exert chief influence on the entire course of world development by its economic construction. Lenin said: 'If Russia becomes covered with a dense network of electric stations and powerful technical equipment, our Communist economic construction will become *a model for the future socialist Europe and Asia*. (Emphasis added.)

Although the Soviet counter-offensive was directed primarily at Communist China, many of its strictures applied to North Korea as well. In the face of obvious Soviet displeasure with its defection, the North Korean régime appeared to abandon precipitately its plan to emulate Peking by "advancing to Socialism and Communism with flying leaps." At the Soviet 21st Party Congress in late January 1959, Kim Il-sung pointedly described his country as proceeding "along the road to Socialism," with "the rich experiences accumulated by the Communist Party of the Soviet Union and the Soviet people always serving as a guide in all our work." At the same time, Pyongyang continued to imitate Peking's "great leap forward" by claiming "miraculous successes" in production and by adhering to hopelessly unrealistic long-term goals. As late as mid-August 1959, Vice Premier Kim Il still spoke of doubling grain output and either tripling or quadrupling industrial output by 1964–65.

Responding to a new Chinese initiative in the fall of 1959, the North Korean régime once more spoke out vigorously in defence of Communist China's unorthodox programmes. After a period of relative moderation and retrenchment, Communist China's leadership had launched a spirited counter-attack against Soviet criticism of the commune and had reiterated the claim that China constituted a model for the underdeveloped nations of Asia. In articles celebrating Communist China's tenth anniversary on October 1, 1959, Foreign Minister Ch'en Yi asserted that "all oppressed nations and peoples . . . see in the Chinese people their tomorrow," and party secretary-general Teng Hsiao-p'ing declared China's experience in "rapidly getting rid of poverty and backwardness" to be *an example of going over from democratic revolution to socialist revolution in a colonial and semi-colonial country and of transforming a backward agricultural country into an advanced industrial country.*" (Emphasis added.)

In marked contrast with the Soviet and most East European delegations attending this anniversary celebration, Kim Il-sung predicted "new and greater achievements in the great leap forward and people's commune movements"; hailed them by implication as "a great contribution to further developing Marxist-Leninist theory and enriching the experience of the international Communist movement"; declared that his countrymen "always learn from your achievements"; and asserted that "no force can break . . . the friendship of the Korean and Chinese peoples based on common ideas and aims." This declaration, in conjunction with the even more candid acknowledgement of the Chinese model by East German delegate Herman Matern (who hailed the commune "as an example . . . for the millions of Asian peasant masses") posed anew the threat of an emerging Asian *bloc* of Communist nations looking to Peking for inspiration and guidance.

Following his abortive October conference with Mao Tse-tung in Peking,

Khrushchev apparently decided to resort to more forceful measures designed to pressure Communist China and its *bloc* supporters back into line. On December 1, for example, he launched a polemical, if oblique, attack on China's commune and "leap forward" programmes in addressing the Hungarian party congress, characterising them as a "distortion of the teaching of Marxism-Leninism on the building of socialism and Communism" resulting from "conceit . . . and mistakes in leadership. . . ." This public criticism was followed almost immediately by a North Korean decision to halt temporarily its own "flying horse" programme, with 1960 designated a "buffer year" in order to correct deficiencies in agriculture and provide a much needed breathing spell in its economic development programme.

Another Soviet counter-measure was the convocation in Moscow in early February 1960 of an unprecedented top-level *bloc* conference on agriculture. North Korea's participation in this conference, which almost certainly levelled criticism at China's communes, was an indication of continued susceptibility to Soviet pressures and, perhaps, of growing disenchantment with Chinese programmes as a solution to its own agricultural problems. The absence of China and North Vietnam, usually regarded as oriented to Peking, and the fact that a speech delivered by Khrushchev on this occasion has never been released suggest that this was the first of a series of multilateral conferences convened by the Russian leader in 1960 for the purpose of "isolating" Communist China within the ranks of the international Communist movement.

Apparently reacting to the pressures applied at this conference and the subsequent Bucharest meeting of world Communist parties in June, North Korea proved to be an early casualty among those who had defended Peking's heretical programmes. In marked contrast to previous laudatory appraisals, North Korean commentary throughout 1960 studiously ignored the existence of China's communes. A striking example of this new subservience to Moscow appeared in Kim Il-sung's message of greetings in observance of China's eleventh anniversary celebration on October 1. Whereas a year earlier he had proclaimed the vitality and creativity of this radical social organisation, the North Korean leader now felt constrained to enter into the Soviet-sponsored conspiracy of silence by ignoring the people's commune in his congratulatory message.

In part responding to this development and in part preparing for the impending summit conference in Moscow, Peking began to exert a number of countervailing pressures in October 1960 in order to maintain its position in North Korea. First was the grant of a loan of some £37 million ($105 million) to finance deliveries of equipment and technical assistance for industrial development. With this new credit, Communist China's total assistance to Pyongyang since the end of the Korean War now exceeded that of the U.S.S.R. Coming at a time of stringency in China's own economic development programme and of similar sizable loans to Outer Mongolia and North Vietnam, this extension of aid indicated a new effort to compete with the Soviet Union for influence in the Asian members of the *bloc.*

Next was the dispatch of a high-ranking military goodwill mission to North Korea in late October for a joint celebration of the tenth anniversary of China's entry into the Korean war. Politburo member and chief of mission Ho Lung utilised this occasion to attack the "modern revisionists" (an epithet directed at Moscow at this stage of heated polemics in the Sino-Soviet dispute) for their "bitter envy and hatred of our country's construction achievements," their "vain attempt to isolate China" and, more pointedly their "vain attempt to sabotage . . . the friendship and unity" of China and Korea. Even more suggestive of a

continuing struggle for influence in North Korea was a curious passage in the report issued by deputy mission chief Lo Jui-ch'ing on returning to Peiping. By contrasting China's consistent "wise" policy of "showing respect" for the leaders of North Korea with the "non-Marxist-Leninist" practice of "great nation chauvinism," he seemed to imply that other *bloc* nations had been guilty of intervening in Pyongyang's internal affairs.

Caught in this crossfire, North Korea's attitude towards Communist China's distinctive programme of Socialist and Communist construction on the eve of the Moscow summit conference displayed marked ambiguity. On the one hand, succumbing to Soviet pressures, it had disavowed the commune not only as a model for North Korean emulation but even as a legitimate form for building Socialism and Communism within China itself. On the other hand, there were indications that Pyongyang still subscribed to a number of the premises underlying Communist China's neo-Stalinist hard-line programme of economic and social development.

The North Korean régime continued to endorse China's "great leap forward" and to implement, although at a somewhat reduced tempo, its own "flying horse" programme. There was continued stress on an integral feature of these related programmes—the construction of small-scale local industrial installations combining "native and modern" technology. There was continued reliance on moral exhortation and revolutionary zeal, rather than material incentives, to stimulate rapid advances in production and construction. In keeping with Kim Il-sung's discovery (after Mao Tse-tung) of "the decisive role played by human consciousness in developing the productive forces," political indoctrination designed "to mobilise the masses" continued to receive priority in all phases of the country's development programme.

Most significant of all was the growing

tendency to characterise domestic policies as the product not of Soviet experience but of the "creative application of Marxism-Leninism" to the special conditions of North Korea. By increasingly stressing "the individuality of North Korea's revolution," it appeared that Pyongyang aspired to a position of neutrality in the deepening Sino-Soviet controversy over the "correct" road to Socialism and Communism on the eve of the Moscow Conference in November 1960.

International Communist Strategy

The Sino-Soviet dispute on international Communist strategy has entailed equally disturbing consequences for the Democratic People's Republic of Korea. Although couched in ambiguous doctrinal terms, this acrimonious public debate has reflected very real and broad differences over policies to be pursued toward the non-Communist world, with Khrushchev advocating a relatively gradual long-term policy of victory through "peaceful co-existence" and Mao Tse-tung countering with a more aggressive, high-risk policy promising quick gains in Asia, Africa and Latin America. Despite uncertainty and equivocation, the North Korean response to these divergent views since the fall of 1959 has revealed a marked predilection for Peking's more militant line in approaching its own number one foreign policy objective — the unification of Korea under Communist rule.

North Korean divergence from Khrushchev's foreign policy pronouncements first came to light in September 1959 when, in contrast with a prior Soviet declaration of neutrality, Pyongyang proclaimed its "full support" for the Chinese People's Republic in the Sino-Indian border dispute. Despite occasional statements admitting the possible value of East-West negotiations, North Korean commentary after Camp David displayed open scepticism of one of the prin-

ciple ingredients in Khrushchev's "peaceful co-existence" policy — his contention that a growing number of Western leaders, specifically including President Eisenhower, were sincere in their desire to reduce international tensions. Echoing Chinese Communist views, Pyongyang's propaganda in October charged that the United States "plans to solve the Korean question by war"; in December launched abusive personal attacks against the American President; and in January 1960 characterised the President's State of the Union Message as a "document of aggression and plunder, reeking of gunpowder."

A number of developments in the spring of 1960 intensified the Sino-Soviet dispute on *bloc* strategy. In April Peking launched a public attack on the theoretical rationale of Khrushchev's foreign policy by reviving Leninist dicta on the inevitability of war, the intrinsically aggressive nature of imperialism, and the need for direct revolutionary action to promote international Communism. The South Korean riots and subsequent overthrow of the Rhee government in April, the collapse of the summit conference in May and the violent Japanese demonstrations in June appeared to cast serious doubt on the efficacy of Khrushchev's détente policy and to lend substance to Peking's view of a rising tide of revolution in Asia. At the same time, the Bucharest Conference in June revealed to other *bloc* parties for the first time the fundamental nature and disruptive effect of the Sino-Soviet dispute. The North Korean response to these developments revealed grave apprehension over the growing rift in Sino-Soviet relations and a consequent desire to remain neutral, and, at the same time, a continuing affinity for Peking's militant policy of unremitting struggle against the West in Asia.

After a significant delay, the Korean Workers Party issued a brief communiqué on the Bucharest Conference which balanced a declaration of "full support of the peace-loving foreign policy of the CPSU based on Leninist principles of co-existence" with an immediate reminder that United States imperialism, the "sworn enemy of the people," remained inherently aggressive. More informative was Kim Il-sung's lengthy Liberation Day speech of August 14, 1960, which launched a new propaganda drive for "peaceful unification" of Korea. Advocating a confederation of North and South for joint development of the national economy, the North Korean leader betrayed the propagandistic nature of this proposal by offering to rescue "our South Korean brothers from starvation and poverty" and contending that "Socialist construction and the happy life of the people in the northern part of the republic are exercising tremendous revolutionary influence on the South Korean people." This stratagem, paralleling an earlier confederation scheme advanced by East Germany, conformed nicely with the Soviet prescription of final victory through "peaceful competition" and Khrushchev specifically endorsed it in a September 23 address to the United Nations General Assembly.

The dominant tone of Kim's speech, however, was one of struggle and militant appeals for direct revolutionary action in South Korea. Employing Chinese Communist invective, he depicted United States imperialism as "the most atrocious enemy of mankind and vicious enemy of the Asian people"; as "intensifying the arms race and aggravating tensions"; and as scheming to establish in South Korea "a military base for provoking another war." The only solution was "an anti-imperialist struggle" of the South Korean people, encouraged and abetted from the North, to compel "the United States aggressors . . . to withdraw." After drawing a parallel between South Korea and Taiwan, Kim asserted that "our people, joining forces with all Asian people, will struggle for the withdrawal of the aggressive United States Army from the whole area of Asia."

Communist China's high-ranking military mission to North Korea in October, noted above in the discussion of domestic policy, made much of this community of national interest. Indeed, when coupled with the charge that "modern revisionists" (*i.e.*, the U.S.S.R.) were attempting to "isolate" China and "to sabotage the friendship and unity" of China and Korea, General Yang Yung's blunt assertion of a special relationship between China and Korea appeared directed as much at the Soviet Union as at the West.

China and Korea are separated by only a river. They are as dependent on each other as the lips and the teeth. What is concerned with one of them is also concerned with the other. The security of China is closely connected with the survival of Korea.

In addition to reiterating a number of Chinese positions in the Sino-Soviet dispute on strategy, the Chinese military spokesman took sharp issue with an earlier judgment of Khrushchev that the United States was "not seeking a military conflict" in Korea. Chief of mission Ho Lung on this occasion characterised "the United States aggressors in South Korea" as "bent on . . . unleashing a new aggressive war, attempting once again to invade the Korean Democratic People's Republic . . . annexing the whole of Korea . . . and launching a new world war. . . ."

The upshot of this new initiative was to swing the North Korean régime even more solidly into line behind Communist China on two key issues of the Sino-Soviet dispute. First was the open espousal of Peking's charge that the "modern revisionists" were engaged in "covering up the aggressive nature of imperialism, beautifying imperialism and . . . denying the universal legality of socialist revolution." Next was the enthusiastic seconding of the Chinese view that revisionism, not dogmatism and sectarianism as implied by Moscow, constituted the most serious ideological devia-

230

tion within the international Communist movement. The reasoning advanced for this assessment was instructive. Within North Korea itself, revisionist elements had engaged in "counter-revolutionary plots" against the Korean Workers Party in the past and were still considered a clear and present danger. As a consequence of carrying on "socialist construction amid the fierce class struggle against United States imperialism . . . and domestic counter-revolutionaries," it was necessary to "arm the working people with hatred against imperialism and class enemies and bring them up as self-sacrificing and ardent revolutionary fighters."

Thus on the eve of the Moscow summit conference in November 1960, North Korea appeared to be following the lead of Communist China in opposing Khrushchev's policy of relaxing international tensions. What is more, the considerations prompting this decision appeared to be strikingly similar to those animating Peking. As a country with unsatisfied territorial claims, it could only view friendlier relations with the West as tending to freeze the status quo. As a have-not nation determined to industrialise at maximum speed, it favoured external tension as a justification for sacrifice and a goad for production. And as one of the satellites plagued by chronic factionalism and purges, it appeared firmly committed to the pre-Khrushchev model of Stalinist totalitarianism.

Recent Trends

Developments at the Moscow Conference and after tend to confirm the existence of strong ideological bonds between Peking and Pyongyang. First, it appears significant that Mao Tse-tung and Kim Il-sung were the only Communist Party leaders in the *bloc* who did not attend this summit conference. More revealing have been North Korea's pointed declarations of friendship and support for Albania, the East European satellite which has consistently backed Communist China in the Sino-Soviet dispute and which, accordingly, has aroused Moscow's ire. In an unusually laudatory article in late November the semi-official government organ *Minju Chosen* asserted that "our two countries are very close to each other, like real brothers, because of common ideology and aims" and that "no force on earth can break the invincible friendship and solidarity between the Korean and Albanian peoples." Moreover, authoritative editorial comment on the hybrid documents issued by the Moscow Conference has slighted Soviet-inspired passages for those expressing the more militant Chinese passages for those expressing the more militant Chinese line.

Most important of all, North Korea has explicitly recognised Communist China as co-leader of the Communist *bloc* following the Moscow Conference. By referring to "the Socialist countries led by the Soviet Union and the Chinese People's Republic," the official organ of the Korean Workers Party appeared to be announcing the arrival of a new stage in intra-*bloc* relations. In view of its previous record of sympathy and support for Communist China, it was fitting that North Korea should reveal what was perhaps the most significant result of the Moscow Conference—the emergence of "polycentrism" as a reality within the international Communist movement.

Bernard B. Fall

POWER AND PRESSURE GROUPS IN NORTH VIETNAM

As in many other Communist states (and quite a few non-Communist ones) there is in the DRV (Democratic Republic of [North] Vietnam) a sharp difference between the theoretical and the actual structure of governmental powers.

Article 4 of the DRV Constitution of January 1, 1960, adequately covers the subject of the theoretical source of power in North Vietnam: "All powers of the DRV belong to the people, who exercise them through the intermediary of the National Assembly and of People's Councils at every echelon, elected by it and responsible to it. . . ."

In actual fact, however, government power is in the hands of several distinct groups, some of which operate within the government structure while some others operate entirely or in part ouside of it. Some of the power groups can be considered as forming part of the "traditional" Communist elite—old party leaders, trade union chiefs, and a sprinkling of military men—while others spring from the ranks of the "New Class"—the Party bureaucrats, the newly urbanised factory workers, and the new managerial class of the largely nationalised sectors of the industrial economy.

As in all Communist states, the actual changes of power are fairly subtle at first and must often be culled from a welter of minor administrative changes or from such seemingly innocuous details as the line-up of political, party, or military leaders at a formal function. It is still a matter of some debate as to whether too much is not often read into such pictures by the "Kremlinologists" who, like the priests of certain older cults, try to forecast the future from such tenuous signs. The fact remains, however, that for the time being the Communists themselves have often chosen that means as a public symptom of a shift of power or of policies within their own camp, as the events in Moscow in October and November 1961 tend to show once more.

Power Groups and Pressure Groups

In order to avoid any misunderstanding in the use of the key terms in this study, a brief statement on definitions will be necessary. Within the frame of reference of this study, a "power group" is an informal body of operators exercising their influence upon the formal structure of government from *inside* that structure; while the "pressure group" may exercise similar influences in a far more inchoate way and from *outside* the formal structure.

In the precise case of the DRV, it is possible to distinguish *two* major policy alternatives subject to pressure or influence from such groups; and a total of *six* power and pressure groups. The two major policy alternatives are: alignment with Moscow or alignment with Peking, with subtle subgradations or compromises between the extremes.

The pressure and power groups can also be divided into two segments respectively:
1. Power Groups:
   (a) The Lao-Dong [*i.e.*, Communist] Party
   (b) The Vietnam People's Army
   (c) The Administrators and Managers
2. Pressure Groups:
   (a) The Intellectuals
   (b) The Urban Labour Force
   (c) The Peasantry

Little can be said about the two policy alternatives that is not already self-evident,

From *China Quarterly*, No. 9 (1962), pp. 37–46. Reprinted by permission of *China Quarterly*..

and was not made even clearer during the memorable debates at the Twenty-second Congress of the Communist Party of the Soviet Union in October–November 1961 in Moscow: North Vietnam, historically indefensible against its northern neighbour, had to walk the tightrope between its ideological preferences and geopolitical and economic realities. This was best shown by Ho Chi Minh's own attitude at the Moscow Congress: while he could not avoid aligning himself on China's "hard" line, Ho nonetheless did not leave Russia when Chou En-lai did but went on a tour of the country instead.

Within North Vietnam's government and Lao-Dong Party structure, the two policy alternatives are represented within every organisation in differing degrees of concentration at various times, the exact degree depending very often upon the changing fortunes of the Cold War.

Peking v. Moscow Wings

The struggle between the two policy wings within the DRV may have gone on as early as the 1920s, when Ho came to Canton from Moscow and Paris, while such men as Dan Xuan Khu joined the Vietnamese Communist movement after training and working with the Chinese Communist Party. Dan Xuan Khu is better known under his present *nom de guerre* of Truong Chinh ("Long March"), fully indicative of his political sympathies.

During the years of war against the French, differences between the two wings were largely immaterial since Moscow was far away and not in a position to help directly in the war effort and, furthermore, was at least in the beginning not particularly interested in helping Ho Chi Minh's cause. With the cease-fire of 1954, the problem immediately became more acute since Chinese Communist influence, hitherto largely limited to military assistance, now also became preponderant in the economic field in the form of huge grants,

loans, deliveries of machinery and goods; and the presence of Chinese advisers in nearly every field of endeavour. From 1954 until 1956, the pro-Chinese wing held the field within the Lao-Dong Party and included many workers and managers, and even some intellectuals—with the Vietnam People's Army under Vo Nguyên Giap representing a stronghold of lukewarm feelings towards Peking.

The peasant rebellion of Nghe-An in November 1956 (of which, significantly, the Army political commissars had warned the Lao-Dong) gave Ho Chi Minh a good pretext to purge the most ardent pro-Peking elements, at least temporarily: Truong Chinh was replaced as Secretary-General of the Lao-Dong by Ho himself, and other minor luminaries of the "Chinese wing" disappeared temporarily from view. But it was obvious that the very presence of China next door did not permit the total elimination of the Chinese wing. Soon Truong Chinh and his friends began their slow climb to new power.

The collapse of the Summit Conference of May 1960 (which, like any other peaceable contact between Moscow and the West, had not exactly been looked upon favourably by Peking) brought a return in force of the Peking clan which now claimed that the C.P.R. had been "clairvoyant" all along in its thesis that one could not negotiate with the "imperialists."

The year 1960 brought about three events which were to influence even further the struggle between the two policy wings: in January a new constitution was promulgated which brought about a far more stringent political control of the government machinery: followed on May 8 (the sixth anniversary of the French defeat at Dien Bien Phu) by the first legislative elections since 1946; and in September of the same year by the third National Congress of the Lao-Dong.

The creation, within the structure of the DRV government, of an "Organ of People's Control" introduced a new element of political surveillance into the administrative machinery; and the reshuffles within the government after the legislative elections of May 1960 clearly showed that the process seemed to favour the pro-Chinese elements: Truong Chinh became Chairman of the Permanent Committee of the National Assembly; while two other pro-Peking stalwarts, Hoang Quoc Viet (head of the Vietnam Confederation of Labour) and Pham Van Bach (the southern guerrilla leader) found themselves in control of the court system and of the "People's Control Organ," respectively.

In fact, the ascendant of the pro-Peking group seemed so strong that at the Party Congress of September 1960 the long-time Prime Minister of the DRV, Pham Van Dong, a scion of the mandarin class and one of Ho Chi Minh's earliest and most faithful followers, stood in danger of losing his post, had not Ho Chi Minh thrown his personal prestige in the balance in order to save his companion.

The hardening of Moscow's relations with the West brought about a closer alignment of the position of the two policy camps in Vietnam and some personnel changes to substantiate the view that the pro-Moscow group was regaining some of its earlier strength. In February 1961, Ung Van Khiêm, the former chief of the Executive Committee for the *Nam-Bô* [South Vietnam] and Vice-Minister of Foreign Affairs, stepped into the post of Minister of Foreign Affairs; while in March 1961, three People's Army Generals: Lt.-Gen. Van Tien Dung, Maj.-Gen. Hoang Van Thai, Maj.-Gen. Dong Hao, well known for their devotion to General Giap and their lack of enthusiasm for Red China, were appointed Vice-Ministers of Defence. On the other hand, Brig-Gen. Nguyên Chi Thanh, a Party fanatic who, as Chief of the Political Department of the People's Army [*i.e.*, Political Commissar-in-Chief] had been known for his unswerving devotion to the Peking line, found himself side-tracked in

the unenviable job as Minister of Agricultural Co-operatives at a time when North Vietnam faced some fairly grim food crises.

The relinquishment in September 1961 of the top political post of Lao-Dong Secretary-General by Ho Chi Minh in favour of Lê Duan, generally considered as at least partly favourable to Peking (or at least not objectionable to it) may be considered both as a renewed sign of weakness on the part of the pro-Moscow wing, or as merely an outward concession without deeper meaning. After all, Ho Chi Minh had once before snatched the job away from a pro-Peking man when he felt that circumstances demanded such a change. It remains to be seen whether the more stringent measures taken against "anti-Party" elements in Moscow will have an echo in Hanoi. Much will depend on Peking's reaction to them.

The Power Groups

As of late 1960, the Vietnam *Dang Lao-Dong* (Workers' Party) counted half a million members throughout the country. This figure compares with a 1946 level of 20,000 and a 1948 figure of 168,000.

The Communist Party thus represents the largest single organisation in the country, encompassing all activities and reaching from the highest councils of government and army to the lowest village in the rice fields. But the Party's ubiquity and numerical strength does not truly express its position of influence within the DRV. That influence is far better evident in the fact that several of the key members of the North Vietnamese régime are at the same time members of the Central Committee (*Tong-Bô*) of the Lao-Dong.

It is in that position that they have succeeded in imposing their imprint upon the whole country: harsh co-operativisation measures, trials of landlords; ideological control of all communication media, etc.

Yet, the Party itself, as has been shown previously, is not a monolith. Not only is it split along the Moscow-Peking axis, but it is also split along age-group lines: there are the "old Bolsheviks" of the calibre of Ho Chi Minh and Ton Duc Thang, in their seventies and dying out fast. Their education is generally broader, for they have not only fought the French but lived with them; to them the West is not merely a Frankenstein myth. That group, small as it was, is being rapidly overtaken by the Party bureaucrats — those whom this writer has called elsewhere the "civil servants, but not the combatants, of the Revolution." These bureaucrats — Lê Duan is fairly typical of them — are those who can be trusted with the reading of morose and long-winded speeches about the new general line; of droning on with interminable production statistics and even higher future economic goals; and of carrying out those tasks with an efficiency untouched by feelings of compassion.

For the time being, like the Soviet Communist Party two decades ago, the Lao-Dong leadership still suffers from the fact that, although pretending to lead a proletarian movement, it still has deep roots in the bourgeoisie. While more recent statistics on the subject have not been published, a 1953 self-critical study of the Party showed that out of 1,855 senior Party positions no less than 1,365 were held by intellectuals or bourgeois, as against 351 positions held by members of rural origin and 139 held by workers. Considering the fact that Vietnam as a whole is 90 per cent. agricultural and certainly less than 1 per cent. "intellectual" (i.e., composed of persons pursuing a liberal profession), it is very obvious that the Lao-Dong, as a power group, cannot claim to have deep roots within the population — even assuming that all 500,000 Party members (out of a population of 30 million in both zones) were fully enthusiastic about the present leadership and political line.

The peasant rebellion of 1956 clearly showed up the weakness of the Party base in the rural areas and in 1957 the Lao-Dong officially changed its aim towards an increase of its urban and intellectual base, apparently considering the peasantry as a whole as "too reactionary."

For a certain time [according to the Vietnam News Agency on April 19, 1957], the Party shall above all increase its strength in the cities and industrial centres, with the aim of recruiting best sons and daughters of the working class. At the same time, attention shall be paid to the development of the Party among the revolutionary intellectuals working at present in various branches of the public services.

It was probably through the massive recruitment drive of that period that the figure of 500,000 Party members was reached. As subsequent events were to prove, that increase in size did not solve the Party's problems of "rapport" with the people at large. It merely multiplied its cadre problem.

The Army

The Vietnam People's Army is a power group perhaps second in size to the Lao-Dong, but surely ahead of it and of any other North Vietnamese organisation in effective power. Recruited largely from among the peasantry but also including units from the cities (such as the 308th Division, recruited in Hanoi) or even from the upland minorities (such as the 316th Division, or the 324th), it can truly claim to have deep roots within the country.

The recruitment of its senior officers also shows a far wider spread than that of the Lao-Dong. While such men as General Vo Nguyên Giap (with his Ph.D. from Hanoi University) can be described as "intellectuals," many other officers were trained in the hard school of the jungle itself, or rose from the lower and other ranks of the French Colonial Army. One of the senior commanders, Maj.-Gen. Chu Van Tan, was a former chief of pirates from the Thô minority and is now President of the Viet-Bac

235

Autonomous Zone—one of the two areas comprising the major part of the mountaineer minority populations. Several other senior officers, such as the now-dead General Nguyen-Son, were trained in China and, like their Party counterparts, tend to espouse the views of their erstwhile teachers.

Thus, the V.P.A. is both more "people-based" than the Lao-Dong and at the same time harsher in the execution of unpopular policies because it perhaps feels more secure in its position in the country than the Lao-Dong does. During the peasant rebellion of 1956, the 325th Division crushed the unarmed farmers with the same iron discipline with which Khrushchev's armour liquidated at precisely the same moment the Hungarian freedom fighters in Budapest. While farm co-operativisation encountered many difficulties among the peasants, the V.P.A. proceeded to man the first true collective farms (or, rather, state farms along the Sovkhoz model) in North Vietnam with farmer-soldiers culled from among the regulars.

It was also the political commissars of the V.P.A., who, meeting in a congress at Hanoi, warned the Lao-Dong of the possibility of a peasant uprising and criticised the Party functionaries for their ignorance of "real conditions" in the country. In fact, like many other professional armies, the V.P.A. had sufficiently shown its contempt for the intellectuals to warrant an open warning from the Lao-Dong's official newspaper *Nhan-Dan*:

. . . there seems to be an excess of prudence [in the V.P.A.] when it comes to entrusting intellectuals with posts or mission in accordance with their abilities. This shows a certain narrowness of mind which operates against the intellectuals. . . .

From the V.P.A.'s viewpoint, developments in North Vietnam have not taken too favourable a turn. To be sure, the People's Army is the *enfant chéri* of the régime, receiving the best food in a period of severe shortages and having first call for equipment, clothing and housing. Its drab wartime and combat uniforms have been replaced by Soviet-patterned issue whose multi-coloured insignia and badges (not to speak of gold-braided shoulder boards not exactly suited to the tropical climate) is almost second to none in the Soviet *bloc*. A multiplicity of specialised military schools assures the V.P.A. of suitable cadre replacements—but still, there seems to be some discontent in the ranks, for in fact, the "civilians" (*e.g.*, the Party and government) had deprived the Army of the rightful fruits of its military victories in 1954 when they agreed to the splitting of Vietnam at the 17th parallel *not* out of military necessity but in obedience to Soviet pressures.

With the prospect of more anti-DRV revolts in the offing (see below) and renewed tension between the pro-Moscow and the pro-Peking factions, the attitude of the V.P.A. leadership may well become a decisive factor in any North Vietnamese power struggle.

The Managerial Elite

The managerial elite, in North Vietnam, is neither large nor proficient. Largely composed of Party faithfuls or discharged army officers, it deserves mention here only because of its many contacts with Soviet *bloc* technicians which give it a singularly important role in shaping North Vietnamese views of the outside world.

Many are the complaints on both sides, with the Eastern European experts privately (and even openly) asserting that the North Vietnamese are "unteachable" and unwilling to accept sound advice; and the Vietnamese (their professional as well as their national pride stung) are not loth to reply that the technicians from the "fraternal countries" are more aloof than even the colonialists of yesteryear and their machinery often less well adapted to local conditions than some of the old French machinery which, though on its last legs, at least has the advantage of being familiar.

The hard fact is that North Vietnam, for years to come, simply lacks the engineering manpower to go with its industrial ambitions and that its Soviet *bloc* supporters are equally loth to loan out personnel whose skills are in short supply at home. For example, as recently as two years ago, the cotton mills of Nam Dinh, which employed forty-seven French engineers and foremen for 12,000 workers, had not one single qualified engineer; while the Quang-Yen — Hongay coal fields which, under French management, had employed more than 150 engineers and foremen, now had to make do with two "technicians" for their 11,000 miners.

For the time being, therefore, the North Vietnamese managerial class can be considered as a "power group" in the negative sense only, *i.e.*, by what it cannot do rather than by what it can do. In many cases it has been made the scapegoat (for, by virtue of its low quality, it is always easy to find some shortcomings in its activities) for all the errors in economic planning made by the régime and the present deteriorating economic situation has resulted in placing a heavy burden of responsibility on its shoulders.

The Pressure Groups

In any totalitarian state, pressure without power is a fragile reed indeed. North Vietnam is no exception to the rule, and those groups among its population which have attempted to influence the course of events outside the accepted channels of the régime, have had to pay dearly for their daring. Of the three major groups in that category, two so far have made the attempt: the intellectuals and the peasantry. The third, the industrial labour force, for the time being enjoys the same privileged position as the Vietnam People's Army.

The intellectuals, at first, had been the most faithful supporters of the North Viet-

namese régime: its firm anti-colonialist stand, its erstwhile lack of corruption, its seeming classlessness, all these contained powerful appeals which the competing southern régime lacks to this day. On the other hand, the harsh police state methods (whose imitation in the South is far more lax), and compulsion to total uniformity in the arts (almost totally absent in the South), form a yoke whose weight, in the long run, is unbearable. The result, in North Vietnam, was a gradual estrangement of the intellectuals from the régime. In disaccord with the Party, distrusted by the Army, many of them soon became guilty of "internal emigration," of *attentisme*.

When the "Hundred Flowers" movement drifted from China to North Vietnam in 1957, a veritable explosion took place in various art forms, which the régime found itself unable to control short of fullfledged measures of repression. By the time the intellectuals had returned to full conformism, many of them had found their way to labour camps along the Bac-Hung-Hai irrigation canal where they were able, according to the North Vietnamese press,

. . . to see for themselves the vast work potential and creativity of the masses . . . [and where the intellectuals] finally understood that culture, literature and the arts spring from the masses and are destined to serve them, for it is the masses who are the most able to assimilate them and judge them. . . .

The peasant, representing 90 per cent. of the country's population and its economic backbone in the truest sense of the term, is both more vulnerable and more powerful than the intellectual pressure group. He is more vulnerable because a government decree, backed up by the ever-obedient People's Army, may deprive him of his livelihood or send him to a working party along the roads and canals of Vietnam. On the other hand, deliberate sabotage of the crops — an act that is as effective as it is suicidal — or the withholding of cattle from deliveries to the cities, can literally bring the country to the brink of ruin.

That is precisely what has happened in North Vietnam in 1961. According to *Nhan-Dan* of June 8, 1961, cattle deliveries had dropped to less than one-half the prescribed rate. Faced with rumours of impending complete collectivisation, peasant riots broke out in several areas and in Haiduong and Cao-Bang, large rice granaries were stormed and burned by the irate populace in April 1961. Coming at a time when natural calamities had reduced the rice crop to almost starvation levels, the DRV government found it more expedient to compromise than meet its peasantry head-on. Promises were made that more of the crop would be left in the hands of the peasants to sell at free market rates and that they would receive priority treatment in the attribution of essential consumer goods. It is unlikely that such concessions are more than a temporary "tactical retreat" in North Vietnam's struggle with its peasantry, but they are nonetheless an interesting sign of the strength of the DRV's peasantry as an informal pressure group.

Some Conclusions

While it is certain that the DRV, like all the other régimes of the Soviet orbit and many other non-Communist dictatorships, has at its command several levers of government which permit it to ride out some severe crises without immediate fear of a major explosion, it has, at the same time, to face the hard fact that is far less monolithic than it would like to be.

The fact that the People's Army is to a large extent loyal to the régime as presently constituted, gives the régime an inner strength which should not be lightly dismissed. On the other hand, that Army, like those of all the other Communist states, is but a tool in the hands of the political leadership. "Zhukovism," in Communist terminology, is a heresy only second to that of Titoism—and neither China nor Russia are likely to be willing to let North Vietnam become another Albania.

The tug-of-war between the Muscovite and Chinese wings of the Lao-Dong Party could, under certain circumstances, assume serious proportions, particularly if the succession to Ho Chi Minh's post were to open up in earnest. For the time being, in any case, neither of the two groups is likely to upset the precarious balance.

This leaves the peasantry of North Vietnam, endowed with a long tradition of endurance of hardships and hopeless rebellion, as the chink in the armour. A succession of bad crops could very well bring it into a state of open revolt with almost bare hands against one of the best armies in Asia, in which case the ultimate result may well be along the lines of Budapest in 1956—unless the West is willing to do something in Vietnam that it has carefully refrained from doing elsewhere.

And that is highly unlikely.

NATIONALISM AND INTERNATIONAL COMMUNISM

The many and frequent quarrels between different nations in the Communist bloc since Stalin's death are symptomatic of the uneasy relationship between nationalism and international communism, two factors that lay at the root of the 1956 crises between Poland and the Soviet Union and Hungary and Russia. More recently nationalism has upset Sino-Soviet diplomacy. The original and foremost upholder of national communism in the bloc was Yugoslavia, and it is fitting that this section should end with a shrewd comment on national communism by Djilas, a Yugoslav, and one of its most enthusiastic exponents. It is on the hard rocks of national rivalry that the ship of communism as a world-embracing ideology may founder in the long run.

Milovan Djilas

NATIONAL COMMUNISM

In essence, Communism is only one thing, but it is realized in different degrees and manners in every country. Therefore it is possible to speak of various Communist systems, i.e., of various forms of the same manifestation.

The differences which exist between Communist states — differences that Stalin attempted futilely to remove by force — are the result, above all, of diverse historical backgrounds. Even the most cursory observation reveals how, for example, contemporary Soviet bureaucracy is not without a connecting link with the Czarist system in which the officials were, as Engels noted, "a distinct class." Somewhat the same thing can also be said of the manner of government in Yugoslavia. When ascending to power, the Communists face in the various countries different cultural and technical levels and varying social relationships, and are faced with different national intellectual characters. These differences develop even farther, in a special way. Because the general causes which brought them to power are identical, and because they have to wage a struggle against common internal and foreign opponents, the Communists in separate countries are immediately compelled to fight jointly and on the basis of a similar ideology. International Communism, which was at one time the task of revolutionaries, eventually transformed itself, as did everything else in Communism, and became the common ground of Communist bureaucracies, fighting one another on nationalistic considerations. Of the former international proletariat, only words and empty dogmas remained. Behind them stood the naked national and international interests, aspirations, and plans of the various Communist oligarchies, comfortably entrenched.

The nature of authority and property, a similar international outlook, and an identical ideology inevitably identify Communist states with one another. Nevertheless, it is wrong to ignore and underestimate the significance of the inevitable differences in degree and manner between Communist states. The degree, manner, and form in which Communism will be realized, or its purpose, is just as much of a given condition for each of them as is the essence of Communism itself. No single form of Communism, no matter how similar it is to other forms, exists in any way other than as national Communism. In order to maintain itself, it must become national.

The form of government and property as well as of ideas differs little or not at all in Communist states. It cannot differ markedly

From Milovan Djilas, *The New Class* (New York, 1957), pp. 173–177. Reprinted by permission of Frederick A. Praeger, Inc., and Thames & Hudson, Ltd.

239

since it has an identical nature—total authority. However, if they wish to win and continue to exist, the Communists must adapt the degree and manner of their authority to national conditions.

The differences between Communist countries will, as a rule, be as great as the extent to which the Communists were independent in coming to power. Concretely speaking, only the Communists of three countries—the Soviet Union, China, and Yugoslavia—independently carried out revolutions or, in their own way and at their own speed, attained power and began "the building of socialism." These three countries remained independent as Communist states even in the period when Yugoslavia was—as China is today—under the most extreme influence of the Soviet Union; that is, in "brotherly love" and in "eternal friendship" with it. In a report at a closed session of the Twentieth Congress, Khrushchev revealed that a clash between Stalin and the Chinese government had barely been averted. The case of the clash with Yugoslavia was not an isolated case, but only the most drastic and the first to occur. In the other Communist countries the Soviet government enforced Communism by "armed missionaries"—its army. The diversity of manner and degree of the development in these countries has still not attained the stage reached in Yugoslavia and China. However, to the extent that ruling bureaucracies gather strength as independent bodies in these countries, and to the extent that they recognize that obedience to and copying of the Soviet Union weaken themselves, they endeavor to "pattern" themselves on Yugoslavia; that is, to develop independently. The Communist East European countries did not become satellites of the U.S.S.R. because they benefited from it, but because they were too weak to prevent it. As soon as they become stronger, or as soon as favorable conditions are created, a yearning for independence and for protection of "their

own people" from Soviet hegemony will rise among them.

With the victory of a Communist revolution in a country a new class comes into power and into control. It is unwilling to surrender its own hard-gained *privileges*, even though it subordinates its *interests* to a similar class in another country, solely in the cause of ideological solidarity.

Where a Communist revolution has won victory independently, a separate, distinct path of development is inevitable. Friction with other Communist countries, especially with the Soviet Union as the most important and most imperialistic state, follows. The ruling national bureaucracy in the country where the victorious revolution took place has already become independent in the course of the armed struggle and has tasted the blessings of authority and of "nationalization" of property. Philosophically speaking, it has also grasped and become conscious of its own essence, "its own state," its authority, on the basis of which it claims equality.

This does not mean that this involves only a clash—when it comes to that—between two bureaucracies. A clash also involves the revolutionary elements of a subordinated country, because they do not usually tolerate domination and they consider that relationships between Communist states must be as ideally perfect as predicted in dogma. The masses of the nation, who spontaneously thirst for independence, cannot remain unperturbed in such a clash. In every case the nation benefits from this: it does not have to pay tribute to a foreign government; and the pressure on the domestic government, which no longer desires, and is not permitted, to copy foreign methods, is also diminished. Such a clash also brings in external forces, other states and movements. However, the nature of the clash and the basic forces in it remain. Neither Soviet nor Yugoslav Communists stopped being what they are—not before, nor during, nor after their mutual bickerings. Indeed, the diverse types of degree and manner with which they insured their monopoly led them mutually to deny the existence of socialism in the opposite camp. After they settled their differences, they again acknowledged the existence of socialism elsewhere, becoming conscious that they must respect mutual differences if they wanted to preserve that which was identical in essence and most important to them.

The subordinate Communist governments in East Europe can, in fact must, declare their independence from the Soviet government. No one can say how far this aspiration for independence will go and what disagreements will result. The result depends on numerous unforeseen internal and external circumstances. However, there is no doubt that a national Communist bureaucracy aspires to more complete authority for itself. This is demonstrated by the anti-Tito processes in Stalin's time in the East European countries; it is shown also by the current unconcealed emphasis on "one's own path to socialism," which has recently come to light sharply in Poland and Hungary. The central Soviet government has found itself in difficulty because of the nationalism existing even in those governments which it installed in the Soviet republics (Ukraine, Caucasia), and still more so with regard to those governments installed in the East European countries. Playing an important role in all of this is the fact that the Soviet Union was unable, and will not be able in the future, to assimilate the economies of the East European countries.

The aspirations toward national independence must of course have greater impetus. These aspirations can be retarded and even made dormant by external pressure or by fear on the part of the Communists of "imperialism" and the "bourgeoisie," but they cannot be removed. On the contrary, their strength will grow.

It is impossible to foresee all of the forms that relations between Communist states will assume. Even if cooperation between Communist states of different countries should in a short time result in mergers and federations, so can clashes between Communist states result in war. An open, armed clash between the U.S.S.R. and Yugoslavia was averted not because of the "socialism" in one or the other country, but because it was not in Stalin's interest to risk a clash of unforeseeable proportions. Whatever will happen between Communist states will depend on all those factors which ordinarily affect political events. The interests of the respective Communist bureaucracies, expressed variously as "national" or as "united," along with the unchecked tendency toward ever increasing independence on a national basis, will, for the time being, play an important role in the relationships among the Communist countries.

Suggestions for Reading

There is now a vast literature on the communist bloc. This selective bibliography concentrates on works that attempt to take an overall, evolutionary view of the communist world, although some of the more significant books on individual countries are also mentioned. Apart from Hugh Seton-Watson's *The East European Revolution*, published in 1950, little of lasting value came out in English before the middle 1950's. This was due in part to the myopia that troubles observers of recent events, and partly to the serious misunderstanding and ignorance in the noncommunist world of Soviet methods until after Stalin's death.

Professor Seton-Watson's *East European Revolution* deserves pride of place among the earlier general works on the Soviet bloc. A pioneer in its field, it remains the clearest account of the involved process of the communist takeover of East Europe after the Second World War. A series of articles by various experts in the *Annals of the American Academy of Political and Social Science* (May 1949) provides a useful complement to Professor Seton-Watson's book, as do Y. Gluckstein, *Stalin's Satellites in Europe* (1952). R. R. Betts, *Central and Southeast Europe, 1945 – 1948* (1951), and *The Fate of East Central Europe*, ed. S. Kertesz (1956). More recent publications include Z. Brzezinski, *The Soviet Bloc* (1960), a worthy successor to Professor Seton-Watson's work, and *Polycentrism*, ed. W. Laqueur and L. Labedz (1962), a treatment of the breakdown of the centripetal bloc system. Since the middle 1950's numerous general articles on the communist bloc have appeared in specialized journals such as *East Europe, Journal of Central European Affairs, Problems of Communism, Slavic and East European Review* and *World Marxist Review*. On occasions a part, or the whole, of a number has been devoted to the communist bloc, as in *Problems of Communism* (May-June 1962).

One of the best general books on economic questions in the communist bloc is N. Spulber, *The Economics of Communist Eastern Europe* (1957). M. Dewar, *Soviet Trade with Eastern Europe* (1951) and J. Wszelaki, *Communist Economic Strategy: The Role of East Central Europe* (1959) pay special attention to Soviet economic predominance in Eastern Europe. J. M. Montias, *Central Planning in Poland* (1962) is an excellent case-study of the Polish economy. I. Deutscher, "Communism's Common Market", *The New Statesman* (July 4 and July 31, 1959) and A. Zaubermann, "Economic Integration: Problems and Prospects," *Problems of Communism* (July-August 1959) deal with recent trends in communist economic collaboration.

Social and cultural aspects of the communist world are treated in I. Lapenna, *State and Law: Soviet and Yugoslav Theory* (1964), *Government and Law Courts in the Soviet Union and Eastern Europe*, ed. V. Gsovski and K. Grzybowska (1959), and G. Schuster, *Religion behind the Iron Curtain* (1954). C. Milosz, *The Captive*

Mind (1953) includes a famous analysis of the plight of the intellectual in a communist régime. A. Buzek, *How the Communist Press Works* (1964) provides an insight into journalism. The role of ideology is ably portrayed in Z. Brzezinski, *The Soviet Bloc* (1960) and expounded more briefly in H. Skilling, "People's Democracies in Soviet Theory," *Soviet Studies* (July and October 1951). E. Goodman, *The Soviet Design for a World State* (1960) contains an interesting discussion of the way in which the enlarging communist world has been fitted into Marxist-Leninist theories of international communist society as interpreted by the Soviet Union. R. Lowenthal, *World Communism: The Disintegration of Secular Faith* (1964) portrays the more recent retreat from ideology in the communist bloc.

Soviet manipulation of the bloc at a more practical level is treated as part of wider surveys of Russian foreign policy in M. Mackintosh, *The Strategy and Tactics of Soviet Foreign Policy* (1962), K. Ingram, *History of the Cold War* (1955), D. Dallin, *Soviet Foreign Policy after Stalin* (1961), and *Readings in Soviet Foreign Policy*, ed. A. Adams (1961). Russia's original domination of Eastern Europe sprang from her participation in the Second World War, which is recorded in M. Gallagher, *The Soviet History of World War II* (1963) and A. Werth, *Russia at War 1941–1945* (1964). Books on the nature of subsequent Soviet influence include *Soviet Imperialism*, ed. W. Gurian (1953) and C. Sulzberger, *The Big Thaw* (1956). Soviet policy as a direct cause of the East European Revolution of 1956 is traced in *Current Soviet Policies II*, the documentary record of the Twentieth Communist Party Congress, edited by Leo Gruliow (1957) and *The Anti-Stalin Campaign and International Communism*, a selection of documents edited by the Russian Institute of Columbia University (1956). *Diversity in International Communism*, ed. A. Dallin and others (1963) brings the reader up to the end of the period covered by the present volume. A very useful survey of the institutional ties that help to bind the communist bloc is given in K. Grzybowski, *The Socialist Commonwealth of Nations: Organisations and Institutions* (1964).

Communist China's role in the bloc is dealt with, for the early years, in *Moscow-Peking Axis*, ed. H. Boorman, A. Eckstein, P. Mosely, and B. Schwartz (1957). More recent Sino-Soviet relations and debates are fully covered in D. Zagoria, *The Sino-Soviet Conflict 1956–1961* (1962) and D. Floyd, *Mao against Khrushchev—A Short History of the Sino-Soviet Conflict* (1964). Albania's status as a European pawn between the two giants is described in V. Dedijer, "Albania —Soviet Pawn," *Foreign Affairs* (October 1951). Vietnam and Korea, two Asian pawns cast in similar molds, are treated in B. Fall, *Street without Joy* (1964) and D. Rees, *Korea: The Limited War* (1964).

The history of Yugoslavia's stormy career in the communist bloc has attracted a good deal of attention. The documentary background of the Russo-Yugoslav dispute is given in *The Soviet-Yugoslav Dispute*, documents edited by the Royal Institute of International Affairs, London, and *The Soviet-Yugoslav Controversy*, ed. R. Bass and E. Marbury (1959). The best secondary account is contained in A. Ulam, *Titoism and the Cominform* (1952). For the working of the Cominform itself in Eastern Europe, A. Ulam, "The Cominform and the People's Democracies," *World Politics* (January 1951) should be consulted. M. Djilas, *Conversations with Stalin* (1962) and V. Dedijer, *Tito Speaks* (1953) provide the opinions of two famous Yugoslavs on their country's ties with the Soviet Union.

Among the many studies of the other countries in the communist bloc, only a few may be mentioned here. E. Taborsky, "Benes and the Soviets," *Foreign Affairs* (January 1949) and P. Zinner, "Marxism in Action: The Seizure of Power in Czechoslovakia," *Foreign Affairs* (July 1956) treat the dramatic fall of Czechoslovakia into communist hands. P. Zinner, *Revolution in Hungary* (1962) and H. Schoenfeld, "Soviet Imperialism in Hungary," *Foreign Affairs* (April 1958) deal with the no less dramatic revolution of 1956 in Hungary. S. Mikolajczyk, *The Rape of Poland* (1948) and C. Manning, *The Forgotten Republics* (1952) do a similar service for the Baltic nations in communist Eastern Europe. The Balkan nations can be investigated in G. Ionesco, *Communism in Rumania 1944–1962* (1964), H. Roberts, *Rumania, Political Problems of an Agrarian State* (1951) and D. Kousoulas, *Revolution and Defeat* (1965). The German problem, which stands apart from all the other questions concerning the bloc, is dealt with in J. Nettl, *The Eastern Zone and Soviet Policy in Germany, 1945–1950* (1951), W. Davidson, *The Berlin Blockade: A Study in Cold War Politics* (1958), *Berlin—Pivot of Destiny*, ed. C. Robson (1960) and H. Kersten, "Ulbricht and the Intellectuals," *Survey* (July 1948).